Questioning the Incarnation

Formulating a Meaningful Christology

T0385615

Questioning the Incarnation

Formulating a Meaningful Christology

Peter Shepherd

CHRISTIAN
ALTERNATIVE

Winchester, UK
Washington, USA

First published by Christian Alternative Books, 2018
Christian Alternative Books is an imprint of John Hunt Publishing Ltd.,
Laurel House, Station Approach,
Alresford, Hants, SO24 9JH, UK
office1@jhpbooks.net
www.johnhuntpublishing.com
www.christian-alternative.com

For distributor details and how to order please visit the 'Ordering' section on our website.

Text copyright: Peter Shepherd 2017

ISBN: 978 1 78535 633 9
978 1 78535 634 6 (ebook)
Library of Congress Control Number: 2016962426

All rights reserved. Except for brief quotations in critical articles or reviews, no part of this book may be reproduced in any manner without prior written permission from the publishers.

The rights of Peter Shepherd as author have been asserted in accordance with the Copyright, Designs and Patents Act 1988.

A CIP catalogue record for this book is available from the British Library.

Design: Stuart Davies

Printed and bound by CPI Group (UK) Ltd, Croydon, CR0 4YY, UK

We operate a distinctive and ethical publishing philosophy in
all areas of our business, from our global network of authors to
production and worldwide distribution.

Contents

The Revd Canon Dr Peter Shepherd was formerly Headmaster of Canon Slade 11–18 CE School in Bolton. He was ordained to a self-supporting ministry, focusing on education, in Chichester Diocese almost 40 years ago, and continues to assist in parochial ministry. Since retirement he has been the SSM Officer for Blackburn Diocese. He has taught Doctrine and Liturgy to ordinands and reader candidates, and is an IME 2 (post-ordination) tutor. He holds Bachelor's degrees in History and Theology, Master's in Theology/Philosophy and Education Management, and a Doctorate in Religious Studies/Theology. He was author of 'Values for Church Schools' (1998) and has contributed chapters and articles to a variety of publications, specialising in providing a rationale for church schools, the theory and development of RE, School Worship and Christian values. Married to Sue, they have two grown-up daughters: Juliette and Penny.

A childish (or child-like?) tale

Although baptised as a baby, as was nearly 70% of my generation, I was not brought up to attend church. Does that mean I was not a genuine or 'proper' Christian? Some would say not. Yet my parents presumably identified in some way, culturally or even nostalgically, with Christianity, or I would probably not have been baptised at all. In the post-War period not having one's child baptised was not the social stigma it had been in the past; it is now, quite rightly, no longer a stigma at all. Furthermore, the organisation of a baptism always requires a particularly positive effort on the part of non-churchgoers. Yet, so far as I recall, the Christian Faith wasn't ever talked about at home and, this time *unlike* many of my contemporaries, I was never sent to Sunday School. I would imagine that, if they thought about it at all, my parents would have shared the view of many working-class folk in the 1950s that religion was acceptable, so long as it wasn't taken too seriously, and that attending church was nothing much more than a life-style choice: 'something that some people like to do'.[1]

Such Christian 'education' as I received was transmitted via State primary school assemblies (the 1944 'act of collective worship' applied) and regular exposure to Bible stories in class. I recall that we began with the story of Abraham in each of my junior years, ending each school year in a different place, depending on the speed with which various teachers ploughed through the Bible: occasionally we reached the New Testament. Presumably, an Agreed Syllabus was in operation; but if it was, I can't imagine that it was followed: Agreed Syllabus makers – statutorily representing a variety of interest groups – would hardly have recommended exactly the same course for each school year. All this explicitly confessional Christian teaching,[2] as that was the form Religious Education[3] took prior to the curiously simultaneous development of a Britain that is both multi-Faith and secular, was neither systematic nor extensive and focused exclusively on the Biblical narratives, with no reference to contemporary religious practice: a child might reasonably have concluded that Judaism came to an end 2000 years ago.

Nor was it particularly educational: pre-Goldman[4] there was limited consideration given to any of the processes which might support the development of a 'religiously educated person', such as the ability to understand religious concepts or critically evaluate arguments. The teacher would read or tell Bible stories, after which we pupils would draw and colour in pictures about them – together with many, many maps - and perhaps even write a paragraph or two. But this exercise was nothing more than a simple retelling of the story in our own words: useful for written English, but quite useless in terms of any proper understanding of the subject matter. Such activities are, sadly, still common in many church-sponsored 'Sunday Schools', not least because 'teachers' are mostly untrained: over the years I have known several who have actually refused Diocesan training on the grounds that 'anyone can teach Bible stories'. As a result many children continue to be taught the Bible, at church and particularly in primary schools where teachers are generalists, by adults who don't themselves understand the complex nature of the Biblical texts. Such limited, superficial and, in my experience, sometimes inaccurate teaching almost inevitably produces adults who may well have high-level expertise in other disciplines, but who have a very undeveloped 'childish' (or is it child-like?) understanding of the Bible and, *a fortiori*, of Christian beliefs: adults who graduate easily from 'the story of Noah's Ark (or water into wine or the Virgin Birth[5] or...) is nonsense' to 'Christianity is nonsense'.

It is, therefore, entirely understandable that, as a child myself, such knowledge and understanding of the Christian Faith that I possessed was patchy and limited. **Yet I can recall quite clearly, although I can't say precisely how old I was at the time (possibly aged somewhere between 5 and 8?), wondering when it would be my turn to be Jesus.** I have never heard this strange idea expressed by anyone else, nor have I ever (before now) written about such an obviously weird, if not wonderful, notion. Nor can I explain how and why this particular thought came to me: somehow I had developed the idea, presumably through the impact these school assemblies and scripture lessons had on me (I cannot think of any other source), that the whole of humanity took turns in being Jesus, one after the other and, I suppose, living that same life over and over again - or perhaps differently: who knows? Fans of Michael Moorcock's 1966 novella 'Ecce Homo'[6] may find my idea ringing bells. To be clear: this was no kind of obsession, nor did I dwell on it in any way. I certainly didn't share it. It was just an occasionally recurring, albeit passing thought that, at the time, seemed pretty obvious to me, but which I fairly soon forgot. Until it recently, once again, came to mind.

Yet today, as physicists speak of a multiverse (an infinite number of universes existing in an infinite number of dimensions, yet all linked) in which, according to the ramifications of 'string' or 'M-theory', every possible event occurs, my odd little idea might not be thought quite so 'mad' or incoherent as it appears at first glance. Although I am not holding my breath that it will eventually become recognised as a great new Christological insight. For many of us, still, saying: 'I am Jesus', is as bizarre as anyone saying 'I am God': which is precisely what many Christians continue to believe that Jesus himself claimed. It is my intention to explore both the meaning and the validity of that assertion.

Subjecting myself to some brief theological self-analysis:

this strange, childish or childlike thought of mine might explain why, having been studying theology 'properly' since A Level Biblical Studies (and then via Bachelor's, Master's and Doctoral Degrees), and never having stopped asking all kinds of bothersome questions since I was drawn into the Church aged 11 by the music teacher at my grammar school who happened to be the local organist-choirmaster (Rest in Peace, Reg), I have always assumed that Jesus Christ ('Son of God', '2nd Person of the Trinity', but certainly Jesus of Nazareth) was, like me, absolutely and utterly human. Indeed, if he wasn't, then he is, in a very significant sense, theologically irrelevant to us and our needs and, most importantly, he was certainly not like us "in *every* respect" (Hebs 2: 17).

Furthermore, if Jesus were 'God', then what was God doing playing at being human: going to the Cross and, unlike every other executed or tortured person in the whole of history, actually knowing that although it might hurt, it would be alright in the end? Precisely the same point is made in the augmented 'Credo' in Bernstein's 'Mass'.[7] It would be rather like me dressing up for a part in a play, being 'killed', and then going home for tea. If the response to this comparison were to be: 'you are breaking an important Trinitarian rule by confusing ("confounding") God (Son) with God (Father)', then I would need to be shown how explaining it like that doesn't break the complementary rule by 'dividing the substance'[8] and so descend inevitably into bi- or duotheism (belief in two Gods).

As a result of my absolute – almost innate – conviction of Christ's 'true humanity' I have never been able to accept, from the time I was that questioning teenager,[9] that Jesus was the child of a miraculous, interventionist conception for, surely, not having genuinely human DNA and genes[10] inherited from a biological father would be bound to compromise any genuine humanity? What kind of human being would it be who possessed DNA and genes only from one parent? With further, more advanced, study of the nature of the Biblical texts I came to understand that the two nativity stories found in Matthew and Luke[11] are not only independent, but obviously different and clearly incompatible.[12] These two stories arose, as Matthew makes explicit, from a deep reflection on the Jewish scriptures: such-and-such a thing occurred "to fulfil what had been spoken by the Lord through the prophet" (e.g. Mt 2: 15), and the specific development of the notion of a virginal conception may well have been influenced or even inspired by the fact that the Greek translation of those Scriptures used by the Evangelists, the Septuagint (LXX), transformed the 'young woman' of Isaiah 7: 14 into a 'virgin',[13] thus offering *carte blanche* to those first Jewish Christians scouring their scriptures for evidence that the coming of Christ (the Messiah) was not only predicted, but altogether special. This process may have been further enhanced by a widespread tendency in the ancient world to ascribe special births to great men. These nativity stories clearly present theological, as opposed to either gynaecological or historical truths, such as in Matthew's recurring theme: 'Jesus as the new Moses' (both had to flee from evil rulers; both came 'out of Egypt').

Yet my conclusion that there are only two genuinely historical aspects of the nativity stories: 1. that Jesus was born (probably in Nazareth) and 2. that his mother was named Mary (and his father may have been Joseph: see Chapter 4 for further discussion), has never stopped me immersing myself devotionally in 'the meaning of Christmas' and benefitting spiritually from that experience. The story of the announcement of the birth of God's Son, himself born in poverty, to nobodies (shepherds) and somewhat dubious and unnumbered astrologers or magicians (*magoi*), rather than to the religious and political elite, is an object lesson in understanding God's priorities and doesn't, for me, need to reflect 'what really happened' in order to be both moving and powerful. Just as it is not at all necessary, for belief in a Creator God, to assert that Genesis 1 provides a quasi-scientific account of the mechanics of creation; nor that calling Jesus the 'Second Adam' requires us to accept that there once was an original 'historical Adam' (although Paul – and Jesus himself – probably believed there was).

Such issues bring us face to face with one of the most fundamental and most disputed problems in Christian theology: how should the Bible be understood? What does it mean to say it is 'inspired'?[14] What is the nature of its 'authority'? What is the relationship between Scripture and Revelation? All these are huge and profound theological topics, each requiring a book devoted to itself: and many have been published over the years. In terms of the concerns and intentions of this study it will be sufficient to point to just three of the most relevant issues, which will be discussed in Chapter 3. Firstly, the variety of ways in which language is used, particularly in the Bible and when we ourselves seek to express 'the things of God' ('doing theology'): why is it that some Christians take as their default position the assumption that such language must normally be understood literally? The second takes the more general linguistic issues one step further, dealing specifically with the question as to how far the apparently 'historical' books of the Bible (particularly, in the NT, the Gospels and Acts) are historical in the sense we understand that designation today and, if not, what literary genre(s) do they inhabit? The third argues that Scripture is the record of God's revelation and not itself that revelation.

So that readers may understand my theological point-of-departure, I should explain that, for me, faith and belief are not the same. I understand 'faith' to represent my trusting relationship with a loving Father-Mother God ['belief-in'], whilst my beliefs are the outcomes of my reflection on that faith in the light of scripture, tradition, experience and reason ['belief-that']. The first refers to an attitude, an affective process; the second refers to a cognitive, cerebral process. Should any think this a curious distinction to make, they might usefully consider its

Biblical pedigree. In the NT the verb *pisteuein* is often translated 'to believe', whilst the noun *pistis* is translated 'faith' and the adjective *pistos*: 'faithful'. In Pauline scholar, David Horrell's view:

> *"It is probably better...to translate...'pisteuein' 'to have faith' rather than 'to believe'...because the words for Paul have less to do with the notion of believing in the existence of, or accepting certain propositions about, and more to do with entrusting and committing oneself to the object of faith.*[15]

If, as many scholars concur, the so-called Pastoral Epistles (1 & 2 Timothy and Titus) are not authentically Pauline (pseudonymous writings), then we are able to view part of the process whereby, from the middle of the first century with increasing divergence in the way Christians were working out just what following Jesus meant, 'faith' gradually changed its meaning-focus from 'trust' to 'belief':

> *"...in contrast to Paul's emphasis on faith as trust and commitment, the Pastorals seem to treat faith more as a body of teaching, which must be safely preserved (e.g. 1 Tim 4: 6; 6: 10; Titus 1: 13). This is often seen as one indication of the later origin of these letters, some decades after Paul's death, when a major concern was to protect and guard the teaching which the original apostles had bequeathed to the church (see 1 Tim 6: 20; 2 Tim 1: 14). Instead of extended theological argument (see, for example, Gal 3: 1 – 5: 1; Rom 1: 18 – 11: 36), theology in the Pastorals seems to be expressed in concise credal statements, which are perhaps reflections of the ways in which crucial Christian beliefs were [later in the 1st C.] being summarised and recited [e.g. 1 Tim 3: 16]."*[16]

This led to a situation, which continues to prevail in many churches, where 'believing-that' came to be more important than 'believing-in'; and the process may be tracked throughout the NT. It is clear from the traditions behind the Synoptics that, for Jesus, faith was not a matter of 'believing the right things', nor holding uncritically to some corpus of religious rules. As important as the Jewish Scriptures were to him, emphasised most powerfully by Matthew (5: 17 – 19), Jesus felt free to reinterpret traditions found in the Torah, such as Sabbath observance (Mk 2: 27 - 28). For Jesus, true faith was expressed through personal familial trust: in him as Master and Lord, and in God as Father (Mt 9: 22; 15: 28; 17: 20; Mk 11: 22 etc.). As we have just seen, this also seems to have been Paul's understanding. The great faith of Abraham, which was pivotal to Paul's (and later Luther's) theology (e.g. Rom 4: 9), was again trust in God, not in a set of beliefs, nor even in a book: not least because in Abraham's time there was no book. Even when, as in Mt 21: 21, 'faith' is opposed to 'doubt', this is clearly not a reference to any kind of intellectual doubting, but to a lack of trust.

As those who followed 'the Way' (the original term for following Jesus) morphed into 'churches' – becoming both more organised and hierarchical – and because these local Christian communities came to do things differently and even believe quite different things about Jesus[17] (particularly after the destruction of Jerusalem in 70CE when it became strategically important to make a distinction between 'Judaism' and 'Christianity': a distinction that had not been particularly significant during the first 20 years or so), Christian leaders began to place much more of a premium on a shared 'faith' (i.e. an established set of beliefs) as an important indicator of Christian identity. So 1 Jn 2: 26 and 2 Jn 1: 7 where the author is concerned that Christians are being deceived by 'heretical' teachers: "Many deceivers have gone out into the world...".

Yet it is surely faith as 'believing in': our relationship with God in Christ, that is of the utmost importance; whereas our beliefs *about* God and Jesus are relatively unimportant.[18] That is because living in an ambiguous universe where some see evidence of design, whilst others – looking at exactly the same phenomena – read absolute randomness and purposelessness, and taking human fallibility and relative ignorance seriously, such beliefs will always be fundamentally uncertain (the opposite of faith is distrust; the opposite of belief is unbelief;[19] that 'doubt' can refer to both just adds to the confusion). There are many Christians who would dispute my view, claiming that 'right belief' is essential for salvation. But a few moments thought shows how foolish and trivial such an idea is: if what we believe is so important then why has God not made everything so much clearer?[20]

As referenced in the previous endnote: John Hick, developing further the theodicy[21] of Irenaeus in his seminal 'Evil and the God of Love', pointed to the necessity for human freedom that there be an 'epistemic distance' (a knowledge gap: 'epistemology' is the theory of knowledge) between God and humanity. The greatest question of all: that of the existence of God, is neither provable nor unprovable: if either were, then all – except the irrational – would hold the same belief. On this, as on many other matters, we are free to decide one way or the other; or free even not to bother to think much about it. If there is a God, and if that God seeks to reveal himself to us, then it is a subtle, rather than an 'in-your-face', revelation. Such ambiguity, caution or hesitancy is the natural outcome of it not being imposed upon us. God's revelation in and through the created order, or indeed through Christ ('revealed' as opposed to 'natural' theology[22]), is never blindingly obvious: some will discern it; others, for whatever reason, will not.

If, on the other hand, God made everything, including himself, absolutely clear, then we would have no choice but to 'bow down and worship' for this would indeed be 'your God':[23] but a God whose majesty so dominated and overwhelmed everything else that human life would inevitably become enslaved to the

Reality. Freedom of knowledge would abolish every other human freedom, including our freedom to be ignorant. Knowing all there is to know would eradicate the essential core of our humanity which, by definition, is finite and fallible. Instead, we have a God who, in self-limiting and abasing himself in humility,[24] 'lets us be'[25] truly human. If, as a result, our beliefs turn out to be wrong, it is hardly our fault. That is why beliefs in themselves are not particularly important, and I can't imagine that the ultimately mysterious Creator of the Universe worries over much about them: certainly not to the extent of giving them any role in human salvation.

It remains a fact that due, not least, to the natural limitations in human knowledge, Christians do not all believe precisely the same things and think in precisely the same way; indeed, there are occasionally quite substantial differences (such as beliefs about determinism versus free will, or the practice and validity of the sacraments – even how many sacraments there are). Who is to adjudicate on what is correct or not: the Pope, the Archbishop of Canterbury, some American Televangelist – or you or me? Churches cannot even agree on which Biblical texts are canonical, or in what order they should appear. One of the greatest intellectual problems posed by 'faith as belief' is that it provides an excuse for believing anything, however bizarre, just because 'my faith tells me to'. In this way 'what I believe' is self-validating: 'you can only be saved if you believe the right things' soon becomes 'you can only be saved if you believe as I do': the self-assured rhetoric of the religious fanatic of any Faith.

Despite the fact that I have developed my Christian faith and formed my beliefs absorbing everything that the Church has thrown at me (even, due to the care and great patience of those curates who had the 'youth-brief' automatically dumped on them, to the extent of being ordained), I have continued to hold to this absolute conviction: Jesus was really human. I have hardly been heretical in doing so, because the genuine humanity of Christ is precisely what the Church has always affirmed. But it has also affirmed his equally 'true' divinity and so, over the years, have I: at least insofar as I have understood what that claim has meant. I have always been aware that, however one imagines or expresses it, the doctrine of the one who is both human and divine is not at all straightforward either to understand or to express: the early Christian Fathers demonstrated that clearly enough by their regular flirtations with 'heresy'.

In recent years, particularly as I have taught Christian doctrine to ordinands and others, and seeking to deal with their evident puzzlement and their questions ('just what is the substance that Christ shares with the Father?'), I have become increasingly clear in my own mind that the classic statements of Nicaea and Chalcedon which speak of the 'divine man' are simply incomprehensible: they are devoid of meaning and thus (I say this technically and not abusively) strictly nonsense. How can we possibly argue that an assertion which we can neither demonstrate nor adequately define can have any meaning? How can we retreat into the concept of mystery and be intellectually satisfied with that? Most basically, how, logically, can a finite man also be the infinite God? It makes no sense. As I don't like being asked to believe no[n]sense, I have now come to 'question the Incarnation', not because I seek to deny it (or to use the common calumny against liberal theologians: that I 'doubt'), nor because I believe it to be fundamentally untrue (although meaning must always precede truth: nonsense can be neither true nor false). **I want to question the Incarnation in the very straightforward, non-pejorative sense of asking: what does it mean to speak of a man who is also God**? If any who read this book are tempted to dismiss my views out of hand because they appear to be reductionist or otherwise heretical, then perhaps they might bear this in mind. I am not denying the Incarnation: I merely want to know what the concept means and what the actuality entailed. Don't you; or do you think you know already?

The Council of Chalcedon (451CE) came up with one way of expressing how 'the Word became flesh'. If that no longer makes sense (if it ever did) there must surely be alternatives? Otherwise I would sooner fall theologically into Adoptionism than into Docetism,[26] even though neither provides a satisfactory answer to the Incarnational question. That is why I am convinced that it is of the first importance to seek to reinterpret or reformulate classical Christology, so that it might make sense and be meaningful and effectively convey that meaning to the generations that are growing up in a world where things like multiverses, the quantum realm and chaos theory are discussed on prime-time TV.

A theological health warning

Arising from my experiences teaching ordinands and trainee Readers, tutoring new curates through the process of 'theological reflection' ('IME 2' in the CE), preaching and leading study groups at church, all of which require keeping up-to-date with the scholarship, some careful thinking and a real preparedness to answer sometimes tricky questions, I have in mind two particular audiences for this book, which uses the scholarly research of many others (for whose insights I am most grateful, particularly those stimulating writers with whom I have entered into dialogue) as a basis for my own proposals for the urgent rethinking of some serious doctrinal issues.

Fellow clergy: those who, due perhaps to time pressures or difficulty in navigating the increasingly complex theological book market, have hardly opened a book of theology since ordination and who, as a result, find themselves totally out-of-date and/or bewildered by the scholarship of the past few decades; there may well be those who are still unsure how to stick their liberal heads over the parapets during a period in which we are witnessing an increasing turn to fundamentalism of all kinds in the Church; those who would share my view that being a Christian doesn't mean we have to stop thinking or otherwise ignore our critical faculties.[27]

Enquiring lay people: particularly, but not only, those seeking to offer themselves for some kind of Christian ministry, who may be totally unaware of the range, creativity and insights of modern biblical and theological scholarship; this group (those 'in the pew') is the majority membership of the *laos* of God (being ordained neither removes clergy from the 'whole people of God' nor does it make them superior members of it[28]); these are those whose exposure to theological thinking has been mainly or wholly through the liturgy, hearing the Bible read, attending to sermons offered for elucidation and encouragement – those who have been, very appropriately, called 'ordinary theologians';[29] some, even many, may feel that the theological 'diet' they have so far received at church via those sermons and the ubiquitous home-study group, has been somewhat bland, majoring rather more in piety than in any rigorous and clear-sighted theological reflection; this is because some clergy continue to believe that too much biblical and theological knowledge can never be a 'good thing', as it must inevitably lead to that doubt from which the laity need protecting at all costs.

This is still a very live issue. Lloyd Geering recalls a conversation he had with a former student friend, who had become a lawyer, back in 1963 following the publication of John Robinson's 'Honest to God' and a follow-up article by Geering himself on the Resurrection: *"[My friend] complained to me, 'I have been a loyal churchman all my life, and I am a reasonably intelligent person. Why have I not been told all this before?'"* Geering comments:

"His complaint was fully justified. I was simply discussing what scholars had been writing about for quite some time, but none of it had ever been heard by people in the pews...A great gulf had been opening up between the thinking of theologians and biblical

scholars on the one hand, and what was still being preached in the churches on the other. It was not that preachers deliberately hid from their congregations what they themselves often learned about in their seminaries; it was rather that pastoral concern for their parishioners had led them to regard the weekly sermon as a way to encourage and comfort its hearers rather than upset them with new and challenging ideas. Unfortunately, this growing gulf between the pulpit and the pew left the congregations in ignorance, with the result that the mainline churches are today suffering rapid decline, as increasing numbers have been drifting out of the churches, feeling that the 'old time religion' is no longer relevant to today's life." [30]

That original discussion took place over 50 years ago, but little appears to have changed: Geering wrote this account only recently. Many Christian lay people continue, for whatever reasons (clerical lack of knowledge or their inability or unwillingness to share what knowledge they have), to live in ignorance about a burgeoning scholarship which has the capacity to impact directly on their understanding of their faith. How, to put the matter bluntly, can lying (even by omission) ever be better than telling the truth? Do not church folk deserve to be given the fullest picture of Christian belief and, if the effects of that experience are at all negative or felt to undermine faith, to be helped through the sometimes tough discipline of revising their understanding? More positively, is that challenge not an aspect of the essential risk that adopting (or indeed denying) a religious faith involves? Why should mature Christians be treated as intellectual or spiritual babes in arms? To all such 'kept-in-the-dark' (and patronised) Christians, I offer what follows as a potential step towards theological freshness and liberation; towards the adoption of basic beliefs about Jesus which do not collide with or contradict other ways of thinking in the modern world.

Christie's research into 'Ordinary Christology' makes it clear that many 'ordinary theologians' are simply flummoxed by much of the Church's teaching about Jesus, both his person and his role as saviour, and find the only way of dealing intellectually with that problem is to think of Jesus either as 'just a good man': an exemplar 'sent by God' for us to imitate, or as God's (possibly unique) messenger, albeit one similar in kind to and certainly not absolutely distinct from, any other of God's chosen human agents. By contrast, there are those, predominantly from the Evangelical tradition, who know exactly what they believe and don't worry over-much about it making sense to them.[31] This tendency to acknowledge problems, but accompanying that with a refusal to consider them any further, seems to be motivated by a fear that the very act of thinking for yourself equates to loss of faith (particularly where faith is treated as a synonym for belief), and so they will accuse the questioning Christian of being a 'doubter' (as opposed to a 'believer'), so failing to recognise that she is no such thing: she is merely a Christian whose beliefs and understanding differ from theirs. This is why 'doing theology', and particularly engaging in 'critical' (as opposed to devotional) bible study, is often seen by religious conservatives as a threat to faith. Ironically, such a stance often evokes a bizarre sense of pride: 'the more difficult something is to believe, the greater my faith must be'. When the mere act of thinking about one's faith is seen to be blasphemous and potentially a spiritually dangerous enterprise, one can only wonder where theology – for Anselm: 'Faith Seeking Understanding' – would be if all Christians lacked a sense of curiosity.

The American ex-fundamentalist, Paul Brynteson, explains such concerns about the dangers of generally knowing too much, not least too much about the Bible:

> *"One can understand why those who ascribe [sic 'subscribe'?] to fundamentalism in their faith journey are often opposed to public*

education and especially higher education. They fear too much critical thinking might lead people away from their faith. My parents and others of my childhood faith often spoke against the 'sins of education', and how too much education caused individuals to leave the faith. How interesting it was to hear a 2012 presidential candidate state such a position. In an hour-long interview with conservative television host Glenn Beck, Rick Santorum said, 'I understand why Barack Obama wants to send every kid to college, because of their indoctrination mills...The indoctrination that is going on at the university level is harmful to our country'...Since the focus of fundamentalism is to tell individuals what to think and believe, they seem to be threatened by higher education with its emphasis of encouraging individuals to think for themselves".[32]

Brynteson further reflects on his own upbringing and the spiritual life-journey which, after many years, led him to take leave of such an intellectually claustrophobic milieu[33] which for him had involved full acceptance of a particularly American form of Millenarianism carrying with it the psychological impact of the *"'left behind' narrative...[which] can lead one to suppress any doubts or concerns about the Bible as being the Word of God"*[34] out of fear of thus being 'left behind' at the Rapture as punishment for one's lack of belief (for them, faith). He tells how, as a result, he lost friends and how those ex-friends quoted biblical texts which (they claimed) "condemned" those who dared query the meaning and (thus the) authority of the Bible. He then quotes an observation of Bruce Bawer, explaining how it fitted his own experience exactly:

"Fundamentalist, evangelical, and charismatic Christianity demands believers not thinkers...no evidence, no logic, no personal experience, nothing can change their minds about 'revealed truth'. Questioning 'revealed truth' in any way challenges the belief system at its core. The more successfully any 'revealed truth' is

challenged, the more vehemently the challenge must be rejected."[35]

In which case, **this book may well require some kind of theological 'health-warning'**, for it is intended not only to encourage thinking, but to encourage the most creative and radical thinking ('radical', here, in the exact sense of 'going back to the roots' – examining and nurturing those which need attention so that new growth may result). It will invite the enquiring and open-minded reader to reconsider those theological 'truths' about Jesus Christ which were 'discovered' and pronounced upon during the first five Christian centuries and which, since then, have been repeated over and over again, virtually as confirmed facts which require no further discussion: that he was/is both human and divine (the 'hypostatic union'), that he and his Father God shared/share the 'same substance' (*homoousios*), and even that Jesus had two wills or minds (dyothelitism). We will ask what meaning these kinds of belief have, and whether there are alternative ways of affirming the 'divine' nature of Christ and the relationship he had/has with God that may be more accessible to Christians 1500 years on. It will argue a case firmly based in Biblical scholarship, undergirded by modern science (insofar as I have successfully managed to grasp the basic principles – I am not a scientist) and philosophy.

The arguments may also be of interest to those who have either abandoned an earlier faith, or never embraced one in the first place yet have an interest in learning more about the religion which lies at the base of their culture and which still, at least for a while longer, informs many of our national political and social structures, as well as many cultural events. Yet the only Christian festivals in Britain today, following the demise of Whitsun (when Pentecost occurs away from the Spring Bank Holiday weekend, it is hardly noticed outside the churches), which impact at all on the consciousness of secular people are Christmas: the great Feast of the Incarnation and Easter, not least because national holidays are still arranged around them.[36] Christmas (and Easter to a lesser degree, because it has neither the 'magic' nor the apparent simplicity of Christmas) has taken on an entirely new set of meanings for most people today as the 'feast' is now dominated by commerce, 'family time', and children, none of which is particularly problematic in itself, but all possess some characteristics which sit somewhat uneasily with the 'true meaning' of Christmas: the birth of a child expressing unconditional love and self-sacrifice existing in and vying with a culture which promotes excess and self-gratification.

Advent is, to all intents and purposes a 'dead duck' so far as secular Britain is concerned, because 'Christmas' now begins in November (after Halloween and certainly by Black Friday,, both of which have successfully made the Atlantic crossing: how much longer before Britons embrace Thanksgiving as well?). Betjeman's poem would probably ring very few bells today (excuse pun): but although 1955 is in many ways a very foreign country, some things remain the same: the 'coloured cards' are still around, although increasingly featuring some unusual and even bizarre 'Christmas' themes:

> "...The Advent bells call out 'Prepare,
> Your world is journeying to the birth
> Of God made Man for us on earth.'
>
> And how, in fact, do we prepare
> The great day that waits us there -
> For the twenty-fifth day of December,
> The birth of Christ? For some it means
> An interchange of hunting scenes
> On coloured cards, And I remember
> Last year I sent out twenty yards,
> Laid end to end, of Christmas cards
> To people that I scarcely know -

They'd sent a card to me, and so
I had to send one back. Oh dear!
Is this a form of Christmas cheer...?"[37]

How is this 'great Feast of the Incarnation' received by many, if
not most, today? We might consider the example of journalist,
author and broadcaster Sir Simon Jenkins,[38] whose father was a
URC Minister. Jenkins was brought up a Christian 'child of the
Manse', but now describes himself as "non-practising" – albeit
still a self-designated – "Christian". He writes:

"Christmas has become a secular festival, booming even as its
origins grow insignificant for most celebrants. It is best left that
way. Like most non-practising Christians, I cannot remember when
I 'stopped believing' in baby Jesus and Santa Claus. My family was
devout and said prayers at Christmas, but I have no recollection of
any switch from belief to non-belief. I regarded, as I still do, such
cultural traditions as integral to a British family and community.
I also loved the specialness of the season, as I rather miss the one-
time 'specialness' of Sunday. What I vividly remember and try to
maintain is the sense of occasion, the awe at the beauty of things
and of music. As for belief, I rely on the little girl who, when asked
if she still believed in Santa, said 'Yes, but only for one more year'.
I therefore treat Christmas with a light touch...we need no myth or
metaphysic to appreciate beauty or to bind our families together in
the commune of humanity".[39]

Is it that children eventually grow out of Christ and they grow
out of Santa Claus (Jenkins links the two), even 'believing' (like
the little girl), at least for a while longer, for the sake of it?[40] How
many churches today have many (or any) children attending
who are above primary school age?[41] Church, in many places, is
mainly for 'little kids and old ladies'.

But Santa Claus isn't real (that is my working assumption), and

Jesus Christ is. Making any kind of conceptual link between the two is an indictment of (at least) the state of Religious Education in schools which has left many inhabitants of this 'Christian nation' below the age of 40 or so possessing little knowledge or understanding of very basic Christian 'facts' (such as why 'Good Friday' is special), as well as representing the abject failure of the Church to engage effectively with the modern world in so many different ways (not the least being attitudes to women and homosexuality which have led many to conclude that the Church is obsessed with gender and sexual matters and cares little for anything else), so that for many today the Church is an irrelevance and its role in society purely aesthetic or ceremonial: it is often the case that when weddings are conducted in church or babies baptised, the main or even whole motivation is nor religious at all, but social and cultural.

The 2015 Report of the 'Commission on Religion and Belief in British Public Life',[42] published just a couple of weeks before Christmas, when many houses were already covered in Christmas decorations: predominantly flashing lights and inflatable Santas and Snowmen, when producers of Advent Calendars and Christmas Cards yet again privileged comic book heroes, footballers and, indeed, any subject that will sell, over any nativity scene, concluded that Christianity, whilst still the largest single Faith, was in terminal decline (with all the implications for 'Establishment' issues). It would appear[43] that between the 2001 and 2011 censuses the number of those who describe themselves as Christian has fallen from an eighth in England and a third in Scotland to just under a half in total. Perhaps paradoxically (or possibly not), it is often reported that where the World Wide Church is actually growing is among conservative Evangelical/Charismatic/Pentecostal congregations which, perhaps, respond to the need of some for a clear, simple and secure set of certainties in their religion.

The logic of this might suggest, to some, that the answer for church growth is for the Christian Faith to abandon its 'wishy-washy' liberalism (particularly found, it is often alleged, in the Church of England) in favour of a full-blooded, unalloyed Gospel message that includes stern judgement, hell (for those outside) and heaven (for those 'like us'). Because, according to self-designated 'Bible-believing Christians' (what precisely is a Bible-non-believing Christian?), that is 'what the Bible says'. I don't intend to discuss the reasons why such conservative Christianities seem to be thriving – that is not my purpose, and 'well done' to them for they are clearly meeting spiritual, emotional and social needs . But I do want to suggest that if there is a problem with 'wishy-washy liberalism', it is more due to its perceived 'wishy-washiness' or 'woolliness' rather than the 'liberal' element itself. We theological liberals need to be bolder, and less apologetic, in explaining just what it is we believe, and why.

After all – and providing an additional rationale for books such as this which seek to stimulate independent creative and progressive theological thinking – according to the well-known and respected writers, Andrew Brown and Linda Woodhead (respectively, religious journalist and academic), commenting on the situation at the turn of the century:

> "Among the ranks of ordinary Anglicans, liberalism was as much a temper and way of life as a belief system – and most ordinary Anglicans were rather liberal."[44]

Yet such liberals have not been well nourished by Churches of all denominations which, for a variety of quite different reasons, reflecting their own denominational priorities and concerns, have sought to restrict what their members should believe to simplistic 'truths'. As we have seen, this has been the tendency ever since 'believing that' became privileged over 'believing-in' towards the end of the first Christian century, and the attainment of a rigid 'orthodoxy' became a prime goal exemplified by, but not limited to, the horrendous post-Reformation 'wars of religion' when Christians killed each other for not believing 'the right things'. It is hardly a surprise, with such an emphasis on the importance of 'correct believing' and with each Christian group so certain their version is correct, that the history of the Church has been a succession of splits. One person's orthodoxy has been another's heresy and, despite the best efforts of ecumenists, that is the way it continues to be (so, for example, Anglicans still cannot officially receive communion in RC churches). Even individual denominations (and, in some cases, individual congregations) continue to have their rivalries, arguments and internal divisions and, despite claims to the contrary, single clear orthodoxies are not easy to find, not least in the Church of England with

"...evangelicals [setting] store by a small set of central beliefs which they could happily recite, and Anglo-Catholics [putting] their faith in rituals and ceremonies... [and where] Liberal reticence to proclaim their faith owed less to lack of conviction than to a concern not to embarrass or coerce anyone".[45]

The response of enlightened laity to such squabbling has been to leave the churches in their droves although, despite what some might think, this does not necessarily entail abandoning their faith.[46] Perhaps a more open-minded Church, one which takes seriously the findings and insights of 21st Century scholarship, might one day be able to welcome them back? Surely, after 2000 years, it is time that people recognised that when it comes to the 'things of God', certainty is unattainable and that different insights might be mutually shared to everyone's benefit rather than being a cause of division. That will not happen until 'believing-in' is once more restored to its rightful and overwhelmingly Biblical place as absolutely superior to 'believing-that'. What, we might even ask, are God's priorities: that we believe 'the right things' about him, or that we develop as loving and compassionate beings, obedient to his will, and rooting actively for his Kingdom?

There have been a few prominent exemplars of Anglican *theological* liberalism creating spiritual apoplexy in conservative ecclesiastical circles, such as the former Bishop of Durham, David Jenkins, whose views were claimed by Evangelicals to have inspired God to strike York Minster, the site of his consecration, with his angry lightning:

> *"For the liberals, and for anyone who believed in the Church as a part of English culture, Jenkins became a beacon in the darkness. He got people talking about Christianity in pubs and workplaces and this seemed to them to reaffirm it as a part of society".*[47]

A little more widespread and persistent has been an Anglican *political* liberalism, exemplified by the publication of the 1985 Report: 'Faith in the City', widely viewed as a direct attack on the Thatcher Government. Nevertheless, Brown and Woodhead's judgement on the state of liberal thinking and its influence on and within the power bases of the Church of England from the turn of the century, allied with (indeed, creating) its then imminent 'decoupling' from English society, is devastating:

> *"The evangelicals' hatred of liberals and obsession with moral purity led them to bind the Church into a commitment to the values of the 1950s, despite these becoming increasingly unpalatable to the rest of society on moral grounds as well as more pragmatic ones. Anglo-Catholics let their opposition to women's ordination cloud their judgement, and exposed a nasty vein of clerical in-fighting over petty privileges and preferment. The 'don't ask, don't tell' policy [particularly relating to sexual matters] by which church leaders had conducted church business for so long was exposed as*

hiding corruption of the sort evangelicals had long suspected. And the liberal elite failed to stand up to any of it. They had been so used to running the show that they underestimated the power of evangelicals operating in the context of the [General] Synod and overestimated the elegant patrician power which they had exercised for so long. By the time they noticed how much just about everything had changed it was too late."[48]

Despite the success of the campaigns for women's ordination and, latterly, consecration in the CE (possibly driven as much by pragmatism – clergy shortage - as conviction), little has actually changed in terms of the pervasive hold on Churches of all varieties of conservatism: theological, biblical and moral. Brown and Woodhead have no doubt of the extent of this increasing conservative hegemony in the CE (together with the apparent perception of many 'conservative' Christians, which may include those who have never had the opportunity to explore their beliefs post-Sunday School, that the way they understand the Bible and doctrine is the norm and that it is modernising liberals who are theologically out of step: and perhaps they are right) when they write of the years following the Lambeth Conference of 1998 at which the Bishop of Enugu, Nigeria, sought publicly to exorcise the Revd Richard Kirker of his homosexuality, when Rowan Williams, as Archbishop of Canterbury, appeared to backpedal on his former support for gays:

"Once Rowan had shown he could be bullied, the conservatives redoubled their efforts to enforce a homophobic line across all the churches of the Anglican Communion";[49] *or put another way: "The liberals and the dons had been robbed of power under George Carey and then robbed of hope by their supposed leader Rowan Williams [... adding] The evangelicals achieved power and then showed they had no idea what to do with it, themselves splintering into contending factions. The Anglo-Catholics were smashed to bits by feminism.*

All that seemed left was worried clergy and ageing congregations huddled in decaying buildings with a kind of grey determination to keep up the show."[50]

The need for some kind of broad liberal revival, particularly if the Church is not to become either totally irrelevant or, like Monty Python's parrot totally dead, is almost palpable.

Before we begin: two final points of clarification

Firstly, in the midst of all the disagreements described above, orthodoxies and heresies, claims and counter-claims, it is important to note that **one issue on which all Trinitarian Christians agree** (although, as we shall see in Chapter 2, not always on the detail) is the Doctrine of the Incarnation: the focus of this book. Indeed, one thing which is almost guaranteed to bring about unanimous condemnation is any attempt – such as this – to 'question' either that doctrine or the historic creeds which proclaim it. Although I have made crystal clear what I mean by 'questioning' the Incarnation, that may not be sufficient to open minds which view the doctrine as being literally beyond question. Within the CE, it may be the one issue which brings Evangelical and Anglo-Catholic together, in which case I may be able to make at least some contribution to ecclesial unity. Yet the central question, the one I am asking: 'what actually does the doctrine mean?' is seldom given much thought, because the main attention of many Christians, and particularly their leaders, has been on other, arguably less central matters, such as who is sleeping with whom.

Yet it is important to understand that during the 300+ years before Chalcedon many different ways of understanding the Incarnation were hotly debated with this or that idea discarded as heretical and occasionally reinstated, at least for a while. It is, perhaps, putting the matter too simplistically, but there is some truth in the claim that had the Emperor not fallen off his horse and died in 450 CE, orthodoxy would have embraced a single nature doctrine of Christ (monophysitism), as opposed to the dual nature which a year later became 'orthodoxy' not least because the new Emperor took a different view.[51] Again, as we shall discuss in Chapter 2, the united 'orthodoxy' achieved at the Council of Chalcedon was really nothing of the kind, as several great churches (thenceforth known as 'non-Chalcedonian') refused to endorse it and went into schism (or, as we shall shortly see: a 'schism-that-possibly-wasn't-really'). Incarnational agreement has never, certainly from the Reformation (after Chalcedon Soteriology became a more pressing concern than Christology about which there seemed to be nothing much more to say) through to today, been absolutely unanimous when one considers the varied proposals, for example, of John Owen, the Socinians, Schleiermacher, the Kenoticists[52] and many others, not least the much derided 'Myth scholars' of the 1970s and 80s. Yet we should not be surprised; we might expect at least some continuing questions and disagreements arising both from the nature of the doctrine itself ('the great *mystery* of the Incarnation') and the nature of the 'evidence' for it.

Secondly, it is important to establish that what I wish to denote by my use of the description **'liberal'** regarding the methodology for this book is the more limited notion of **an enquiring and critical**[53]**approach to matters of faith which considers the evidence and follows it fearlessly wherever it may lead.** The broader aspects of liberalism (political, moral and so on) may or may not arise from this (some liberal theologians may be quite conservative on moral issues), but those are not my main concern here. I wish to establish ways of seeking to understand the person of Jesus which don't require us to eschew our ability to think the issues through, calmly and carefully, and without feeling any need to 'toe a party line' or otherwise believe something just because we are instructed to do so. What this means for our use of the Bible (obviously the first and most important staging post in any investigation into the life and meaning of Jesus) will be explored in much greater detail in Chapter 3, but it is important to emphasise at this early stage that, despite the views of 'Bible-believing Christians', an open exploratory approach to the biblical text does not necessarily reduce or in any way demean the Bible's authority for Christians. It is rather a question of understanding the nature of that authority correctly. Biblical authority is to be found not in any allegedly inerrant information to be found therein, nor because the text is itself God's direct revelation, but rather because it is the (very human and necessarily fallible) record of God's revelation in Christ and, as such, the *fons et origo* of Christian faith, to which we need constantly to return in order to appropriate that original revelation (Christ, not the Bible) for ourselves, and to enable us to interpret and proclaim it anew to each generation.

Is such a way of proceeding in any way impermissible or disrespectful? Quite the contrary: the Anglican tradition in particular has always accepted that 'reason' – we might say: 'using our God-given brains' - has a role in theological method. Indeed

> "...*almost all theologians would be prepared to allow some place to reason, and the question at issue concerns the extent to which reason may enter as a formative factor...[but] we should never relinquish the ideal of a reasonable religion, in the sense of one whose content has been subjected to the scrutinising and corrective exercise of critical reason".*[54]

Or in the words of a scientist-theologian:

> "*The human quest for meaning and purpose draws on both our inner and outer experiences and reflects on them with both intuitive insight and rational thought – in other words, through the creative*

27

interaction of faith and reason. Throughout most of the Christian theological tradition, faith and reason have been companions on this journey of life; they have been seen as complementary and not contradictory...the fracturing of this relationship is a relatively recent phenomenon, occurring over the past three hundred years, and is primarily a product of Enlightenment rationalism and Cartesian foundationalism...We now recognise that fact and value cannot be separated, for all facts are value laden, contextual truths, It is interpretation (hermeneutics) that transforms raw data into meaningful fact, by placing that data in a meaningful theoretical context, which is itself value laden".[55]

Finally, a very apposite warning was given by Archbishop William Temple:

"...revelation can, and in the long run must, on pain of becoming manifest as superstition, vindicate its claim by satisfying reason".[56]

In other words, if not entirely rational in the sense that every religious claim is founded on some unquestionable metaphysic or some other ground which can be objectively demonstrated (when dealing with the things of God we must always recognise the possibility that we have come face-to-face with divine mystery – inevitable when God is inherently mysterious,[57] but which should never be used as an excuse for obfuscation), then our beliefs should 'satisfy reason' and most certainly not be irrational. Otherwise the content of our faith is bound to be equated with superstition, and theology would deserve to be consigned to the intellectual dustbin alongside alchemy and astrology. Attending church would then be the equivalent of avoiding walking under ladders, consulting the stars, or taking out a spiritual insurance policy. We should not be invited, as was Alice in 'Through the Looking Glass', to believe 'six impossible things before breakfast', although sometimes we may feel that is precisely what some sections of the Church are inviting us to do, thus facing Locke's criticism:

> *"He that believes without having any reason for believing may be in love with his own fancies, but neither seeks truth as he ought nor pays the obedience due his maker, who would have him use those discerning faculties he has given him, to keep him out of mistake and error".*[58]

Reason, reasonableness, and the ability and willingness to use our 'discerning faculties' lie at the basis of all scholarship which properly proceeds on the basis of evidence and argument, not on the basis of what we would like, or what we have already decided, to be the case: and so should our theology, if it is to remain intellectually respectable. It is never sufficient just to say: 'The Bible says...', or even, as a bishop once told a clergy friend: 'The 39 Articles say...'!

If, despite areas of growth, Christianity, particularly in the developed world, is in decline, it may well be the outcome of the Church continuing to parrot old slogans, and even older ideas, in a context where people are much better educated, and also less biddable, than they were, and who have concluded that the way many Christian doctrines are traditionally presented is often, not only incomprehensible, but irrelevant to their modern lives: that what they are being called upon to believe is often unreasonable or even irrational, both defying and denying 'common sense'.[59] Just have a discussion with any intelligent, interested and often sympathetic agnostic in your local pub, or perhaps after a Carol Service. Such folk are often drawn in by the mystery of the Incarnation at Christmastide, but, in the end, because it is presented in such an ultra-simplistic manner (because Christmas services are often full of children, it is sometimes difficult – particularly for those churches which have abandoned Midnight Mass – to find the opportunity to present a 'meatier' theology), dismiss it as just 'something for the kids'. Just like Santa Claus who manages to visit all the children of the world in one night, so the Magi 'followed a star' to a specific site: "...and, there, ahead of them, went the star that they had seen at its rising, until it stopped over the place where the child was",[60] where they found a baby who never cried,[61] and probably didn't wet his nappy either.[62]

So is it possible that what many have 'grown out of' is not particularly the doctrine of the Incarnation *per se* (insofar as they think about it and, in thinking about it, understand it), but the way it continues to be expressed: repetition, without any interpretive comment beyond piety, of old 'supernatural' stories (which Jenkins – inaccurately - calls 'myth' and – accurate only in part - 'metaphysics')? But if such folk were helped to recognise the Christmas stories as what they are: a profound exercise in Incarnational theology (seeking to express our understanding of Christ and, thus, of God; for Christians, Christ will always be the 'way into' God) rather than history, such 'grown-up' "non-practising Christians" (ending this introduction where I began: in what sense is a Christian who doesn't practise, a Christian?[63]) might come to understand and appreciate the meaning those stories artfully conceal, and through them come to recognise the God who offers that meaning for their lives. Put simply: might a reinterpretation of the doctrine of the Incarnation prove a crucial element in the resurrection of Christianity? We begin our discussion by considering the problems both implicit in and raised by the classic formulations.

Notes

1. Levitt A. '"The church is very important to me." A consideration of the relevance of Francis' attitude towards Christianity scale to the aims of Church of England aided schools', in 'British Journal of Religious Education', (1995)

quotes a mother interviewed as part of a research project in Cornwall: *"I believe in God, you don't need to go to church, Christian I suppose I'd call myself...I have a belief. I let the children evolve their own."* Levitt then comments: *"What is typical about this mother and son is their acceptance of religious education in schools and tolerance* **to those who are religious as long as they are not proselytizing**"; she terms this 'normal' religion: *"a residual feeling of guilt, but not enough to make her ever attend church, and a determination not to force her own children to attend, but to leave it up to them"*; it is often assumed, she claims, that *"...those with a residual faith will turn to it again in time of crisis. In the course of the research six of the mothers had such crises...All of them said it made them think about God but only those who already had a church connection turned to a particular church. However, rather than their faith being increased [by the crises] it was more often diminished"*; what people with a residual faith have lost is *"their capacity to use, or listen to religious language"*; as a result: *"Their children had experienced religion as an optional activity out of school. They did not associate religious practice with hypocrisy, but simply saw it as something some people like to do"*;

2. From the widely adopted 1945 Surrey Agreed Syllabus: "The aim of the Syllabus is to secure that children attending the schools of the County...may gain knowledge of the common Christian faith held by their fathers [sic] for nearly 2000 years; may seek for themselves in Christianity principles which give a purpose to life and a guide to all its problems; and may find inspiration, power and courage to work for their own welfare, for that of their fellow creatures, and for the growth of God's kingdom": cited Hull JM 'Agreed syllabuses, past, present and future' in Smart N & Horder D (eds. 1975) 'New Movements in Religious Education' p. 100;

3. Then most commonly called Scripture or Bible or Religious Knowledge, and even 'Divinity', although this latter was

probably found more in fee-paying or grammar schools;

4. Ronald Goldman ['Religious Thinking from Childhood to Adolescence' (1964); 'Readiness for Religion' (1970)] was one of the pioneers of a properly educational approach to Religious Education, specifically applying Piaget's theories of childhood cognitive development to the teaching of Bible stories, although such ideas have much wider, yet still often disputed, applications;

5. More accurately termed 'virginal conception';

6. Novelised 1969, in which a time traveller takes on the role of Jesus of Nazareth, because the real Jesus was too inadequate, physically or mentally, to be 'the real Jesus', and goes to the cross in his place;

7. Based on the Roman Latin Liturgy this theatre piece was written for the opening of the newly constructed '[JF] Kennedy Center for the Performing Arts' in Washington DC, and premiered 8th Sept 1971; in the 'Credo' the baritone soloist sings: "And you became a man. You, God, chose to become a man. To pay the earth a small social call. I tell you, sir, **you never were a man at all.** Why? **You had the choice when to live, when to die. And then become a god again**...You chose to die, and then revive again. You chose, you rose alive again. But I, I don't know why I should live if only to die" (Additional texts: Stephen Schwartz & Leonard Bernstein);

8. "And the Catholick Faith is this: That we worship one God in Trinity, and Trinity in Unity; **Neither confounding the Persons: nor dividing the substance.** For there is one Person of the Father, another of the Son: and another of the Holy Ghost. But the Godhead of the Father, of the Son, and of the Holy Ghost, is all one: the Glory equal, the Majesty co-eternal": extract from the *Quicunque Vult*; this merely underlines how difficult it is to keep to these 'rules' which seek to both link divinity and humanity, whilst also keeping

them appropriately separate, so that, in terms of the Trinity, we often fall into the twin heresies of either tritheism or modalism;

9. I recall reading Leslie Weatherhead's newly published 'The Christian Agnostic' (1965) which includes a section entitled 'Virgin Birth' and feeling liberated by comments such as: "...I should recommend the Christian layman [sic] to put the idea of the Virgin Birth into the imaginary mental drawer to be labelled, 'Awaiting further light'"; "Divinity is not proved by having one parent instead of two"; "The Doctrine...may have begun as a rumour" (ibid. pp. 70 – 71); in retrospect I don't find such comments particularly insightful (although I can see why a naïve yet inquisitive teenager, unimpressed by being asked to believe such things as virgins becoming pregnant, might) and I set out my own arguments in Chapter 4 below;

10. DNA: the chain of 'links' which determine how the different cells in the body function; contains two copies of 23 chromosomes, one from the mother and one from the father; genes: parts of the DNA which determine both how cells live and function, and the fundamental traits inherited from parents;

11. Mark has no interest in any such narrative, introducing Jesus as an adult; John's *Logos* theology, stating directly in 1: 14 that "the Word became flesh" (clearly believing that no explanation was required), obviates the need for one;

12. The Holy Family could not *both* return to Nazareth from Bethlehem 40 days after Jesus' birth, from where Jesus then grew up (Lk 2: 39 – 40), *and* move again from Bethlehem to Egypt (presumably two years later: Mt 2: 16), and then – apparently for the first time – move to Nazareth; it is, perhaps, surprising that so many faithful Christians, well-versed in the nativity stories, don't appear to recognise this obvious discrepancy;

13. In Isaiah 7: 14 the Hebrew *'almah* means 'young woman' (usually of marriageable age, not a young girl – see also Gen 24: 43; Exod 2: 8; Prov 30: 19), but connotes nothing whatsoever about the state of virginity; the Heb term for 'virgin' is *bethula* and, presumably, had Isaiah specifically meant 'virgin' he would have used this word; but in the LXX translation of the Hebrew of Isaiah 7: 14 *'almah* became *parthenos*, as in Gen 24: 43: so *parthenos* was used by the LXX both to translate *bethula,* 'a virgin' and also to translate *'almah*, a 'young woman who may or may not be a virgin'; the woman in 7: 14 is likely to have been both present at the time and pregnant (although there is no suggestion that this pregnancy is miraculous; simply 'look – this woman is pregnant, and by the time her child is...'); the translators presumably chose *parthenos* because it was a word capable of a fairly wide range of meanings although, in Greek culture, 'virgin' was the predominant meaning; that is the meaning which Bible translators – following Matthew's intentions - have continued to provide for Mt 1: 23 in order to reflect and reinforce the specifically Christian doctrine of the virginal conception to which Isaiah 7: 14 is actually making no reference at all (Isaiah's prophecy was clearly directed at the current situation of King Ahaz); interestingly, most modern translations of Isaiah 7: 14 either use 'young woman' or give it as an alternative to 'virgin' so that anyone who turns back from Matthew to Isaiah will find two different words; 'The Jewish Annotated New Testament' (eds. A-J Levine & MZ Brettler, OUP. 2011) suggests that "behind Matthew's account [is] a midrash similar to Jewish ones concerning the miraculous birth of Moses [who] was supposed to have been born, as he was conceived, without pain (hence his mother was not subject to the punishment of Eve); when he was born the house was filled with light; and he was said to have been born already circumcised" (p. 4); a useful reminder

that what we call 'the Old Testament' is first and foremost the Jewish scriptures, and Christians must use it with care, caution and integrity;

14. This is often the way that 2 Tim 3: 16 is understood, although 'God-breathed'(*theopneustos*) is capable of a range of interpretation; in fact, the verse goes on to say that scripture is "useful (*ophelimos*) for teaching...", not 'essential' or even 'necessary', as is often implied (e.g. in Article 6 of the 39 Articles Scripture is said to contain everything "necessary to salvation"); furthermore, a variant reading, as "every scripture" instead of "all scripture" on which James Barr comments: "When we say 'all scripture' we picture the entirety of the Bible. If the meaning is 'every scripture', then the word 'scripture' does not designate the entirety of the Bible; rather, it is a word for each individual passage or sentence". Barr J (1984) 'Escaping from Fundamentalism' p. 1;

15. Horrell DG (2nd Ed. 2006) 'An Introduction to the Study of Paul' p. 79;

16. ibid. p. 133;

17. One of the earliest 'heresies' was the view of some, perhaps many, Jewish Christians that Jesus was entirely human; groups like the Ebionites wanted to keep Jewish practices and identity in the face of the growing Gentilisation of the Church; for them, Jesus was sent by God to fulfil the Jewish Scriptures; therefore to belong to the people of God, one needed to be Jewish (Sabbath, Kosher, Circumcision etc); Jesus was special because he kept the Law perfectly; but was certainly not divine, because only God was divine;

18. This is not to say that what we believe is totally unimportant: (i) true belief is clearly better than false belief, and so it is important to continue to work to ensure that whatever we believe about God, Jesus etc. is as true as it can be (given our finitude and the ambiguities of existence); (ii) if our beliefs

lead to immoral actions (e.g. the murder of 'unbelievers'; the exclusion of gays etc.) then it is self-evidently right that we should review those beliefs as to their truth or falsehood – if God is love (merciful, compassionate etc.) then **clearly real truths about God would never lead to evil actions;** theology is only 'true' when it correctly represents the character of God;

19. In religious terms atheism claims there is no god, and agnosticism that there is no way of knowing (not 'I'm not sure');

20. An old comedy sketch by Peter Cook and Dudley Moore (in BBC TV's 'Not only...But also' broadcast in the 1960s) has the two tramp-like characters discussing this very issue – wouldn't it be wonderful (says Dud) if God were to push the clouds aside and, "in a golden ray of sunshine", give us a wave and say 'Hello, I'm here'; the reason he doesn't do so (replies Pete, the supposedly brighter one) is that it would 'debase the coinage': or in 'theology-speak': "God must be a hidden deity, veiled by his creation. He must be knowable, but only by a mode of knowledge that involves a free personal response on man's part, this response consisting in an uncompelled interpretive activity whereby we experience the world as mediating the divine presence. Such a **need for a human faith-response** will secure for man the only kind of freedom that is possible for him in relation to God, namely cognitive freedom, carrying with it the momentous possibility of being either aware or unaware of his Maker" (Hick J [1966] 'Evil and the God of Love' p. 317);

21. From *theos* 'God' and *dike* 'justice: the specific form of theology which seeks to defend or 'justify' the goodness and omnipotence of God in the light of the experience of evil and suffering: 'how can a completely good and all-powerful God allow such appalling things to happen?'

22. "Natural theology provided the traditional way of

formulating the relation between faith and reason...[natural theology] allowed theological discourse to get started... beginning from universally accepted premises, it sought to establish some basic truths, such as that God exists, that he is beneficent, that the soul is immortal, and perhaps some other matters. This provided a basis on which revealed theology could take over and lead into a fuller understanding of these matters – for instance while natural theology might show that God is, and that he is beneficent, only revealed theology could go on to expound his triune nature" Macquarrie J (2nd Ed. 1977) 'Principles of Christian Theology' (henceforth 'Principles') pp. 44 – 45; 'natural' theology is thus that reflection which is based on our observation of the world and our place in it, involving both *a priori* and *a posteriori* arguments – to put it simply: what we can work out for ourselves without the benefit of revelation which is that information 'provided' (somehow) by God;

23. 'Meekness and Majesty' Graham Kendrick;

24. Macquarrie J in (1978) 'The Humility of God' makes the insightful point that the Lat. *humilitas* and *humanitas* were both derived from *humus*: 'the earth' and that, as such, God is essentially quite 'earthy'; "in conferring the gift of existence on others than himself, God limited himself and took upon himself a commitment which already opens the way that leads to the incarnation and the passion" p. 1;

25. Macquarrie J 'Principles' p. 109: the term 'letting-be' (or 'releasement': *Gelassenheit*) via Meister Eckhart and Heidegger; the risk arises from the freedom with which God has endowed the created order; analogous to the parent who nurtures a child and then eventually lets her be herself – a self which might horrify and so break the heart of the parent;

26. 'Adoptionism': that God chose and then adopted the human Jesus to serve his purposes – that would certainly concur with the Jewish notion of 'Messiah': the 'anointed' or

'chosen' one; 'Docetism' from the Greek *dokein* 'to seem' or 'to appear to be': Jesus only appeared to be human;

27. "From my perspective of almost 40 years' parish ministry, it does not at all feel that it is 'easier now to believe in orthodox Christianity with intellectual integrity than it was' [quoting from the Bishop of Worcester's somewhat negative review of Robert Reiss's (2016) 'Sceptical Christianity']. Quite the opposite. Isn't the elephant in the room for the Church of England's Renewal and Reform programme that actually it does no good just to repeat the same message more loudly, because for many people in our society the Christian faith as traditionally expressed no longer rings true." Letter to the 'Church Times' from Canon Andrew Norman (28th October 2016, p. 21);

28. I once heard a member of the clergy refer to the laity as 'muggles'; any reader of Harry Potter will understand just how demeaning that title is;

29. Astley J 'Ordinary Theology: Looking, Listening and Learning in Theology' (Ashgate 2002), and Ann Christie's PhD 'ordinary' Christological research (including both 'person' and 'work') has been published as 'Ordinary Christology' (Ashgate 2012), well worth reading as a valuable study of how some 'ordinary' churchgoers answer the question: 'Who Do You Say I Am?'; for a brief introduction to this important way of doing theology see the Grove Booklet 'Taking Ordinary Theology Seriously' (2007) by Jeff Astley and Ann Christie: "this is a lay theology, not only because it is shared widely by the whole people (*laos*) of God, but also because it typifies the non-expert...[Therefore] those of us who are engaged in Christian communication, pastoral care and worship – and indeed in every other form of Christian conversation, leadership and relationship – need to listen... **Ordinary theology is the theology to which every Christian pastor, preacher and teacher must relate.** We need to know

about the beliefs and values of those for whom we care and those who are forced to listen to us, and get some sort of handle on their patterns and modes of thinking, believing, and valuing": 'Seriously' p. 5;

30. Geering L 'Foreword' to Hunt RAE & Smith JWH (eds 2013) 'Why Weren't We Told: A Handbook on "progressive" Christianity' pp. xv – xvi;

31. Comments made by Christie's interviewees include: "I don't really think. My faith is just there"; "I know what I believe and I don't wan't to…[voice trails off]"; "I really don't want to explore it"; "I've always said that I didn't want to go too deeply into it, because…um…I think people would soon lose…um…you know…if you looked into it too much"; "I sometimes think it's better not thinking [laugh] because it is harder to believe…I don't feel that I need to know" (cited Christie A 'Ordinary Christology' [2012] pp. 153 – 4); on the specific issue as to whether the doctrine of pre-existence undermines the humanity of Christ, Christie's evangelical group, whilst being aware of this possibility, were "not unduly troubled by the issue. They do not have the same need or desire an academic theologian might have to resolve, through rational argument, the tensions or contradictions inherent within the claims being made" (ibid. p. 73);

32. Brynteson P (2013) 'The Bible Reconsidered: A Journey from Fundamentalism to Progressive Christianity' pp. 5 – 6;

33. "…I began to apply reason and experience to scripture. This was blasphemy in my family and in evangelical Christianity. With great fear for my own soul, I allowed my mind to quietly and privately question the scriptures wondering all the time if, as a consequence I would be left behind if the rapture came;" ibid. p. 32;

34. ibid p. 32;

35. ibid pp. 5 – 6 [citing Bawer B (1997) 'Stealing Jesus: How Fundamentalism Betrays Christianity' pp. 8 – 9];

36. With Easter following, at least for a few years more, a frustratingly mobile lunar calendar many schools, in order to avoid spring and summer terms of uneven lengths, are now just taking Good Friday and Easter Monday (legal 'Bank Holidays' rather more than religious occasions), and taking their 'Easter holidays' mid-April and regardless of the actual date of Easter;

37. 'Advent 1955';

38. 'Should we tell children that Santa Claus doesn't exist?': a dialogue between Simon Jenkins ('Yes') and Amanda Craig ('No') in 'Prospect' (a Left-leaning monthly magazine on politics, economics and society) January 2016, pp. 26 – 27; despite the title, the debate is much more focused on aspects of the 'Biblical' nativity (Santa is hardly mentioned); it may be that the authors equate the story of Jesus with that of Santa Claus;

39. art cit p. 26;

40. "I told this story [of Santa Claus] to my daughter and she said, 'I believe in Santa Claus.' I also asked her if she believed in the Easter bunny and she said, 'Yes. I'm a kid, so I believe in everything'." Kaplan E (2014) 'Does Santa Exist: A Philosophical Investigation' p. 3: children believe in everything and anything whilst they are children, but as they grow up they "put an end to childish ways" (1 Cor 13: 11), in which category religious belief is often placed!

41. "...the main reason for leaving the Church of England and the Church of Scotland is death, not displeasure. It is their failure to compensate for the mortality of existing members by recruiting their offspring which explains why these denominations have declined" Bruce S (1995) 'Religion in Modern Britain' p. 69;

42. Published 7th Dec 2015, The Woolf Institute, Cambridge; chaired by the Rt Hon Baroness Butler-Sloss and including Rowan Williams among the patrons;

43. From the 'Executive Summary' p. 6;

44. Brown A & Woodhead L (2016) 'That Was The Church That Was' p. 19;

45. ibid p. 19;

46. See Aisthorpe S (2016) 'The Invisible Church' for a fascinating survey of Christians who have found it more productive and meaningful to live their faith away from churches;

47. Brown & Woodhead op cit p. 49;

48. ibid. p. 62;

49. ibid. p. 198;

50. ibid. pp. 205 – 206;

51. "If we needed any proof that doctrine does not fall down from heaven, Theodosius' horse should suffice. The annulment of the decision of the 'robbers' synod' of 449, the convening of the Council of Chalcedon, and in general all orthodox Christological statements since then are in debt to Theodosius' horse (or perhaps to the gopher that dug the hole in which the horse stumbled). In order to insist that doctrinal development is guided by God in such a way that we can guarantee it is absolutely correct, one would have to claim that God determined that Pulcheria should reign, that Theodosius should fall and die, that the horse should stumble, and that the gopher should dig. This is a bit much to expect of even the staunchest believers in divine Providence" Gonzalez LJ&CG (2008) 'Heretics for Armchair Theologians' p. 150;

52. Gk. *kenoo* 'to empty' hence Kenoticism: the idea, developed in 18th Century Germany, that the divine Son "emptied himself" of his divinity "taking the form of a slave": Phil 2: 7;

53. From the Gk. *krino*: 'to judge/decide' so regarding the biblical text: making judgements about author, date, context, authorial intentions, historicity etc.

54. Macquarrie 'Principles' pp. 15, 17;

55. Simmons EL (2014) 'The Entangled Trinity: Quantum Physics and Theology' pp. 121 – 122;

56. Temple W (1934) 'Nature, Man and God' p. 396;

57. Otto's *'mysterium tremendum fascinans'* ('the mystery which both overwhelms/terrifies and draws us') in 'The Idea of the Holy': first published in 1917 as *Das Heilige - Über das Irrationale in der Idee des Göttlichen und sein Verhältnis zum Rationalen* [*The Holy - On the Irrational in the Idea of the Divine and its Relation to the Rational*];

58. Philosopher John Locke (1632 – 1704) 'Essay Concerning Human Understanding' (1690) IV. xvii. 24;

59. The Anglican Church Times' leader comment ('Not healthy yet', 27/5/16 p. 16) on the Report by Dr Stephen Bullivant ('Contemporary Catholicism in England and Wales', published May 2016, with data on religious affiliation extrapolated from the annual British Social Attitudes surveys: the report included figures for Anglicans, Methodists and Baptists as well as for Roman Catholics) was brief, terse and to the point: "...evangelism is not working";

60. Mt 2: 9: how does one literally follow a star? astrologers and users of horoscopes do so metaphorically (there is an obvious clue here); and how does a star stop?

61. "...the little Lord Jesus no crying he makes": 'Away in a Manger', William J Kirkpatrick, 1895;

62. Thus the 2nd Century Gnostic, Valentinus, believing that matter was evil, argued that Jesus never needed to use the toilet: "He was continent, enduring all things. Jesus digested divinity; he ate and drank in a special way, without excreting his solids. He had such a great capacity for continence that the nourishment within him was not corrupted, for he did not experience corruption"; fragment from the 'Epistle to Agathopous' cited in Layton B (1987) 'The Gnostic Scriptures' p. 239;

63. As sociologist of religion, Steve Bruce, has incisively put it:

"Imagine someone tells you that he is a big football fan. You ask if he is a member of a supporters' club and he says not. You ask which team he supports and he is unsure. You ask when he last went to a match and he says he has not been for twenty years. He also admits that he never reads reports of games in the papers, changes channels when football comes on the television, cannot name any prominent footballers, and never plays himself. At some point in this inquisition **it becomes clear that 'football fan' here is being used in an unusual manner**": Bruce op cit p. 47.

Chapter 1

Problems inherent in the traditional Doctrine of the Incarnation

Why Christological reformulation is an essential task: a case study in the construction of metaphysical conundrums[1]

It may be thought by some that the mere idea of formulating a 'Christology for today' is at best misconceived or unnecessary, at worst blasphemous. After all, 'The Truth' (God's truth) was pronounced at Chalcedon, wasn't it? Jesus Christ was and is both God and Man, in a hypostatic union of two natures - what more is there to say? This rather complacent tendency (complacent in the sense that no attempt is made to question these past formulations as they are) may be illustrated by the October 2014 'Agreed Statement on Christology' made between the Anglican Communion and the Oriental Orthodox (one of the 'Non-Chalcedonian') Churches.[2] Back in the mid-5th Century a schism arose between those Churches which supported Chalcedon's two-nature Christology and those who continued to embrace (because it seems to have been the prior 'default' position) a one-nature (either a more nuanced 'miaphysitism' or rather less so 'monophysitism': Gk: *physis/phusis* – 'nature'[3]) understanding of Christ.

In his brief introduction to this Agreement, Bishop Geoffrey Rowell (Anglican Co-Chairman) points to a range of *"ecumenical encounters and dialogues of the last half-century or so...[during which] there have been notable efforts to resolve this ancient division"*. This particular Agreement is the "latest" and has been built "on earlier theological agreements". In this latest Agreed Statement we read that despite the prior classic disagreement, these churches now,

"...following the teaching of our common father Saint Cyril of Alexandria...can confess together that in the one incarnate nature of the Word of God, two different natures, distinguished in thought alone...continue to exist without separation, without division, without change, and without confusion"[4] (echoing many of the phrases of the Athanasian Creed).

Bishop Rowell (rightly, I am sure) celebrates this ecumenical agreement which appears to offer a compromise position or, rather, a position which enables two previous, apparently contradictory, views to be reconciled: although, as we shall see, when seeking to differentiate between mono- and mia-physitism the issue is not quite so straightforward. It is not the case (and according to the Agreement never, apart from the Eutychian heresy, had been the case) of believing that there was *either* one nature in Christ *or* two, but rather that there is *"one incarnate nature of the Word of God"* in which there are *"two different natures, distinguished in thought alone [which] continue to exist without separation..."*: in essence, and using Cyril's terminology, 'one out of two' (*eis ek duo*). If this is a correct analysis, then one might reasonably ask what the 5th Century 'schism'[5] (which included the Miaphysite Oriental Orthodox as well as the more extreme Monophysites) was all about. Furthermore, one still might even more reasonably ask: 'what, precisely, were they talking about?' Those who drew up this Agreement speak as though they have a precise and uncluttered understanding of both a divine nature and a human nature, and also of the (apparently distinct) "one incarnate nature of the Word", without ever considering the philosophical difficulties of positing the union of two very different (so one assumes from the other language used) and possibly entirely contradictory concepts.

Indeed, the fundamental problem is that the language and concepts of the 5th Century are treated as *a priori* 'givens', acceptance of which bypasses the need to question either the assertions themselves or the way in which they have been expressed. Whatever it may mean to say so (and meaning doesn't seem to have bothered the authors of this Agreement, just as it didn't over-bother their forebears: they all seem to believe that they are dealing with fully comprehensible concepts), Jesus Christ was ontologically one (*homoousios*) with God and a person who possessed two (or is it just the one, or some combination in which 'two' is actually one?) natures. The argument (if one may call it that) put forward in the Agreement, when based on this quite uncritical acceptance of the Councils ('because the Church Fathers said this, it must be correct'), might sound superficially logical, even though it draws unanimity out of a previous set of contrary positions (one nature or two or...?) which were, in the 5th Century, taken so seriously as to create a formal schism between churches.

In the Agreement, the hypostatic union is recognised as a "mystery" (in which case, how can we speak of it at all?) in which

"...those among us who speak of two natures in Christ are justified in doing so since they do not thereby deny their inseparable indivisible union; similarly, those among us who speak of one incarnate nature of the Word are justified in doing so since they do not thereby deny the continuing dynamic presence in Christ of the divine and the human, without change, without confusion".

To give proper credit in a situation where they appear to be cleverly reconciling two positions which had been previously thought irreconcilable (or were they: perhaps the 'Miaphysites' have been orthodox all along?), the writers point out that they

"...recognise the limit of all theological language and the philosophical terminology of which it makes and has made use... [adding] We are unable to net and confine the mystery of God's utter self-giving in the incarnation of the divine Word in an ineffable,

inexpressible and mysterious union of divinity and humanity, which we worship and adore".[6]

Such theological modesty is to be commended: as we shall see, the 'apophatic horizons' of any doctrine should be respected.

Nevertheless, particularly in an age where theology forms part (or should form part) of critical scholarship: being prepared to follow the evidence wherever it leads and not being constrained by prior positions, there is something just a little disconcerting in reading that Jesus Christ is 'this-and-that', particularly when, because it is a divine mystery, we do not really know what 'this-and-that' actually means. Would it not have been better to enquire into what the classic doctrines were seeking to express in the language and concepts they used at the time (aims and intentions), and then consider whether other language and concepts (methodology) might be more meaningful today, rather than just parroting the past? After all, this Agreement was reached in 2014.

To briefly summarise a somewhat confusing 5th Century debate, confusing, not least to the modern mind, because the Greek words used: *'mia'* and *'monos'*, appear to be synonymous, meaning 'one', 'single', 'only'; however, *'mia'* can mean also mean 'united' and so could imply a more cautious or conservative form of *'mono...'*: that the natures were truly and equally united into one without one or the other predominating:

1. Jesus Christ was thought (somehow) to be both human and divine and the classic Christological heresies were those positions which went too far in one direction or the other (too divine or even too human);
2. Chalcedonian orthodoxy was 'dyophysite': Christ was said to be 'made up' of two distinct natures, human and divine, brought together in a personal ('hypostatic') union of the Divine Word with the man Jesus of Nazareth;

3. 'miaphysites' understood humanity and divinity to be united in Christ in one nature, but in such a way as to be 'without separation, confusion or alteration';

4. this Christological position arose as a response to (Antiochene) Nestorianism (although scholars today wonder whether alleged heretic Nestorius was ever himself 'Nestorian') which made such a distinction between the human and divine natures that it might seem that two separate people 'lived' in the one Jesus Christ; Nestorianism was condemned at the Council of Ephesus in 431;

5. whilst some Chalcedonians thought that a 'miaphysite' position could be interpreted in an orthodox manner, others saw it as a form of the subtly different 'monophysitism'; equally, some 'miaphysites' condemned Chalcedon as being just another version of Nestorianism; they wanted to stick rigidly to Cyril's formula: "one nature of the Word of God Incarnate";

6. the equal and opposite heresy to Nestorianism was that of Eutyches (together with the earlier and equally docetic Apollinarianism) who taught that the divine and human were so tightly united that Christ's humanity was absorbed into his divinity (like 'a drop of vinegar in the ocean'); this was anathematised at Chalcedon in 451 and, as we have seen, equally rejected in the recent Agreement as being at all representative of miaphysitism;

7. true 'monophysites' were those who believed that, after the Incarnation, Christ possessed only a single nature, either (predominantly) divine, or some synthesis of divine-human, but one in which – in true docetic fashion – the divine would always predominate;

8. historically, 'Monophysitism' refers primarily to the position of those (especially in Egypt and to a lesser extent Syria) who rejected the Council of Chalcedon; the

moderate members of this group, however, maintained a 'Miaphysite' Christology that was adopted by the Oriental Orthodox Churches; as we have seen in Point 7 of the recent Agreement, the Oriental Orthodox reject the label 'Monophysite' even as a generic term, although it is to be found extensively in the historical literature;

9. after Chalcedon, the Monophysite controversy (together, as ever, with many other factors) led to a lasting schism between the Oriental Orthodox Churches on the one hand, and the Western and the Eastern Orthodox Churches on the other; the Christological conflict between monophysitism, dyophysitism, and their various subtle combinations and derivatives, lasted from the third through to the eighth centuries and left its mark on all but the first two great Ecumenical Councils.

In the light of modern historical research and ecumenical discussions, the Miaphysite and Chalcedonian positions appear to differ mainly in their understanding of the key term 'nature' (*physis*) rather than in their basic Christologies (thus making agreement more possible); but other smaller differences of interpretation or emphasis also existed. When we explore the original disagreements we find that, in the two great theological 'schools' of ancient Christianity,[7] Alexandrian thought was supportive of a 'One Nature Christology' which sought to explain how the Eternal Word (*Logos*) became incarnate as a man, whilst the Antiochenes tended towards a 'Two Nature Christology' (beginning with the humanity of Christ and then seeking to explain how the Jesus of the Gospels was united with the Word: an idea which had reached its expressive apogee in John 1) as represented by such as Diodore of Tarsus and Theodore of Mopsuestia, for whom Christ's humanity and divinity were united in a single *prosopon* ('person'). Here the union was seen to be like that of body and soul – or even man and wife: although united, the two separate 'elements' always remained recognisable, with the presence of the Logos in Christ being similar to the presence of God's grace in a person.

As with all the ancient debates about Christology and Trinitarian theology there were tremendous problems posed by language: its use and meaning, not to mention translations between Greek and Latin. For Cyril of Alexandria *'physis'* represented a concrete reality; so the ascription of two natures potentially gave two separate persons (sometimes unhappily described as a 'panto-horse' Jesus). This was further complicated by the fact that, for Cyril, *physis* was almost, if not quite, the equivalent of *hypostasis* (the word which came to be used for 'person'), and not, as later, 'nature'. This meant that later monophysites (true 'one-nature' believers) could, and did, claim Cyril's authority for their position. However, for the Antiochenes 'nature' was somewhat less concrete, so that two natures could unite in an external reality. For example, Nestorius was understood to be saying that Christ was two persons, one human the other divine, with no real union, just a 'mechanical' conjunction, so Christ was both 'Son of God' who was omniscient and 'Son of Man' who suffered and wept: a representation which also resulted in Jesus having two wills or minds, because their philosophy tied those to a 'nature' rather than to a 'person'. As, from our position in the 21st Century, we consider these esoteric debates about the nature of Jesus Christ, we might be wondering exactly what was going on – and why.

As we shall shortly consider in more detail, we must also reckon with the influence of Hellenistic philosophy on theological development:

"...in his effort to make philosophical sense of the Incarnation Cyril employed categories whose home is Plotinus and Apollinarius. The Plotinian picture of human nature is of a being that has, as it were, his head in heaven and his feet on earth. On the one hand he is an

intellectual perfect spirit, and on the other he has emotions and feelings and a body. How can both be fitted together into a single person? This problem is addressed in Enneads 3: 6 entitled 'The impassivity of the unembodied'. For Plotinus the immateriality of the soul excludes any influence upon it of bodily or emotional states. His conclusion is stated clearly, 'that the Intellectual Essence, wholly of the order of Ideal Form, must be taken as impassive has already been established' [so] even the human soul is not entirely immersed in the body...In other words there is always part of every human being that rises above the emotions of the lower soul and the body. The presence of the impassible spirit in the body/soul is not proof of its having lost its impassibility. Cyril's knowledge of Hellenistic literature was considerable and...he may have read Plotinus...After all there was a flourishing Neoplatonic academy in Alexandria...His language...rather suggests some acquaintance with the Enneads as he offers a similar solution to the same problem as faced Plotinus. The presence of the impassible Word in a human being composed of body and soul to form one person need not threaten the divine immutability and freedom from passion and sin".[8]

It is arguable that Cyril's reaction to Nestorius went so far in the opposite theological direction as to completely undermine Christ's humanity and thus blur the distinction between Father and Son:

"Cyril's Christ remained an abstraction, his humanity so much part of the divine world as to be unrecognizable in human terms... There was no Biblical ring in his thought...".[9]

As I have already argued: that would generally appear to be the case with 'orthodox' Christology – however it is expressed, Christ's humanity is inevitably compromised.

"The problem in all this was that Cyril was drawing much more heavily than he realised on extreme One Nature doctrines...In forming his ideas, he was entranced by a phrase that he believed had been written by...Athanasius, who had supposedly spoken of Christ as **'one Nature (mia phusis) of the Logos of God Incarnate'.** *Through Cyril, this idea became the basis of emerging Christian orthodoxy. The problem was that the text in question was forged, and the idea actually came not from Athanasius, but from Apollinarius...Based on these spurious texts, the Alexandrian tradition became ever more committed to the ideas of One Nature".*[10]

For Cyril

"The Word, having united to himself hypostatically in an ineffable and inconceivable manner flesh animated by a rational soul, became man and was called son of man...While the natures that were brought together in true union are different, yet from them both is the one Christ and Son...the Godhead and the manhood, by their ineffable and indescribable coming together into unity, perfected for us the one Lord and Christ and Son."[11]

Although he accepted that the Incarnation consisted of the joining of two natures (human and divine), Cyril asserted that once the Word had become 'enfleshed' in Jesus there was only one nature: the human and divine natures were continuous with each other and ran into one. So although Christ possessed two natures, God the Word was the only active subject. Cyril even went so far as to suggest that Christ 'suffered impassibly' (a semantic contradiction) on the cross. As

"...an exponent of the 'Word-flesh' scheme, [Cyril] thought rather in terms of two phases or stages in the existence of the Logos, one prior to and the other after the incarnation. The Logos, as he liked to say, 'remains what He was'; what happened was that at the

incarnation, while continuing to exist eternally in the form of God, He added to that by taking the form of a servant. Both before and after the incarnation He was the same Person unchanged in His essential deity. The only difference was that He who had existed 'outside flesh' [asarkos] now became 'embodied' [ensomatos]. The nature or hypostasis which was the Word became enfleshed [sesarkomene]; henceforth the Word was 'incarnate'". [12]

In order to understand all this, it is important to recall that Cyril's understanding of 'nature' was of a 'concrete individual' (as noted, almost like '*hypostasis*', although this alleged synonymy has been disputed). So what existed after the (hypostatic) union was just one nature: the 'enfleshed nature of the Word'. There was no division in the Incarnate One although the humanity was still real (including a rational soul) and this was, perhaps, the crucial distinction with monophysitism:[13] the notion that Christ had a single (divine) nature after the union of deity and humanity in the incarnation, and not two, although we should note that although the true monophysites found talk of two natures in Christ after the incarnation unacceptable, they never specifically denied the fullness of the humanity (as monophysites have often been charged with doing). Cyril thus

"...spoke of the two aspects of Christ's being as two 'natures' or 'hypostases', or even 'things' [pragmata]. The humanity was as real as the divinity, and the modern allegation that he regarded it as a collection of purely abstract qualities conflicts with his express language. So, if Christ was one, He was 'one out of two' [eis ek duo]: 'the single, unique Christ out of two different natures'... There has been...'a coming together of things and hypostases', and Christ is 'one out of both'. But since the Incarnate was none other than the eternal Word in a new state, His unity was presupposed from the start...[in other words] the Lord's humanity became a 'nature' or 'hypostasis, i.e. a concrete existent reality...in the

nature or hypostasis of the Word. It never existed on its own...but from the moment of its conception in Mary's womb it belonged to the Word, Who made it His very own. The body was the body of the Word, not of some man, and in the union the two constituted a single concrete being".[14]

So

*"What can we learn from this controversy, which seems **so technical and alien from a modern perspective**? First, the argument over the nature of the unity of Christ revealed that Cyril and Nestorius understood words like hypostasis and prosopon in significantly different ways. In the background of the debates about Christ were dimmer and more confused arguments over the meaning of such words. Often one side assumed that their meaning of a word was correct, without appearing to realise that it was precisely that meaning which was being contested...[also] there were not only contested words but more general contested ideas [e.g. 'union', 'conjunction' etc.]...However, with Nestorius' claim that Cyril's Christ was a mixed unity, and Cyril's counter-claim that Nestorius' Christ was two, it became very difficult to find any common ground...Secondly, both Cyril and Nestorius recognised the importance of being able to say that in becoming incarnate the Word was in some sense related to all humanity...Finally, both Nestorius and Cyril were concerned with the implications that Christology had for everyday piety, liturgy and human behaviour. They may have followed these implications in rather different ways, but neither thought that theology was an armchair profession".*[15]

The authors of Chalcedon themselves saw their statement primarily as a commentary on and appendix to the Nicene (i.e. Nicaean-Constantinopolitan) Creed. Inevitably, theologians had their views misrepresented by their opponents: Chalcedon

"*...was not so much a corrective to Cyrilline teaching as a ratification of his true opinion against caricatures that had been advanced in his name [and] elements in the decree...which are often said to be Antiochene because Cyril does not affirm them with conviction are at least as incompatible with the attested statements of Antiochene authors and...their father is more likely to be a heresiarch who is second in notoriety only to Arius – Apollinarius of Laodicea...[who] had fallen under the censure of the church before any charge was laid against Theodore or Nestorius, but, whereas every doctrine that was peculiar to these last two was rejected at Chalcedon, this assembly not only ratified his teaching that 'the same' being who was man was also God, but prepared the way for a vindication of his dictum that the Word was the proper subject of the passion, a doctrine which was not espoused by the writers whom we commonly style 'Antiochene', and which even Cyril cannot affirm without periphrasis*".[16]

Yet Chalcedon was hardly an Antiochene-Alexandrian compromise. In Henry Chadwick's view: "*because of its mosaic character, the definition had something for almost everyone other than Eutyches and the ultra-Cyrillians*".[17] However, in practice,

"*...each faction tended to caricature and exaggerate the positions of its enemies. After Chalcedon had issued its diplomatic and elaborately considered analysis of the divinity, some critics returned to their Palestinian homeland with the alarming news that the Nestorians had triumphed, so that now believers would be required to worship two Christs and two Sons. Furious listeners launched a bloody revolt against the triumph of the Two Nature heresy...On the other side...Christians knew that Apollinarius had taught the single nature in Christ, so that any later belief that erred too far in the direction of stressing the One Nature must be Apollinarian, however significant the distinctions with that older creed*".[18]

In the end "['our common father'] *Cyril's greatest contribution to doctrine was the formula that he devised in opposition to Nestorius, that of the hypostatic union...[in which] two different natures came together in a 'union according to hypostasis' (henosis kath' hypostasin), a dynamic unity, 'and from both arose one Christ, one Son'''*.[19] This 'formula' was eventually (at Chalcedon, after Cyril's death) to prevail over all others although, at the time, it provoked considerable opposition. It just goes to show how, what eventually became solid orthodoxy, never to be doubted, was once a very tenuous position. Here lies the root of the claim (in this recent Agreement) that Cyril was the "common Father" to both the (eventually) orthodox (represented here by the Anglican Communion) and the Miaphysite positions; but Monophysites can also claim this pedigree. The point is that Cyril's thinking could be interpreted in such a way as to be able to support them all: in which case, what does that say about the clarity given to the issues under debate, either then or now?

Revisiting these arguments today, I ask: do they make any sense at all? Are the various subtle distinctions at all meaningful? Is Cyril a "common father" only insofar that what he said and wrote was so imprecise, ill-defined, arguably inconsistent and certainly capable of multiple interpretation, that (often subtly) different Christological positions were all able to hail him as their source and inspiration? There was, in fact, a nice (and perhaps wisely deliberate?) ambiguity in the writings of the Father of the phrase 'hypostatic union', the 'common father' of erstwhile schismatic Churches, and one who was himself a one-naturist: a fact that Chalcedon went on to ignore. Certainly, the schism which caused so much animosity and mutual despising in the 5th Century was somehow able to be declared 'not really a problem at all' in the 21st. What had changed in substance, apart from a new willingness to seek reconciliation? But the bottom line is this: how could the various protagonists be so sure that they were correct in their analyses of the nature of Jesus Christ, to the extent of designating some 'orthodoxy' and others 'heresy'?

Yet despite these complicated verbal jousts, which today may more bemuse than inform us, it has been the case that, throughout most of Christian history, the Christological (and Trinitarian) doctrines as formulated during the 4th and 5th Centuries (using Greek language and philosophical concepts) have been *"the unquestioned – and unquestionable – touchstone of truly orthodox faith and teaching"*,[20] and remain the official teachings of most, if not all, Christian denominations (illustrated by the regular liturgical recital by congregations of the 'Nicene' Creed with its *'homoousios'*). That is presumably why Anglican theologians can happily agree with their Oriental Orthodox counterparts that, despite the apparent difference in a doctrine Rowell describes as "central to the Christian faith",[21] sufficient common ground can be salvaged in which to argue that it was not actually a disagreement at all but, rather, a misunderstanding.

Such abstruse thinking is reminiscent of the Reformation debates about the nature of Christ's presence in the Eucharistic elements, which was equally opaque and often verging on the bizarre: what is the actual difference between transubstantiation and consubstantiation[22] if neither means anything much at all, not least because they depend on an Aristotelian understanding of reality, that is in any way demonstrable? Wisely the Orthodox Church and, to a degree, the Anglican Communion[23] have been content to avoid speculation about the 'mechanics' of the Real Presence of Christ in the Eucharistic elements (not least because the idea of 'transubstantiation' didn't appear until the 4th Lateran Council in 1215, after the Schism between East and West, and so was viewed with suspicion by the Orthodox), and believe Christ's Eucharistic presence to be a mystery 'which only God understands'.[24]

Reviewing the verbal manoeuvrings of the 5th Century it is easy to see both how misunderstandings and confusions were possible, and why solutions were sought in theological hairsplitting. What, after all, is the difference between someone consisting of one nature, or two natures, or even one out of two natures, if the actual nature or natures are a mystery? And was it a union, conjunction or what?[25] Furthermore, if the Incarnate Christ represents a totally new state of being (the divine human), what can we, with and from our purely human and finite state, ever say about that? But the central question is this: whatever conclusion one reaches about Christ's nature, is that conclusion really compatible with a 'true humanity'?

These, and other, questions are the reasons why

"...for many scholars as well as laypeople these classical Christological formulas are cast in a language that is obscure, abstract, and far removed from the experience of faith. In addition, critics say that the Christology of the old creeds comes close to losing sight of the concrete reality of Jesus of Nazareth in a maze of metaphysical speculation. Even theologians who disagree with these critics will acknowledge that the classical Christological creeds must be interpreted and not merely repeated."[26]

Indeed, Karl Rahner, one of the Roman Catholic Church's greatest 20th Century theologians, went so far as to assert that these classic formulations are not the final word for theological reflection, but should be treated as points of departure.[27] I intend to take him at his word.

Why we need to reinterpret the outcomes of the Great Councils

We will now consider six issues which make the **construction of a 'modern Christology'**: a Christology based not in ancient and outmoded philosophies, but on modern scholarship and informed biblical exegesis, at least a reasonable, and possibly even for the sake of mission, an essential endeavour.

The 'Chalcedonian Definition'

The so-called 'Chalcedonian Definition', the purpose of which was to resolve differences in interpretation of outcomes of the Council of Nicaea, particularly the concern to have a balanced way of asserting both the humanity and the divinity of Christ, was not a definition in any modern sense (a 'statement expressing something's essential nature' or 'the meaning of a word', "semantic clarity, linguistic precision, or careful circumspection" concerning which Sarah Coakley adds: "...*and we have already seen how Chalcedon apparently fails to deliver all of these*"[28]). It was not meant to provide a 'definitive' blueprint of the nature of Christ, such as a diagram of a human body ('as you can see, this bit is...that bit is...': that would, in any case, be as impossible as mapping the mind, as opposed to mapping the brain). In all these senses, Chalcedon tells us hardly anything about the nature of Christ, such as what (an) *hypostasis* or (a) *physis* actually are, or how they relate to each other.[29] Rather, based on Christian experience, philosophical reflection, and meditation on the Scriptures, it sought, not so much to define, as to place limits around what might be said about Jesus, so that what was said would be clearly identifiable as 'Christian'. So to say that Jesus was a great teacher or a good man is not sufficient for Christian discourse, and thus fails the Chalcedonian 'test'. Furthermore, Chalcedon provides not just a simple boundary ('you can say this, but not that'), but what Coakley[30] calls an 'apophatic horizon'.

Coakley[31] understands **'horizon'** (Gk. *horus*) in the Patristic sense with its meaning ranging across ideas such as 'boundary', 'horizon' and 'limit' to 'standard', 'pattern' and (monastic) 'rule'. Thus a Christological 'horizon' was established by the great Councils which, having ruled out of order the three heresies of Apollinarianism, Eutychianism, and Nestorianism, went on to establish a boundary beyond which, should we trespass, we are in danger of taking ourselves outside of valid 'Christ-talk' altogether, although, as Coakley notes, there will always be "forays backwards and forwards".[32] This image of people trying to push at a boundary, occasionally moving forwards and occasionally (being repelled?) backwards, is a very appropriate analogy for the development of Christian doctrine.

The term '**apophatic**' refers to the so-called 'negative way' in theology (*apophemi* is 'to deny': prioritising what cannot be said about God over what can be said: it is easier to say what God is not than to say what God is) and its purpose is to remind us that we should be humble enough to admit that what we don't know about God and his ways is much, much more than we do or can ever know. In the words of one of the Cappadocian Fathers who made such significant contributions to the development of Trinitarian theology:

> "*But to comprehend the whole of so great a subject as this is quite impossible and impracticable, not merely to the utterly careless and ignorant, but even to those who are highly exalted, and who love God, and in like manner to every created nature; seeing that the darkness of this world and the thick covering of the flesh is an obstacle to the full understanding of the truth...For it is one thing to be persuaded of the existence of a thing, and quite another to know what it is*".[33]

Recognising this, the authors of Chalcedon provided

> "*...an abstract rule of language (physis and hypostasis) for distinguishing duality and unity in Christ [as well as] presenting a 'riddle' of negatives by means of which a greater (though undefined) reality may be intimated*".[34]

Coakley also uses the phrase "**linguistic regulation**" as pointing to another, albeit linked, intention of Chalcedon: the Fathers sought to reaffirm the previous Councils and particularly their own affirmation of the "biblical narratives of salvation" and then *"to provide a regulatory grid through which to pass them interpretatively"*[35] so establishing a kind of 'vetting process' for acceptable Christ-talk. When Christians talk about Jesus, that talk ought (for example) to involve some notion of 'true humanity' and 'true divinity', and their connection; although recalling the apophatic nature of what can be said we should be cautious in claiming to understand exactly what this kind of talk actually means: its 'cashability' is limited. Whilst we may believe we understand the nature of 'true humanity', what of 'true divinity': can human language ever express its meaning? Nevertheless, not least for the purposes of sharing the Faith, we must try: so just as Christian talk of God will normally be Trinitarian in its formulation, Christian 'Jesus-the-Christ-talk' (Christology) has employed the twin 'labels': 'humanity' and 'divinity', and the classic Christological endeavour and dilemma has been to steer a path between the two without losing hold of the 'content' (the essential meaning) of either: just as the Trinitarian dilemma has been how to successfully hold modal and social models in tension. The classic heresies were those ideas which went too far in one direction or the other. Thus we might say that **these classic doctrines provide the 'grammar'** (i.e. the rules) for our God (or Christ)-talk, **not necessarily a precise and permanent vocabulary**, not least because the meaning of words tends to change, leading, for example, to the modern problem of conceiving of God as three 'persons': an idea which seems today to imply the existence of some kind of divine committee and, ultimately, falls into tritheism. Because much of the Christological and Trinitarian vocabulary is firmly embedded in Christian tradition and liturgy, we might feel it more effective (in terms of communicating the Faith) to hold onto, rather than change, certain specific terminology (such as 'the divinity of Christ') whilst seeking to reinterpret what it might mean. That will be my approach.

We can, therefore, accept that the Great Councils of the 4th and 5th Centuries, whilst not providing a detailed analysis of Christ, at least provided some ground-rules as to how we might speak of him 'Christianly'. Yet while there was evidently some kind of special connection between Jesus and Father God which Christians ought to proclaim, the crucial Christological question we should be addressing is how that connection is best characterised, defined and expressed when it is proclaimed (does it, for example, make sense?) and what it means, whilst bearing in mind the constraints embodied in the concept of an 'apophatic horizon'. As Coakley points out: if Chalcedon is understood to be

"...the primary bar of ecumenical engagement and discernment in Christological matters [then] its 'apophatic' horizon...could shelter many more alternatives than later official clarifications, East and West, would appear to allow; and its character as 'horus' could perhaps find greater understanding in circles of the West, a development that would chasten expectations in some analytic philosophical quarters, but...release spiritual and theological creativity in others".[36]

Perhaps some boundaries require greater effort in the pushing?

Philosophy and Language

Directly linked with the above is the nature of the philosophies employed and the language used by theologians during the first Christian centuries, particularly contrasted with those in use today. Theology will normally be embedded in some philosophical context, presupposition or assumption, explicit or implicit, whether that is recognised or not. Theology isn't some kind of 'pure' mental activity totally separated or immune from any other idea: if it were it would be incomprehensible and unable to be expressed. The question is rather: how much is the 'shape' or content of theology influenced by these other ideas? Is the relationship one of master, slave or happy partner?

Those ancient philosophies (mainly Platonism, Aristotelianism, or some mixture of the two[37]) which so influenced the thinking of the Early Church will not mean much to modern Christians. How many of those who regularly recite the Nicene Creed (in context and original conception, an anti-Arian[38] tract) really understand what it means to say that Christ is *homoousios* (of one substance/consubstantial) with the Father? Extrapolating from Christie's research in 'ordinary Christology', probably not many.[39] The relationship between theology and philosophy is both mutual and complex: sometimes in alliance, sometimes antagonistic. Justin Martyr, referring to the thought of Plato and the Stoics, agreed that they shared in the Logos that was in Jesus, whilst Clement of Alexandria believed that philosophy *"assists towards true religion as a kind of preparatory training for those who arrive at faith by way of demonstration"*.[40] Tertullian was not so sympathetic ('What has Athens to do with Jerusalem?'): for him philosophy represented *"the world's wisdom, that rash interpreter of the divine nature and order"*.[41] As noted above, theology has always tended to partner to some degree the philosophies of its day in order to express its ideas with as much clarity and meaning as possible; and, particularly in the first Christian centuries, theologians sought, through an analysis of scripture influenced by those philosophical assumptions, to create a coherent and satisfying account of the Faith which would find acceptance in the intellectual milieu of the day. This effort has not always succeeded yet, without the potential clarity of ideas and expression it can bring, we are in danger of falling into murky waters. A phrase pervasive in hymnody of a certain type:[42] 'Jesus is God', is actually a gross oversimplification of what Christian tradition has claimed. Technically it is the Apollinarian heresy, with its tendency to Docetism, which was developed on the basis of, and so circumscribed and governed by these very Hellenistic philosophies, and many theologians today would not accept it without some kind of qualification.[43]

Clearly, there were philosophical elements of the Christological and Trinitarian debates which went way over the heads of some of the participants in those great Ecumenical Councils: not many bishops, particularly those from the West who spoke Latin rather than Greek, had a clear understanding of *homoousios*, if such clarity was ever available. Indeed, there was considerable disagreement about its meaning, not least because the word itself had been anathematised in the 3rd century as being intrinsically modalist.[44] Furthermore, there was considerable variation in the meaning of words such as *hypostasis* and *ousia* (which, at one stage, were synonyms, before becoming used, respectively, for what was three and what was one of God) during the 3rd – 4th Centuries. At Nicaea some of the bishops clearly preferred *homoiousios* (denoting similarity rather than identity), a term with which Arius probably could have lived – which is equally probably why it was rejected by the proto-orthodox. Things are not much different in the modern world, although professional theologians (if not bishops) are often competent philosophers as well: some, like Macquarrie and Hick, originally trained as philosophers, although that doesn't automatically make their ideas accessible. For example, John Macquarrie's theology (set out in his magisterial work of systematic theology: 'Principles of Christian Theology'[45]) is undergirded by and embedded in the two modern philosophies of existentialism and ontology[46] and it is not always easy to grasp the profundity, the subtlety or the importance of Macquarrie's thought without having at least some basic understanding of these two philosophies.[47]

The other side of the coin of this problem: the nature of the language, is even more fundamental. When using philosophical terms (such as *homoousios*) just how did the Conciliar Fathers expect that language to be understood? It is probably anachronistic to make the kind of clear and delineated linguistic distinctions used by philosophers today, although it would be somewhat patronising to think that they would not have been able to recognise the difference between language used literally and that used non-literally. Much Patristic biblical exegesis was non-literal: typological, analogical, anagogical and so on. But without some clear and explicit reference to usage (as, for example, in Aquinas' writings on analogy which is described, interestingly, as *analogia entis*: 'analogy of *being*' – thus relating it to ontology), it seems likely that they would have understood their application of philosophical terms to God to have (at least) some realist (or 'literal') referent: Christ was truly, not merely analogically or symbolically, *homoousios* with the Father; divine and human natures 'really' came together in Christ. In the essay cited above, Coakley also asks what we mean by 'literal' (as in a 'literal incarnation'), and whether the Fathers of Chalcedon would have understood what they were saying to be literal in a modern sense: firstly:

"...the 'Chalcedonian 'Definition' – as Nicaea and Constantinople before it – takes for granted the achievement of salvation in Christ and then asks what must be the case about that Christ if such salvation is possible. In that sense Chalcedon is much more like a 'transcendental argument'...for Christ's divinity and humanity than an empiricist investigation of the evidences of Jesus' historical life".[48]

She then points out that

"...the assembled bishops at Chalcedon resisted at one point the Emperor's demand for greater 'precision'...[Chalcedon] does not... intend to provide a full systematic account of Christology, and even less a complete and precise metaphysics of Christ's makeup".[49]

Presumably, if it had had this intention, it would have struggled even more over the appropriate language to use.

In view of the fact that much patristic theology was contextualised within a philosophy, a range of philosophies, or a philosophical framework, which have now lost their currency, and was often couched in a pre-modern understanding of the use of language (as being somehow 'descriptive' of God) and its relation to meaning, many of the doctrines formulated 1500 years ago or, to be more exact, the manner in which they were expressed, have inevitably lost much of their meaning. So it's worth posing the question: if we were seeking to answer Jesus' question: 'Who do you say that I am?' for the first time and in our modern culture, what sort of answers might we come up with, and in what philosophy/language/concepts might they be expressed?

Biblical Criticism

It is impossible, unless the Christian is wilfully blind ('I don't want to think about this') or takes shelter in some bastion of anti-intellectualism ('I know what the Bible means, and I don't need any scholar to tell me otherwise', sometimes accompanied by: 'they're not really Christian, in any case') not to take account of the development of the modern critical study of the Biblical texts which has raised some very difficult, albeit stimulating questions, the most obvious of which concerns the accuracy (or 'truthfulness') of the accounts of the life and words of Jesus. In the view of one American scholar:

"Jesus would not recognize himself in the preaching of most of his followers today. He knew nothing of our world. He was not a capitalist. He did not believe in free enterprise. He did not support the acquisition of wealth or the good things in life. He did not believe in massive education. He had never heard of democracy. He had nothing to do with going to church on Sunday. He knew nothing of social security, food stamps, welfare, American exceptionalism,

unemployment numbers, or immigration. He had no views on tax reform, health care (apart from wanting to heal leprosy), or the welfare state. So far as we know, he expressed no opinion on the ethical issues that plague us today: abortion and reproductive rights, gay marriage, euthanasia, or bombing Iraq. His world was not ours, his concerns were not ours, and – most striking of all – his beliefs were not ours. Jesus was a first-century Jew, and when we try to make him into a twenty-first century American we distort everything he was and everything he stood for." [50]

The process by which Jesus' words and deeds were handed down by word of mouth (the oral tradition) before taking a relatively fixed form in the Gospels (and possibly also in certain other written documents such as discrete passion narratives, smaller pericopae, or the hypothetical text 'Q'[51]) covers a relatively long period: say, around 40 years from the crucifixion to Mark, during which it is very difficult to be sure how far such traditions underwent change. Hence concerns to develop criteria for judging authenticity. When Jesus is said to have done this or said that, then it is possible that he didn't, or didn't exactly, say or do what has been recorded (this is to leave aside those narratives which may entirely be the theological constructs of the Evangelists such as the nativity stories or the Cana narrative – on which see further below). Virtually all scholars accept that none of the Evangelists was an eye-witness of the life of Jesus, although that doesn't exclude the possibility or even likelihood that the traditions they used included eye-witness testimony in some shape or form.[52] That is why research into the oral tradition has been seen as a priority by many NT scholars, and originally undergirded the development of Form Criticism. In a very helpful survey of several quite different approaches,[53] Eric Eve concludes that

"...the proper approach to the Jesus tradition should lie somewhere

between the extremes of credulity [believing everything is true] *and scepticism* [believing nothing is true]. *This follows from three theses about oral tradition and memory that flow from our study: (1) oral tradition typically exhibits both stability and change; (2) collective memory reflects both the impact of the past and the needs of the present* [e.g. the Form Critical insight that an event or saying may have originated in the life – the *Sitz im Leben*[54] - of the early Church, rather than in the life of Jesus]; *and (3) individual memory (insofar as it can be distinguished from social aspects of memory) is both generally reliable and capable of being seriously misleading"*.[55]

Mapping this process successfully depends on having a proper understanding of what many Christians have tended to take for granted: the nature, role and effectiveness of memory in transmitting those early traditions. Bart Ehrman has recently focused his attention on 'memory theory': how memory, both individual and collective, works:[56]

"Our own memories are, on the whole, reasonably good. If they weren't, we wouldn't be able to function, or even survive, as human beings in a very complex world. We count on our memories for the thousands of things we do every day...But we forget a lot of things as well...Even more disturbing, we misremember things... It happens to all of us. And it happened to everyone who has ever lived. Including the followers of Jesus. Including the ones who told stories about him. Including the ones who heard those stories and the passed them along to others. Including the ones who heard those thirdhand stories and told them to others, who told them to others, who told them to others, who then wrote the Gospels. Each person in that link of memory from Jesus to the writers of the Gospels was remembering what he or she had heard. Or trying to do so... [But] memory is not simply about individuals... [it] also involves groups of people as they remember what has happened in

their collective past... [and] it is astounding how we, individually or as a society, have different memories of events and people from the past, and how often our recollections of important moments and figures are so far removed from historical reality... [Ehrman then considers American collective memories of Lincoln and Columbus, asking why a Lincoln who authored some – what today would be considered - extraordinarily racist statements,[57] is now considered a "champion of civil rights"]... When we remember the past, whether we are thinking simply our individual thoughts or are reconstructing our previous history as a collective whole, as a society, we do so, always and necessarily, in the light of our present situation. The past is not a fixed entity back there in time, It is always transformed in our minds, depending on what our minds are occupied with in the here and now... [is it] necessarily a bad thing if stories were changed as they were told and retold [?] Don't we often change a story based on the context in which we were telling it? And based on the people we are telling the story to? And based on what we find to be most important, fascinating and gripping about it? We are not necessarily doing something deceitful when we change stories. We are often doing something very useful: telling a story in the light of the situation at hand and the needs of the people we are speaking with. Would it have been any different with the early story-tellers who were passing along memories of Jesus? The study of memory is thus not only about seeing what gets changed over time: it is also about the people who remember things the way they do. It may be possible to look at how later memories of Jesus were presented to their audiences to help us understand what the storytellers considered to be the most important points for their own contexts. And by doing so, we may be able to appreciate better what these storytellers and their hearers were dealing with and experiencing in their worlds... [Finally, memories] are socially constructed...various social groups have shaped the memory. The societies we live in...determine how we remember the past. These memories are thus not only about what happened, but also about the

*contexts and the lives of those who cherish and preserve them. That
is why, for example, the Reformation is remembered so differently
by fundamentalist Christians and hard-core Roman Catholics; or
why the legacy of Ronald Reagan or of Malcolm X is remembered
so differently amongst different social groups in [the USA]... [T]
here are different kinds of memory. And people remember things
differently.*[58]

The basic issue is this: memories can be reasonably reliable,
although not absolutely accurate representations of the past,
which is never a "fixed entity back there in time",[59] but they
are also very fallible: subject not only to their innate frailty
(our forgetfulness), but also to the way we may, sometimes
inadvertently, sometimes deliberately, modify them to suit
particular situations or audiences.[60] Just think of your own
memories of events: might they be blurred, exaggerated, fitted
to the occasion of recall? For example, the memory of a dead
person may, due to sensibilities ('never speak ill of the dead'), be
embellished to make him/her more 'saintly' than they actually
were in real life? And what would be the state of your memories
were they to be handed on by family and friends (or enemies!)
for 30 – 40 years?

It has often been claimed that in pre-literate societies
(societies in which most people cannot read, and in which
books are the preserve of the rich), particularly societies in
the ancient world, memory was much more efficient than it is
today. In the modern world we don't need to memorize vast
amounts of material, because we can turn to a book or to the
Internet. In societies where that was not possible, people were
much more adept at remembering and so the oral transmission
of memories was much more accurate. We can, therefore, be
confident that those memories which 'made it' into the Gospels
are extremely reliable, not least because those memories were of
the first, indeed ultimate (eschatological), importance to Jesus'

followers. As noted, this case has been strongly made by Richard Bauckham:[61]

"...the Gospels...embody the testimony of eyewitnesses, not of course, without editing and interpretation, but in a way that is substantially faithful to how the eyewitnesses themselves told it, since the Evangelists were in more or less direct contact with the eyewitnesses, not removed from them by a long process of anonymous transmission of the traditions".[62]

Whilst there is neither need nor space to examine Bauckham's proposals in any detail here, suffice it to say that many, if not most, non-Evangelical scholars would question (i) the basic evidence that there was such a close temporal relationship between eyewitnesses and Evangelists; (ii) whether we can assume that eyewitness evidence is always 'good' evidence: after all, there are legal cases today in which the testimony of witnesses is found to be different or even contradictory.

So even if the Evangelists had direct access to those who personally witnessed the words and deeds of Jesus (and that is a matter of debate), how reliable was that evidence, and is it true that ancient memories were far better than modern memories seem to be? *"Unfortunately, decades of intense research have shown that this idea is probably not right at all."[63]* In Chapter 5 ('Distorted Memories and the Life of Jesus'[64]) Ehrman accepts that there is clear evidence that some people have phenomenal memories (either naturally so or through *"using methods that have been around since Greek antiquity"[65]*) and that memories are necessarily more important amongst non-literary people. Nevertheless he questions whether that must necessarily entail that such people had better – more efficient and effective – memories. Ehrman cites research which suggests that so far as the brain itself is concerned (that seat of our memories) there is no significant differences in neuronal structures either between people of different periods of history or people of different races. As opposed to a literate society in which information can be constantly checked by reference to what has been written down, traditions in an oral society are lost as they are replaced: *"oral cultures do not remain the same over time, but change rapidly, repeatedly, and extensively"*:[66] there is no way of checking current against prior information.

The idea that pre-literate societies had the ability to remember their traditions better is just an assumption: one that both neurobiological research into memory function and modern anthropological studies suggest is incorrect. Ehrman concludes:

> *"...oral traditions change as they are told and retold from one person to another. They change every time they are told. If what we have in the Gospels are not eyewitness reports...but accounts in circulation, not just for weeks and months, but for years and decades, then almost certainly they were changed. We know in fact that they were changed, because we can compare different accounts of the same words or activities of Jesus and find discrepancies... But the study of memory does not have to be concerned only with such negative findings, with memories that appear to have been 'distorted' over time. It can also be very positive, not simply to determine which memories are true to history, but also to see what they can tell us about the groups of people who were passing them along to others. Different people, and groups of people, remember things differently, as the present they inhabit affects their memories of the past they recall."*[67]

In what sense may the Gospels be said to contain **accurate memories** of Jesus? A memory

> *"...is **not a photographic record** of what actually took place, but a construction based on the original encoding of experience, the relating of that experience to oneself and others according to narrative frameworks and conventions supplied by one's cultural*

*context, and the need to make sense of the past in the light of the present and of the present in the light of the past. This does not mean that memory is radically unreliable; clearly for most everyday purposes it is anything but that; but **it does mean that what is remembered cannot straightforwardly be equated with what actually happened**. While it is most unlikely that the general course of Jesus' ministry would be seriously misremembered by those who witnessed it, and while it is highly likely that at least some details of striking events and sayings would also be retained with reasonable accuracy, distortions, reinterpretations, blending and confusion of separate incidents and even of the source of material apparently remembered would inevitably have occurred. To this must be added the tendency of oral narration to simplify, exaggerate and dramatise, to prefer stark contrasts and conflict, the need of oral poetics to cast its material in memorable form, and the tendency of both oral tradition and social memory to render the past usable in the present by relating it to other parts of the tradition by such means as keying, framing and metonymic reference. This doesn't mean that the historical Jesus is forever lost to us, but it does mean that even under the most favourable conditions in which we suppose eyewitnesses to have played a key role in stabilizing the tradition, the Jesus who lived and walked and breathed in Galilee may be glimpsed only through a distorting lens."*[68]

Another helpful way forward is proposed by Dale Allison: instead of focusing on the individual details of Jesus' life, we should be more interested in the cumulative evidential weight of those details. So, for example, Jesus may not have healed this particular person in this particular way, but the weight of detailed evidence in the tradition allows us to say that, on balance, it is entirely reasonable to believe that Jesus did, rather than did not, heal people, although we must also recognise that, without clear and unambiguous primary evidence, these are bound to be fairly subjective judgements. Yet again, it is about how memory 'works':

> *"Given that we typically remember the outlines of an event or the*
> *general purport of a conversation rather than the particulars and*
> *that we extract patterns and meaning from our memories, it makes*
> *little sense to open the quest for Jesus by evaluating individual*
> *items...in the hope that some bits preserve pristine memory. We*
> *should rather be looking for repeating patterns and contemplating*
> *the big picture. We should trust first, if we are to trust at all, what*
> *is most likely to be trustworthy...What matters is not whether we*
> *can establish the authenticity of any of the relevant traditions...but*
> *rather the pattern that they, in concert, create. It is like running*
> *into students who enjoy telling tales about their absent-minded*
> *professor. A number of those tales may be too tall to earn our belief;*
> *but if there are several of them, they are good evidence that the*
> *professor is indeed absent-minded".*[69]

Morna Hooker concurs with an approach which prioritises breadth over detail:

> *"If we concentrate on the whole rather than on the details...we shall*
> *find that we know quite a lot about Jesus, even though we might not*
> *be able to reconstruct with certainty any of his sayings or actions.*
> *It is clear, for example, that he spoke with impressive authority,*
> *even though there is considerable doubt about the exact form of all*
> *the stories demonstrating that fact. It is beyond question, also, that*
> *he taught in parables, however difficult it may be to reconstruct*
> *them, or to be certain about their original meaning. Few scholars, if*
> *any, have doubted that the centre of his teaching was the Kingdom*
> *of God – though what he might have meant by that phrase is again a*
> *matter of dispute. He also performed various miracles, even though*
> *we may disagree about precisely what happened or how. Again,*
> *while various stories and sayings may or may not be 'accurate', it is*
> *clear that he befriended those on the outskirts of society and that he*

offended the religious and political leaders. It seems clear, too, that he called men to be his disciples – though whether or not there were twelve in the inner circle is not so certain – and that he demanded – and inspired – remarkable devotion on their part. It is indisputable that he was put to death by the Roman authorities – though to what extent the Jewish authorities were involved is far from clear – and that his followers came to believe that he had been raised from the dead, though how and where they came to that conviction is now impossible to say."[70]

Writing specifically about the oft-contested historicity of the Fourth Gospel, Horsley and Thatcher[71] take a similarly broad perspective, recognising that communication in the ancient world was predominantly oral (with implications for the role and use of written Gospels, understood here as 'texts-in-performance'), and arguing that *"the Gospels as **whole stories** (with speeches) are more reliable as early sources than are particular sayings or episodes, on which previous study has focused".*[72] They make an important distinction between 'verification' and 'verisimilitude' (which has a range of meanings from 'an appearance or semblance of truth' to a 'likelihood' or even 'probability' [Lat *verisimilis*: 'probable': *verus*: true, *similis*: like]), suggesting that whilst it is impossible to verify the detail of the Jesus-story, the Fourth Gospel overall has *"considerable historical verisimilitude"*,[73] although not all scholars would agree with this assessment, some doubting that the 4th Gospel contains much in the way of historical material at all, particularly the extended 'sermons' of Jesus, so different from the pithy Synoptic sayings.

Bearing all this in mind **what, therefore, *can/do/might* we know from the biblical accounts about Jesus?** Allison discerns a number of broad patterns about which we can be reasonably certain:[74]

1. "Jesus made uncommonly difficult demands on at least

some people";

2. Jesus was "an exorcist who interpreted his ministry in terms of Satan's downfall";

3. he spoke of God as Father;

4. he composed parables;

5. he came into conflict with the religious authorities;

6. Jesus believed that he had "a starring role in the eschatological drama" which was to unfold.

Anything much more than this is a matter of faith, not evidence. Some Christians might not like that: but it is the direction in which the thrust of much modern critical biblical study is leading us. We must accept that there will always be a degree of agnosticism concerning the Biblical 'Life of Christ' and that what we know is much, much less than what we don't know.

The Jesus of History and the Christ of Faith

We live in a modern scientific and technological world, far distant not only from the world which produced these doctrines, but also from the even more different world of Jesus. If the Faith is to maintain any credibility, or even be understood today, then we must (continually) reassess the way we both understand and express it, using the best intellectual tools at our disposal. So if Jesus was (as the Church has declared to be orthodoxy) genuinely human, then the findings of historians, albeit limited by the relative paucity of comparative sources, must surely affect the way we understand him. During the period of classic creedal formation when there certainly were allegorical and other non-literal interpretations of the Bible, it was still generally assumed that the Gospels provided an accurate account of the life of Jesus, although these early Christian scholars were well aware of various inconsistencies, and of the significant differences between the Synoptics and John.[75] But, as we shall shortly argue, none were historians as in our modern understanding of that discipline; but that is no longer the case. Thus inevitably undergirding and influencing modern Christological proposals and also the interpretation of the NT, has been the so-called search or quest for the 'Historical Jesus': the man who lived in Palestine around 2000 years ago. Just what kind of man was he? What evidence do we have? What are the outcomes of research? The answer to all these questions is, despite years of endeavour, mainly disagreement and inconsistency, although that is little different from many other historical enquiries:

"At any given time people who appear to be equally competent, well-trained, and respected scholars disagree fundamentally about many of the most crucial issues. Such disagreements can easily inspire and justify scepticism on the part of the outsider as to whether any of the parties really have beliefs that are strongly grounded. Even where there is consensus at present among scholars, a degree of scepticism seems justified if one looks at the history of the discipline, for it seems clear that what was widely accepted by one generation of scholars is often doubted or rejected by the next."[76]

"Is the historical Jesus best understood as a Jewish rabbi, who, like other rabbis, taught his followers the true meaning of the Law of Moses? Or as a Jewish holy man, who, like other holy men, could claim a special relationship with God that gave him extraordinary powers? Or as a Jewish revolutionary, who, like other revolutionaries, urged an armed rebellion against the Roman imperialists? Or as a Jewish social radical, who, like other social radicals, promoted a countercultural lifestyle in opposition to the norms and values of the society of his day? Or as a Jewish magician, who, like other magicians, could manipulate the forces of nature in awe-inspiring ways? Or as a Jewish feminist, who, like other feminists, undertook the cause of women and urged egalitarian structures in his world. Or as a Jewish prophet, who, like other prophets, warned of God's imminent interaction in the world to overthrow the forces of evil and bring in a new Kingdom in which there would be no more

suffering, sin and death? All these options have their proponents amongst competent scholars who have devoted years of their lives to the matter yet cannot agree about some of the most basic facts about Jesus, except that he was Jewish".[77]

Most scholars recognise three main 'quests' for the historical Jesus. The aim of the 18th - 19th century liberal Protestant approach (the First Quest) was to free the historical Jesus from the dogmatic formularies of the Church. But after Schweitzer's famous critique of the project (in 'The Quest of the Historical Jesus', 1st Ed. 1906), scholars turned their attentions elsewhere. Indeed, Bultmann argued that the historical Jesus was irrelevant for faith, distinguishing the historical Jesus ('Proclaimer') from the historic Christ ('Proclaimed'). Ultimately, in Tyrrell's well-known words, these 'questers' were *"looking back through nineteen centuries of Catholic darkness [to see] only the reflection [of their own] Liberal Protestant face[s] seen at the bottom of a deep well":*[78] we will always find the Jesus that is most congenial to our presuppositions. The 'Second Quest' is often dated from a lecture given by Kasemann (a pupil of Bultmann) in 1953 who not only believed it was practically possible to reach some limited historical conclusions about Jesus, but also that it was theologically essential to do so: there needed to be at least some continuity between the Jesus of History and the Christ of Faith. The Third (and ongoing) Quest placed a heavy emphasis on Jesus' Jewish and apocalyptic-eschatological contexts, adding to that an interest in social and economic issues, the use of non-canonical sources (such as the Gospel of Thomas), the use of interdisciplinary approaches, and so on. Probably best-known (at least popularly) is the work of the so-called 'Jesus Seminar' which infamously used coloured beads to designate which words and deeds of Jesus were considered by participants the most or the least authentic: the results were generally negative.

Although these 'Jesus historians' often came up with portraits of Jesus greatly at variance with each other, their findings, whether Christians liked it or not, were bound to impact on our theological understanding of Jesus:

> "What does it mean that, until relatively recent times, our dominant theologians have put Jesus into a Christological straitjacket, that they have, despite their protests otherwise, been docetists of a sort [i.e. not taking the human Jesus seriously enough] for whom Jesus' humanity was above all a philosophical problem? And what should we think when we learn that these theologians defended their Christological opinions primarily by appeal to biblical texts having to do with Jesus' identity?...Those who subscribe to Nicaea should be anxious, for the historical Jesus did not think of himself what they think of him. To be sure, his identity, like that of the rest of us, cannot be restricted to his self-conscious evaluation, whatever we judge that to have been. Jesus must be more than the sum of his own thoughts. Still, traditional, orthodox christologies have assumed that Jesus was fully aware of his own godhead and spoke accordingly, whereas modern criticism has, in the judgment of many of us, exterminated this possibility. The orthodox tradition thus needs to acknowledge that the revisionist christologies of the last two centuries have been partly occasioned by advances in knowledge. There has been good cause to rethink some things."[79]

Why such an impact? Because Jesus was 'truly human', living at a particular time, in a particular place, amongst real people, and in a religious, cultural, political and socio-economic context which modern historians have opened up considerably but nowhere near completely. Although the assertion that Jesus was (also) divine is theological and not historical (it cannot be demonstrated using the tools of historical research), whatever we may wish to say about his theological, ontological and existential significance must surely be based on that real life, insofar as we can recover it. It was this real man who, around 2000 years ago, gave rise to

Christian faith: somehow or other. So we cannot simply divorce the 'Christ of Faith' (a theological assessment: the Risen Lord as believed in by the Church, expressed in and through the New Testament documents, and the focus of Christian discipleship today) from the 'Jesus of History' (an historical assessment: the man who lived in Palestine around 2000 years ago and who was crucified by the Romans), but neither can we simply equate them. The critical question is: just what is the relationship between the two? Is it a close relationship: the 'picture' presented of the Christ of faith is much the same as and faithful to the real person, or is it distant: the 'picture' presented of the Christ of faith is quite different from the real person, because it has taken on/absorbed additional theological assessments of his person and work? A very illuminating discussion of the nature of this relationship is to be found in two linked essays.[80]

In 'Is the Christ of Faith also the Jesus of History?' SJ **Patterson** argues[81] that it is important to distinguish very clearly between the two. Obviously the 'Christ of Faith' arose from the 'Historical Jesus' (as I have argued above) but, because the history has become overlaid with theology, the resultant 'Christ of faith' seems to present a very different 'picture' to that of the 'historical ('real') Jesus', insofar as we can discover/recover this historical person. Put simply: the Gospel narratives are neither history nor biography in the modern sense and although research has found strong similarities with the Hellenistic *bioi* (stories of great people), 'Gospel' is virtually a genre of its own – kerygmatic (proclamatory) theology/christology in narrative form. As a result, claims Patterson, some Christians, unable or unwilling to deal with this tension between the historical and the theological, have come to 'inhabit' two totally dissimilar worlds simultaneously (they persuade themselves that both can exist without any contradiction): the world of their experience which being both rational and scientific works according to regular predictable 'laws' and, in which, when you are ill, you go to the doctor and take medicines. This is seen over against the 'world' of Jesus which is full of miracles and awesome happenings and where, if you are ill, you have the demons cast out. They treat this latter world as if it were just as 'normal' (and, they assume, just as 'historical' and 'real') as the first (the one they really inhabit), although it is a world

"…where things happen that do not happen in normal life. But this seems normal. After all, Jesus is the divine Son of God. He is an exception, one of a kind. Who could not see this; he walks on water".[82]

So he asks:

"Did Jesus really do astonishing things and is this why people should believe in him? Or is this an illusion that masks another, more important reality: that faith begins in another, less astonishing, more ambiguous, and ultimately more challenging way?".

His conclusion: the simple equation of the Jesus of history with the Christ of faith (and vice versa) is

"…a Christian conceit that allows us to think that we believe what we believe because history itself proves we are right [when the Gospel material is hardly 'historical' at all in any modern sense of the concept i.e. in terms of its purpose and evidential value]. It is a conceit we can no longer afford in an increasingly plural and divided world…".[83]

Patterson concludes:

"Our Gospels are a mix of history and interpretation, myth and reality. These two poles – history and interpretation – work together and must be held together. The historical reminiscence, however it

survives, is [just] the memory of an experience in history – the words and deeds of a real human being. The interpretation, whatever its form, is the expression of faith that says in these words and deeds one can encounter something more than the human being. One can [somehow] encounter God in a real human life. History and interpretation, they always work together, interpretation always claiming the presence of revelation, history always recalling the moment and character of that revelation. In this sense [and in this sense only] the Christ of faith is the historical Jesus; the historical Jesus is the Christ of faith".[84]

We may compare and contrast CA **Evans** 'The Christ of Faith is the Jesus of History'[85] who argues that *"the Christ of Faith [really] is the Jesus of History"*. What is believed reflects the reality – at least, to a degree:

"Strictly speaking we cannot without qualification equate the Christ of faith with the Jesus of history. The two are related; they overlap. But they are not the same. Much that Christians believe about Jesus, what is usually called Christology, reflects theology that is simply not open to historical examination... Nevertheless, a qualified equation is possible... [The 'Christ of Faith'] *includes a number of historical components, some of which are very important...* [So the 'Jesus of history'] *overlaps with key theological elements in Christology...behind the creed, behind the faith claims of the Christian movement, is history...It was the actual events that awakened faith and later prompted theological enquiry"*.[86]

In practice, each of these scholars reaches the same basic conclusion (that you cannot simply identify or equate the Jesus of History with the Christ of Faith) although Evans takes a more positive view of the connection than does Patterson.

Whether or not we judge the connection between the Christs

of faith and of history to be close or distant, if we fail to take the work of historians seriously, we fall inevitably into some form of Docetism or some other heresy which undermines Christ's humanity: one of the characteristics of being human is that we all have a history. Christologies not firmly rooted in history (so far as that is possible) are in danger of being both too speculative and irrelevant to a faith based, not on philosophical musings, but in historical realities: the two key points of which are Jesus' crucifixion and the birth of the Church.[87] More to the point, it allows or even encourages us to overlay or otherwise infuse our Christologies with our own preferences and prejudices: we come to believe in the Jesus Christ who best fits our theological preconceptions and meets our religious needs. Of course, 'Jesus historians' are equally capable of constructing their own Jesuses who may turn out to be completely irrelevant to faith: for example, a wholly 'eschatological Jesus' – who turned out to have been completely wrong about an imminent End – is hardly a good starting point for a modern faith, although there are ways we can cope theologically with that understanding that Jesus was a man of his times, sharing the particular beliefs and outlook of his fellow Second Temple Jews. In the end, whatever conclusions about Jesus we come up with, they stand a greater chance of being true to the real man when we utilise the best intellectual tools available to us, and not rely on 'this is what I choose to believe'. Perhaps potentially risky for faith; but then faith itself is a risky business.

The main lesson we have to learn from these 'quests' is, as James Dunn has argued in the first magisterial volume of his 'Christianity in the Making' Project[88] that the 'real' Jesus, the 'Jesus of History', the 'Jesus as he was', the man who lived 2000 years ago in Palestine, is fundamentally inaccessible to us today. There is a great deal about that real life we can never know (not least the 30 years or so before Jesus' public ministry) and, hard as it is for some, we need to reconcile ourselves to that fact. All we can ever know is the 'Jesus as he was remembered' through the impact he had on his followers, while each experience and the memory of it will have been unique to the person. Simon the Zealot's[89] memories may have been tinged with and moulded by disappointment that Roman rule was not only still solid, but had killed the one who was to have brought liberation. Nevertheless, we recall that memories are not photographic records, and can't be simply equated with 'what actually happened'.

Nevertheless, despite its intrinsically subjective nature and the myriad ways it has been transmitted, the memory of Jesus is still considered by Dunn to have been, by and large, the very 'Jesus as remembered' by his disciples. The Synoptics (at least) have been informed by genuine memories, although those memories will have undergone some degree of transformation. Taking account of the life-changing effect Jesus clearly had on those who actually knew him, and even though their memories are not directly available to us (only indirectly via the tradition: that which has been 'handed down'), we can still make some reasonable judgements about the kind of person Jesus actually was and, to some extent, how they (and perhaps even how Jesus himself) understood his purpose and meaning. However, no objective picture (one independent of these memories) of Jesus is possible; even today we can never produce a totally objective picture of any historical character, although modern historical methodologies have given us greater access to and better and more diverse tools for dealing with evidence: but that evidence still has to be interpreted. So biographies of any great figure of history may well reach quite different conclusions about the person - personality, successes/failures, assessment of character - some even markedly so, not least because every such history will be affected to some degree or other by the bias, assumptions and abilities of the author; just as the differences in the Synoptics reflect the theological agendas of the individual Evangelists.

Therefore, we must accept not only that 'subjective' memories of Jesus are the only kind of memories available to us, and further that even those memories can only be seen through the prism of oral tradition, and may well have been yet shaped by the Evangelists and their theological concerns (including their incipient Christologies). However, it is just as important to note that to label them 'subjective', despite the way those memories were managed over a 40+ year process, doesn't in itself entail their being intrinsically unreliable, although some may have been more accurately transmitted than others - hence still the need for some kind of 'authentication criteria': for example, the 'criterion of embarrassment' assures us that Jesus was baptised by John, a fact the Church would probably have preferred to forget (not least because there are hints in the 4th Gospel that the followers of John were seen as rivals to the followers of Jesus as late as the end of the first century).

When we take history seriously we must accept that there is no neutral, faith-free portrait of Jesus to be had, however much we might wish it otherwise. Some Christians will refuse to accept this judgement because they believe that to do so would rob their faith of anything 'solid' to hold onto. As a result they cling blindly to the view that the Gospels accurately (indeed, inerrantly: 'gospel truth') represent the 'true' Jesus in every detail: if it is reported that he did this or said that, then that must be what happened (sometimes even irrationally dismissing an evident contradiction as 'no contradiction at all...it might seem contradictory to us, but not to God'). For them, if it is not literally and historically true, then all is lost. That is wrong and is very much the result of putting one's theological head in the sand. It is entirely possible to hold to some degree of historical scepticism or agnosticism and still be very positive about our ability to understand the 'Jesus event'. Whilst we might not be entirely sure whether this happened or that was said, we nevertheless have a picture that is generally and sufficiently valid for faith: we find that the 'Jesus-as-remembered' has been remembered well enough, and that memory transmitted well enough, to provide a basis for our commitment – even when, as Hooker put it: *"Historically [a story] may be a complete invention, while nevertheless conveying the truth"*.

Dale Allison offers an example of a non-historical, yet theologically faithful and theologically truthful narrative, in the story of the Temptations of Jesus:

> *"I concluded, as have so many others, that the story is haggadic fiction, and that it arose out of Christian reflection upon Scripture. And yet it dawned on me one day, it is scarcely bereft of memory. The story rather preserves a series of likely truths about Jesus – that he was a miracle worker, that he refused to give self-authenticating signs, that he thought himself victorious over demonic forces, that he could quote the Bible, and that he had great faith in God. Here, then, we have a narrative about events that probably never happened, a narrative that nonetheless rightly catches Jesus in several respects. It thus illustrates the fact…that fiction can indeed preserve the past, as in modern 'historical fiction'."*[90]

It is the theology rather more than the history which sustains, nurtures and illuminates our faith.

Indeed, if faith were to rely entirely upon the historians, then it would be a frail thing indeed; yet, equally, ignoring the historians would be a mistake. There is a commensurate negative aspect or risk to this: in our finite situation it must always be possible that history could radically impact, if not on our faith in God, at least on the beliefs which arise from that faith. To take a couple of ridiculous examples: if historical research determined beyond reasonable doubt that Jesus never existed or that he did exist but was a serial killer, then we might well need to think hard about what it was we believed about him. But, if someone then said: 'whatever the evidence I will not believe it', they have already begun to depart from reality, and their faith becomes a toxic mix of personal dreaming and wishful thinking, which they often use 'Biblical authority' to defend, because it refuses to come to terms with the 'groundedness' of life: like those who flatly refuse to believe that science and the scientific method have nothing to tell us about God, the Bible, or even that the Bible is more trustworthy in its portrayal of creation than science.

So although Jesus was a real man, in a real place and time (etc.), there is an important sense (as the relative failure of the Jesus of History 'project' has demonstrated) that we can never know all that much, or certainly not as much as we would like to know, about him: what he was like, what he believed, except in quite general terms – we don't even know what he looked like. The 'real Jesus' is, without access to Michael Moorcock's time machine, beyond our ability to fully grasp and recover. What we do know and this, for most Christians, is sufficient, is what his first followers thought about him, although those thoughts have tended to be expressed more in theological than in historical terms. McKnight sums up the matter well:

"Jesus is by nature, because of the history of who he was and who he has become, theological. The Jesus of Allison, who is a variant on Albert Schweitzer's apocalyptic Jesus, is, even if he is not the completely orthodox Jesus, a theological Jesus. The remembered Jesus of Dunn, too, is a theological Jesus, even if he is a bit closer to the orthodox Jesus than Allison's. Tom Wright's end of exile Jesus, Dom Crossan's sagacious, counter-cultural, non-apocalyptic Jesus, and Marc Borg's religious genius, non-apocalyptic Jesus are also theological Jesuses. And the Jesus we construct is the Jesus we more or less believe in".[91]

We might represent the situation thus: there are many Jesuses:

1. **Jesus the man** who lived in Palestine 2000 years ago: we have very limited knowledge of him →

2. the many **Jesuses of History** each of which may be (much)
    more or (much) less true, in various respects, to the reality
    (the life of the man), but none is, nor could ever be, an
    exact representation of 'what really happened', and none
    to the extent that historians are able represent the life and
    thought of a more modern character for whom a greater
    degree and quality of evidence is available; yet still, for
    whom, a totally 'objective' portrait is not available →

3. the **'remembered Jesus'** (from original eye-witness
    memories, via oral tradition, to the Gospels) →

4. the **Christ of Faith** as established from the writing of the
    NT documents (beginning with Paul), up to and beyond
    the great Councils, and embraced by millions today →

5. the **error**: to assume that all of the above may be equated
    →

6. the **problem**: to judge the exact nature of the relationship
    between the real man, the memories and the Gospel
    portraits of him, and the Christ of Faith: just how small
    or great is the 'gap' between the Jesus of History and the
    Christ of Faith? (a simple example: the man → the God-
    man; or even the man → God 'in human form' – whatever
    that might mean). So are we really to imagine that the
    historical Jesus knew he was God although, if he was and
    didn't know it, how could that be ('surely God would
    know he was God?' is the very question which gave rise
    to Kenoticism as a proposed solution to the problem)?

Modern Science

Our penultimate reason for commending a new approach to
Christology is the rather obvious one that there are many modern
scientifically-based disciplines which were not available in and
to the ancient world and which would shed considerable light
on the issues the classical theologians were seeking to address:
particularly psychology (study of the mind) and anthropology

(study of humanity), as well as the mainstream sciences. After all

> "...if God is in fact the all-encompassing reality Christian faith proclaims, then what science says about nature, whether physical, chemical or biological, can never be irrelevant to a deeper experience of God."[92]

The most obvious question for **psychology** concerns the orthodox understanding – on which Chalcedon was somewhat ambiguous - as to whether Christ had two 'wills' (or, as we might say today, 'minds': the bases of the human will): human and divine, and how they operated together. It would probably seem to many moderns that the idea of a person having two minds or wills is either just plain silly, or is otherwise referring to a pathological mental condition. It obviously didn't seem that way to these early Christian thinkers who would have had only a limited understanding of the elements of what we know today as human psychology. Patriarch Sergius of Constantinople (supported by Pope Honorius 1 and Emperor Heraclius) proposed a compromise solution (the *Ecthesis*) which affirmed two natures but one *energeia* (action/energy) which sought to solve the problem of the divine Christ and the human Christ disagreeing with each other. But at the Third Council of Constantinople in 681 (the 6th Ecumenical Council) it was decided that because a will properly belongs to a nature, rather than a person, Jesus must have had two wills and, furthermore, on the soteriological basis that 'the unassumed is unhealed', Christ must have had a human will (as well as a divine will) hence 'orthodoxy' was **dyothelite** (*thelein*: 'to will'). To protect against the idea that the human and divine wills might ever be in conflict, it was asserted that the human will was always subordinate to the divine will (or, as I have argued above, that the divine always overwhelms the human). The Council also affirmed that in Jesus were two *energia*; it is less than clear whether "*earlier church fathers would have been* *so quick to accept the reified natures, each complete with its own proper will and working...".*[93] The medieval theologians continued to think through some of the implications of Dyothelitism as, against the challenge of Islamic theology, they tried to achieve greater metaphysical sophistication. So, for example, Thomas Aquinas, John Duns Scotus and William of Ockham employed the technical term *suppositum* (an independently existing, ultimate bearer or sustainer of properties): Christ's individual human nature is sustained by the Logos as the *suppositum,* so there are two wills. However, this is not without its problems (and modern theologians have offered correctives), not least its quasi-Nestorian elements: can a single person really 'contain' two separate, and arguably contradictory, natures?

Indeed, can any person have two minds (wills, consciousnesses), beyond the metaphorical: 'I'm in two minds about this'? As already noted, this would seem to entail an abnormal psychology:

"It looks as if it could be explained, or at least understood, on the basis of some sort of psychological analogy – though the analogy with schizophrenia is by no means encouraging".[94]

And again:

"Two wills in one person would be a pathological condition, and this was surely not what the church wanted to say about Jesus Christ. Willing belongs to the self or personal centre, and although Chalcedon spoke of two natures, it acknowledged one person, and therefore a unitary willing. No doubt human nature has a plurality of desires, and these may conflict with one another, but this is something different from willing".[95]

If Christ did have two wills and the divine will always prevailed, then it must be asked whether this does not diminish, or almost evaporate, his humanity – would there be any 'real' human mind left at all?:

> *"The human mind was so much overshadowed or absorbed by the divine that though it was there, it made no difference. The chief reason why any of the ancients wanted to acknowledge a human mind in Christ was that it could sluice off the human passions which can only with danger (they thought) be ascribed to the Godhead"*.[96]

In other words, an unintended consequence of Constantinople III was yet again, despite Rahner's contention that

> *"...the 'human nature' of the Logos possesses a genuine, free, spiritual, active centre, a human self-consciousness, which as creaturely faces the eternal Word in a genuinely human attitude of adoration, obedience, a most radical sense of creaturehood..."*,[97]

to undermine the genuine humanity of Christ.

But, as Donald MacLeod puts it:

> *"His human nature certainly did not exist in an I-Thou relationship to his divine nature: such an understanding would plunge us into the most unambiguous Nestorianism"*;[98]

and as James Buswell Jnr explains:

> *"...[we] cannot deny that the wording of the decision of the [sixth] council seems to imply that a 'will' is a substantive entity, like a hand or a foot. Yet I do not believe that such an opinion can be dogmatically asserted as the actual meaning of the council. We are familiar with the tendency of human expressions, not only towards literal reification or hypostatization, the tendency to regard an abstraction as a substantive entity; but we are also familiar with the tendency of language towards metaphorical reification. I cannot*

prove that the implications of the wording of the third council of Constantinople were merely metaphorical and not literal, although in my opinion a case could be made for such a conclusion".[99]

Metaphor or not, we might well add that the Synoptic narrative seems to show a single (if enhanced?) human mind at work in Christ (although John is more ambiguous, as the single human mind becomes, particularly in the 'I am' sayings, more like a single divine consciousness). Clearly there were, and are in the light of modern science, still serious problems with the classical Christologies that require resolution, particularly the precise nature of Christ's 'human nature'. Put simply: how can true humanity really exist alongside and combined with divinity; won't it be neutered, overpowered or even eradicated by its divine 'partner'?

As for the **mainstream sciences**: whilst in the 19th Century biology (particularly the theory of evolution) had the greatest impact on theology, today it is physics: in particular the two theories of relativity (first 'special' then 'general', incorporating a new understanding of the nature of gravity) and quantum mechanics (or quantum theory[100]). These theories have undermined[101] the traditional Newtonian universe and thus its 'mechanic God' who keeps everything 'ticking over' with miraculous interventionist adjustments as necessary. However, the truth revealed by such innovative ideas and confirmed by experimentation is, as one might expect, much more subtle. At least one significant difference between our time and the ancient world is that we live in an age where scientific research has greatly increased our knowledge and understanding of our universe, and continues to do so at a seemingly exponential rate: we don't just know more; we know far, far more, not only about the very large (cosmic realm), but also the very small (quantum realm). It is incomprehensible how any Christian in this modern age can (as many do) ignore the findings of modern science.

The Greek term *kosmos,* although (in the NT, 182 times) referring mainly to the 'world' can be used to denote everything that is: the whole creation, although there are actually only two such NT usages: Col 2: 8, 20. Although many early scholars were perfectly aware that the world was round, in most cultures the idea of a flat earth generally obtained for many years:[102] a view to which a few creationist diehards continue to adhere, despite the evidence (such as photographs of the Earth seen from space). This is precisely the point: once we ignore evidence which 'stares us in the face', our beliefs are on a very slippery slope, and will be rightly criticised and even mocked (hence Russian cosmonaut – and, apparently, a member of the Orthodox Church - Yuri Gagarin's alleged comment in April 1961 that he'd been round the Earth 'looked and looked but still hadn't seen God'). The idea that God's abode was 'above'[103] with the human realm sharing the Earth with the place of the dead ('Sheol'/'Hades': not necessarily hellish) 'below' – the cosmology which lay behind Genesis 1 – was widespread in the ancient world and, astonishingly, continues to be the kind of picture of the universe held by some Christians even today. Some ancients, to the intellectual shame of such moderns, took a more sophisticated view, but even they did not (and how could they?) comprehend just how vast the universe is; and the concept of a multiverse would probably have been beyond their ability to grasp – as it is for most of us today. For even today the mind boggles at the vast distances not only between planets, but particularly between stars and, even more, between galaxies – which are themselves to be counted (if we could) in the billions. How can we possibly think that these kind of scientific discoveries are irrelevant to the way we 'do' theology? So, for example, writing of Heisenberg's work on the 'quantum leaps' of electrons which appear to have no precise 'place' to be at all and so seem unreal, the Italian physicist Carlo Rovelli explains that it is *"as if God had not designed reality with a line that was heavily scored, but just dotted in with a faint outline"*.[104]

It is easy to portray the Church as obscurantist and anti-science, but that is simply wrong.[105] For instance, the Church's opposition to Galileo was not intrinsically about his science, but about the question of authority, not least the personal authority of Pope Urban VIII, who had initially supported Galileo, but now feared not only for his own position, but also for that of the Church and the Bible. When Galileo observed that the earth went round the Sun this not only went against the Church's view that the Earth and humanity formed the pinnacle of God's creation, but it also appeared to contradict the Genesis accounts which were judged to be making a similar point. It is both noteworthy and encouraging that, in the 1990s, Pope John Paul II formally apologised for the way Galileo had been treated. As noted, a similarly apparent 'science v. faith' controversy famously broke out in the late 19th Century following the publication of Darwin's (1859) 'Origin of Species', and still rumbles on in the form of the modern – but, in my view, somewhat futile - Creationist/Intelligent Design debates.[106] Today, most Christians are relaxed about the current scientific consensus regarding the Big Bang, evolution, the age of the Earth, and so on.[107]

It is clear that the findings of the scientific academy will inevitably impact on the theological academy; if that is not understood, then our theology is in danger of becoming mere speculation, introspection and sophistry: and totally irrelevant to the 'real world'. So when John Macquarrie comments on the scientific principle of entropy and decay:

"Let me say frankly...that if it were shown that the universe is indeed headed for an all-enveloping death, then this might seem to constitute a state of affairs so wasteful and negative that it might be held to falsify Christian faith and abolish Christian hope",[108]

then this is a significant statement, for it suggests the possibility that science has the capacity to 'wreck' faith. I don't myself agree with Macquarrie on this occasion, for even if creation finally dies (as surely it must in the end?), then that does not mean that it has not served its purpose as the context for producing beings of such consciousness and spiritual development that they can recognise, worship and enter into a relationship with their Creator.

A particularly sharp (theologically) and very current example of how science and theology may engage positively may be found in the potential impact on our beliefs about both God and Jesus of the **discovery of intelligent life elsewhere in the universe**. It may have been Nicholas of Cusa (1401–1464), or possibly his close contemporary, the Franciscan Guillaume de Vaurouillon, who was first to suggest that life may exist elsewhere in the universe, and discussion was further encouraged after the Reformation by Bishop John Wilkins' '*A Discovery of a New World: or a discourse tending to prove, that t'is probable that there may be another habitable world in the Moon*' and by John Ray's '*The Wisdom of God Manifested in the Works of Creation*'. In these only-just-modern times such writers could have had no idea of the vastness of the physical universe. It was as the space-age was developing that W Burnet Easton Jr[109] pointed to the likelihood that there is intelligent life elsewhere in the universe and examined the implications for Christian faith if there were. His basic claim was that the idea of God may even be enhanced by such a finding (the astronomer Herschel had apparently asserted: "*If one world glorifies God, more worlds glorify him all the more*"), but he also acknowledged the 'downside' for theology. What if that alien life turns out to be more advanced than us? That might well raise questions about our relationship with God in general and the Incarnation in particular. If we find intellectually, morally and spiritually advanced/superior civilisations elsewhere in the universe:

"*Can we still believe that a God who is responsible for all these worlds cares enough about the rather backward bipeds on this tiny speck in space, to incarnate himself in a man, Jesus of Nazareth, who is the Christ?"*.

Furthermore:

"...if man is only one of nobody knows how many intelligent beings on isolated planets scattered all over the universe – and perhaps a very inferior one at that – it suggests that Christianity may be only an immature and very parochial faith of a more or less primitive form of human development".

A more recent exploration of this theme has been by Methodist theologian-astrophysicist and Principal of St John's, Durham, David Wilkinson.[110] Beginning with an historical account of the search for evidence of alien life, and particularly now the work of the SETI (Search for Extraterrestrial Intelligence) Project,[111] Wilkinson reminds us of the staggering size of the universe: our Milky Way Galaxy containing 400 billion stars, our observable universe (and who knows how much larger the parts of universe we cannot – and, due to the relative 'youth' of the universe and the limits of light-speed, could never – see is?) containing 200 billion galaxies, with an unknown number of galaxies and possibly even more universes beyond that, perhaps even intersecting with ours via different dimensions. Since the first planet was discovered (1988) which orbited another star, it has been estimated that around 10% of stars are like our Sun and that about 20% of that 10% have at least one Earth-like planet orbiting them – based on the estimated figures above, then the observable universe is likely to contain around one and a half thousand billion, billion habitable planets. Wilkinson poses the obvious question: what chance is there of there **not** being life somewhere else? The theological issue is this: if there is life elsewhere then that life is part of God's creation and so will be in some kind of relationship with their Creator. Wilkinson, for his part, suggests that other intelligent beings, if they exist, are likely to be "good, fallen, and looking for grace",[112] and discusses three theological models:[113]

1. *"God becomes incarnate as a human being and dies on the cross to offer redemption for the whole Universe. This is universality from particularity...As nothing of the fullness of God [as per Colossians 1] was left out of Jesus, so nothing is beyond his reconciling work. So the work of shedding blood on the cross is for all things"*; criticisms of this model include its arrogance in assuming what happens on Earth can affect the whole Universe or that, somehow, humankind, amongst the whole of creation, 'deserves' redemption – he quotes CS Lewis' view that mankind is not "the sole end of Nature".

2. *"...multiple incarnations and multiple redemptive events. This is universality by particularity; that is, God offers salvation by particular acts in lots of different places. It locks together revelation and redemption and makes the assumption that aliens have fallen in the same way as have human beings"*. The main theological principle undergirding this proposal is that God comes to us as we are, not as we are not. God's revelation to alien beings will be appropriate for them. So perhaps there could be many different 'incarnations' or other 're-presentations' of God's Word; but it would be the same Word that was incarnated (or whatever form of presence works), and the same salvation won. As Prof. John Polkinghorne put it in a newspaper article (hence the non-scientific language used): *"If little green men on Mars need saving, then God will take their little green flesh... He will do what is necessary"*.[114] The main criticism of this view is that it is fundamentally speculative: we simply do not have the knowledge, either in terms of science or in terms of theology, to be able to say; nevertheless,

the model does fit with what Christians claim to be the nature of God – love and concern for his whole creation.

3. Origen presented Christ's redeeming work as a transcendent action which gradually impacts cosmically as its effects reverberate across the Universe; that the redemptive act occurred on this planet is due to the fact that it had to occur somewhere: *"As Christ is the one through whom all things were made and all things hold together, the significance of the historical Jesus on Earth extends to the history and destiny of farthest reaches of the Universe"*.

What Wilkinson doesn't discuss is the possibility that there is intelligent life elsewhere which actually doesn't need salvation, because it hasn't 'fallen'. Is it not possible that, if God's original creation was truly 'very good', some forms of life have maintained that goodness, and live in a happy fulfilling relationship with their Creator, as it was always meant to be? Perhaps we humans are the only ones who have 'messed up', so requiring an incarnation-type 'intervention'? Such issues have also been explored via poetry[115] and hymns.[116]

Some Christians may well believe (as an Evangelical student once told me) that even raising this issue is a waste of time and totally irrelevant to Christian faith and belief. But is that really so? My student would have taken the view, garnered from a more or less literal approach to the Bible and reflecting the 'exclusive' paradigm to be found (along with inclusivism and pluralism) in a Christian 'theology of religions',[117] that salvation is only for Christians, and possibly even only for 'true' Christians (like him?), all of whom are both (literally) earth-bound and include only a small proportion of humanity. But surely that is a far too narrow concept of God?

"God's love is cosmic and all-embracing, and Christians should rejoice that they see it on this small planet, expressed in the person

*of Jesus...[This exclusive] interpretation of the gospel...is hardly good news for the vast majority of the world's population at all... Christian morality is largely fixated on matters related to sexual conduct, and cares most about keeping rules, but is not greatly concerned with caring for all life on the planet or about seeking justice for the poorest people of the world. As for the rest of the universe, that is irrelevant. There are 100,000 million stars in our galaxy, and 100,000 million galaxies in the observable universe. But they are all irrelevant, and human beings, on this rather peripheral planet, are the central, perhaps the sole, objects of God's interest in creation. When God ends human history, the whole universe will cease to be – **a conclusion that is in stark contradiction to virtually all science teaching in the educated world. This interpretation of the gospel...seems to me rather negative, morally limited, and anti-scientific...**"[118]*

Or, as Macquarrie put it (in the context of a broader discussion about angelic beings):

*"Man is sometimes afflicted with a sense of loneliness on his little planet, the only 'existent' upon earth, perhaps just an accident in the cosmos. But if the Christian doctrine of creation is true, then man is no accident, and presumably he is not alone. **He must be one of countless races of beings on which the Creator has conferred being, and some of these races must, like man himself, have risen to consciousness and freedom whereby they can gladly cooperate with God.** Some must have moved further in the hierarchy of beings, so that they constitute higher orders of creaturely beings. The doctrine of the angels opens our eyes to this vast, unimaginable cooperative striving and service, as all things seek to be like God and to attain fullness of being in him...[it also] directs our minds to the vastness and richness of the creation, and every advance of science opens up still more distant horizons. **Any merely humanistic creed that makes man the***

measure of all things or regards him as the sole author of values is narrow and parochial. The panorama of creation must be far more breathtaking than we can guess in our corner of the cosmos, for there must be many higher orders of beings whose service is joined with ours under God".[119]

Indeed Wilkinson quotes with approbation the view of the highly-esteemed Astronomer Royal, Lord Martin Rees, that the search for extraterrestrial life is humankind's "greatest quest" and underlines that with the assertion that "the discovery of any form of extraterrestrial intelligence would be one of the greatest events in the history of mankind".[120] He suggests:

"Perhaps at its very core is the question of what it means to be human. If the human species is just one intelligence among many in the Universe, then some think that our cosmic status is somehow different to our being the unique seed of consciousness...[but whether SETI is successful or not, these issues] are fruitful rather than destructive for religious belief".[121]

So if, as theologians ('ordinary' or otherwise), we want to understand and seek to explain God's plans for his creation, then we surely must take scientific theories into account – after all the subject matter: 'Creation', is the same. We need to understand that just as

"...the 'theological' and 'scientific' beginnings are not exactly simultaneous, as we cannot know whether God's initial act of creation is identical with the creation of this universe. So also the end points are not co-terminus, as God's consummation of the universe is God's initiative and not a matter of scientific prediction".[122]

Quoting Eberhard Jungel's: *"In the death of Jesus Christ God's 'Yes' which constitutes all being, exposed itself to the 'No' of the nothing...*

and in the Resurrection, this 'Yes' prevailed over the 'No'", Weaver comments:

> *"So there is the possibility of humans being taken out of the descent to hostile non-being and being caught up in the Being of God who is on the way to God's goal of a new creation. Through cross and resurrection the arrow of redemption ends in resurrection and renewal for the whole cosmos"* [123]

Does this address Macquarrie's concern noted above?

Particularly if we were to adopt a panentheist[124] understanding of God: that God transcends but is also present in his Creation, then we may reflect that either God will radically transform that creation ('a new heaven and a new earth') or that our and its destiny lies beyond the merely physical realm (but is creation 'merely physical'? what is the nature of the quantum realm – is it at all 'spiritual': we shall discuss this below)? This is – as ever - a massive topic, so I will now point to the thinking of three modern theologians in whose work the scientific dimension is taken very seriously.

Rob Bell: author of 'Love Wins', an American evangelical pastor – a recent book is 'What we talk about when we talk about God' (2013): Chap 2 'Open' is almost entirely devoted to a reflection on the outcomes of modern scientific discovery. For example:

> *"We live in a very, very weird universe. One that is roughly 96% unknown…To be closed-minded to anything that does not fit within predetermined and agreed-upon categories is to deny our very real experiences of the world. We're here, this is real, subatomic particles travel all possible paths and then choose one when observed, and there is no precedent for such a thing…Now it's true that religion can lead people to be incredibly closed-minded…[but also] to believe that this is all there is and we are simply collections of neurons and*

atoms – that's being closed to anything beyond that particular size and scope of reality. But to believe that there's more going on here, that there may be reality beyond what we can comprehend – that's something else".[125]

Bell, here, is not denying what the scientists have found; rather, he is arguing that their findings about our "weird universe" are the point at which serious theological thinking can 'take off'. It is by thinking through those discoveries that we can begin to form a coherent picture of a reality which doesn't exclude God, but encourages us to understand that science itself ultimately points towards that kind of reality:

"...when I'm talking about you, I'm talking about the paradox at the core of our humanity – that we're made of dust and stars and energy and patterns of planks and yet, as it's written in the Psalms, we've been crowned with glory and honour":[126]

scientific talk and theological talk, though different, complement each other.

John Polkinghorne: formerly Professor of Mathematical Physics at, and also President of Queen's College, Cambridge University who, after retirement, was ordained an Anglican priest:[127] so

"...the final chapter of every story told by science, whether concerning individual beings, or the universe itself, ends in death. Within the naturalistic context of science, which can only offer a 'horizontal' account corresponding to the continued unfolding of the present process, no ground can be discovered for belief in anything lying beyond death. All must eventually end in seeming futility. Human beings die, on a time scale of tens of years. The universe itself will die, on a time scale of many billions of years. From the point of view of physics, this prevalence of futility is a

consequence of the second law of thermodynamics, decreeing an inevitable drift from order to disorder. From the point of view of biology, evolutionary process requires the death of one generation as the price of the new life of the next...[However, a theological account] includes a 'vertical' dimension, corresponding to trust in the eternal faithfulness of God, and that introduces a motivated element of hope...Since [this] hope is not a natural expectation, science does not have any direct power to speak about it, either for or against. In this fundamental sense, the context of science is irrelevant to theology's task of eschatological thinking. Yet in a subsidiary sense, the context of science has a relevance to which careful attention needs to be paid. While the basis for the hope of a destiny beyond death lies in divine faithfulness – for the Christian manifested and guaranteed by the resurrection of Christ – the detailed form of discourse in which that hope is expressed may rightly be influenced by scientific understanding. The reason for this lies in the fact that a credible account of another life beyond this one has to include within it elements of both continuity and discontinuity in relation to life in this world...Science has a legitimate role to play in helping theology to explore [such issues]...This is particularly true of eschatology, with its concern for the nature of the world to come. No doubt there comes a point in eschatological speculation at which 'wait and see' is the best advice to follow. Yet modest exploration of rational possibility, capable of being assisted by insights derived from the context of science, is worth pursuing as far as it may prove possible to do so".[128]

Regarding '**continuity**':

"The notion of the soul as being an information-bearing pattern may not presently amount to much more than offering a toy of thought with which to play, but I believe that it serves to show that the acceptance of human psychosomatic unity, so natural in the context of science, does not deprive one of the idea of a carrier of

continuing identity".[129]

And '**discontinuity**':

> "...*it does not seem incoherent to believe that God could bring into being a new kind of 'matter', endowed with such strong self-organising principles that it would not be condemned to a thermodynamic descent into chaos. Theology can envisage this new form of 'matter' as arising from the divine transformation of present matter, redeeming it from its otherwise inevitable end in cosmic futility. On this view, the eschatological destinies of human beings and of the whole universe lie together in the world of God's new creation (Romans 8: 19 – 21). This new creation is not a second divine attempt at 'creatio ex nihilo', an action which would seem to imply the ultimate irrelevance of the first creation, but rather it is a 'creatio ex vetere', the transformation of the old into the new".*[130]

David Wilkinson's 'Christian Eschatology and the Physical Universe' (2010), although difficult for non-physicists (like me), is well-worth struggling with, as it deals with all the most significant issues so well. Having set out the current scientific views about the end of the Universe ("ending in futility"),[131] he summarises the (on the whole) "limited" responses of those he terms 'theologians of hope',[132] particularly those of Polkinghorne and Russell (of which he approves), and Moltmann and Pannenberg ("disappointing"). For Wilkinson, the Resurrection of Jesus is pivotal to any understanding of the End,[133] with two questions leading the field: the relationship of the resurrection to the physical sciences and the status of modern NT scholarship.

We may reasonably conclude, therefore, that scientific advances, particularly those made over the past century such as Einstein's theories of relativity and, now, the possibility of finding the physicists' 'Holy Grail': a 'Theory of Everything' in which, at last, general relativity (dealing with the very large) may be unified with quantum theory (the very small), a theory which will no doubt framed in the most elegant mathematics, just as the created order is itself both elegant and beautiful, will inevitably impact on our understanding of God,[134] particularly on the great theological issues of God as Creator (the Beginning) and thinking about Eschatology (the End). This is the exciting task which scientists and theologians can share: the continuing struggle to understand the great mysteries of the universe and particularly that greatest mystery of all which is God. We are one small part of the universe seeking to understand both itself and everything else: the greatest adventure of all. My rather more limited aim in later chapters is to show, using what these new insights can offer, how God might be understood generally to 'operate' in and on his creation, and how he did that specifically in the Incarnation.

As we have seen, **Quantum Theory**, which has the benefit of massive experimental success leading to many life-changing applications (such as the development of computers) which we now take very much for granted, has shown that reality, at least at the level of fundamental particles, doesn't work in the manner which traditional Newtonian physics would have us believe. Here predictability is impossible; all is radically uncertain (hence the Heisenberg Uncertainty Principle) and random.[135] So uncertainty is not just the result of ignorance on our part; it is *"written into the fundamental nature of reality"*.[136] Such ideas are not without their own problems (and hence, theologians must use them with a certain amount of caution), not the least being just how the unpredictable micro-world *"gives predictable, measurable answers when interrogated by our macro-world"*?[137] and, as Wilkinson points out: *"it is difficult to see how God working at the uncertainty of the quantum level would affect the everyday level"*.[138]

Setting such dilemmas aside for the scientists to argue over, we may at least conclude that God works in a rather complex universe (far more complex than we previously thought) and does so in quite unusual ways, for which the metaphor of the 'great mechanic' (or even that of the potter dabbling with his clay[139]) is no longer appropriate. The implications for re-imagining how God interacts with the universe are exciting, challenging, and potentially very creative as expressed, for example, through Process Theology, where

"...*God is not only the background to this reality [i.e. creation] and part of its evolution, but God can also be changed by the world; God is in process (as is the world), actively experiencing the world, sharing our own experiences with us, influencing us as we influence God. Each event is a product of the past, the present action and God. God therefore interacts in the world, but has no power to change it and cannot override free will...In process ideas, the world is incomplete and developing, and God allows this to happen as part of the freedom given to creation, and to individuals within it. Everything is travelling towards an end point, a future which is both unknown and has as its goal God...This would mean that God has formed a cosmos where the future is genuinely uncertain, even perhaps to God... Perhaps, even, chance is necessary for creation:* **creation must explore every avenue and all possibilities to find the best way.** *Conceivably, this is God's plan to care for creation using chance to explore all the possibilities at the limits of the physical world. Quantum indeterminacy gives the universe the opportunity of an open future and of a free relationship between created and creator...[So] the role of chance in quantum challenges our concepts of God and human freedom. So quantum mechanics could be the perfect subject for those who believe they are in a relationship with God, yet are free to act; those who believe that they are loved and that their actions matter in the world; those who accept the radical outcome of science that the world may not be as predictable as previously thought*".[140]

Furthermore, as Goldingay puts it:

"Divine sovereignty is...a subtler affair than it first seems. A dialectical relationship obtains between divine decision making and human decision making. While nothing happens outside Yahweh's control or outside parameters Yahweh lays down, and some things happen because Yahweh makes explicit decisions, many things happen in part because human beings respond to Yahweh in the way that they do".[141]

This is a rather more satisfying rendering of Ward's concept (discussed further below) of "divine-human synergy": how God cooperates with humanity. God is in charge, but not in any way that compromises human freedom and action; God works alongside us and the whole created order to bring good, so far as is possible and within the creative 'rules' he has made, out of our multifarious fumbling, hesitant and incompetent ways of 'screwing things up'.

Another 'game-changing' insight of modern science is so-called '**chaos theory**'. Whilst quantum theory deals with matters at the sub-atomic level, chaos theory (like Newtonian physics, which it also limits in eschewing predictability in anything except the most simple of systems) operates at the macro-level and posits that

"...most systems in the world are extremely sensitive to the circumstances around them, so much so that the slightest disturbance [as in 'the butterfly effect'] will make them act in a radically different way [entailing that] after a short time a system becomes essentially unpredictable".[142]

Indeed, in Wilkinson's view: *"chaotic systems have a great advantage over quantum systems in that their effects are felt at the everyday level"*[143] then referring to Polkinghorne's insight that God may well *"work in the flexibility of these open systems as well as being the ground of law. God's particular activity is real, but it is hidden"*.[144]

However, as Wilkinson points out: not being able to predict the future with certainty doesn't require us to conclude that the future is fully open (i.e. literally anything can happen) so that nothing can be known about it (even by God), but rather that any predictions we might seek to make (e.g. about the weather) are severely limited. Keen-eyed observers of the biblical texts will be well aware that the writers had no problem with the idea that even God did not know the future: in 1 Sam 15: 10 – 11, 35 God is said to have been sorry that he had made Saul king; had God known the future, then he would have known that Saul would make a mess of things and would not have made that appointment in the first place.

It may have seemed in the 19th Century that religion and science were implacably opposed, even mutually contradictory. That view is no longer possible to sustain and the sooner Christians and atheists accept that, the more enlightened (and enlightening) our theologising (and, for the atheist movement, anti-theologising) is likely to be. So we might want to ask a basic question: in the light of the modern human and natural sciences, does the notion of a man who was also God make any sense? We will explore some possible answers a little further on.

The Moral Status of Doctrine

Finally, and much more briefly, for many Christians today the traditional models for understanding Jesus are *"perceived as ethnocentric, patriarchal, misogynist, anti-Judaic, exclusivist and triumphalist"*.[145] There are not only philosophical and hermeneutical concerns, there are moral concerns as well: many Christians are rejecting the 'penal substitution' atonement model as immoral. Equally some Christians would regard the Roman Catholic prohibition of artificial methods of contraception (re-expressed in Pope Paul VI's 'Humanae Vitae' of 1968) immoral in the effects it has in the developing world (many RCs in the developed world ignore the prohibition) by, for example, allegedly undermining the battle against Aids, or creating large families which parents are unable to support.

The theologian Paul Badham makes a very simple comment which might usefully inform all our doctrinal thinking: *"If a doctrine offends our highest moral feelings, that is a powerful reason for rejecting it..."*.[146] Some might have come to believe that the most offensive aspect of traditional Christology is the implicit denigration of Jesus' humanity (as in the dyothelite subordinationism) which is unable, without an 'injection' of 'divinity', to serve the purposes of God in whose image we were created. Indeed, particularly (but not exclusively) in relation to Atonement, theologians – apparently committed to the idea of Incarnation, where the human condition is shown to be good enough for the Word to 'descend' into it - have spilled acres of ink seeking to show just how pathetic: morally, intellectually and spiritually lacking, human beings are. If that were true, then surely God would not touch humanity with the proverbial bargepole, and Incarnation would not have occurred?

If we could come up with a better way of showing modern people how Christianity can provide a living faith in the 21st Century, without coming into conflict with obvious scientific truths about the universe, without seeking to defend clearly immoral doctrines, and without the need to believe the impossible; rather than continuing to wallow in the language and concepts of the 5th, then it just may be possible to engage in effective mission, in which people are not encouraged to disconnect their brains as they enter church. Such a challenge not only validates, but actually invites, the project of reformulation, not least because much of what emerged from the 4th and 5th Century discussions is enormously problematic.

Notes

1.   This fairly technical section may be omitted, should the reader find herself becoming bored, without any loss to

the overall argument; however, staying with it may help explain my basic concern in writing this book: why should we be asked to take metaphysical conundrums at face value?

2. 'The Agreed Statement on Christology of the Churches of the Anglican Communion and the Oriental Orthodox Churches' in 'The International Journal for the Study of the Christian Church', 2015, Vol. 15, No. 3, pp. 159 – 185; Introduction by Geoffrey Rowell ('note on background and context') p. 159; Agreed Statement pp. 160 – 163; 'Theological Reflections' by Sergey Trostyankiy (Sophia Institute of Byzantine and Orthodox Studies) pp. 163 – 185;

3. In Point 7 (of 10) of this Agreement it is stated that the term 'monophysite' "which has been falsely used to describe the Christology of the Oriental Orthodox Churches, is both misleading and offensive as it implies Eutychianism. Anglicans, together with the wider *oikumene*, use the accurate term 'miaphysite' to refer to the Cyrilline teaching of the family of Oriental Orthodox Churches, and furthermore call each of these Churches by their official title of 'Oriental Orthodox'. **The teaching of this family confesses not a single nature but One Incarnate united divine-human nature of the Word of God.** To say 'a single nature' would be to imply that the human nature was absorbed in his divinity, as was taught by Eutyches" ibid. p. 162;

4. cited ibid. p. 161, point 2;

5. This is the very word used by Rowell in his introduction referring to that which the Agreement was intended to resolve: ibid. p. 159;

6. Point 4;

7. It is somewhat misleading to call them 'schools', as there were no institutions as such – rather "the patronage of certain individuals within the church, and the development

of different ecclesiastical and theological factions, led to networks of relationships and allegiances that go along with preferment and partisanship" (OD Crisp and F Sanders [eds 2013] 'Christology Ancient and Modern' Introduction p. 1);

8. Meredith A 'Christian Philosophy in the Early Church' (2012), pp. 110 – 111;

9. Frend WHC 'Rise of the Monophysite Movement' p. 125;

10. Jenkins P (2010) 'Jesus Wars' p. 59;

11. Quoted ibid. p. 58 note qualifiers 'ineffable', 'inconceivable' and 'indescribable';

12. Kelly JND (5th Ed, 1977) 'Early Christian Doctrines' p. 319;

13. The term was not used until after Chalcedon;

14. Kelly op cit pp. 319 – 320;

15. Ludlow M [2009] 'The Early Church' p. 204;

16. Edwards M. (2009) 'Catholicity and Heresy in the Early Church', p. 170;

17. Chadwick H (2003) 'The Church in Ancient Society' p. 581;

18. Jenkins op cit p. 67;

19. ibid. p. 58;

20. Pelikan J (1999) 'Jesus Through the Centuries' p. 58;

21. op cit p. 159;

22. Transubstantiation: the 'substances' (innermost reality: an Aristotelian concept) of the bread and wine are transformed into the substances of the body and blood of Christ; consubstantiation: the substances of each co-exist;

23. Being a broad community without a distinctive (Anglican) set of doctrines (it has more a distinctive theological method), and being both Catholic and Reformed, there will be many individuals who will subscribe to Roman Catholic doctrine, just as there are those clergy who – despite their ordination vows – use the Roman Eucharistic Rite;

24. In the words of St John of Damascus: "The bread of communion is not plain bread but bread united with

divinity";

25. The 2014 Agreement goes on (Point 5) to speak of rejecting any teaching "which separates or divides the human nature, both soul and body in Christ, from his divine nature, or reduces the union of the natures to the level of conjoining and limiting the union to the union of persons and thereby denying that the person of Jesus is the single person of God the Word." Equally, "both sides also agree in rejecting the teaching which confuses the human nature in Christ with the divine nature so that the former is absorbed in the latter and thus ceases to exist". Indeed, once again, all that is happening is that the ancient debates are being re-rehearsed, this time with care being taken not to raise issues which 1500 years ago might have caused division, without any consideration at all being given to the question: does any of this make sense?

26. Migliore DL (2nd Ed. 2004) 'Faith Seeking Understanding' p. 164;

27. Rahner K (1965) 'Current Problems in Christology' in 'Theological Investigations' Vol 1, pp. 149 – 200;

28. Coakley S 'What Chalcedon Solved and Didn't Solve' in Davis ST et al (2002) 'The Incarnation' p. 160;

29. Coakley supplies a list of questions which Chalcedon didn't answer: ibid. pp. 162 – 163;

30. ibid. p. 144;

31. ibid. p. 160;

32. ibid. p. 162;

33. Gregory of Nazianzus (329/30 – 389/90) from his Second Theological Oration, sections IV & V;

34. Coakley art cit p. 161;

35. ibid. p. 145;

36. ibid. p. 163;

37. The 2nd Century the Platonic and Aristotelian traditions came together as Middle Platonism, and this was the

dominant philosophy until, during the 3rd Century it gradually morphed into Neo-Platonism (particularly associated with Porphyry and used by Augustine), although the Cappadocian Fathers – in the late 4th Century - made use of both;

38. Arius was the 4th Century 'heretic' whose row with his bishop eventually led to the Council of Nicaea in 325;

39. Christie A op cit pp. 164 – 165;

40. Clement 'Miscellanies' I (v);

41. Tertullian 'On Prescription against Heresies' viii;

42. e.g. in the worship song 'Meekness and Majesty': "..the Man who was God"; it is important to recognise that worship songs are not meant to provide rational explanations of theological conundrums – they are more to do with our affective than cognitive states (the heart rather than the head); however, as they are one of the primary ways in which 'ordinary' Christians learn their theology, we should take them seriously as potential sources of error due to that very simplicity which makes them attractive and accessible;

43. See e.g. Mackey J (1979) 'Jesus: the Man and the Myth' p. 212;

44. 'modalism' (sometimes known as Sabellianism after its 3rd Century advocate) is one of the two major Trinitarian extremes (the other being tritheism) which claims that God's triunity is simply an expression of roles, forms and modes under which he has acted, rather than being intrinsic to his God-self; Trinitarian thinking has always sought a pathway between these two extremes;

45. Macquarrie himself was always very positive about the relationship of philosophy and theology although, when writing in the 60s and 70s, he described the "present mood between theologians and philosophers [as] one of suspicion and standoffishness, as each remembers the injuries which his discipline has received or is supposed to have received

at the hands of the other [and he concludes]... The fact that there may have been distorted relations in the past does not mean that there cannot be healthy relations, or that the two disciplines must go their separate ways in sulky isolation. This, I believe, would be most unfortunate, and would heighten still more the fragmentation of modern culture" ('Principles' pp. 22 - 23);

46. In its technical sense 'ontology' (from *'ontos'* 'that which is') is the study of 'being', 'existence' and other related ideas ('becoming', 'reality' etc.), a branch of what is termed 'metaphysics' ('after Physics', a reference to Aristotle's writings); we shall consider further below how 'being' (or 'Being') can have a role in explicating both divine and human nature;

47. Defined: 'Principles' p. 23; Macquarrie's declared "method of interpretation" was to "try to illuminate the symbolic language of revelation with an **existential-ontological language** drawn from contemporary philosophy, though this language will in turn be illuminated by the symbols of faith" ('Principles' p. 38; he sets out this method in detail on pp. 182 – 186);

48. Coakley art. cit. p. 159;

49. ibid. p. 161;

50. Ehrman B (2012) 'Did Jesus Exist?' p. 335;

51. A hypothetical source ('Quelle' is German for 'source) posited as an explanation for the material which Matthew and Luke have in common, but which is not found in Mark

52. See e.g. Bauckham R (2006) 'Jesus and the Eyewitnesses: The Gospels as Eyewitness Testimony';

53. 'Behind the Gospels: Understanding the Oral Tradition' (2014);

54. 'life situation': used in the sense of identifying the genuine context of a saying or event e.g. in Jn 9: 22 the parents of the blind man healed by Jesus were frightened to affirm that

healing on the grounds that "...the Jews had already agreed that anyone who confessed Jesus to be the Messiah would be put out of the synagogue" and the technical Greek term *'autosunagogos'* is used; this seems to be a reference to the so-called 'Heretic/Test Benediction' – the official formula by which Christians were expelled from synagogues; but that didn't actually exist until 85 – 90CE (prior to the writing of the 4th Gospel, but way after the time of Jesus: see also 16: 2); we may therefore conclude that the 4th Evangelist has artificially and anachronistically transposed something which existed in his day, and not much longer before that, and which was affecting the contemporary Church, back into his Jesus-story;

55. Eve op cit p. 178;

56. Ehrman B (2016) 'Jesus Before the Gospels';

57. "I am not, nor ever have been, in favour of bringing about in any way the social and political equality of the white and black races...and I will say in addition to this that there is a physical difference between the white and black races which I believe will forever bid the two races living together on terms of social and political equality" quoted ibid. p. 6;

58. ibid. pp. 3 – 8, 13 – 14, 20;

59. Consider how news stories change as they are retold, particularly transmitted via uncontrolled and uncontrollable social media; or how people can leave a meeting with quite different accounts of what transpired (often formal 'minutes' have to be agreed just in case they have misreported any facts or resolutions); in a literate society at least the most recent report can always be checked against and compared with its predecessors;

60. Ehrman quotes Maurice Halbwachs (ibid. p. 7): "... collective memory is essentially a reconstruction of the past that adapts the image of historical facts to the beliefs and

spiritual needs of the present";
61. Bauckham R op cit;
62. ibid. p. 6;
63. Ehrman op cit p. 66;
64. ibid pp. 179 – 226;
65. ibid. p. 179;
66. ibid. p. 183; Ehrman presents an extensive study of the Sermon on the Mount in order to illustrate the points pp. 195ff;
67. ibid. p. 226;
68. Eve op cit p. 181;
69. Allison DC (2009) 'The Historical Christ and the Theological Jesus' pp. 62 – 63;
70. Hooker M 'Foreword: Forty Years On' in Keith C & Le Donne A (2012) 'Jesus, Criteria, and the Demise of Authenticity', p. xv; this collection of essays provides a trenchant critique of the so-called 'authentication criteria': those criteria adopted by scholars since the 1960s by which they seek to judge the authenticity of particular sayings or actions recorded of Jesus in the Gospels (did Jesus really say/do this?; the whole basis of the work of the Jesus Seminar); this particular group of essayists claims that such criteria (e.g. the criterion of dissimilarity) either need root and branch revision or complete abandoning, as they are both too simplistic and potentially misleading; Hooker continues: "The search for the 'authentic' is in fact a strange conceit. For what makes a saying or story 'authentic'? Since Jesus spoke in Aramaic, and the Gospels are written in Greek, the record of them inevitably takes us at least one remove from the original, for **all translation involves interpretation**. We have to reckon, too, with the interpretation given to the saying or story by the early Christian community, which handed the tradition on, as well as with that given to it by the evangelist. And what makes a tradition 'inauthentic'?...

Historically [a story] may be a complete invention, while nevertheless conveying the truth. It has been said of Winston Churchill that half the things attributed to him are untrue – but are nevertheless true!" ibid. pp. xv – xvi; in other words – Jesus may not have actually said x, but x is, nevertheless, truly representative of his teaching;

71. 'John, Jesus and the Renewal of Israel' (2013);
72. ibid p. 92;
73. ibid p. 120;
74. Allison op cit pp. 63ff;
75. e.g. the chronological placing of the cleansing of the Temple, the day of crucifixion etc.;
76. Evans CS 'The Historical Jesus and The Jesus of Faith' (henceforth 'Historical') pp. 321 – 322;
77. Ehrman B 'Lost Christianities' pp. 95 – 96;
78. Tyrrell G (1913) 'Christianity at the Crossroads' p. 44;
79. Allison op cit p. 85;
80. In Moreland JP et al (eds. 2013) 'Debating Christian Theism';
81. pp. 447 – 457;
82. ibid. p. 447;
83. ibid. p. 447;
84. ibid. p. 455;
85. ibid. pp. 458 – 467;
86. ibid. pp. 465 – 466;
87. Historians continue to disagree over whether the Resurrection can ever be understood as an historical 'event': "It might be argued that Jesus' burial marks the end of what we can say about the historical man with any degree of plausibility. Christian claims regarding his Resurrection, however, have been so crucial in determining the future of his movement that a book on the historical Jesus which did not examine the Resurrection would be lacking an important element. Although the event itself is not open to historical investigation, we can at least **examine the effects**

of the Resurrection on Jesus' earliest followers" Bond HK (2012) 'The Historical Jesus: A Guide for the Perplexed' p. 166;

88. Dunn JDG (2003) 'Jesus Remembered';

89. Assuming that 'Zealot' (those committed to free the Jews from Roman occupation – which may, in any case, be an anachronistic reference, as it is likely that the 'Zealots', as a coherent group, didn't come into being until the end of the 1st C.) is a correct translation of *zelotes*, which may just mean 'zealous' in a religious sense;

90. 'It Don't Come Easy: a History of Disillusionment' in Keith C & Le Donne A (2012) 'Jesus, Criteria, and the Demise of Authenticity', p. 191;

91. McKnight S 'Why the Authentic Jesus is of no use for the Church' in Keith and Le Donne op cit pp. 173 – 174;

92. Mooney C 'Theology and Science: A New Commitment to Dialogue' in 'Theological Studies' 52 (1991) p. 316;

93. DeWeese GJ 'One Person, Two Natures: Two Metaphysical Models of the Incarnation' in Sanders and Issler (eds. 2007) 'Jesus in Trinitarian Perspective' p. 124;

94. Hanson AT (1984) 'Two Consciousnesses: The Modern Version of Chalcedon' Scottish Journal of Theology, 37, p. 474;

95. Macquarrie J (1990) 'Jesus Christ in Modern Thought' pp. 166-7;

96. Hanson RPC cited by Hanson AT art cit. p. 476;

97. Rahner K 'Current Problems in Christology' in 'Theological Investigations' Vol 1, p. 97;

98. MacLeod D (1998) 'The Person of Christ' p. 201;

99. Buswell JO (1962) 'A Systematic Theology of the Christian Religion' Vol 2 pp.53 - 4;

100. "mathematical formulations provide fundamental assumptions for understanding our universe, assumptions made about the historical development and composition of

our universe when humans were not around at the time; advancing technology designed using these theorems such as quantum mechanics has ultimately given rise to tangible scientific applications idealistically aimed at securing the future of humankind; however, scientists can only formulate what has 'happened' historically based on past or current data and a perception or interpretation of that data using present technology: not unlike your theologians": private comment made on my text by Dr Lesley Cookson (research chemist);

101. "Newton's theory is not really wrong; it merely has a limited range of validity". Davies P (1983) 'God and the New Physics' p. 220;

102. Held by such as Plutarch (1st – 2nd C. CE) '*De Facie in Orbe Lunae*' and Cosmas (6th C.) '*Topographia*', over against e.g. John Philoponos (5th – 6th C); however, "...it was generally accepted in European thought by the seventh century that the earth is spherical (*mundus est figure sperice seu rotunde*)." Evans GR (2014) 'First Light: A History of Creation Myths from Gilgamesh to the God Particle' p. 44;

103. One of my favourite hymns as a child, sung at infants' school, was 'There's a friend for little children above the bright blue sky' (Albert Midlane, 'Good News for Little Ones', Dec. 1859; The hymn published in memory of John Stainer): I imagine that, at 5, I would have taken the words literally and searched for Jesus and God 'up there'; but, at least, aged 5, one has some excuse;

104. Rovelli C (2014) 'Seven Brief Lessons on Physics' p. 15;

105. For a very accessible survey of the positive relationship between Christianity and science during the Middle Ages see James Hannam (2009) 'God's Philosophers: How the Medieval World Laid the Foundations of Modern Science';

106. See McCalla A (2006) 'The Creationist Debate';

107. For a very straightforward account of the issues within an

historical context see Jean Dorricott (2005) 'Science and Religion', or particularly good at identifying the issues and explaining them is GK Straine (2014)'Introducing Science and Religion: A Path through Polemic'; a more advanced study is John Weaver (2010) 'Christianity and Science';

108. 'Principles' p. 356;

109. 'Life on other Planets' in 'Science and Religion' ed. Ian Barbour pp. 324ff (from which the following quotations are taken);

110. 'Science, Religion and the Search for Extraterrestrial Intelligence' (2013);

111. See Paul Davies 'The Eerie Silence: Searching for Ourselves in the Universe' (2010);

112. Wilkinson op cit p.163;

113. ibid pp. 167ff;

114. The Observer, 11th August 1996;

115. Alice Meynell (1847 – 1922) 'Christ in the Universe' (pub. 1917);

116. Sydney Carter's 'Every Star Shall Sing a Carol';

117. The theological assessment of other Faiths: see the paradigm (exclusivist, inclusivist and pluralist – to which was later added 'particularities') established by Alan Race: Race A. (1983) 'Christians and Religious Pluralism';

118. Ward K 'The Philosopher and the Gospels' pp. 25 – 26;

119. 'Principles' p. 237;

120. Wilkinson 'Science, Religion and the Search for Extraterrestrial Intelligence' p. 1;

121. ibid. pp. 2 – 3;

122. Weaver op cit p. 232;

123. ibid pp. 232 – 233;

124. 'panentheism', 'all in God' suggests that God, although distinct (transcendent) from his creation, nevertheless operates within and through creation (immanent); contrasted with 'pantheism' 'all God', that God and

creation are identical; all this is opposed to 'traditional theism' which separates God and Creation and limits God's action to special interventions;

125. op cit pp. 79 – 80;

126. ibid. p. 55;

127. For a convenient digest of his thought see 'The Polkinghorne Reader' ed. Thomas Jay Oord (2010);

128. John Polkinghorne (2008) 'Theology in the Context of Science' pp. 102 – 103;

129. ibid. p. 105;

130. ibid. p. 107; other particularly useful books by Polkinghorne include 'Reason and Reality' (1991), 'Quantum Physics and Theology: An Unexpected Kinship' (2007), 'Science and Religion in Quest of Truth' (2011), the very straightforward 'Questions of Truth' (2009 – co-written with Nicholas Beale) which provides 51 responses to questions "about God, Science and Belief" and, particularly relevant to this topic: 'The God of Hope and the End of the World' (2002);

131. Chapter 2; "The end of the Universe in scientific terms is both simple and very difficult to predict" p. 12;

132. Chapter 3;

133. Chapter 5 is entitled 'Reclaiming the Resurrection in its Cosmological Setting';

134. By way of example: Einstein famously said, in relation to the roles of chance and irrationality within 'creation', that 'God does not play dice with the universe': yet "in modern physical theory, rationality is reflected in the existence of fixed mathematical laws, and creativity is reflected in the fact that these laws are fundamentally statistical in form… The intrinsically statistical nature of atomic events and the instability of many physical systems to minute fluctuations, ensures that the future remains open and undetermined by the present. This makes possible the emergence of new forms and systems, so that the universe is endowed with

a sort of freedom to explore genuine novelty...Is this not to admit an element of irrationality into the world?...But one man's irrationality is another person's creativity...For those, such as process theologians, who choose to see God's guiding hand rather than genuine spontaneity in the way the universe develops, then stochasticity can be regarded as an efficient device through which divine intentions can be carried out. And there is no need for such a God to interfere directly with the course of evolution by 'loading the dice'..." Davies P. (1992) 'The Mind of God' pp. 191 – 192; the title is taken from the presumably ironic final sentence of Stephen Hawking's 'Brief History of Time': "If we find the answer to [why it is that we and the universe exist] it would be the ultimate triumph of human reason – for then we would know the mind of God" (1988 p. 175);

135. As John Polkinghorne commented in an interview with the *Church Times*: "...there are intrinsic unpredictabilities present in physical processes – that is to say, unpredictabilities not due to the fact that we can't calculate accurately, or measure precisely; they are just there"; 9th October, 2015, p. 26;

136. Wilkinson D (2015) 'When I Pray What Does God Do?' p. 150;

137. ibid. p. 149; Wilkinson contrasts the inability to know both the position of an electron and its velocity with the ability to know both of a cricket ball;

138. ibid. p. 153;

139. cf. Gen 2: 7, Isaiah 45: 9 – 12; 64: 8; Jer 18: 1 – 11;

140. Straine GK 'Introducing Science and Religion: A Path Through Polemic' (2014) pp. 84 – 85, 122 – 123;

141. Goldingay J (2014) 'The Theology of the Book of Isaiah' p. 133;

142. Wilkinson op cit p. 155;

143. ibid. p. 160;

144. ibid. p. 161;
145. Hodgson P (1994) 'Winds of the Spirit' pp. 234, 236 – 243;
146. 'Making Sense of Death and Immortality' (2013) p. 64.

Chapter 2

The Christological Problem Defined

Not only human, but also...[1]

To set out the modern dilemma as clearly as possible: despite the (at least semi-) docetic language which continues to pervade expressions of Christian belief and piety (and is certainly to be found 'lurking' in much popular hymnody), one might reasonably assume that all Christians – some, perhaps, needing the occasional 'nudge' in that direction – unless they embrace some full-blown docetic heresy, would agree that Jesus Christ was genuinely human: this despite the fact that many seem quite unaware just how belief in a literal virginal conception might undermine that claim. So whilst 'proving' Christ's humanity might not appear to be a Christological need today, having been of some importance prior to Chalcedon (why else would the Fathers have felt the need to emphasise it?) when Alexandrian docetic impulses were often stronger than the Antiochene emphasis on Jesus' humanity, that old dilemma is still hiding 'in the wings'and is often to be found in the Church's liturgy.[2]

The most intractable problem, arising from the great Councils and certainly taken for granted by many Christians (not least because it is formally 'orthodoxy'), is the assertion that the 'truly human' Jesus was, not only human but also 'truly divine'. Yet this latter assertion would seem to render the 'death blow' to any serious consideration or understanding of Jesus' humanity, despite reassurances (or unconsidered assumptions) which one commonly hears from the pulpit, or other pronouncements of Christian ministers and leaders, that the two are perfectly compatible. Why is that?

If we take, as an example, the ideas expressed in the *Quicunque Vult:*[3]

"For the right Faith is that we believe and confess: that our Lord Jesus Christ, the Son of God, is God and Man; God, of the Substance of the Father, begotten before the worlds: and Man, of the Substance of his Mother, born in the world. Perfect God, and Perfect Man: of a reasonable soul and human flesh subsisting; Equal to the Father, as touching his Godhead: and inferior to the Father, as touching his Manhood. Who although he be God and Man: yet he is not two, but one Christ. One, not by conversion of the Godhead into flesh: but by the taking of the Manhood into God. One altogether, not by confusion of Substance: but by unity of Person. For as the reasonable soul and flesh is one man: so God and Man is one Christ."

According to the Athanasian Creed, Jesus Christ is

1. (Perfect) God and (Perfect) Man (although the nature of those perfections remains undefined);
2. "of the substance" (*homoousios* – 'same substance': the outcome of Nicaea, although not a particularly stable nor, indeed, much revisited concept for many years following) of both God (*per* God) and his mother (*per* Man) – simultaneously two different kinds of 'stuff', presumably either mixed or conjoined in some way (this was to become an heretical headache);
3. "...begotten before the worlds" but also born "in the world" (do the two together imply some kind of 'injection' of divinity into humanity?). We read in the modern version of the Nicene Creed[4] that Christ was "...eternally begotten of the Father...begotten not made..."; and from the earlier Book of Common Prayer (BCP): "...the only-begotten Son of God, Begotten of his Father before all worlds...Begotten not made..."; thus we may deduce that 'eternally begotten' and 'begotten before all/the worlds" are synonymous expressions.

'Begotten' is a translation of *gennao* which, in the NT, carries a range of meaning: 'father' (43 times, mainly in the Matthaean Genealogy i.e. the 'begetter of'), 'bear'/'was born' (42 times e.g. Mt 1: 16, 2:1; Lk 1: 13, 1: 35 etc.), 'child' (twice: Jn 8:41; 1 Jn 5:2), 'bear a child' (once: Gal 4: 24), 'breed' (once: 2 Tim 2: 23 – here metaphorically: 'breeding quarrels'); also 'bring', 'conceive', and 'parent'. In other words, virtually all references are to the act of birth/breeding children. Yet in Acts 13: 33, Paul, speaking of Jesus, quotes Ps 2: 7 ("You are my Son, today I have begotten you"), as does Hebs 1: 5 and 5: 5: this is a Davidic psalm where, in context, David is declared the 'son' (so Paul/Luke and the author of Hebrews are likening Jesus to David) and where 'begotten' denotes not a physical birth but the selection/choice/anointing of David as King. A probably later variant reading of Lk 3: 22 (God's words at Jesus' baptism: "You are my Son, the beloved, with you I am well pleased") has "...You are my Son, today have I begotten you", which is probably yet another attempt to explicitly link Jesus and David (through a scribal change of wording) and, as such, would fit well with, although doesn't require, an adoptionist view of Jesus. After all, David was never said to have been born 'Son of God', but only became so having been chosen following the failure of Saul's kingship. So the act of 'begetting' may be used both literally and metaphorically. It would seem obvious that, with God, the notion of a literal begetting of any child is simply bizarre, and to be equated with the crude notion of the Greek, Roman and Hindu gods siring children, either with their own kind or with mortals.

But as used in the NT and after of Jesus, not just 'begotten', but (the) 'only begotten' (Son): a translation of the Gk *monogenes*[5] which, in the ancient world, carried two main meanings:[6]

1. "Pertaining to be the only one of its kind within a specific relationship", as in Hebrews 11: 17, referring to Isaac as Abraham's only son: although Abraham had other sons,

Isaac was the only one with his first wife Sarah and so was the official 'son' (or, we might say, 'heir') and, in this sense, the 'only' son - but not literally so. In terms of the Biblical narrative, Isaac was Abraham's successor, just as Jacob was his: hence God was the "God of Abraham, Isaac and Jacob" (Mk 12: 26). So *monogenes* could carry a meaning similar to that in Hebrews: that, of all God's 'children', Jesus, in Christian understanding, is the heir, and this is clearly how the author of Hebrews understood the matter (Hebs 1: 3). Yet Paul claims that all Christians are "children of God and if children then heirs, heirs of God and joint heirs with Christ" (Rom 8: 16 - 17) – thus signalling at least some degree of continuity 'with us'. It is also the case in some passages that the Jews are heirs (with certain caveats) and that Christians are also Abraham's "offspring" (Gal 3: 29). It is clear that the idea of God's 'heir' (*kleronomos*), one who would be '*monogenes*' in the first sense, is used very imprecisely in the NT. The straightforward meaning of '*monogenes*', as used of the children of the widow of Nain and Jairus, is that they each just had the one child. If it is in this sense that Christ was '*monogenes*', then that would require us to understand the term virtually literally: God really had only one Son (he only 'impregnated' one woman!). But, as we shall consider further below, there is a problem in seeking to take this concept literally: how can one be born and yet not created (as in the carol 'O Come All Ye Faithful': 'begotten not created' – Christmas carols are awash with heretical utterances)? Inevitably, what was 'begotten not created' would not be a creature and, therefore, not human at all (as all human beings are, by definition, creatures). To argue that Jesus was a 'different kind of human being' in that he was 'generated' directly by God, not only undermines any concept of his 'true humanity', but places his birth squarely in the Roman 'demi-god' category (Father God, human mother). Put briefly, neither *'gennao'* nor *'monogenes'* can be understood literally of Jesus if we are to protect his 'true humanity'.

The now somewhat old-fashioned English translation of *'gennao'* (and hence *'monogenes'*) as 'beget' (Middle English 'begetten') carries twin meanings:

a   "To procreate or generate offspring" (i.e. any birth): this meaning would also fit with the literal sense of most uses of *'gennao'* and also *'monogenes* (1)' above. But is the notion that God made Mary pregnant (the 'virginal conception') meant to be taken literally? According to many Christians (however God's action is understood) the answer would be affirmative: Jesus was as much God's son (*gennao*) as the little girl was Jairus' daughter (*gennao*) and, like her, the only one (*monogenes*), albeit not conceived in the normal way. If this were literally true then Jesus was apparently 'born' twice (although 'born' is really only appropriate for the second): once 'in heaven' and once 'on earth' (the former an eternal action of God the Father; the latter through the 'operation' of God's Spirit). The clear implication in the Athanasian Creed is that 'begotten' means something different to 'to be born' (or else 'born' would have been used twice) and we have that warning tag-line: 'begotten not made'. In which case, we can only wonder what Christ's origin in eternity might mean as, indeed, the additional notion that Christ and God are 'co-eternal' – one was not prior to the other – piling on the incomprehensible concepts (having sought to distinguish between a temporal and nontemporal understanding of divine generation, Eusebius of Caesarea followed his theological mentor Origen in insisting on its mysteriousness). The Nicene Creed emphasises this difference: "eternally begotten of the Father" (the BCP equivalent is "Begotten of his Father before all worlds" i.e. 'in eternity'). But what does the idea that Christ was "eternally begotten of the Father" ('only' or otherwise) actually mean? For surely any act of 'begetting' must, virtually by definition, make the begetter prior to the begettee (subject→action→result), although we may note that for such as Eusebius the issue was not about temporal intervals at all, but about a relationship of origin and derivation? Nevertheless for those who might argue that 'priority' is only an issue for time, and not for eternity then, because (by definition) we can have no idea what 'eternity' is (just as we can have no concept of 'infinity'), that falls into the category of yet more things we affirm but cannot explain (something theologians have been quite adept at doing). Furthermore, what are we to make of this clear distinction between begetting and making (creating): the one not being the other? What is actually involved in the act of 'begetting' (remembering that the most obvious meaning of 'beget' is to give birth) that is not, in effect, 'making' or 'creating'? We have to understand that once the Church had decided that Christ was *homoousios* with the Father – ontological identity – then the question of 'where did Christ come from' (i.e. the meaning of 'begotten') is completely misjudged if we think of it as a word which seeks to explain how Christ was 'produced' because he is 'the same as God' ('*homoousios*' with the Father; God and Man; the Second Person of the Trinity – unless our 'social' trinitarianism falls into tritheism). In developing Trinitarian thought, unity was combined with diversity (the one and the three) in order to seek to explain the Christian experience of God (as Father, as Son and as Holy Spirit). Essentially (and this is the other message of 'Trinity') God and Christ are both (co-eternal) one (eternal); that is fundamentally what the Creed of Nicaea was seeking to express: "the only-begotten; that is, of the essence of the Father". The use of 'beget', then (regardless of its meaning today), is just a way of providing some degree of separation between Father and Son (just as 'procession' was used for the origin of the Holy Spirit to which the Western addition of *'filioque'* just makes the situation even more opaque: Father ☉Son☉ Spirit), which is the fundamental 'mystery' of the Trinity but which, sadly, gives us not the slightest aid in protecting the genuine humanity of Jesus. That, therefore, continues to be the main dilemma: we cannot protect Christ's humanity by not taking 'beget' literally, but neither can we protect it by understanding the term to denote (as some kind of device to render 'identity within diversity') the 'essential' ('of the essence') unity of Father and Son. Indeed, the obvious conclusion is that these words quoted from the Athanasian Creed fatally undermine the genuine humanity of Christ – despite the attempt to deny that by making him not only *homoousios* with God, but also with Mary: the fundamental problem of a 'two natures' doctrine (and it's worth recalling that a 'single-nature' ['monophysite'] understanding of Christ predominated for many years up to the unfortunate death of Emperor Theodosius in 450, and the calling of the Council of Chalcedon in 451 by his successor Marcian, at which the 'dual naturists' triumphed).

b   Rather different is 'beget' as "to cause" or "produce as an effect". It is entirely possible that the deployment by the authors of the Athanasian Creed (who wouldn't have been aware of this more modern meaning) of the helpfully vague term: *'monogenes'* was seen as a way of combatting the Arian view (still around in some shape or form in the 6th Century) that Jesus was created. Thus 'begotten', implying 'not made' might, taking 'beget' with this latter meaning, reinforce the idea that Jesus was an effect where God was the cause, but posing exactly the same dilemma as noted above: (1) both equal (as God) and inferior (as Man) to the Father: is either contradictory or requires a Christ who was dual (as the Church decided he was, even to the extent of having two wills/minds – dyothelitism): again, hardly human, in the way we understand humanity; (2) God *and* Man: he is singular as a Person, but dual in substance (nature); a short question will suffice as commentary: what on earth does this mean?

How to explain this duality of humanity and divinity (which the Athanasian Creed doesn't bother to do) has been a problem for Christian thought from the earliest days, which is why so many have failed in the attempt to hold these two apparent opposites together, even in some kind of creative tension. Yet holding both together may not actually be an option: is it conceptually viable to affirm both humanity and divinity in the same person – can a man also be God? Christianity has lived with this question for nigh on 2000 years, but has made little effort to explain it. That is the complacency often linked with orthodoxy: 'we believe X; we cannot tell you what it means; but we require you to believe it too, if you want to be one of us'. It may be the case that before the emergence of the modern critical study of the Bible, and its effect on theology, it was easy to understand this as a divine mystery – something which is, by definition, impossible to understand and must be believed. I would argue that in the modern developed world, with religion seen by many as somewhat irrelevant to their lives, where we do have a wide range of critical and intellectual tools, together with a vast and growing bank of knowledge about the early Christian world, available to us, that is no longer a realistic nor a desirable option.

What does it mean to say Jesus was divine?

Just asserting the two natures in the fashion of the Athanasian Creed doesn't actually solve the intrinsic problems, not least the logical ones: God is (by definition) infinite, omniscient, omnipresent (and so on); humanity is the precise opposite: finite, limited in knowledge and confined to one space at a time. So how can anyone – even God – defy logic and be both infinite and finite, omniscient and limited in knowledge, omnipresent and located, all at the same time? To claim that would literally be illogical nonsense, on par with Lewis Carroll's 'Jabberwocky',[7] and as for those who say simply (simplistically) that God can do anything: we fall inevitably into a 'Wonderland theology': believing six impossible things... As a result, the formal expression of the way both humanity and divinity can be attributed to Jesus Christ has come close – on formal examination – to being incoherent and virtually incomprehensible.

So can these, arguably illogical (and, hence, meaningless in the exact sense) assertions be reinterpreted into fresh ways of thinking, whilst holding onto the 'grammar' (and even some of the vocabulary) or 'governing intentions' of traditional Christology: the fundamental idea that, however we might express it, the man whom we call Jesus the Christ had the closest of relationships with God? Indeed, so close was this relationship that many of those met by Jesus felt (somehow) that they had been met by God himself. The Council of Nicaea judged this to be a relationship of ontological identity (*homoousios*), and although even then, as we have seen in the potential of *homoiousios*, that was not the only way of portraying it, it was to become the orthodox (implying, 'the only') way of understanding Christ across the Church, embedded in the Nicene Creed for example, and so there will always be those who would argue that no reinterpretation is needed; it is all perfectly clear: Jesus Christ

"...although he be God and Man: yet he is not two, but one Christ. One, not by conversion of the Godhead into flesh: but by the taking of the Manhood into God. One altogether, not by confusion of Substance: but by unity of Person. For as the reasonable soul and flesh is one man: so God and Man is one Christ".

All I am saying is that it is not actually clear at all!

The central philosophical question is this: what actually does the doctrine of the Incarnation mean? What, in particular, is a divine-human person (a human being who is [somehow] touched by divinity to the extent that the fullness of that idea requires us to use the word 'divine' of him), one who "is not two, but one...one altogether, not by confusion of Substance, but by unity of Person"? What would such a person look like – what would be his or her identifying characteristics? Sadly

"...it has not proved possible, after some fifteen centuries of intermittent effort, to give any clear meaning to the idea that Jesus had two complete natures, one human the other divine. The paradoxical character of the idea is evident. In order to be genuinely and fully human Jesus must have had all the attributes that are definitive of humanity, and in order to be genuinely and fully God he must also have had all the attributes that are definitive of deity...A being who lacks any of [the divine] attributes [such as omniscience, omnipresence etc.] is not fully God...[and how can someone who has a body be omnipresent, or how can a creator be a creature? etc. etc.]...The question, then, that has so vexed theology and that has never been satisfactorily answered, is how a historical individual, Jesus of Nazareth, could have both sets of attributes at once..."[8]

This also raises the question of the nature of incarnational language: what Wittgenstein-type of 'language game' is being played?

Put simply: no one, not even God, can be both God and not-God, not least because the nature of logic is such that even God cannot be illogical (despite what some Christians may believe, God cannot make two and two equal five). As the 4th Evangelist tells us: the *'Logos'* was not only *with* God but *was* God (Jn 1: 1). The Greek concept of *'Logos'* (as used both by the Jew Philo of Alexandria and the Christian John, referencing the creative Word 'at the beginning') connotes 'reason' and (of course) 'logic'. If 'the Word' ('which is God') is by definition logical, then God cannot be other than logical; just as God, as *'Sophia'*, cannot be other than wise. This is the central reason why a man cannot be God: because to be human is, among other things, to be 'not-God'. It is logically impossible to be simultaneously 'God' and 'not-God', just as it is logically impossible to be anything else and its contrary. Similarly, no one could be both human and not-human unless, perhaps, it were some kind of hybrid; and this is not what the Church has ever proposed. In any case, a hybrid would not be 'fully' or 'genuinely' human either and, furthermore, any hybrid – by nature physical - would need to consist of two creatures: those which exist within creation rather than 'outside' it.

It is noteworthy that the Chalcedonian Fathers, having asserted that Jesus had all the divine and all the human attributes, did not bother (or weren't able) to explain how and, as we have seen, virtually every attempt to do so was judged heretical either because it compromised Jesus' humanity or his divinity. Similar questions can be asked of the more modern notion of **Kenosis** (that the 2nd Person of the Trinity took 'shore leave' and 'emptied himself' into the human being who was Jesus of Nazareth) which was explicitly intended to resolve the divine-human dichotomy:

"Is God without the attributes of God still God? In what sense was Jesus incarnate if he lacked the characteristics in virtue of which God is God?...[How could] a self-existent being...ever cease to be

self-existent...But even if that could be made clear, the idea of half-divinity still has major problems, For the divine moral attributes are infinite, and how can infinite qualities be embodied in a finite human being? A finite being cannot have infinite attributes...". [9]

So the problems are not simply linguistic, they raise issues of logic as well and, as such, appear to be inherently contradictory. [10]

It may seem surprising that in the 21st Century it is not Jesus 'divinity' which needs protection, but his humanity which, particularly in liturgy [11] but also in many other areas of Christian life and witness, is being constantly undermined: although probably without much popular awareness of that. To take a simple, yet somewhat obvious, example: should Christians pray *to* Jesus (rather than *through* Jesus)? Due perhaps to carelessness or an apparent lack of sensitivity to theological nuance, there are always some intercessors who follow, or even themselves use, the introduction: 'Let us pray to the Father', and then proceed to begin their prayers: 'Dear Lord Jesus Christ...'. Many appear to give this issue little thought or, when they do so, just assume that as 'Jesus is God' it is perfectly right to offer prayer and praise to him. We may note James Dunn's book: 'Did the first Christians worship Jesus?' (2010) and his conclusion:

*"**No, by and large, the first Christians did not worship Jesus as such**...Christ is the subject of praise and hymn-singing, the content of early Christian worship, more than the one to whom the worship and praise is offered. More typical is the sense that the most (only?) effective worship, the most effective prayer is expressed in Christ and through Christ. That is to say that we find a clear and variously articulated sense that **Jesus enables worship – that Jesus is in a profound way the place and means of worship**... The only one to be worshipped is the one God".* [12]

There seems to have been an early 'high' view of Jesus expressed through worship/devotion (e.g. 2 Clement [c. 140 – 160 CE]: *"We must think of Jesus Christ as we do of God"*; Pliny the Younger [d. 112CE] writing to Emperor Trajan: *"... [Christians] pray to Christ as a God"*). Nevertheless, even if the very first Christians did not *worship* Jesus directly (i.e. contrary to Pliny's view) it is quite clear that they held Jesus in the highest esteem. It is worthy of note that Clement doesn't say: 'we must think of Jesus Christ as we do of God...because he is God': in other words, Christ is attracting some of the 'value' of the divine (on which further discussion below) and that they held a view of Jesus as mediator (a 'conduit' for prayer or, as later liturgies would understand it: praying *to* the Father, *with* the Son, *in* the Spirit) and some clearly offered their prayer to him, although others, such as Origen in the 3rd Century due perhaps to his alleged subordinationalist Christology, felt this was wrong and that it should be discouraged, although he recognised its devotional value.

However, it would be wrong to think that those first Christian generations felt that Christ was a passive conduit: he was seen also to be worthy of devotion (of some kind – and this is the point) himself. As time went on there grew an

"...intense devotion to Jesus, which includes reverencing him as divine [and which] was offered and articulated characteristically within a firm stance of exclusive monotheism...At an astonishingly early point, in at least some Christian groups, there is a clear and programmatic inclusion of Jesus in their devotional life, both in honorific claims and in devotional practice".[13]

Clearly that presented the emerging Christian Faith with a problem: Christ was seen to be (*somehow*) 'divine'. Already before the end of the first century both Matthew and Luke had Jesus born via a virginal conception in the power of the Holy Spirit, and the Johannine paradigm went even further in denoting Jesus the incarnate Word, existing before creation. But he was obviously not the 'Father' – yet there is still only one God. Adding the Holy Spirit to the 'mix' (e.g. Lk 1: 35; Mt 28: 19) made things even more complicated: how could Christians pray to God and Jesus, and to the Holy Spirit as well, and not desert their monotheistic roots?

This helpfully reminds us that the development of the Doctrine of the Trinity was driven, not by abstract reflections on the nature of God, but much more by Christian experience and liturgical practice. Nevertheless, one of the issues raised by the 'Arian' dispute was: if (as Arius claimed) Christ was a creature, then any worship directed to him would be idolatrous. One solution, rejected by the 'orthodox', was to take what would become known as the modalist-Sabellian view: that the one God has revealed himself in different ways, but these are not true distinctions within the Godhead. In this way, praying to God/Father/Christ is the same as praying to God in one of his 'guises' or roles. This question about worship is just one of the practical issues thrown up by Christological discussion. The Church has always formally addressed prayer to God "through Jesus Christ our Lord" (or as it is sometimes put: "In the power of the Spirit and in union with Christ, let us pray to the Father"[14]), which actually makes more sense if Jesus 'isn't [exactly] God' – just as some Catholics may pray to the Saints (particularly Mary) believing them not to be divine but, nevertheless, possessing the capacity to mediate with God on their behalf.

So this central issue will pervade the argument which follows: **how can Christians say what they want to say about Jesus, fully and without dilution, without essentially denying (despite their denials of so doing!) that he was 'truly human'?** How can the humanity of and divinity of Christ be affirmed together? Or, more specifically: can the continued use of ontological categories ever offer us a truly human Christ, or are these categories in need of re-interpretation, or perhaps even replacement? Put bluntly: was Jesus really God or divine (is to call Jesus 'divine' the same as calling him 'God' or not, in which case what is the difference?) in any metaphysical sense? Bearing in mind that whilst few Christians are explicit docetists, many may be implicit docetists (singing lustily at Christmas: "Veil'd in flesh the Godhead see..."[15]) who deny, in what they say and believe about Jesus, his genuine humanity, we might find these potentially overwhelming issues easier to approach if begin with a simple question (albeit one which is particularly significant because many Christians maintain the ontological divinity of Christ on the grounds that he himself claimed that status): did Jesus really think of himself as divine and, if not, what are the implications of that?

Firstly, the relevant biblical texts, in the main from the 4th Gospel, are agreed by almost all serious contemporary scholars (both conservative and liberal) not to be the *ipsissima verba*[16] of Jesus, but rather express the theological views of the writers. The Revd. Prof. CFD **Moule**, one of 20th C. Anglicanism's greatest NT scholars and an Evangelical, wrote in his classic book on Christology: "*Any case for a 'high' Christology that depended on the authenticity of the alleged claims of Jesus about himself, especially in the Fourth Gospel, would indeed be precarious*".[17] For James **Dunn**: "*... there was no real evidence in the earliest Jesus tradition of what could fairly be called a consciousness of divinity*".[18] Brian **Hebblethwaite** (a major defender of orthodoxy in the 'Myth' debates of the 70s and 80s) claimed: "*...it is no longer possible to defend the divinity of Jesus by referring to the claims of Jesus*";[19] whilst David **Brown** (the great modern defender of Kenosis: 'Divine Humanity', 2011) affirms: "*...there is good evidence to suggest that [Jesus] himself never saw himself as a suitable object of worship...[it is] impossible to base any claim for Christ's divinity on his consciousness once we abandon the traditional portrait as reflected in a literal understanding of St John's Gospel*".[20] Finally, the late and very orthodox Archbishop of Canterbury, Michael **Ramsay**, asserted simply and directly: *"Jesus did not claim deity for himself"*.[21]

The response of modern evangelical scholarship to this widespread historical scepticism as to how many of the words placed on Jesus' lips by the Evangelists actually originated there, has often not been the, perhaps anticipated, brisk (or brusque) denial, but rather a

> *"...retreat from a dominical authority for their belief [in a literal incarnation] to the highly debateable argument that Jesus' words and actions implicitly [rather than explicitly] claim deity"*.[22]

In other words: claims to divinity, whilst not explicitly made by and of Jesus (at least in the Synoptics) are thought to be implied both by Jesus' **authoritative words** (e.g. forgiving sins) and his **mighty deeds** (e.g. the miracles he performed). Yet neither the authority to forgive sins, just as in the Church a priestly 'absolution' is offered on God's behalf,[23] nor the 'power' to perform miracles – which are themselves open to a variety of interpretations – require 'divinity'. Yet God, presumably, can delegate his authority to whomsoever he chooses without that vicegerent being confused with him (although such confusion is often found in the OT – see below), just as throughout the ages rulers have delegated their authority to others without losing their ultimate right to/ownership of that authority. Certainly, the ancient world is full of stories of alleged miracle-making, as are Christian texts, both canonical and non-canonical, and particularly the Acts of the Apostles. Yet in none of the cases cited in Acts, all reminiscent of the miracles of Jesus (including the ultimate: raising the dead), is the miracle-worker deemed to be divine. Why, then, should Jesus be thought to be divine on the basis of his miracles, and not Peter, Paul et al, let alone the miracle workers of the OT, some of whom also raised the dead (1 Kings 17: 17 – end; 2 Kings 4: 8 - 37)? It merely begs the question to claim that whereas Jesus did these things through his own divine power, these others performed their miracles by invoking his name.

Furthermore those who have studied the history of doctrinal development are well aware that the outcomes of Nicaea, Constantinople and Chalcedon followed acrimonious debates involving dense philosophical argument combined with the often insidious impact of both 'secular' political and ecclesiastical agendas. It seems clear, therefore, that the assertion of Jesus' divinity was one made by the Church, not by Jesus himself and, further, that the two characteristics (authority and miraculous powers) often thought to demonstrate divinity do not require that particular conclusion. That is why, as a humanly-constructed (rather than 'revealed' – whatever that may mean) doctrine, the claim that Jesus was ontologically divine must, as with any other theological claim, be open to critical examination, for although these considerations do not invalidate the Church's claims, they do invite the entirely reasonable questions: how valid (or useful) was that initial ecclesial designation/interpretation; and what do such claims (about a divine human being) mean?

Instead of slavishly holding on to formulations created in a different age and culture, just because they have been deemed 'orthodox' (in some cases, only just), we should re-visit the issues with which they struggled and seek to re-evaluate the way they reached their solutions, not least because we know much more about the nature of the scriptural documents and the 'Jesus of History' (with associated historiographical issues) than they did, and perhaps most significantly, we are not so circumscribed by particular philosophical methods.

Doing Christology today: a preliminary proposal

There are many theologians today who are reconstructing classical Christology with

"...varying degrees of radicalness. Some wish to remain true to the so-called 'governing intention' of Chalcedon and their 'official reconstructions' give great import, if not normative status, to the dogmas of Nicaea and Chalcedon. Others, however, propose abandonment of the classical dogmas altogether and a complete reform of Christology. Since Christology and soteriology are intimately related it should not surprise that soteriology too, has been the subject of fierce debate in recent decades". [24]

As we noted above:

"...even theologians who disagree with these critics [of Nicaea and Chalcedon] will acknowledge that the classical Christological creeds must be interpreted and not merely repeated". [25]

The common error (made, to a degree, in the first of the above quotations) is the assumption that we must either accept or reject the "dogmas of Nicaea and Chalcedon" because they are either right or wrong. The issue is far more subtle and nuanced than this: it is not so much whether these doctrines 'correctly' represent the 'truth' about Jesus or not but, rather, recognising what was probably the single coherent insight of the Logical Positivists: that meaning precedes truth and that something cannot be true (or false) if it lacks meaning, the important issue is whether the various doctrines make sense to us today in the manner and mode in which they have traditionally been expressed.

The proper question is not: 'is Christ really *homoousios* with the Father?', but: 'what does it mean to say that Christ is *homoousios* with the Father?' What meaning and what truths is this kind of language seeking to express, and is it successful in doing so? It is only when the meaning of an assertion has been clarified that one can proceed to ask whether or not it is true. The corollary of this is the need to explore whether the language and concepts used 1500 years ago, if they really do fail to deliver meaningful assertions (assertions that we can understand and which make sense to us), may be maintained in their traditional formulation (e.g. the assertion that Christ is both human and divine) but interpreted rather differently; or whether both the assertion and the language in which it is couched should both be totally rejected. If we feel, as do I, that the classic formulations (both the assertion and the language used to express it) should be preserved, because they are so engrained in Christian life and liturgy that they provide the 'grammar' of Christology such that without them we would lose hold of the roots of faith and belief, then the next obvious question is this: if the category of metaphysical ontology is unhelpful today in expressing the relationship between 'Father' and 'Son' (in that it fails to provide any beliefs that make sense in and to the modern world), what other categories might take its place?

My proposal is to explore two linked categories for explicating the nature of Jesus Christ's relationship with God. First, a **'functional unity':** the idea that God and Christ were one and united in their soteriological work, similar to the way the OT prophets did the work of God. Just like these prophets Jesus spoke God's Word (without the tag: 'Thus says the Lord...'). Even if it were agreed that Jesus – like John Baptist – was "more than a prophet", then it is that 'more' which requires further elucidation. That 'more' might be expressed by saying that not only did Jesus speak God's Word: he did so, so effectively that he was, to all intents and purposes, that 'Word': the very *Logos* of God. Jesus was certainly understood, and may well have understood himself, in the role of the Prophet. Jesus of Nazareth did God's work and spoke God's Word on God's behalf, and so there was a unity of purpose and action. The concept of 'Messiah' explicitly denotes one who is 'chosen' or 'anointed' by God, one who is God's 'agent' or 'functionary' (the term itself is less than felicitous, but it does the job). Even the use of the title Messiah

(Christ) underlines this functional unity.

Secondly, a **'symbolic unity'**: where the symbolizandum (that which is symbolised) is represented (re-presented: 'presented again') in such a way by the symbol that the symbol itself is treated 'as if it were' the symbolizandum. The essential point is that the symbol is **not** the symbolizandum, but that it attracts the 'value' and 'meaning' of the symbolizandum and thus some of the reverence directed towards it in the same kind of way that in the OT the identity of God's agent is often blurred with that of God. Macquarrie explains the way symbols 'work' using the philosophy of existence in combination with that of ontology, showing:[26]

1. that an effective symbol (positively or even negatively, such as the way a Jew might respond to a swastika) evokes some kind of response in us such as awe, reverence, loyalty, humility, and that this is the same kind of response we might make to the symbolizandum: we might say that it touches us at the roots of our existence;

2. that the symbol also conveys (and this is the reason why it evokes any response at all) something of the 'being' of the symbolizandum.

If we understand a symbol to be something which stands for (or re-presents) something else, then we can see it shares something of the methodology of analogy and metaphor: it seeks to illuminate meaning and express truth by taking something which is understandable and graspable univocally (literally), and applying it to something else which is more opaque, complex or otherwise difficult to comprehend. Many symbols are natural and 'universal' (water, light, bread); other symbols are 'particular' (the Christian Cross, created not only because that was how Jesus died, but because it has taken on salvific significance; we may note in passing the different theological emphases of a cross and a crucifix). 'Universal' symbols have the capacity to work for anyone (but may not do so); 'particular' symbols work for particular people: for example, in Roman Polanski's comedy-horror film 'The Fearless Vampire Killers' (1967), a Jewish vampire is not deterred by a cross. All symbols have come to be or have been generated by mainly (but not completely – there is a rationale behind choosing a Cross) non-cognitive factors such as feelings, intentions and, like much other non-univocal language, they are connotative (suggest, hint) rather than denotative (define). We might say that an effective symbol 'touches' us in our 'innermost being' (the 'subjective' existential dimension) but, in order to do so must 'contain' and 'transmit' something of the 'being' of the symbolizandum (the 'objective' ontological dimension).

Each of these complementary ways of constructing a Christology will be explored in more detail in Chapter 7, but before we proceed to build our argument towards that end, the ground needs to be cleared and the proper foundations laid (that's a metaphor which, as we shall see in the next chapter, is a significant tool in religious language), after which we can begin to address the Biblical issues, before proceeding to tease out the theological.

Notes

1. Once again, this technical section may be omitted;
2. So, for example, the Collect for Corpus Christi (the CE's "Common Worship: Services and Prayers for the Church of England' [henceforth CW] p. 407), is directly addressed: "Lord Jesus Christ", being quite untypical among such prayers normally addressed to "Almighty Father" or "Heavenly Father" or, simply, "God", thus implying that it is right to pray to Jesus 'as God'?
3. The first two Latin words of the so-called Athanasian Creed (composed some years after the death of Athanasius):

'Whosoever wishes...'

4. The so-called Nicene Creed was not actually the 'Creed of Nicaea' (325AD), but developed from that together with the creed arising from the 1st Council of Constantinople (381); the Creed of Nicaea had: "...begotten of the Father (the only begotten; that is, of the essence of the Father)...begotten not made...; the Creed of Constantinople had: "...begotten of the Father before all worlds (aeons)...begotten not made";

5. In the NT *'monogenes'* is found in Lk 7: 12 (the widow of Nain's 'only' son); 8: 42 (Jairus' 'only' daughter); Jn 1: 14, 18, 3: 16, 18, 1Jn 4: 9 (Jesus as God's 'only' son) and (as noted above) Hebs 11: 17;

6. Walter Bauer's 'Greek-English Lexicon of the New Testament and other Early Christian Literature' (Ed. Rev. 2001);

7. 'Through the Looking Glass' (1871);

8. Hick J in Okholm DL & Phillips TR (eds) (1996) 'Four Views on Salvation in a Pluralistic World' p. 55;

9. ibid. p. 57;

10. MM Adams deals with the alleged contradictions to be found in the doctrine of the Incarnation in 'Christ and Horrors: the Coherence of Christology' (2006) pp. 113 ff.; for a spirited – if somewhat strained - defence of the logical nature of the doctrine of the Incarnation see Morris TV (1986) 'The Logic of God Incarnate';

11. Further examples are to be found in the regularly recited text of the liturgical 'Gloria in Excelsis': (i) Jesus Christ, as well as being addressed as 'Lamb of God' and 'only Son of the Father' is also explicitly called 'Lord God', just as God the Father was earlier so addressed, suggesting that just as the Father is 'Lord God' (in the OT YHWH is 'the Lord' – treated virtually as a personal name for God; in Gen 2: 4 & Ps 59:5 'YHWH Elohim' is 'the Lord God'), so also is Christ 'Lord God'; (ii) Christ is "seated at the right hand of the Father"; although (obviously?) this usage is metaphorical,

the implication is clearly bitheistic: there would have to be two Gods for one to be able to 'sit' separately from the other (as in many pictorial representations of the Trinity); later on in the 'Gloria' we find (again, addressed to Christ): "you alone are the Holy One, **you alone** are the Lord" which is a blatant contradiction of the earlier designation of the Father as (also) 'Lord'; the point is that such usages are theologically crude (in the sense of being simplified/simplistic; we cannot expect either theological consistency or precision in such texts); nevertheless, they represent the kind of ideas many Christians regularly and uncritically 'soak up' in their devotional lives, and so come to assume as coherent beliefs;

12. Dunn, pp. 150 – 151;
13. Hurtado L 'Lord Jesus Christ: Devotion to Jesus in Earliest Christianity', pp. 3 – 4;
14. e.g. CW p. 282;
15. 2nd Verse of 'Hark the Herald Angels Sing', Charles Wesley, 1739; it has been argued that the biblically-focused Wesley would never have been unorthodox in his expression of Christian faith, and that this is a reference to Hebrew 10: 20: "...the new and living way that he opened for us through the curtain [veil] (that is, through his flesh)...", where curtain/veil (i.e. Jesus' 'flesh') is a means of entry rather than a disguise; even if that is what Wesley had in mind, the allusion (perhaps, inevitably, because it is a reflection of a fundamentally docetic orthodoxy) still implies that the 'flesh' is an addition to, rather than fundamental to, Christ – the divine takes on something not 'natural' to divinity – and so undermines any true humanity just as much as 'hidden'; it is my argument that 'orthodoxy' (or rather, the way it is often expressed) itself undermines Jesus' humanity;
16. Scholars speak variously of the *ipsissima verba Jesu* (the very/actual/exact words of Jesus), the *ipsissima vox Jesu* (the

very voice of Jesus i.e. these might not have been his actual words, but they are true to the kind of things he said) and the *substantia verba Jesu* (these words convey the substance, main points or gist of his message); whilst few scholars, these days, would argue that all the words of Jesus as set out in the Gospels are exactly those which he spoke (some would argue that none are), how one categorises Jesus' sayings is still a matter of debate, and scholars use a variety of authentication criteria in order to reach their conclusions;

17. Moule CFD (1977) 'The Origins of Christology' p.136;

18. Dunn J (1980) 'Christology in the Making' p. 60;

19. Hebblethwaite B (1987) 'The Incarnation' p. 74;

20. Brown D (1985) 'The Divine Trinity' p. 108;

21. Ramsay M (1980) 'Jesus and the Living Past' p. 39;

22. Hick J in Okholm DL & Phillips TR (eds. 1996) 'Four Views on Salvation in a Pluralistic World' p. 54;

23. In the pericope (a particular form of a story tradition) of the healing of the paralytic (Mk 2: 1 – 12) the scribes point to the "blasphemy" of anyone offering forgiveness other than God, to which Jesus replies: "the Son of Man has authority on earth to forgive sins"; there is no suggestion here that the authority belongs to the Son of Man by right – simply the statement that he "has authority" - and the most obvious interpretation is that the authority has been given to him by God cf. Mt 7: 29//s; when Jesus is asked the direct question (Mk 11: 28//s) he actually refuses to answer (11: 33), although it is not altogether clear why that is;

24. Christie A 'Ordinary Christology' p. 5;

25. Migliore DL op cit p. 164;

26. Macquarrie J 'Principles' pp. 139 ff.

Chapter 3

Clearing the Ground

Playing the correct language game

How is language used in the Biblical texts or in any other kind of religious context such as liturgical usage? Should we expect it to be used any differently from the way we use language in normal everyday life? Is there something unique about Biblical or theological language? Many would argue that no language (not even the language of 'existence'[1]) can be used univocally ('one voice' - literally) of God, because the Creator is not a creature and the only context in which literal language 'works' is in relation to 'things' within creation (even if some of those 'things' are abstract concepts, such as hope and love). This does not mean, however, that religious language is somehow *sui generis*, and can only be understood by those privy to its esoteric secrets; that because it is the 'Word of God' it must be, by definition, both different and distinct and comprehensible only to 'those who believe'. Rather, it is to affirm that God and his ways cannot be adequately described using human language, simply because we speak the language of 'mortals', not even that of 'angels' (cf. 1 Cor 13: 1), and certainly not that of God (whatever that may be).

When we use particular concepts of God, we may use them analogically.[2] To call God 'Father' implies not a biological relationship, but a loving one (for those who have had negative experiences of a father, it may not connote that, and so other more helpful analogies need to be available: perhaps God as Mother, or Brother/Sister/Friend – any description that points to the closest of relationships?). The only language we have is human language, and we have to make that work for us, even if it sometimes means stretching words and concepts to their limit as we often do when seeking to talk of God. The mistake made by many Christians is either to ignore or forget that.

Normally, we use language, often quite instinctively, in some very different ways. For example, a man who cheats on his wife may be called a 'rat'; yet no-one would expect him to have a tail and squeak. A soldier may be described as a 'lion on the battlefield' yet, again, we would not search for a mane and a capacity to roar loudly: it is simply a way of expressing his bravery. These examples are metaphors. The Bible is full of examples of God (and his agents) being described using non-univocal language such as this: "The Lord is my Shepherd" (Ps. 23: 1: another metaphor) does not invite us to think that God really does keep a flock of sheep as a hobby; whilst "he will be like a refining fire and like fullers' soap" (Malachi 3: 2b – here the word 'like' signals a simile) doesn't mean that God's messenger is going to be made of a (strange) combination of fire and soap, but that he will have that same kind of cleansing/ purifying effect. The popular metaphor that God 'is a Rock' doesn't require us to put on our climbing gear to reach him. All this is obvious: language is complex, very often nuanced, and certainly not always literal.

A focus on language, how it is used and what it might mean, dominated 20th Century philosophy which comprised "very largely the story of this notion of sense or meaning."[3] The rather limited so-called empiricist approach to language which developed among the 'Vienna Circle' of philosophers known as 'Logical Positivists' during the decades following the First World War (a response to Wittgenstein's ground-breaking 'Tractatus Logico-Philosophicus'[4]) understood meaning to have a simple correlation with a word: 'this is a brick' (this reddish rectangular hard thing). In their view a word stands for and equates to the object. So, they concluded, if you cannot point to (demonstrate objectively) the object 'named' (such as God), then the word has no meaning. Any meaningful designation requires either verification or falsification. If you make an assertion (compare:

'John is in his room' with 'God is in heaven'), can you show what would either prove or disprove it (in this case the first is easy; but the second clearly problematic). Because if an assertion (a statement of alleged fact) can be neither verified nor falsified, then it is literally nonsense. What, then, could either prove or disprove the assertion: 'God exists'?

As a result, the Logical Positivists concluded that all religious language was literally nonsense, in that it possessed no meaning. This one-to-one equivalence of object-language may seem obvious and because it is actually the way that language is taught, it may also seem quite reasonable. Nevertheless a little further thought shows us that reality is much more complex: not all words are mere labels. Instead of employing such arbitrary and limiting definitions, the later Wittgenstein came to believe that it is more sensible to consider how words are actually used (sometimes called 'functional analysis' over against the earlier 'verificational analysis') as language is, in practice, used in many different ways. To do this requires studying the actual use of language in its own characteristic context; only then can you judge how valid any assertion is: whether or not it makes sense, and only after that can you move on to ask whether it is true. We must allow the discourse to speak for itself – in Wittgenstein's words: we must *"show the fly the way out of the fly-bottle...*[for] *philosophy may in no way interfere with the actual use of language...it leaves everything as it is"*.[5]

Language is essentially social because it has developed naturally in and through society: *"Our language can be seen as an ancient city; a maze of little streets and squares, of old and new houses, and of houses with additions from various periods; and this is surrounded by a multitude of new boroughs with straight regular streets and uniform houses"*.[6] Because language is a natural phenomenon, nothing can be excluded from its use. In approaching language all one can do is observe and classify the way it is used, not seek to curtail that use by *a priori* rules. Reacting to the empiricist demand for proof of **meaning** the functional analysts asked about language's **use or function. The meaning of an assertion was to be found in the way it was used.** This is not to say that they were uninterested in meaning, rather that they wanted to offer a *new concept of meaning.* The way forward was to approach each sentence as an individual case and with no preconceived definitions of its significance; in so doing we may well find that the meaningfulness of a sentence may be quite independent of the question of whether it is empirical (i.e. verifiable by the senses) or not. Of course, language may be misused or used out of context: *"Philosophical problems arise when language goes on holiday".*[7] Wittgenstein himself used the analogy of the way strands of rope combine to form a strong rope, but the strands at one end do not always extend all the way to the other; he also used the notion of 'family resemblances' and pictured language as being like a number of handles which looked alike, but which caused different things to work.

As language has developed naturally, so have linguistic rules and conventions: in fact, just like a game. But to understand any game, you must first understand the rules. So learning a language is like learning how to play a game: just as there is an enormous variety of games played in human society, so there is an almost open-ended number of possible **'language games'**. Each of these is, according to Wittgenstein,[8] embedded in a particular **'form of life'**[9] that is not necessarily visible or comprehensible from outside, as are some games: American Football may, to those who don't know the rules, be mistaken for Rugby Football. Wittgenstein did not expand on these two concepts in any systematic way; indeed, he used the terms very loosely. But perhaps the very notion of a 'game' is a warning not to be too precise: some, but not all games have common elements (such as using a ball), although they often have overlapping characteristics (keeping a score, for example). But we seldom sit down to *learn* the rules of any game before we start playing it;

we tend to pick them up as we go along: as we experience the game itself. Furthermore, some 'games', like being humorous, depends on some knowledge of the person telling the joke, and particularly on our ability to recognise that it is a joke (if we don't we may be offended). Some games have their own special vocabulary (you can't be 'off-side' in cricket) and it is important to only use words in their correct context as well. Thus the question of 'Messiahship' is only relevant in the Judaeo-Christian tradition and wouldn't have any meaning in (say) Hinduism - this point serves to emphasise that language expresses something of the life of a group. The language is actually an activity of the group: this, perhaps, is what is meant by the term: 'form of life', which may involve other activities, customs and rituals not immediately evident to or understandable by the outsider. Indeed, we have to operate within the Form of Life, to live in it, and experience it from the inside before we can become competent 'players'.

Religious language can only be properly understood in situations and contexts where it is actually being used. It is not the role of philosophers to tell us which games we can 'play'; rather they should concentrate on trying to make sense of the games which are being played. Religion might be considered a Form of Life within which different language games are 'played': think, for example, of an act of worship, where in the space of about an hour, many different 'games' are played: the language of devotion, the language of creeds (which may itself involve different games: the language of history ["he was crucified under Pontius Pilate"] side-by-side with the language of theology or even mythology ["he sits at the right hand of God"]), 'performative' language that actually brings things about ("I baptise you..."), and so on.

When we take the trouble to look and see, we find that religious language is actually being used in many different ways. People often focus attention on just one way: the imparting of information or the assertion of facts (the **cognitive** use of language) because it seems most obvious, and so make the mistake of thinking that all religious language is about beliefs and other forms of religious assertion, such as creeds. But a mono-focus on the purely cognitive use of language is misleading and limiting. Religious language, as with any language (except perhaps that of pure science and technology) is used affectively as well. Indeed, language-use may be both **affective** (arouse, evoke, change emotions and attitudes - to do with feelings) and **effective** (it enables believers to live out their beliefs - to do with action), as well as being used to transmit information. But the use of language within religious behaviour (private and public, individual and collective e.g. worship, habits, customs, lifestyle etc.) is generally not the argumentative, fact-claiming cognitive kind: in fact, many people take their beliefs for granted (perhaps they shouldn't, but they do). After all, you don't go to Church to hear arguments about the existence of God: those are assumed in the form of life which is the Church.

Wittgenstein suggested that religion has to do with living one's life by a picture, but this 'picture' shouldn't be seen as a mental image; rather it is more of a framework by which we order and make sense of our lives. He also spoke of a 'grammar' of a Form of Life – in this sense the Form of Life is religion, and the grammar is theology (or any type or religious discourse). Taking the discussion further, as happened in the 1950s, faith itself may be understood as a 'blik',[10] and the process by which we come to faith (or lose it) is mysterious. We shall discuss this important concept later on in this chapter.

Playing a new kind of game

Whether religious language games are always used in the way that their players imagine is another matter. Participants in the non-realist 'Sea of Faith'[11] movement appear to be playing the same 'game' as any other Christian: they use the same kind of language, indeed the same formulae ("In the name of the Father..."), but are they actually following the same ('grammatical') rules? In many cases ('non-realism' is a theologically diverse movement) Christian non-realists may appear to be atheistic,[12] explaining that 'God' doesn't refer to any objective, external reality, but only to our highest human ideals. For many 'Sea-of-Faithers' there is no 'spiritual reality'; all reality is material. As Anthony Freeman put it:

> *"Now I have decided to change my use of the term God. Instead of referring it to a supernatural being, I shall apply it to the sum of all my values and ideals in life...Ever since we embraced just one God, he has always been in fact the sum of all our ideals. The only difference now is that we are able (or should be able) to accept that this is what he is, without having to claim for him an independent supernatural existence.*[13]

and then my life-long friend, Tony Windross:

> *"The God at the heart of Christianity is often used as a sort of explanation-of-last-resort, a God-of-the-gaps. But inevitably, as the ability of human beings to explain things gets ever greater, the need to wheel him in diminishes; and the current position seems to leave little for him to do apart from start the universe off...[a better way of thinking may be] to recognise that all of us have depths in ourselves...These depths are what yearn for the profound and the glorious, and are not fed by the banal or the superficial. They are what is reached when we respond to music or art or poetry – or religion, which is a way of organising our search for what is most real or significant...Believing in God might be said to be 'falling in love with life'; afterwards nothing seems the same again"*.[14]

So 'God' (and, thereby, God[15]) becomes another word for our greatest ideals or our sense of profundity, the point being that this 'God' is to be found *only* 'in us' and not 'out there' or 'outside us'. In that sense, God is 'not real' or, rather, is only as real as our ideals. Perhaps put even better: God is real in the same way that our ideals are real. Although, like God, our ideals are of the greatest importance to us, and may include values that people would literally die for, they have no objective reality (*extra nos*). Some find it difficult to understand how such people can continue to call themselves 'Christian'.[16] Many 'Sea of Faith' networkers are ordained Christian ministers: Freeman and Windross are both Anglican priests. 'Sea-of-Faithers' continue to live recognisably Christian lives, including attending or leading worship and, if they are clergy, it is entirely possible that their congregations are not even aware of their 'humanist' views, because they continue to use the same kind of language as any other Christian: just using it in a different way.[17] But don't we all.[18] Sometimes 'non-realism' is called 'radical theology' but it is nothing of the kind: it actually detaches itself from the roots of Christian faith. Perhaps it would provide helpful context to what follows to make it clear that in the Christological explorations which follow, I am entirely 'realist' and that is how my proposals should be understood.

It should be clear from the above discussion that one issue with which language game theory cannot help us is the question of truth-claims. Language game theory may help us to decide whether a particular assertion is meaningful in a particular context, but it cannot help us to move on to say that it is true (or false), particularly in a post-modern world where truth is often understood to be relative: 'this may be true for you, but it isn't for me'. As noted, some might claim that language games, particularly of a religious type, are not meant to impart cognitive (or more particularly, metaphysical) information at all. Rather, the aim of such games is to shape attitudes or to seek to express our 'bliks' or our feelings. But to pursue this kind of argument can have the effect of treating the meaning of religious utterances as nothing more than the role they have in the lives of the users, as members of a society or group in which that language game is played.

While asking 'what does it do for them?' is a good starting point, it is not the whole of it. We should expect our religious statements both to make sense, and to express something that is both real and true.

If it is to be taken seriously as a way of communicating ideas about reality, religious language can't be limited to those 'playing the game': religious people, for that would make any form of evangelism pointless, as we could only talk to ourselves. But we do 'have a gospel to proclaim': that God did come to us (somehow) in Christ and, so, if our language is to be meaningful, it must be meaningful, not only to us, but in the broader public sphere as well. It is, therefore, essential that this Gospel be proclaimed in language that makes sense in the (post-) modern age; that it uses expressions and categories that have the potential to convey meaning to anyone who wishes to hear us.

That is the crucial problem when using expressions such as 'Jesus Christ is divine'. Are we really intended to understand that literally? Or, put rather better: what does it mean to understand such assertions literally? This is the central Christological problem for today: to say that Jesus Christ is both human and divine, and to understand that statement literally runs into all kinds of philosophical (and theological) problems. Over the years, the main Christological heresies have been those which either diminish or deny the humanity of Christ (Docetism and its offshoots) or his divinity (Adoptionism and related ideas), and that has come about because of the difficulty of expressing 'the mystery of the Incarnation' in meaningful language. If our language is to be meaningful both to those within and those outside the Church, then we must take care to understand its nature and, hence, the kind of ideas it is expressing; and particularly whether those ideas are meaningful. For only then can we move on to claim that they may be true.

Awareness of the nature of the language being used and how it conveys meaning is particularly important when we come to the central doctrine of the Incarnation: that Jesus Christ was/ is both human and divine. In 1977 John Hick edited 'The Myth of God Incarnate', a set of essays arguing, more by implication than directly – the main problem with the collection – that incarnational language falls most naturally into the category of 'myth'. Then, some years later, Hick wrote 'The Metaphor of God Incarnate' (1993; 2nd ed. 2005), thus suggesting that he had come to find the use of the linguistic tool, 'metaphor', rather more illuminating. If it is correct that no language used of God can be literal, then the use of categories such as 'ontological' or 'functional' – which we shall explore further below - in apparent opposition to each other for describing Jesus' relationship with God, is not meant to suggest that one is correct and the other incorrect. The most we can say is that one usage makes more sense (i.e. creates meaning) for us than the other. Those Christians (and sadly there are many) who complain that talk about Christ ('merely') as agent of God (so-called 'functional' language) undermines belief that he is *homoousios* with the Father ('ontological' language), are rather missing the point: the central truth (the 'actuality') about Christ resides not in the various philosophical terms utilised by theologians, but in the fact of his closeness to God. The expression of that truth, and nothing else, is the cardinal aim of Christology and the crucial question is this: does this actuality require some expression involving identity, or would some other expression be both better (in terms of meaning) and more accurate (in terms of truth)?

Theories, Models and Christology

As we shall discuss further in the next section, truth lies in the actuality, not in the way that actuality is presented or expressed: the expression is not itself the reality. This is the mistake many make concerning the doctrine of the Incarnation (or any other doctrine) – actually the ame mistake as the Logical Positivists – that the words equate to the reality. What is said really is it: the Word (whatever that is) became Incarnate (whatever that means). This is why whatever we say about Christ (again, as with any other doctrine, such as 'penal substitution') should be understood more in terms of a model than a theory.[19] Theories are descriptive and denotative of reality: so the two theories of relativity seek to set out the nature of physical reality and their predicted outcomes have been confirmed by experimental data.[20] Conceptual models, on the other hand, are suggestive and connotative; they are more equivocal than univocal. As opposed to a model, say, of a building, which is to all intents and purposes that very building on a much smaller scale (although without many of its real features, like the plumbing) is not a description of 'how it is'; it is an illustration or 'picture' which seeks to illuminate what its essential features and aspects are, and what they may mean. Models, therefore, are never right or wrong, they are either more or less appropriate and-or helpful; their only link with reality is allusive and referential. In this sense, they belong to the family of metaphorical and symbolic language rather than to the 'factual' demonstrative language of science (although even the language of science and maths can sometimes seem to fall into poetry and mysticism: we sometimes speak, for example, of the 'beauty' or 'elegance' of equations).

This distinction is worth examining further because for many Christians, saying that Christ is 'homoousios with the Father' (reasserted every time the Nicene Creed is recited), is clearly understood as a demonstrable theory on all fours with some scientific theory: we have examined the evidence and this is the result. It is a statement of 'fact', something that is 'real', 'what we believe to be the case', 'what happened' 2000 years ago. A similar view is taken of the Trinity: Jesus Christ (the man Jesus of Nazareth who was joined in hypostatic union with the Word) is (really) the Second Person of a Triune God. The point becomes clearer when we consider the scientific method: that which deals with the realities of the Universe, and so potentially covers every aspect of it – which obviously includes the man Jesus, but equally obviously not God. Of course, this method is not restricted to scientists and is used, informally and perhaps unknowingly, by most of us most of the time in our normal transactions with the world.

We begin by our attention being drawn to some aspect of the world which we then seek to understand and, in understanding, hope to make predictions about future occurrences. The Sun 'rises' and 'sets' each day (the risings and settings, by the way, are not real but simply our perception of what happens from where we are); but it does so at different times. Before modernity it was believed (on Biblical authority) that the Sun circled the Earth; now we understand, through scientific observation, that the reverse is true. That finding is now so self-evident that only the diehard denier of evidence would disagree. Once that was understood, it became possible to make certain predictions: not only the very simple one (replacing the notion that God personally sets the Sun and Moon 'in their courses': Ps 33: 6 cf. 104: 19) that the Sun will – barring a cataclysmic event of which we will get eight minutes notice – rise and set tomorrow, but the much more complex prediction of precisely when that will happen each day and in each place. Today, exact sunrise and sunset times, wherever we are, are available at the touch of an 'app'.

Such a process is also part of our ordinary domestic lives: we may 'set our watches' by the milkman; we know to have a Gin & Tonic ready for our partner when s/he arrives home from work. So we form a hypothesis which we then test and, as a result of that testing, we formulate a theory which is assumed to be true until further testing falsifies it; in which case the hypothesis is modified and tested again. This theory ultimately replaces the hypothesis, which has now been confirmed (until new information undermines it: with the present state of our scientific knowledge it would take a very brave person to claim that a particular theory will always apply). We make simple predictions on this kind of basis all the time: 'I'll need to have the Gin & Tonic ready for 6.00 pm because s/he always arrives home then'. Such predictions may occasionally prove to be wrong (if there are traffic jams or delays on the train), and although odd aberrations can be tolerated without the need to adjust the basic hypothesis, any theory we formulate, even by incorporating a basic amendment ('occasional events may cause delay'), may eventually need rather more considerable adjustment. If I have the Gin & Tonic regularly available for 6.00pm and my partner begins to arrive equally regularly at 5.00pm, then I need to update my information and revisit my theory. The explanation: 'I now finish work an hour earlier' requires me to adjust my basic hypothesis until it adequately fits the known facts. Thus an hypothesis may be either right or wrong, and a theory worked out on the basis of what at least initially appears to be a correct hypothesis will be provisionally true until it is then verified by regular experience ('the optimum time for Gin & Tonic is 5.00pm'), or it may be modified to fit the facts more precisely ('from now onwards she will always arrive home at 5.00pm because she finishes work at 4.00pm'), or it is replaced by a somewhat different theory deemed to be a better overall representation of observational reality ('her timing is all over the place, so I'll just keep a bottle of white wine in the fridge').

A scientific example will further help clarify a range of related issues, including distinguishing theories and models, similarities and differences between scientific and theological methodologies, the nature of proof and truth claims, and the claims of revelation over against observation. We saw above just how fundamentally important Einstein's two theories of relativity have been for modern science and how they have enabled scientists to radically reconceptualise the nature of the universe, particularly the space-time relationship. Astronomical observations, made in 1919 of the area of space 'close to' (from our point of observation) the Sun during an eclipse, showed that light rays were deflected or distorted by the Sun's gravitational effects and, in confirming General Relativity, demonstrated conclusively that Newton's understanding of gravity, though empirically correct in many cases (it had fitted the then known facts, and continued to fit some of them), was conceptually wrong: gravity was not the previously reified 'invisible force' that attracted objects to each other; it is an effect (of the warping of space-time) which we experience. This was a ground-breaking conception. Yet it is entirely possible that in the future even such game-changing theories may themselves need to be refined, substantially modified or even completely replaced, as with any other theory for which past 'clearly demonstrable facts' have been made redundant by new findings.

Up to this time it had also been generally assumed that the only stars which existed within the universe were those which formed our own 'Milky Way' Galaxy, with the rest of the universe an empty void. This universe was believed to be both static and stable, in that it had no beginning and would have no end: it was considered, to all intents and purposes, both spatially and temporally infinite. Yet General Relativity predicted an expanding universe. Einstein's solution was, perhaps, surprising: rather than remain stubbornly loyal to (have faith in?) his theory, he changed it in order to fit these prior assumptions. Perhaps in a manner similar to that in which some religious people may temper their views when they come across inconvenient and apparently incontrovertible 'facts', but do so only insofar as to protect their main thesis: such as the way that Creationism has morphed into Intelligent Design where one can still stand by a fairly literal understanding of Genesis 1, whilst allowing some degree of acceptance of modern scientific findings: the 'having-one's-cake-and-eating-it' syndrome. Einstein added a 'cosmological constant' (represented by the Greek letter *lamda*) to his theory, making it at once both more complex and less elegant: a useful 'fudge factor' or just 'fine tuning' according to one's perspective, but one which allowed the universe, once again, its stability, albeit at the expense of altering the original theory. This is a useful warning not to be too hasty in changing our thinking when our observations do not immediately match our theories: perhaps it is our methods of observation (or the gathering of other forms of evidence) which require improvement.

During the 1920s astronomer Edwin Hubble and colleagues showed that the assumption that our galaxy and the universe were, in effect, identical was incorrect. It became clear when observing the Andromeda nebula (Lat. *nebula*: 'cloud': the 'smudge'-like *nebulae* were, when viewed through the telescopes of the day, thought to be clouds of interstellar gas) that it was itself composed of millions of stars. Initially, some thought such nebulae represented those parts of our galaxy where new stars were born; it soon became apparent (through the measurement of stars of variable luminosity) that such 'clouds' of nascent stars were, in reality, separate and mature galaxies: in Andromeda's case (the nearest galaxy to our own), some 2.537 million light years distant. As a result of such observations, our understanding of the size of the universe was again dramatically transformed. Moreover, further research showed that these galaxies were not 'floating' steadily in space, but were moving apart. The universe was not static, but expanding – just as Einstein had predicted, but had refused to believe. Einstein happily removed the cosmological constant from his theory, expressing his regret that he ever put it there in the first place. Scientists were also presented for the first time with evidence that the universe had a beginning, leading ultimately to the current consensus (at least, reasonably so) of the 'Big Bang' theory.

The new prevailing (albeit temporary) view came to be that the expansion of the universe (caused by the initial energy 'thrust' of the Big Bang) was in the process of slowing down (just as other objects in motion eventually tend to slow down), and that ultimately the Universe would collapse in upon itself. However, much more recent research into dying stars (*novae*) suggests that the expansion of the universe, rather than slowing down, is actually speeding up, and so yet another theory has had to be abandoned. And not only that: as the universe expands one might have expected it (as when pouring water into a squash concentrate) to become less dense; yet further research has shown that its density is actually being maintained. Scientists have no idea (yet) why that is, and so in 1998 postulated the existence of what they call (at least for the present) 'dark energy': here 'dark' refers not to colour, but to the simple fact that they don't know what it is (so 'darkly' mysterious), and 'energy' refers to the fact that it (whatever it is) is somehow 'pushing' the galaxies away from each other. As density is stable, it would seem that new dark energy is being created all the time, so that it is apparently self-replenishing. Quantum theory (which Einstein didn't like: 'God does not play dice...') is now being called into service in order to explain what is going on: in quantum physics elemental particles are understood to come in and out of existence, providing energy as they do so. However, current predictions do not match what is being observed, and the difference in scale is enormous (a 'google': 1 followed by 100 zeros); thus 'dark energy' remains dark.

There is even more to this recent journey of intellectual exploration: back in the 1970s astrophysicists had discovered that not all the universe was made of the same kind of 'stuff': in fact, the matter out of which we and the stars are formed (atoms themselves made up of electrons, protons and neutrons) makes up just 4% of the universe; newly 'discovered' matter was, as later with energy, labelled 'dark' – thus 'dark matter', which was seen to provide the additional gravitational force required to hold galaxies together. However, even 'dark matter' couldn't account for all the mass detected in the universe, and it has recently been calculated that dark matter makes up around 25% or so of universal mass, whilst dark energy accounts for an enormous (up to) 75%. In 2020 the Euclid Project is planning to launch a new observational device which will be far more efficient than the great Hubble telescope, able to observe one and a half billion galaxies. Euclid will enable astrophysicists to measure how these various forms of matter have expanded over time and provide an enormous range of data sets against which the range of current theories may be evaluated: some will then presumably be 'binned', whilst others are again modified. One finding may be that the general theory of relativity, whilst 'working' from our Earth-bound base, may not apply across the universe, and a new way of expressing the concept of 'relativity' will need to be found. Scientists admit (happily or otherwise) that they now understand much less about the universe than they thought they did (the concern of physicists at the beginning of the 20th Century had been that there was nothing much left to be discovered), and now await a 'new Einstein' to provide an overarching theory which may itself have only a limited life as yet more and more new discoveries are made.

As can be seen from this brief (and somewhat simplistic) survey, the 21st Century is set to be an exciting time for both science and theology: the former as the great mysteries of the universe come to be better understood; the latter as light is shed on the wonderful combination of simplicity and complexity that is God's creation. If one were able to measure such things we would doubtless find that we have learned more about the universe over the past hundred (or the past 50 or even 25) years[21] than in the whole of prior human history; and it is surely not impossible that, in a hundred years' time, we may be able to say the same thing: human knowledge (if not human wisdom or human morality; leading to the most pressing question of our day: is intelligence left to its own devices inevitably fatal?) is increasing at an exponential rate.

It would be interesting to discuss whether the same thing might be said of our explorations into theology: have our knowledge and understanding of God increased over the

Christian centuries – significantly, a little or at all? Some Christians would be firm in their view that the 'Faith' has been unchanging and probably, in practice, correctly so: for despite the continuing plethora of new theological books, these 'words about God' (*logoi theou*), at least so far as the fundamentals are concerned, have been pretty much unchanged, unchanging and, indeed, unchangeable since the formulation of the Christian Creeds. All that most theologians have done since then is to 'tinker' with some (admittedly important) details, 'crossing Ts and dotting Is', but have not engaged in much radical re-thinking of the basics. In any case, whatever Christian theologians say or write continues to be judged by the Churches against those very 'classic' formulae, and rejected virtually out of hand (as in the 1977 'Myth' controversy) if they differ in any significant way from 'orthodoxy'. It wasn't until relatively recently that a churchman could safely propose the absence of a Hell without suffering ecclesiastical penalties (FD Maurice lost his Chair at King's London in 1853 for so doing) and still today the accusation of heresy waits in the wings to be deployed against 'modernists'.[22] It seems almost unbelievable that the shadow of the Inquisition is still with us in the 21st Century.

Those Christians holding to the conviction that there can never be anything radically new to say about God are exactly like those early 20th Century scientists who believed that they had discovered everything. Yet this is not, for them, about either discovery or observation: they claim they know everything there is to know (certainly all they need to know), because it has been revealed to them; hence the very rash and somewhat intellectually arrogant theological equation (see further below) of the Economic with the Immanent Trinity (God is exactly what God appears to be – but how could we ever know that?). As God has already told us everything, there is nothing new to be said about the Incarnation or any other major doctrine. Indeed, if anything really new *is* said, it must – almost by definition - be heresy: exactly the same view that the Church took of Galileo's discoveries and which it had eventually (and somewhat embarrassingly) to retract. For those who take this view the final pronouncements of the Chalcedonian Fathers are as valid to them as those of Newton were to those pre-Einsteinian scientists.

That is precisely the problem: Newtonian physics has now been shown to be inadequate in exactly the same way that modern critical Biblical study and other new theological insights (such as panentheism and a passible God[23]) have exposed the quite understandable limitations of Patristic thought, dominated by Greek philosophy and the impact of that on the interpretation of Jewish Scriptures. Although theologians such as Rahner have 'given permission' for the classic formulations to be taken as points of departure rather than ends in themselves, only relatively few theologians have been prepared to take him at his word and engage in the risky adventure of following the evidence wherever it leads. Still today many books of theology offer essentially nothing more than a rehash or even direct restatement of prior positions – the equivalent of a modern scientist seeking to hold onto a Newtonian universe, or Canute attempting vainly to hold back the sea. Scientists today would condemn any of theirs who did such a thing; the Church on the other hand celebrates its theological Canutes as "Defenders of the Faith". The 'shock-horror' publication (a brave initiative of SCM Press) of 'The Myth of God Incarnate' in 1977 led to the headline in the Anglican Church Times: "Seven Against Christ?"[24] (at least the editor permitted a question mark), whilst the fairly swift publication of the rebuttal, 'The Truth of God Incarnate' (ed. Michael Green),[25] was reviewed with precisely the Canute-like headline above - this time with no question mark.[26]

The Church of England in particular continues to tie itself in bureaucratic and theological knots in order to provide for those who, despite living in a modern world in which acceptance of such things is commonplace, cannot accept either the leadership of women or the practice of homosexuality (each view based upon uncritical interpretations of Biblical texts, such as in the first instance those relating to 'Headship'). 'The world', puzzled by what it considers old-fashioned and discriminatory views, treats the Church with disdain; by way of response the Church prides itself on not giving in to 'cultural fads' and offers byzantine theological reasoning for these various positions ('a male Christ cannot be represented by a woman' demonstrates a woeful misunderstanding of symbolism) which few outside its 'club' can understand and even less care about. As a result it leaks membership – and wonders why. Church leaders still call for yet more and more missionary and evangelistic activities, whilst basing them on the same tired and often meaningless theologies.

It is surely a paradox that, in a modern world almost drowning under the weight of new knowledge, the worldwide Church (particularly and notably the Church in the Developing World) continues in the main to look backwards? New thinking is deemed damaging to faith and ecclesiastical (and other Faith) conservatisms and fundamentalisms are on the rise: Anglican Primates walk out of, or simply refuse to attend, Communion meetings which include the 'heretical' Episcopal Church of the USA (ECUSA), and support the alternative 'orthodox' GAFCON.[27] Most sadly, there appears to be an increasing gulf between those 'conservative' or 'fundamentalist' Christians and those who espouse more 'liberal' or 'modern' views.

The Roman Catholic radical scholar (formerly a priest and monk), John Dominic Crossan, a founder member of the 'Jesus Seminar', has spent his life exploring much the same kind of issues as this study, focusing in particular on the Jesus of History. His writings have provoked an enormous, virtually 'black and white', reaction, with many critics basing their complaints on reports rather than the writings themselves ('I haven't read the book but I know it is wrong'):

"I read an article entitled 'Scholar Sees Jesus as Revolutionary' in our local newspaper. I was outraged at the statements you made... MANY, MANY born again Christians, along with those Bible scholars who have made intensive studies of the Bible, have a much different picture of our Lord than you have...You state that Christ was an illiterate peasant, for example. Don't you realise that Christ was God in human form...the one who created ALL things and that His knowledge did not have to come from university/theological training! He knew, and knows ALL things and such knowledge is far above what you or I or any human could EVER possibly know!"[28]

Contrast this letter:

"It is the theologians and researchers like yourself who make my Sunday mornings meaningful. After our Sunday sessions, the whole class feels more comfortable about facing the polarised world of fundamentalism. Thank you for your work and the work of the Jesus Seminar. Your research, your interpretations, and your honesty are appreciated."[29]

A further letter to Crossan came from the same kind of people – in fact, a group from England – who, together with "nonchurchgoing professionals", as I suggested in my introduction might be interested in this study, here offering both a rationale and a warning:

"Most United Kingdom clergy...take for granted that Jesus said or did everything that is recorded in the Gospels. Our group finds it increasingly irksome having to endure sermons and lectures which ignore the most elementary conclusions of biblical scholarship. Living with the gap is challenging. On the one hand, it enables us to speak with nonchurchgoing professionals about Jesus and his followers in ways which do not insult their intelligence and integrity. On the other hand, the paradigm shift has such radical

consequences for normal church discourse and worship that very few church people can face them."[30]

It is entirely possible that the "very few church people [who] can face" new ideas may be assisted in their journeys of exploration by introducing them to books (perhaps like this?) which not only explain how the modern critical approach to the Bible works, but also explore carefully and diligently the theological implications of such studies.

Nevertheless, the transition (the "paradigm shift") can be tough and personally disorienting. Peter Enns describes such an epiphany whilst watching a Disney children's film ('Bridge to Terabithia') on a plane journey:

> *"It wasn't fair. I wasn't ready. How was I to know that the company that gave us Mickey Mouse, Goofy, and Son of Flubber would venture deep into a religious debate? I was just minding my own business at thirty thousand feet over the Midwest and was caught off guard. Me – a professional Christian, a seminary professor paid to think right thoughts about God and to tell others about them. But after a long trip, my orthodoxy shield was resting at my side. I was unarmed..."*[31]

The subject of this epiphany?

> *"The idea that the Creator of heaven and Earth, with all their beauty, wonder and mystery, was at the same time a supersized Bible-thumping preacher, obsessed with whether our thoughts were all in place and ready to condemn us for eternity to hell if they weren't, made no sense – even though that was my operating (though unexamined) assumption as long as I could remember..."*[32]

And the outcome?

Since I have outed myself as someone who is okay with questions about the faith. I can't tell you the number of private conversations I have had with people – often virtual strangers telling me about their secret questions and thoughts. They seem haggard and worried. Even frightened. Taking a risk like this could mean being branded for life, that person who 'used to have such strong faith' but is now just another doubter who 'doesn't know what she believes any more'. Church is often the most risky place to be spiritually honest."[33]

We might think that mere idea of the Church of Christ being a "most risky place to be spiritually honest" is a horrendous thing to say; but it is the experience of many people. It is difficult to see how this gulf between (what we might call for shorthand purposes) 'conservatism' and 'liberalism' can ever be bridged or such an impasse worked through, not least because their relative positions represent passionately-held, yet often quite contradictory beliefs, and also because they arise from fundamentally different ways of understanding God, the Bible, the nature and role of revelation, and the impact of reason on that understanding. My own attempts over many years to discuss Jesus, Creation and other matters with conservative Christians have led me to the very sad conclusion that it is most often an exercise in futility: our assumptions are just so different, we are like 'ships passing in the night'. As we shall see in the next section, it is often extraordinarily difficult to find any basics on which we might agree: even the premise that God loves us is contentious because some will insist that God loves only some of us. In a recent discussion my partner-in-dialogue claimed that God really hates atheists, members of other Faiths, women who 'pretend' to be priests, and homosexuals: and he based this assertion on his reading of the Bible. These currently 'unloved' could be embraced by God's love if they only 'changed their ways' and repented of their current life-styles: in other words, if they believed as he believed.

Yet despite this combination of insularity, exclusivity and special pleading (via privileged revelation), many 'conservative' Christians appear to want to understand creedal assertions in much the same way as scientists understand theories: as expressions of reality which describe and denote 'what happens'. Yet a moment's thought tells us that the scientific method is not the kind of process which would normally be applied to theological or, perhaps particularly christological claims: such as that Jesus Christ did not have a human father, or that he walked on water, or that he is "of the same substance" as Father God and so on. Of course, theology isn't science (despite its traditional ascription as 'Queen of the Sciences'): the subject matter is (at least, to a degree) different, as are its concepts and its methodologies. Christians might put it this way: theology is about the Creator; science is about the Creation. But there is obvious overlap between Creator and Creation, and so an equally obvious one between science and religion. Nevertheless, there are those scientists who view theologians as those who deal with pseudo-knowledge as opposed to their own clearly 'real' domains, just as there are some Christians who view science with suspicion and disbelief because it appears to them to undermine or even deny their religious beliefs. There are also many Christian scientists, just as there are many Christians in general who accept the findings of science and seek (as do I) to incorporate those ideas into their understanding of God. Although their main foci are different (scientists explore the nature of the universe; theologians explore the nature of God) science and theology share a number of concerns: the twin search for meaning and truth; the aim to establish what is real over against what is false, and so on. They also share certain methodologies: the application of experience and rational thought to their respective problems; the examination of evidence be that fossils or religious writings, mathematics or archaeology.

There is one highly significant difference: whilst scientists (at least, the less fundamentalist ones) regard even the apparently most secure theories as essentially provisional (what they tell us represents 'fact' only for the time being, until – as in the examples above – new information comes to light which shows the theory to be in part or wholly incorrect), many Christians today would rebel against the idea that there could ever be any new insights or new information which might make us reconsider and amend our religious assertions. This is because they regard their beliefs as 'eternal verities': truths which never change, because they are from a God who is both changeless and truthful. This kind of thinking arises from a fundamental misunderstanding of the nature of revelation (which we shall consider further below): firstly, that revelation consists of scripture itself (the Bible *is* Revelation), rather than revelation being that to which scripture witnesses (the Biblical writings bear witness to the Revelation, but are not themselves that Revelation) and, secondly, that the content of revelation consists of a series of infallible propositions about people and events combined with 'regulations for living', rather than a person (for in revelation what God reveals is nothing other than himself). To recognise this alternative way of understanding scripture: non-propositional and personal, requires us also to recognise that the revelation (in and through the 'Christ-event') always comes to us indirectly (it was direct only in and to the people and events witnessed by Scripture) and, as such, requires interpretation – we cannot apprehend that original revelation directly, we can only explore and consider its relevance to us.

This is not to say that we cannot apprehend or evoke God directly now, although the Church has always maintained that that most intimate form of our relationship with God – prayer – is properly mediated "through Jesus Christ…" (except, perhaps, the Lord's Prayer in which Jesus himself urged his friends to pray directly: 'Our Father…' and 'The Grace' which embraces the Trinity; neither of which in traditional usage conclude with 'through...'). A Christian normally approaches God through Christ, just as those of other Faiths approach God through their own discrete 'systems'. Yet a certain type of Christian will often claim that it is not only possible, but salvifically imperative, to have an equally intimate relationship with the 'living Jesus' himself: 'you must have a personal relationship with Jesus', or 'you must invite Jesus into your life'. Apart from being an expression of piety (or, less likely in such cases, some form of symbolic theology), it is difficult to be sure just what 'having a personal relationship with Jesus' or 'inviting Jesus into our lives' (or indeed the declaration that Jesus is 'alive'[34]) might mean in either (philosophical) ontological[35] or (linguistic) literal terms. Certainly, of those (who clearly believe that even ordination is not sufficient evidence of true Christian commitment) who, over the years, have urged me to take such 'necessary' steps, none has been able to express the characteristics of this relationship in comprehensible language (language which makes sense), and often end up by asserting (sadly, in a somewhat superior manner) that the experience is *sui generis*: only those who have it can know and understand it. If you haven't had it, then you've still some way to go in your proto-Christian life for, according to them, it cannot yet be authentic. Of course, the idea of having a relationship with Jesus or inviting Jesus into our lives makes perfect sense when understood non-literally as, for example, an expression of our commitment to God through Christ.

Perhaps such claims, if they are meant to be taken literally or have an ontological referent, are based on the idea, simplistic to the point of inaccuracy even in traditional Christology, that Jesus (really) is (equates to) God: so a direct relationship with God and with Jesus is one and the same thing. But if the relationship with Jesus is understood to be somehow separate from the relationship we have, through faith, with God, then how is that to be characterised? Ultimately it implies an interpretation of the

Trinity verging on, if not fully, tritheistic: 'I have relationships with each of the Persons' (so, yet again, the 'substance' is divided). I am not implying that the claim to have a 'real' personal relationship with Jesus is either meaningless or false, yet if it is the case that it cannot be expressed in any meaningful way, how can such a claim be either true or false? It might be what some people believe, and may inspire and enhance their faith; but as to whether it is a genuine personal relationship (a relationship between two centres of consciousness, such as that which is always available with Father God in prayer) they may be deluding themselves, as well may my friend who believes he has regular personal conversations with God, in which God genuinely provides him with information. Some people hold similarly strong and convinced beliefs about astrology and the fact that his arises from a fervent and absolutely genuine religious faith doesn't automatically mean that it is, as an alleged 'fact', any less self-delusional. But (again, in terms of symbolic theology) it may be that the imagined relationship with Jesus or conversations with God are just other ways of both picturing, entering into and developing that essential relationship with Father God (for whom Jesus is the definitive symbol), which is the properly immutable centre of Christian faith. In other words, to say 'I have a personal relationship with Jesus' actually means 'I have a personal relationship with God' (if any were to argue that they have separate relationships with God and Jesus then they are in danger of 'dividing the substance'). In terms of a symbolic Christology (Chapter 7) that makes perfect sense (for the symbol attracts the value and devotion due to the symbolizandum); but I doubt if many who use this kind of language see it in this way and so, probably unwittingly, inevitably fall into one of several Christian heresies.

Returning to our necessarily indirect interpretations of God's original revelation in Christ: they, by their very nature, are never fixed and immutable (only the original revelation is that, in that it has occurred; that occurrence can only be mediated to us as we cannot experience it directly), but must be continually renewed and 'owned' within and by the community of faith. Only God, not God's alleged propositions or rules, is the changeless Truth; but for that Truth to be meaningful and relevant, it needs to be accessed by each generation afresh, and that is done through the Church's scriptures and traditions. Such an understanding of revelation enables us to consider issues relating (for example) to moral or ecclesial concerns to be reassessed in the light of that original revelation. The Biblical text says 'x': but how might 'x' be understood today taking account of the Church's experience, its understanding of God's continuous guidance through his enabling Spirit, undergirded by the findings of modern critical scholarship? We might conclude, for example, that God's only concern about sexual relations, rather than who does what with whom, is that they are always loving and never abusive: in which case, we might further conclude, that sex itself is neither a moral nor a proper theological issue, and that the Church should stop obsessing about it.

Some (particularly some of the more trenchant atheistic scientists) might claim another important difference: science can be proven; theology cannot. But a little further thought exposes the weaknesses of such an argument: as we have just noted, scientific theories are always provisional. They only amount to proofs until the next observations overturn them. We can be very certain about all kinds of things, but we can never be absolutely certain: so there is an element of 'faith' even in scientific claims. Although scientific and theological assertions are different in almost every way, what they have in common is that they are both offered as truth claims – they each assert something about reality (and equally something about their contraries), and although the former seems rather easier to demonstrate than the latter, for those who believe both to be the case, they are equally valid claims, although may be judged variously to be 'more or less certain'. If we take one of the greatest of all human questions: that of the origins of the Universe, we may note that although scientists have added enormously to our knowledge as to 'what occurred', just as theologians have helpfully reflected on the implications of faith in a Creator God, one vital element of that occurrence cannot be definitively proven despite what either scientists or theologians believe: that is the question of **purpose** (in Christian thought the element of 'design' as expressed in the teleological argument: Gk. '*telos*' is 'end', 'purpose', 'goal'). Is the existence of the universe something that has come about (an accident: Lat. '*accidens*', present active participle of '*accido*': 'happen' i.e. 'it just happens') or is it intentional and purposive? Whatever view we hold on this great question as to 'why is there something rather than nothing?' (the question often attributed to Liebnitz) it cannot be proven, and it is difficult to imagine how either view ever could be proven, not, at least, in this life.[36]

There is yet another very significant difference between theology and science: immutable religious truths are thought by those who hold them (and correctly, as they are bliks: again, further below) to be immune from empirical testing (the nub of scientific activity), although those making such a claim tend to do so on the basis that evidence is not needed when making claims about God, because we are dealing not with empirical 'discoveries' at all but with the outcomes of a privileged revelation: indeed, to be a Christian one *must* believe such things (exactly as expressed) and, furthermore, to be absolutely certain about them; not to do so is to 'doubt' or 'have a weak faith'. As a result, beliefs in (actually about) God or Jesus, as set out historically by the Church (and in the language and concepts used by the Church at the time) are often regarded by the 'faithful' as settled and absolutely certain truths, to be accepted by Christians even if rejected by others ('it is their loss'). For their part, these others may see this kind of thinking as Christians choosing to believe what they wish to believe, in which case the rest of us can safely ignore them, until their beliefs impinge negatively on matters we take seriously.

For the 'true believer' the great offence against faith is actually to use this 'scientific' (modern critical) method: to ask questions, to examine Christian 'theories' (which, of course, they are not) and to make judgements upon them – do they make sense, are they moral, does the evidence (in, for example, the Biblical witness) actually lead to such a conclusion? That is judged not only sinful, but salvifically perilous; but it is the inevitable outcome of privileging 'believing-that' over 'believing-in'. Gregory Boyd (now senior pastor of a church in Minnesota, USA) writes of his experience of being a member of a fundamentalist church with such an emphasis, not only on faith as 'believing-that' (however bizarre or illogical such beliefs may be), but also on the commensurate importance for salvation of 'having certainty' (views which Boyd began to challenge after doing university courses in biology and biblical studies):

"If God is pleased by our ability to make ourselves feel certain that a particular set of beliefs is true, then a person is going to be pretty much locked into whatever beliefs they were initially taught to believe...How likely is it that people will change their beliefs if they think salvation and damnation depend on whether they can remain as certain as possible that what they already believe is true? Not much. But this means that a person's set of beliefs will be determined by circumstance – where they were born, who raised them, what proselytiser first persuaded them, and so on. Is this really how our beliefs should be determined? Over the years I became increasingly convinced that there is something seriously screwed up about this certainty-seeking concept of faith. Look, what it means to believe in something is that you believe it is true. But if you're really concerned that what you believe is true, then you can't leave that belief to chance. The only way to determine if a belief is true is to rationally investigate it. Which means you have

to doubt it. It is simply impossible for people to be concerned that their beliefs are true unless they're genuinely open to the possibility that their current beliefs are false...I'm convinced that the idea that faith is as strong as a person is certain, combined with the house-of-cards way of embracing this faith [i.e. take one piece away and it all falls], is behind most of the faith struggles Christians have today. In fact, I am convinced it is the main reason so many of our young people abandon the Christian faith and the main reason most nonbelievers today don't take Christian truth claims very seriously. Among other things, certainty-seeking faith, combined with the all-or-nothing way evangelicals typically embrace it, is simply no longer viable in the postmodern world in which we live".[37]

No doubt the Fathers of the Early Church believed (had they used this kind of language) that their 'theory' of a 'hypostatic union' was not only true (and they were absolutely certain about that), but that it was based on clear 'evidence': the evidence of the Scriptures. But those Scriptures, as we shall see in the next section, were not evidence in any proper sense of that term: they were the ideas and beliefs of Christians developed on the basis of their reflection on their personal faith in Jesus Christ (however that arose) and their interpretation of the Hebrew and, latterly, the increasing number of Scriptures designated 'Christian' (the New Testament). They had no empirical evidence which could be tested, and upon which predictions could be made ('if another like Christ appeared with such-and-such characteristics, then we may need to adjust our "theory" of the Trinity to that of a Quaternity'). If, as is often claimed, the Christ-event is literally unique: a 'one-off', then there is nothing that can be tested (we have nothing against which to test it), and nothing which can either confirm or refute that claim: most obviously, if Christ is that literal 'one-off' then how could we possibly understand what that entails, as a 'God-man' could never be part of our understanding of the world in which we live? Logical Positivists would say that renders such claims nonsensical; I would rather say that they suffer, for the purposes of Christian mission, an even greater fate: they are matters of opinion or belief which some people have, and which are impossible to demonstrate to others who do not share the same beliefs. Worse still, they are often incomprehensible (and even celebrated as such: 'so great is our faith...'). As a result people are being asked to accept views about God and Christ which make little or no sense, and which are based only on 'what I choose to believe, because I want to... and I invite you to do the same': hardly a solid platform for evangelical outreach.

No theological language is univocal, because no univocal language can be used of God. Therefore, despite what Athanasius *et al.* believed, even ontological categories should not be taken literally. What, actually, is the *ousia* (substance, being)[38] of God which Jesus is supposed to share? Indeed, would not the 'substance' or 'being' of God (whatever that is) be significantly different from that of a 'human being' (again, whatever that is)? Although we may note Macquarrie's view, to which we shall return, that [Holy] Being becomes manifest in and mediated through (the) beings;[39] yet even with Macquarrie's customary clarity, language strains to express the mystery that is God and, we might add: also the mystery that is humanity.

There are many difficulties – both linguistic and philosophical - for any who wish to insist that Christ is (literally) 'of the same substance' as the Father: how could we possibly know that (it is certainly not directly expressed in scripture, and much depends on how John's 'Word'/*Logos* is understood): but, most significantly, what does such a statement mean? To base everything on *homoousios* is to say, in effect, that Christ's nature (which we don't understand) is the same as God's (which we equally don't understand). We therefore seek to find the meaning of one obscure concept in another that is equally obscure. This is to play a language game only with those 'like us': no wonder so few others ever listen.

That is why we need to replace traditional expressions of Christology with inevitably more limited and cautious assertions and ideas based on such evidence as we do have (such as Jesus' impact on those he met, demonstrated not only by the scriptural witness but also by the existence of the Church and its continuing life in Christ), and couched in language that is at once much clearer and much more readily understandable. All those Patristic assertions made about Christ, whether he had two natures or one, two wills or one, were expressions of religious belief, presented as ways of understanding the significance of the 'Christ-event'; they were not the outcome of a tested and confirmed hypothesis, leading to a demonstrable (and falsifiable) Christological 'theory'. That is also why it is far better to understand assertions of Christian belief as models (helpful or unhelpful; evoking and connoting) rather than as theories (right or wrong; denoting demonstrable realities). So on the related doctrine of 'atonement' or 'soteriology' (the other side of the Christological coin): was Christ's death in actuality a ransom paid to an objective 'real' Devil, or a genuine victory over (equally) 'real' demonic forces, or a proper and very 'real' payment by way of satisfaction to a divine (quasi-feudal) overlord in order to assuage God's 'real' anger at a sinful humanity? Or are such ideas explanatory, albeit allusive models arising directly out of their various cultural and historical contexts?

Put at its most basic: we mistake the nature of theological language if we understand it to express literal realities. Furthermore, we must always make a distinction between the experience or reality, on the one hand, and the ways in which those are expressed, on the other: for the one is not the other; the expression is not the actuality, it is the medium through which we seek to understand and share the actuality. The most we can say about the meaning of *homoousios* is that it seeks to express the truth that Christ shares the closest of relationships with the Father: but what the actual nature of that relationship is will always be, at least to some extent (no doubt as for all of us), a God-shaped mystery, in the proper sense of the word. But, as we need to say something about it, if only for the purposes of mission and proclamation, we should use the most meaningful language available in which to do so, and the language of ontology (at least, as a purely abstract concept) is not that. That is why we have to interrogate the language of the Bible in precisely the same way; because how it expresses ideas is often complex and opaque, and its meaning is not always as obvious as it may first appear.

Interpreting the Biblical Text: History, Bliks and Scriptural Inerrancy

We might reasonably criticise a biographer of Churchill who gets his 'facts' about Churchill wrong (such as date and place of birth; positions held in Government etc.), who misquotes (or goes so far as to make up) his war-speeches, and who makes basic errors concerning the conduct and progress of the Second World War. We would be even more disturbed if the biographer actually invented stories, particularly if he claimed that Churchill's defeat of Hitler had been due to the intervention of (say) angelic beings.[40] Our expectation, whilst recognising that different authors are likely to make different judgements about *interpretations* of their subject (what was the character of Churchill like; which were the main causes of the First World War?), would unquestionably be that those matters we might conveniently call 'historical facts' (such as the periods during which Churchill was in Government; the date and place of the assassination of Archduke Franz Ferdinand[41]) would, having been based on the evaluation of the best evidence using the best critical tools, be accurate: that the written history described as faithfully and as accurately as possible 'what really happened'.

Even if it couldn't present with similar certainty the reasons why such an event happened, or why a person took a particular action, at least those reasons proposed would be rational: the political demise of Margaret Thatcher probably wouldn't be assigned to the machinations of black magicians.

Yet even modern history has the capacity to take on some mythic tendencies (stretching the technical category of myth just a little), arising both from the fragility of memory, our bias and our preferences (what we would have liked to have happened, and so what we may come to believe did happen). Jenny Diski reminded us that for later generations

> "...receiving the recollections of their parents or grandparents, or reading the historians, the past is a story, a myth handily packaged into an era, bounded by a particular event...anything that conveniently breaks the ongoing tick of time into a manageable narrative. Those people, who were alive during the period in question, looking back, call it a memory – memory being just another instance of the many ways in which we make stories."[42]

The twentieth century itself, no doubt like other periods in the past when those who lived through the period were still alive providing their often augmented memories, offers several different examples of how certain historical episodes have been 'handily packaged', including 'the myth of the Blitz' (how it wasn't all that bad really and we all 'hung in there' having great fun), or the 60s themselves (it was all sex, drugs and rock and roll, with the permissive society immortalised in the quotation attributed to Grace Slick: "If you remember the 60s, you weren't there"). Yet those 'myths' ('what we prefer to remember': views of the past which have been romanticised or idealised with the passing of time) can be fairly easily set aside by the more sober judgements of historians based on solid evidence, as well as the effective retrieval of rather more realistic personal memories: (i) the reality of the Blitz was terror, confusion and the predictable negative effects of Government incompetence on the poor and apparently dispensable; (ii) most of us growing up in the 60s noticed very little difference from what had gone before, except greater affluence and, I would add, better music.

Even in the modern world, with the benefits of really comprehensive sources of information and far superior techniques of record keeping, the way we recall events (or the way we *choose* to recall events) can begin to vary from, or otherwise distort the actuality (person or event), within a very short period, and certainly change very significantly by a generation or so of the person/events themselves: a similar period to that which separated the life of Jesus from the written Gospels. Telling stories about one's own life or that of our communities, or pursuing our most passionate concerns, involves a complex and diverse set of practices, and is never a totally objective exercise: we tend to recall those things that are important to us rather more easily than we recall those less important facets of our lives, and we do so in such a way that the recalled content is shaped to fit our prejudices and preferences, and so meets our current needs. Sometimes this involves a deliberate manipulation or 'massaging' of the 'facts'; sometimes it is almost instinctive: 'my schooldays were the happiest/worst of my life': but were they really, or did 'rose-tinted spectacles' (or the contrary) predominate?

Historians today may well include such stories among their sources, but they will do so with appropriate cautionary warnings, recognising (as we discussed earlier) that memories are not only essentially fallible, but also that the recalling of events, particularly difficult or significant events, is not always the best guide to 'what really happened', not least because every memory is based in a particular perspective (literally in some cases: 'just how clearly did you see the accident from where you were standing?'). In short, memories are selective and tend to be selectively deployed depending on how well they serve a particular purpose (CVs and obituaries – our life summaries – may enhance, even creatively re-draw, some memories and ignore or drastically edit others). Memory selection is often biased, and bias almost inevitably results in a one-sided story: just read any politically partisan newspaper where stories which impact negatively on the preferred Party may not even be run. Any ideologically driven agenda, political or religious, will be prone to selectivity and bias (there is no great conceptual distance between pursuing a political programme and evangelism; each seeks to 'win hearts and minds'): anything said or written will be geared to achieving certain outcomes rather than seeking to establish a neutral, 'there are two sides to this argument', conversation. The Evangelists are no exception: they had a Gospel to proclaim, and did so in the most effective way possible. Their aim was not to provide a dispassionate, objective account of the life of Jesus 'based on clear evidence'; rather it was to express their joyous understanding of God's great work of deliverance both in the light of the Jewish Scriptures and as revealed in the man Jesus, and they did so through the lens of their experience of resurrection faith.

Bearing these considerations in mind, we move to our first focus: the question 'how far do the Gospels and (Luke's) Acts, or the apparently historical narratives of the OT, intend to, and how far do they actually, provide straightforward 'factual' accounts of the life of Jesus, the missionary work of Paul, or the lives of Abraham and Moses, in the sense of 'historical' used above?' Apart from any variations in properly interpretative matters (the assessment of character, intentions, causation and such like), do they tell us 'what really happened'; are they as accurate as we would expect a modern historical study or biography to be? When someone (particularly Jesus or Paul) is quoted, are those quotations accurate (we have independent access to many of Churchill's speeches, but, apart from Paul's letters, we have no similarly direct access to what either Jesus or Paul said – so far as we are aware, Jesus never wrote anything); or are their words, as was common in ancient historiography, the construction of the authors? Where written sources (of whatever literary generation, such as the relationship between alleged-'Q' and the Gospels of Matthew and Luke) are based on memories, how selective are those memories, how accurate are they (in portraying 'what really happened'), how and how far have the Evangelists edited them, and against which kind of criteria?

Most scholars agree that both Matthew and Luke used the Gospel of Mark as one of their sources, and it is instructive to explore the ways in which they did so, particularly the editorial changes they often made to Mark's text which can provide clues to their literary and theological interests and intentions. Should anyone claim that Matthew or Luke received a version of a particular pericope via an independent oral tradition or some other source (rather than from Mark) then, whilst that is always a possibility (we cannot know for sure), it pushes the question as to why a story might have been circulating in different versions one stage further back: the issue itself is not avoided. To take a reasonably straightforward example: Mark tells the story of the healing of the daughter of the Syrophoenician woman in 7: 24 – 30; Matthew gives his version in 15: 21 – 28.

In Matthew's account the Syrophoenician, a simple foreigner, a Gentile, becomes a Canaanite, one of Israel's classic enemies, the original 'sitting tenants' from the post-Exodus entry of 'the Jews' into 'their' Promised Land; so Jesus doesn't just help a foreigner, he helps an enemy: a theme similar to Luke's parable of the Good Samaritan, where an enemy helps a Jew (whose plight had been ignored by two fellow Jews).

Mark doesn't tell us how the woman addressed Jesus, but Matthew is very explicit: Jesus is "Lord" and "Son of David" (a messianic title, even though the woman herself is not Jewish). Further, in Mark the disciples have no role; indeed, there is no indication that they were even there (the implication of "he set out...and did not want anyone to know he was there" is that Jesus was alone); but in Matthew (where discipleship is an important theme, with Matthew frequently pointing out just how useless and obdurate Jesus' then-followers were) they intervene in a quite unpleasant manner: "Send her away". In Mark, Jesus' reason for not wanting to respond to her request is that "the [unspecified] children" have to be "fed first"; Matthew (writing, probably in Syria, to encourage and support Jewish Christians struggling to define themselves against traditional Judaism) seems clear that Jesus was (originally?) "sent only to the lost sheep of the house of Israel"; as Jesus clearly changed his mind, that wasn't to be the final word on the matter, yet the re-assertion might have been of some comfort to his Jewish-Christian audience, and may hint at what Jesus himself really thought (see further below).

Finally, we may note two small and relatively insignificant points: (i) Mark concludes his story by having Jesus say, quite vaguely: "For saying that, you may go"; whilst Matthew is again much more explicit: "Woman, great is your faith" (did Mark not want to overpraise a gentile?); (ii) Mark then tells us that the woman went home and found her daughter healed, whilst for Matthew the healing takes place "instantly"; Mark may well have shared that understanding and was making the point that the woman didn't find out until later. We mustn't overthink such things; not everything we read in the Bible is packed full of meaning.

It is a good general rule for the student of the Bible (and particularly important for the preacher) to bear in mind not only the role and function of a particular pericope in the way in which the ministry of Jesus is being presented to us (why did the Evangelist choose to tell this particular story; and why tell it in this particular way?[43]), but also its possible place in the 'life situation' of the Evangelist's community (what connection does the story have to the circumstances and concerns of the particular church in and for which the Gospel has been shaped and written?). Similarly, for OT texts: what were the circumstances of the post-exilic/Second Temple Judaism in which most of the documents were either composed or had their final editing, and how did those situations affect and otherwise impact on the final version of the text? One might even ask in which of the two contexts a particular story originated. In the case of Gospel pericopae: was it the Jesus-situation which is the subject of the story, or was it the Church-situation at the place and time of writing? It is possible that some stories may have been created either by the Evangelist or by others within his community, and then artificially inserted into the evolving literary 'Life of Christ' which (probably) began with Mark. In this way Jesus could be used to justify or otherwise explain issues which were troubling the early Church or which were matters of controversy or even dissention. One obvious example is the reference in John 9: 22 to Jesus' followers being ejected from the synagogue: as already noted, a formal Jewish procedure which didn't actually exist at the time of Jesus, or the reference in Mt 16: 18 to a 'Church' when it may be argued that Jesus had no intention of 'building' a Church although, obviously, one came to exist before the Gospels were written and 16: 18 thus provided its rationale.[44]

Equally, the Evangelists may have created (or excluded) particular narratives in order to further, support or justify their own theological purposes: again as already noted, prime examples include the distinctive nativity stories of Luke and Matthew which have virtually nothing in common (this evidence alone, if any more were needed, places a major question mark over their historicity). Each story was crafted in order to express the understanding that each Evangelist had of the significance and also, perhaps, the nature (and thus the origin) of Christ, although this latter question seems to have been of limited interest and importance to them, because neither Evangelist makes anything more of his birth narrative, just as John never revisits his 'Word' theology. That Luke didn't include the story of the Syrophoenician-Canaanite woman at all is surprising in view of his well-known interest in stories about women (e.g. Luke 7: 36 – 8: 3). He obviously knew the story, because he knew Mark's Gospel; so it is entirely reasonable to consider the possible reasons for him omitting it. Was it because he didn't wish to collude in the further transmission of a portrait of an apparently unsympathetic, even heartless, Jesus who has to be cajoled to heal; a Jesus who, furthermore, not only changes his mind, but appears to have had his mind changed;[45] or, rather worse, shamed into thinking again by the woman's heart-felt plea? These few examples show clearly how naïve it is to take the view that the Evangelists told their stories simply on the basis that 'they happened': the process of selection and writing up was much more complex.

It is apparent that Matthew has not only augmented his version of the Syrophoenician encounter; he has changed it in some quite significant ways. Therefore, it is reasonable to ask why Matthew didn't copy Mark almost verbatim (as he sometimes does): what was going through his mind as he altered the text before him, and what his motives were for doing so? Is this primarily a story about a healing or is it a story which aims to provide a rationale for opening up the gentile mission, perhaps against those in Matthew's Church who were still urging caution. Indeed, Matthew's amended story may have contributed towards, or even arisen from, the debate in his own community: one which might have been out of step with other Christian Churches (the evidence suggests, as we saw above with reference to the Ebionites, that some groups of Christians fiercely maintained their allegiance to Judaism, certainly into the 2nd Century and possibly much later). We can see on which side of the argument the Evangelist (if not Jesus) stood in Mt 28: 19: "Go therefore and make disciples of all nations...": are these the *ipsissima verba* of Jesus or an expression of Matthew's view, and representative of the eventual consensus of the Church?

So, Matthew argues: 'Yes. Jesus was sent to us Jews first; but this story shows how his mission took on a universal focus and we should follow suit: [perhaps implicit] just as the rest of the Church is doing'. This is because, by the time Matthew was writing, the Church was predominantly Gentile: while it maintained its most valued Jewish roots (particularly the OT), its identity was becoming increasingly separated from Judaism (a process exacerbated by the destruction of Jerusalem and the Temple in 70CE) and that would have been a matter of regret, and perhaps even anger, for many Jewish Christians who hadn't ever considered that 'being a Christian' would eventually mean ceasing to be Jewish.

Some have understood this episode to mark a genuine turning point in Jesus' own understanding of the scope of his mission: that he originally saw himself as having been sent only to the Jews, but came to understand (perhaps through this very encounter) that God had a more universalist agenda. If Jesus valued the Prophet Isaiah, particularly the Second Isaiah and his 'servant songs' (as we shall see: there are several indications that this was the case), then such a theme would have been very familiar to him: "Here is my servant, whom I uphold, my chosen, in whom my soul delights; I have put my spirit upon him; he will bring forth justice to the nations...I have given you as a covenant to the people, a light to the nations..." (Isaiah 42: 1, 6b), with which we might compare Luke's 'Song of Simeon' (the *Nunc Dimittis*): "...a light for revelation to the Gentiles and for glory to your people Israel" (2: 32): here Luke is saying: 'Jesus, from the time he was a baby, had a universal mission', not least because there is no doubt that direction is where Luke's own priorities were to be found.

However, as morally satisfying as any movement from

exclusivism to inclusivism may seem, the theory doesn't immediately appear to be compatible with the narrative in Acts (e.g. Acts 15; supported by Paul's own testimony in Galatians 2), which claims that Paul had to fight hard to open up mission to the Gentiles. If universalism had been Jesus' position and intention all along, and Peter *et al* would have known that, why would his followers have felt the need to make such a big issue of it? That in itself might suggest that Jesus never actually had a vision beyond the "lost sheep of the house of Israel". Particularly if he expected an imminent End, Jesus may have had the much more limited aim of creating an Isaiah-type 'remnant' of faithful Jews patiently and prayerfully waiting for God's irruption into history. Craig Evans suggests that Jesus was seeking to establish *"a community of disciples committed to the restoration of Israel and the conversion and instruction of the Gentiles..."*.[46]

If Evans is correct, then while Jesus may have had outreach to Gentiles in mind, it would have been of the kind in which they were to be converted to Judaism. This might explain the controversy in the early Church: it was not that Gentiles were not welcome to join the Jesus movement; it was that some (like Peter and James – and Jesus?) believed they had to become Jews first: rather naturally perhaps, because 'Christianity' (followers of the Christ) wasn't at that early stage thought by its own members to be separate from Judaism. It was a new movement within Judaism, but not a new religion. It was this act of conversion that Paul opposed, not least for pragmatic reasons: the requirement to follow certain Jewish practices (such as circumcision and dietary laws) may well have put off potential converts, although he cites plenty of theological reasons as well throughout his letters. The distinction is between a Jewish community which includes converted Gentiles (which is mainly how it began), and a 'Christian' community which included both Jew and Gentile on equal terms: "There is no longer Jew or Greek..." (Gal 3: 28 cf. 2: 14), and which eventually became separated from Judaism:

a situation which was well in process by the time Mark wrote, and which had been completed, or was near to completion, by the time that Matthew and Luke were writing. That is why it is crucial to take account of the situation which obtained, as stories which may well have originated in the ministry of Jesus (but some may equally not have done so) were further edited by the Evangelists.

The Syrophoenician-Canaanite woman and similar stories involving a positive view of Gentiles (such as the healing of the Centurion's servant: Lk 7: 1 – 10; Mt 8: 5 – 10) may have been told for the express purpose of showing that Jesus himself had been in favour of extending God's mission to the Gentiles and, furthermore, that he purposely established a Church over and against the Judaism he himself inhabited, even expecting it to become an alternative Faith. On the other hand, these may not have been his intentions at all. Again, some Christians might rebel against the idea that Jesus was either religiously or culturally exclusive, or that he was ever wrong about anything; but as a fallible human being and a man of his time and place he may have been both.

How, then, should this particular story be understood? As a straightforward 'historical' description of one of Jesus' healings (in this case, an exorcism; albeit one which seems almost incidental to the narrative); or something entirely different: a story seeking to commend a particular direction for Christian mission, something which forwards the theological agenda of the Evangelist, originally Mark, and then as modified by Matthew? The short answer is: we can't know for sure; we must use our understanding of the nature of the text and its origins, and also of how the world operates, in order to make our own judgements about what is most likely. In so doing we may bear in mind that the whole issue of exorcism will be understood by many today in a way markedly different to that of Jesus and his contemporaries (as well as that of some contemporary Christians) who believe(d) that the world was infested by evil spirits and that they were/ are fighting a war against demonic and other spiritual powers (in Matthew the daughter was being "tormented by a demon"). Furthermore, precisely what is represented by the description of this spirit, in Mark, as 'unclean' or 'impure', particularly when 'inhabiting' a "child" (in Matthew no age is indicated), and how might such a diagnosis be explained today? It may seem almost too obvious to mention, but the Evangelists were not writing for us in the 21st Century developed world; they were writing for their own communities either in Palestine or wider afield, focusing on their own particular situations, needs and priorities, and their narratives were formed and shaped to that end. This kind of narrative is not and was never an exercise in the discipline we call history. Stories were selected and even constructed (i.e. invented) in order to pursue particular theological agendas and to assist in the effective proclamation of the 'Good News' (*evangelion*: 'gospel'). And, in their historical context, there was nothing whatsoever wrong with that: problems only arise when we seek to impose our own modern historiographical and ethical standards (e.g. regarding plagiarism or the adoption of another's identity: as with the Deutero-Pauline letters) on a different age and culture.

This question of historical accuracy becomes particularly sharp and contentious when it comes to descriptions of allegedly miraculous happenings, particularly those known as 'nature miracles' (over against healings which are both more subtle and more complex), as the supernatural and the historical do not make good bedfellows. Did Jesus really feed 5000 people with a very limited, but supernaturally augmented, supply of food; did he really turn plain water into wine (and why? in a world of great pain and suffering it seems a very trivial miracle)? In the light of our discussion above concerning variety in linguistic usage, are such stories not capable of entirely different interpretations?

For example, **the feeding of the 5000** may be more accurately interpreted as another case (compare the pericope of the raising of the son of the widow of Nain [Lk 7: 11 – 17] with Elijah's raising of the son of the widow of Zarephath [1 Kings 17: 17 – end] where, despite some differences in detail, much of the thematic structure of the two stories is identical) portraying Jesus as a prophet, like the prophets of old, but even greater (5000 compared with a mere 100) – in this case Elisha (2 Kings 4: 42 – 44): "...but his servant said, 'How can I set this before a hundred people?' So [Elisha] repeated, 'Give it to the people and let them eat, for thus says the Lord, 'They shall eat and have some left'. He set it before them, they ate, and had some left..."; thus Mark 6: 30 – 44 and //s: "...And all ate and were filled; and they took up twelve baskets full of broken pieces and of the fish..."; again, some differences in detail, but the overall structure and intentions are much the same. Or the story may be a symbol or prefiguring of the Eucharist: in Chapter 6 of John's Gospel the account is followed by a prolonged and profound meditation on the "bread of life" – positively contrasted with the manna in the wilderness. It may show the superiority of the bread Christ offers to that offered after the Exodus; or it may be seen to celebrate God as giver of 'all good things'.

The **Cana** pericope may be understood (variously) as a prefiguring of the eschatological 'wedding banquet of the Lamb' (as in Rev 19: 6 – 9; 21: 1 – 5), or the similar glorious feast of the Kingdom that is to come (cf. Mk 14: 25; Mt 26: 29; Lk 22: 18) when the wine will be extraordinarily good and abundant. It may be a theological reflection on the 'marriage' between God and Israel (as in Isaiah 61: 10 – 11; 62: 1 – 5) portraying the restoration of that bond in Christ; Jeremiah (33: 6 – 16) had warned that the bridal song would not ring out again until the nation had been purified by the "righteous branch" which would spring out of David's line, and the nation renamed: "the Lord our Righteousness". It is possibly a parabolic representation of the superiority of the Christian Eucharist over Jewish rites (John explicitly points to the prior purpose of the water jars used), and thus of Christianity over Judaism (to establish the superiority of Christianity over Judaism was clearly one of the motives of several of the NT authors). It may making the simple point that in Christ there is a far deeper purification of human life, or the equally simple idea that Jesus himself is the 'new wine' of the new Kingdom. All of these are possible interpretations of that apparently straightforward story.

Such stories (like the birth narratives) are primarily or even entirely theological. They may have no historical core whatsoever; or that core, as in many legends formulated through the ages, may be so remote that it is virtually impossible to recover (such as with the historical King Arthur or Robin Hood, although in these particular cases the motivation for developing the stories will have been political or simply romantic rather than religious). The question: 'what meaning may we find?' is far more appropriate than 'did it really happen?', not least because this latter question portrays a naïve understanding of the nature of the texts (that they are descriptions of 'what happened' rather than expressions of faith). If any do seek to argue that Jesus really turned water into wine, then they need to recognise that doing so would be more magical than miraculous, and that the nature of such an event would, again, undermine his humanity – human beings cannot do things like that (except as an illusion): water cannot be turned into wine (it would be a chemical impossibility: wine is made from grapes) and, as we have seen, to argue 'God can do anything' is to beg the central Christological question.

There are also interpretations of otherwise agreed historical events which (as with any form of proper historiography) may be challenged: for example, hardly any reputable historian would claim that Jesus' death was not by crucifixion, because the evidence for that, both internal and external, is so strong. But what part did the Jewish leaders play in that death? Was the claim that they took the lead, as set out in the Passion narratives, merely an emollient attempt on the part of Christian writers, following the Roman-Jewish War (when being thought Jewish might be dangerous), to exonerate the Roman authorities and so avoid problems with them, by drawing a clear line between Judaism and the emerging Christian Faith?[47] That might also explain Paul's call for obedience to the ruling authorities (Romans 13: 1 – 7), for although the Romano-Jewish War (66 – 73CE, with Jerusalem sacked in 70) had yet to occur, the signs of the times were there to be read. It certainly seems that Paul himself eventually fell foul of the Roman authorities despite, at least according to Acts, being a Roman citizen.[48] Because it is impossible to know, as an allegedly historical 'fact', who was primarily or even completely responsible for Jesus' execution (the only 'evidence' available is that presented by the Evangelists – there is no contemporary Roman record – and, as argued in the linked endnote, there is every reason to believe that the accounts are driven by other than historical concerns[49]) we can do little other than speculate on the basis of what we do know. As Governor of Judaea, Pontius Pilate was well known for his brutality, seen by the Roman authorities as necessary in such a troublesome province (that was why Judaea was under direct Roman rule, rather than under a local puppet such as Herod); it is possible, but not likely, that Pilate would help the Jewish authorities, but not unless to do so were in his own interests. Furthermore, crucifixion was a punishment usually reserved for political agitators and other criminals who offended against the Roman State: the Gospel narratives claim that Jesus was thought by Pilate to be innocent of any such offence – what is less believable is that Pilate would care less.

It seems much more historically likely that Jesus was killed by the Romans as a potential, if not actual, political agitator (with or without any input by Jewish leaders); such a view of Jesus might have been generated by what is presented in the Gospels as the 'Palm Sunday' entry into Jerusalem[50] and/or the 'cleansing of the Temple'[51] (all public events with political implications, even if Jesus didn't see them or intend them to be seen as such) or by other events such as represented in the 4th Gospel (after the feeding of the 5000) by the crowds wanting to make Jesus King (Jn 6: 15). A non-citizen (and, sometimes, even citizens) probably didn't need to do or say much to fall under the suspicion of the Roman authorities due to their continuing paranoia about potential rebellion. Overall, it seems reasonable to conclude that modern historiography, where we expect a considerable degree of accuracy in what is written, is quite different both in purpose and methodology to that of the ancient world. Biblical history in particular, as noted by Patricia Dutcher-Walls,

"...constructs an account of the past that uses conventions, approaches, and principles of its ancient time and context. Biblical historical books communicated about events, people and interactions, dates and chronology, geographical and environmental factors, and causes and consequences, all in ways that made sense to their ancient audiences"[52]

Yet for many Christians today, the Bible is a history book on par with (and probably more accurate than) any modern example because as its source is God, no human memories are involved. They feel able to conclude that it narrates events (including the time when the sun and moon 'stood still' as Joshua fought the Amorites: Josh 10: 12 - 14[53]) exactly as they occurred. In particular, the stories of Jesus, from the birth at Bethlehem to the Cross at Calvary, not only describe 'what really happened', but include the *ipsissima verba*[54] of Jesus, including all those from the Cross, even though no one Gospel includes them all.[55] The Acts of the Apostles is deemed to be the history book *par excellence* (generations of schoolchildren – and their examiners - have used it to plot the 'missionary journeys' of Paul), not least because it (allegedly) includes the first-person eye-witness testimony of Luke (in the so-called 'we' passages[56]), and even though what it narrates about Paul's various itineraries and experiences is often at odds with the information given in Paul's own letters.[57]

The assertion made above that the Bible includes a variety of literary genres and, in particular, that the apparently straightforward, historical narratives are nothing of the kind, is often seen as exhibiting a lack of faith: 'God has told the story as it was; God would not lie'. For such folk, God has (somehow) provided the Biblical text: perhaps not precisely in the direct-revelation manner as believed by Muslims and Mormons of their scriptures but, nevertheless, God has so inspired the Biblical writers that their writings may not only be thought of as genuinely God-given, but also – because of that - straightforwardly factual. The writers produced the text, and may well have written what they believed to be their own ideas; but the content of what they wrote was, in effect, provided by God himself who controlled both the process and the content. We may note, for example, the view of Stephen Davis:[58]

> "I believe that God superintended the writing of the texts that Christians call the Bible...It seems that in order for the Bible to accomplish God's purposes, God would have to (1) ensure the protection and preservation of God's basic message to humankind (e.g. by putting it into a text); (2) superintend the process of compiling that book (including deciding on the canon of that text); (3) ensure that this text could be properly interpreted (e.g. by creating a tradition of interpretation like 'the rule of faith'); and (4) ensure its authoritative interpretation and application by creating an institution (the church) designed to do that very thing. And I believe God did all four."[59]

If all that were the case, then a huge range of questions follow:

1. what precisely was the process by which God "superintended the writing of the text" (this goes to the root of the meaning of 'Biblical inspiration') and how far does that compromise human freedom? Were the biblical authors mere puppets to whom God 'dictated' the text and, if so…

2. …how then do we explain inconsistencies and contradictions within the text? Surely, if God were personally responsible for those texts, there would be no such discrepancies?

3. further, just what is the "basic message" which God wanted to convey? Christians would surely have good reason to assume that it would be a message of love, but how does that relate to those parts of the OT when God is presented as quite immoral, such as 1 Sam 2: 25 where it was "the will of the Lord" to kill Eli's sons; or the God of Noah who, having regretted creating humanity, decided to wipe them out, not by a 'click of the divine fingers', but by the painful and sadistic method of drowning (why do we persist in telling that story to children?); or God ordering death and destruction even on innocents (e.g. Josh 6: 21, 24; 8: 24 – 25)?

4. still further, why are there so many textual variants if God was personally responsible for the text – clearly the 'superintending' did not extend to the copyists which, in itself, means that we cannot be confident that we have the authentic original text in any case;

5. are we to imagine that all the canonical discussions in the early church were just 'window-dressing' because God had already decided what the canon of scripture would be and, somehow, ensured that his preference was implemented? And again, how was that done?

6. what is 'proper interpretation' when there have been, and continue to be, multiple interpretations of the text?

How do we know which interpretation is God's as, for example, in the antinomian or 'works' v. 'faith' debates in the NT? Where does God 'stand' on slavery (seemingly approved of e.g. Titus 2: 9 - 10), homosexuals (to be put to death: Lev 20: 13) and women (to be silent in church: 1 Cor 14: 34)?

7. in a continually divided Church where does an "authoritative interpretation" actually lie – what of those areas where churches disagree (e.g. is God 'in favour' of infant baptism, or not)?

The fundamental criticism to be made of Davis is that he makes these claims only on the basis that this is what he 'believes', presumably as a matter of faith. He makes no attempt to make a case for them, providing examples and argument which could be examined and interrogated by other scholars. "I believe God did all four" is not, in any sense, a scholarly claim: it is an *a priori* premise; it is either an opinion he chooses to hold for religious reasons or something he can't help but believe (see further below on the nature of 'bliks'). It is difficult to know quite what kind of evidence would count either for or against the assertion that *"God superintended the writing of the texts that Christians call the Bible"*. Certainly there can be no empirical evidence: there is, after all, no absolutely compelling evidence (evidence which would lead all unbiased intelligent thinkers to the same conclusion) for the existence (or non-existence) of God, the proposed 'author'. An even more fundamental issue is this: what exactly does textual 'superintendence' involve? Ensuring that the narratives are correct and without error, or that the texts would be preserved, or that God appropriately dictated the material, or what? Furthermore, while both Davis and I have concluded (possibly for quite different reasons) that there is a God, even that belief cannot be, *per se*, the basis for any further claims that God acts in particular ways: such theological ideas will be worked out using a range of different methods: our interpretation of scripture, use of our reasoning faculties and so on. We might choose to believe that God does this or that, but we cannot successfully demonstrate it, particularly to those who don't believe in God in the first place. This is the nature of faith: that we trust in "the assurance of things hoped for, the conviction of things not seen" (Hebs 11: 1).

Furthermore (a point often ignored by 'fundamentalists' of whatever hue), even 'the Bible' itself, even if it were to be agreed that 'the Bible' had a common author and could be treated as a single work of literature (I understand it to be a library: a collection of books by different authors written at different times for differing reasons), doesn't make Davis' claim: as we have seen, the author of 2 Timothy merely states that scripture is inspired by God (or 'God-breathed'), and that claim is capable of multiple interpretations, not least because at the time of writing there was no NT canon in existence. Neither the Evangelists nor Paul claim that anyone else is responsible for their writings: in fact, Luke states explicitly that his Gospel is the end result of the traditions handed on to him by "eyewitnesses and servants of the word" (Luke 1: 1 – 4), whilst the 4th Evangelist (or the author of the appended Chapter 21, if not the same person) also states that the Fourth Gospel is based on eyewitness testimony (Jn 21: 24 – 25), although that claim is disputed by many scholars (not only because it appears in an appendix, but also because John's narrative is so different from the earlier and fairly common Synoptic witness). Davis and others may claim that although the biblical authors believed that they were writing their own accounts, that is not actually what happened, because they were (unknown to them) being 'supervised' by God. But that cannot be demonstrated: it is just a point of view.

Davis' stance is, as noted above, what philosopher Richard Hare termed a 'blik': an unverifiable belief or world view – 'the way I see things'. In Hare's parable, a university don (fellow or tutor) believed that all the other dons were planning to kill him (which is presumably why Hare calls him a 'lunatic'); his friends work hard to disabuse him of this (crazy) idea,[60] organising a party to which the 'lunatic' and all the other dons are invited; at the party they are all perfectly kind and civil towards him: so, his friends tell him (after meeting them one by one), "'*You see, he doesn't really want to murder you; he spoke to you in a most cordial manner; surely you are convinced now?' But the lunatic replies 'Yes, but that was only his diabolical cunning; he's really plotting against me the whole time, like the rest of them; I know it I tell you'. However many kindly dons are produced, the reaction is still the same.*"[61] Hare's explanation is both insightful and relevant to our argument:

"*Now we say that such a person is deluded. But what is he deluded about? About the truth or falsity of an assertion?...There is no behaviour of dons that can be enacted which he will accept as counting against his theory [that other dons are planning to kill him]; and therefore his theory...asserts nothing [in that it can be neither verified nor falsified]. But it does not follow that there is no difference between what he thinks about dons and what most of us think about them – otherwise we would not call him a lunatic and ourselves sane...[so] it is very important that we have the right blik...It was Hume who taught us that our whole commerce with the world depends on our blik about the world; and that differences between bliks about the world cannot be settled by observation of what happens in the world. That was why, having performed the interesting experiment of doubting the ordinary man's blik about the world, and showing that no proof could be given to make us adopt one blik rather than another, he turned to backgammon to take his mind off the problem*".[62]

What Hare is arguing (as part of the early 1950s debate on theology and falsification published in the philosophical journal 'University') is that it is not simply a case of an assertion being either true or false, and so subject to reasonable debate during which the opposing sides set out the arguments for and against. The lunatic is particularly "deluded" (although for the logical positivists his very claim is meaningless in that he will allow nothing, no facts or other evidence, to count against it), because many, if not most others, would have a 'normal' blik (understanding/perspective) about dons, one which is significantly different from his: so different, that it seems reasonable to describe his particular blik as 'lunatic'. In which case, we might dismiss what he says as the ravings of a madman. Perhaps the same kind of response might be given to anyone who clings on to a belief regardless of the evidence against it ('verificationalists' would say: 'he is talking nonsense'). But as silly as it might seem, that particular belief has an overwhelming impact on his life (he can't go out for fear of dons) and because it forms one basic way that he perceives reality it probably affects other judgements as well, not to mention the deleterious effect on those who are subject to his constant suspicion. That is why – as Hare remarks – "it is very important that we have the right blik".[63] Wrong bliks can be dangerous for everyone involved.

Hare illustrates this with a further example: when he is driving his car, whilst it sometimes occurs to him that his steering might fail, he believes (he has this blik: a trust in the quality design and build of his car) that it will not: "*I just have a blik about steel and its properties, so that normally I trust the steering of my car*".[64] If, however, he developed the opposite blik, although his friends might think him silly, it would make a real difference to his life: in this case he would never drive again. "*Yet I should hesitate to say that the difference between us was the difference between contradictory assertions. No amount of safe arrivals or bench-tests will remove my blik and restore the normal one; for my blik is compatible with any finite number of such tests*".[65] The central point is this: a blik is not an explanation of some fact or other (as the empiricists tended to understand it), and it is a mistake to see it as such; but nevertheless,

> *"...without a blik there can be no explanation; for it is by our bliks that we decide what is and what is not an explanation. Suppose we believed that everything that happened, happened by pure chance. This would not of course be an assertion: for it is compatible with anything happening or not happening, and so, incidentally, is its contradictory. But if we had this belief, we should not be able to explain or predict or plan anything. Thus, although we should not be asserting anything different from those of a more normal belief, there would be a great difference between us; and this is the sort of difference that there is between those who really believe in God and those who really disbelieve in him".[66]*

Bliks are strange. They are not the outcome of rational thought: we don't work out our bliks by a process of discernment and reflection. They are more 'instinctive' (although to use this word is, to a degree, to misuse it because they are not instinctive in the sense that – say - our fear of the dark is instinctive) or 'natural' than they are deliberate. They are often 'black and white', in the sense that once we have adopted our blik, we fail to see anything against it, although we are fully alert to the problems with (what we may call) our anti-blik. A good illustration of this is any particularly strong 'innate' political conviction (as much as with a religious conviction): we are 'died-in-the-wool' Socialists or Tories. As such, we acknowledge nothing against our own position, but we see everything against our opponents' (it is at once amusing and sad to see debates in the House of Commons wherein neither side will see any good whatsoever in their opponents' arguments, when common sense might suggest that there are pros and cons on either side, and further that there are pretty obvious compromises which might be reached).

Sometimes our bliks are so passionately held that we will abuse or even physically attack our opponents on the streets.

Nothing will make us change our stance: no argument, no facts, and not even persuasive friends. Indeed, they may well cease to be friends if they ever become too persuasive! It may even be (and I have personal knowledge of such folk) that I support a particular political party even though, if it came to any rational analysis (which I avoid), it would turn out that I disagree with every single one of their policies: indeed, truth be told, I support the policies of their opponents. Nevertheless, I stay with them because they are (somehow) 'mine', or perhaps reflect my social/cultural background. Bliks are often very tribal: you are either 'one of us' or my enemy: hence the rather aggressive 'conversations' between militant atheists and equally militant Evangelicals.

Some bliks may be positive (for example, an utter and innate conviction that the poor of the world must be saved from their poverty – this may be a blik insofar that there are no rational arguments proffered: 'the economic advantages of reducing poverty over against the economic advantages for keeping it'). Yet others may be negative and destructive: the conviction that Jews are evil and must be exterminated: we may note that most anti-Semites are impervious to argument. Once we hold a particular blik, it will impact on many other areas of our lives: if we believe that the Biblical narrative is literally true, then we assign scientific accounts of the origin of the universe to the work of the Devil (in whom our blik requires us to believe) and we agitate and campaign for 'creationism' to be taught as part of the science syllabus in our schools. Indeed some Christians are so concerned that research into the Jesus of History is dangerous for faith, that they believe it is best avoided.[67] So our bliks determine how we explain the world. Anti-Semitism explains all the problems of the world as originating and persisting in the existence of Judaism. Therefore the only logical conclusion (bliks have their own internal logic) is to exterminate the Jews.

However, the essential problem with bliks is that (even if we are not mad) we cannot easily control them. Our world views (including whether or not we believe in God) are, as we have seen, generally formed not as (but not completely ruling out) the outcome of pure rational thinking: very few people become religious believers having studied a course in comparative religion, or by sitting down and thinking carefully through the theological issues; then, having weighed up the arguments, reach a conclusion and start to attend church. But neither does religious faith arise from a vacuum. We tend to be (or not be) religious, and hold (or not hold) a religious world view as the result of our upbringing and life experiences. More negatively, they may be the result of some degree of 'brainwashing': I recall a pupil who, in the context of class discussion, poured out a racist diatribe during which it became clear that he was parroting the views of his parents, not least because when asked why he regularly sat next to a boy from an African heritage, he responded that it was because 'he is my mate'. Nevertheless, his blik remained unchanged, even when socialising with his friend of another race. Bliks are not rational, and may even appear quite irrational.

Once we come to hold that position of faith or unfaith (that blik), we tend to fit all else around it: it provides sense and meaning to our lives, and is the basis upon which we explain many other things, such as the religious view that whatever occurs, good or evil, it is the 'will of God': in which case everything that happens (including the suffering of innocents) is God's will. Whatever views we adopt, we will hear nothing against them; indeed, those who disagree must be evil or mad. We will not only allow nothing to count *against* our blik; we will allow nothing to count *for* any opposing blik. Our bliks are generally immune from argument on the grounds that, to us at least, they are self-evidently correct. That is not to say that faith-bliks are invulnerable to damage, or even total destruction – they are certainly not: plenty of people have come to lose faith in God due to experiences as seemingly trivial as boredom, or as life-changing as the suffering of a loved one. As Hare points out: bliks may change. Nevertheless, whilst we hold them they seem blindingly obvious to us although they may seem odd or even mad to others (so Richard Dawkins entitled his most famous anti-religious tract 'The God Delusion', in which he states that religious people are deluded and delusional) and we cling on to them with considerable tenacity. That is presumably why self-ascribed people of faith are able to kill others whilst shouting the slogan 'God is Great': an obviously immoral, irreligious and deluded action to any reasonable person. But not to those who hold to it. This reminds us that whilst bliks are not verifiable (they are not explanations), they may be wrong and they may be falsified, although the nature of a blik (and its dominant role in our world view) is often such that its holder will ignore anything which might reasonably be thought to count against it. That was the point of Hare's extreme depiction of the 'lunatic with the blik about dons'.

When Davis bases his whole scriptural exegesis on the foundation that *"God superintended the writing of the texts that Christians call the Bible"*, he is essentially expressing his particular blik (or perhaps a sub-blik; the overriding blik is his faith in an unseen God): the way he sees things. There is no way of verifying his blik, but that is the nature of a blik. Some might respond to me: but surely, just as Davis has a blik about divine supervision of the Biblical text, so you too have a blik that the Bible has purely human authors? This may seem reasonable: Davis holds his blik about God and the Bible, whilst I hold a different one. But further reflection suggests that is not actually the case: for we each hold our views on Biblical authorship for quite different reasons. Whilst I share Davis' overriding blik (at least, to an extent – see below) that we live in a universe divinely and providentially created (for although that particular blik can be neither verified nor falsified, it is far from being insane; it is –

as Hare has made clear: like many bliks – as valid as its contrary; of course, it may be wrong, for we can have perfectly sane, but still quite wrong, bliks), so far as the Bible is concerned, and quite unlike Davis, I do not start from any *a priori* position about its authorship and then seek to build my arguments on that (the deductive method). I begin by examining the (now) enormous range of evidence and proposals of over 200 years of Biblical scholarship, considering and making critical judgements about them. I argue my case (therefore not a blik; because we don't feel the need to argue for our bliks: we just have them) that the Bible is a purely human creation: perhaps inspired, although to say that raises many difficult theological issues, not the least being what is meant by inspiration, and how such interventionist inspiration might compromise human freedom. Mine is thus the *a posteriori* route (the inductive method). To put it at its most basic: Davis believes what he believes as a matter of faith (and there is nothing particularly wrong with that), whilst I reach my view having first examined the evidence: my trust in God is a matter of faith for me; my view on the writing of the Bible is not.

So far so good. Where, however, Davis' view (and others like it) can become particularly problematic is when his blik is seen to be inviolable: nothing can count against it. Again, my position cannot be compared with his: I hold an opinion based on the evidence and I recognise the possibility that I may have misinterpreted that evidence and, faced with new evidence, I may change my mind. My view on Biblical authorship is not blik-like at all, because if it were, I would never accept there could be any evidence against it. Indeed, should the evidence take me in a different way, I would happily adjust my view. But even if I adjusted it to the extent that it duplicated Davis' blik (I came to believe that Davis' blik is correct), mine would still not be a blik in the way that Hare has proposed, because I would still seek to interrogate it. It would not be – we might say – a 'heartfelt' and precious belief. It would just be the way I see things whilst the evidence stands as it does: it is a provisional theory.

The more important question is not 'can Davis' view be verified?' (it cannot) but can it be falsified – is there anything that would count against the belief that God supervised the writing of the Bible? As we have seen, the lunatic will not accept that any behaviour counts against his blik about murderous dons. Regarding my own (kind of) blik about God's existence – I accept that I may be wrong (which means it may not be a blik at all), although I don't think so (that is its blik-likeness); I do not think that Dawkins et al are right, but I recognise the possibility that they may be. That is the nature of our ambiguous existence: we cannot know such things, either one way or the other, for certain (theologically there is the need for that 'epistemic distance' between God and humanity). I might be criticised by some Christians as somehow lacking in faith, as they could never not believe in God: that is an entirely blik-like position, but at the same time a major misunderstanding of the nature of faith. My own belief in God is blik-like only insofar that I cannot conceive of any situation in which I would believe the contrary (and, occasionally, as an intellectual exercise, I have tried) although, as already noted, even though I cannot conceive that situation doesn't require me to claim that there could never be one (and that is where my blik trembles on the very edge of blikdom). It would differ only in the sense of recognising that because God's existence cannot be proven beyond doubt, then even people of faith should recognise that we may be wrong. Indeed, the whole nature of faith is that it is not based on absolute certainty: if I have faith in my surgeon, it recognises that whilst I trust her to treat me effectively, a whole range of situations might prevent that. If I knew beyond doubt that my surgeon will do everything correctly, then that would not be faith, it would be knowledge.

I am not seeking to imply that Davis, and Christians like him, are lunatics: their view concerning the writing of the Bible is clearly an important article of faith for them, and not at all in the same category as the one who believes that everyone is out to kill him. Furthermore, I simply don't know whether they would continue to hold their blik against any and all evidence to the contrary[68] but, if that *is* the case, then their view would fit with any and every situation, and so asserts nothing. If one believed that God 'superintended' the writing of the biblical text and will accept no shred of evidence against it, then there can literally be no further discussion: that is just the way they see things. Yet I do think that there is considerable evidence (as we shall see below) to suggest that they are wrong: not the least being that if God did superintend or otherwise organise the writing of the scriptures, then he clearly didn't make a very good job of it:

> *"The logic of biblical inerrancy is palpable. If God is omniscient, and if he is the author of the scriptural text, it follows that the text cannot contain mistakes, whether in content or form. If it should be found to contain errors, through some indiscernible will of its author, it remains problematic that an omniscient, omnipotent, and perfectly good being should be content to allow errors to have come into existence in his written work...there is a family resemblance between biblical inerrancy and the problem of evil; both the inerrantist and the theodicist are faced with the dual difficulty of making intellectual sense of the problem, and defending the character and competence of the God in which each believes".[69]*

In other words, it is entirely possible (I think most likely) that Davis and many others are holding a wrong blik concerning the Bible (although not, in my view, about God) and, for a Christian biblical scholar, that – if true – is serious, not least because any exegesis based on a wrong understanding of the nature of the Biblical text is likely also to be wrong. One of the central problems with any *a priori* premise is that if it is unsound (or plain wrong), so too are any arguments which use it for their foundation: if God did not superintend the writing of the scriptures then making the claim that he did so is likely to lead the Biblical exegete down a number of blind, or even destructive, alleys. This may again be demonstrated by the two current controversies which appear to be tearing the Anglican Communion apart: women and homosexuality (particularly this latter). If God has supervised (whatever that means) the writing of the Biblical text, then it is clear that God is both anti-gay sex and also against the ministry of women: for that is the straightforward reading of the OT and Paul. If, however, these are the views of human authors and do not represent 'what God thinks', then those Christians who criticise (or, particularly, demonise) gay Christians and women priests have got it entirely wrong. That, theologically and ecclesiologically, is very serious indeed: if the Church is misreading God's intentions, then it is not following its own vocation to be disciples of Christ, the one who proclaimed a loving and (within the culture of his time) inclusive God. That is why *"it is very important that we have the right blik"* but, by the very nature of bliks (we don't choose our bliks), it is not altogether clear how we can ensure that.

The previous discussion touched on the particular matter of so-called Biblical inerrancy:

"The logic of biblical inerrancy is palpable. If God is omniscient, and if he is the author of the scriptural text, it follows that the text cannot contain mistakes, whether in content or form...".[70]

This represents the claim that the Bible is not only (literally) true, but is incapable of error. Its classic expression is the assertion that the story of the six-day creation in Genesis 1 is an entirely accurate description of the actual processes by which the universe came to be. For those who take such a view, this both contradicts and trumps the findings of modern science and is often the prelude to further claims that, for example, humans walked with dinosaurs (when the scientific view based on empirical evidence is that dinosaurs died out well over 60 million years before humanity began) and that the Earth, rather than being 4.5 billion years old, is probably little more than 6000 years old ('Young Earth Creationism'). Any suggestion that science is right on such matters, and the Bible wrong, cuts to the heart of Biblical authority:

> "...I recall our pastor teaching that, if Genesis 1 wasn't literally true, then 'the whole Bible is a book of lies!' So, as far as I was concerned, my entire faith was leveraged on my ability to survive this class [in evolutionary biology] with my faith in young-earth creationism intact."[71]

As one might expect, there exists a variety of expressions of biblical inerrantism, although all have basically the same thrust - the Bible is true, authoritative and contains no mistakes or contradictions (and should never be questioned[72]):

> "The Bible is the Word of God written; it is the revelation of the truths of God conveyed by inspiration through his servants to us. As such it is infallible and without error...We conceive the Bible to be in actuality the very Word of God...We define inerrancy as meaning 'exempt from error' and infallibility as 'incapable of error'...Such inerrancy and infallibility apply to all of scripture...It is truth" (The Assemblies of God); "The Bible is the only inspired, infallible, and authoritative Word of God" (The Community Bible Church, Montevideo, Minnesota, USA); "God has spoken in the scriptures, both Old and New Testaments, through the words of human authors. As the verbally inspired Word of God, the Bible is without error...the ultimate...to be believed in all that it teaches, obeyed in all that it requires, and trusted in all that it promises" (The Evangelical Free Church of America); "...[the] scriptures of the Old and New Testaments are verbally inspired by God and inerrant...are fully trustworthy and of supreme and final authority

in all they say" (Wheaton College, Illinois, USA).[73]

Although all these quotations come from American sources, they would be echoed by many, if not most, British Christians who identify themselves as Evangelical. The Evangelical Alliance's 'Basis of Faith' does not appear quite so direct and unambiguous as the above: this declares belief in *"the divine inspiration and supreme authority of the Old and New Testament Scriptures, which are the written Word of God – fully trustworthy for faith and conduct".*[74] Although this is a somewhat more measured statement, potentially open to a range of interpretation (what does it mean to 'be inspired', to be "fully trustworthy" etc.?), nevertheless, when pressed, many British Evangelicals would revert to claims similar to those of their American brothers and sisters.

It is of particular interest that Davis claims he is not a Biblical inerrantist, not least when he adds:

> *"...but I do affirm that the Bible is 'infallible', where I understand this to mean something like 'does not mislead us in matters that are crucially related to Christian faith and practice'"*[75]

for he seems now to be contradicting himself. I cannot see any substantial difference between something which is inerrant (doesn't make mistakes; makes no error) and something which is infallible (doesn't make mistakes; doesn't fail): the words are broadly synonymous. Clearly, Davis is using 'infallible' here in a very particular way: something which doesn't "mislead" rather than 'something which isn't wrong' or 'something which is incapable of error'. We might compare the doctrine of papal infallibility, where the Pope is thought to be preserved from the possibility of error

> *"...when in the exercise of his office as shepherd and teacher of all*

> *Christians, in virtue of his supreme apostolic authority, he defines*
> *a doctrine concerning faith and morals to be held by the whole*
> *Church"?*[76]

Here, the issue is more to do with the nature of authority than with doctrinal certainty, although perhaps the same motive is to be found in Davis' writings, except that instead of an authoritative Pope it is the authoritative Bible for which infallibility is claimed. If the Bible were infallible (or supervised by an infallible God), then one would expect not to find any contradictions and inaccuracies within it: but there are many. This is precisely what I mean when I claim that whilst Davis cannot verify his claims, they seem easily falsified. What puzzles me is why anyone should wish to make such a claim in the first place, particularly in light of the many demonstrable contradictions and discrepancies in the text: why does the 'authority' of scripture have to rest on God's 'supervision' of it, rather than recognising its innate, albeit more limited, authority as the valid mode of transmission of God's revelation in Christ (at least the NT)?

Regardless of the pros and cons of this argument, again, Davis' position is entirely subjective, because it is as much a matter of opinion as to what constitutes "*crucial* [matters] related to Christian faith and practice", as is the judgement about what might count as 'misleading' (a vague term in itself): does he mean 'inaccurate' or 'wrong'? But the main reason for describing these views as subjective or blik-like is that there is not a shred of evidence for any of Davis' claims. To take just one example: after Jesus' birth, was he taken to Nazareth or to Egypt? If the answer is 'both' when did that happen and how is it that neither Matthew nor Luke knew of the alternative destination – did God withhold different information from each of them? Further, is this a 'crucial' issue for faith, or not?

Davis describes his position as representing a "hermeneutic of trust" (sometimes contrasted with the somewhat disparaging phrase: 'a hermeneutic of suspicion' as, I imagine, my own approach would be so described) which he summarises as accepting what the Bible says *"unless I find convincing evidence not to do so"*.[77] Again, it is not clear what might constitute such evidence: Davis offers no examples. For Davis this 'trusting' attitude is held by

> *"...those who hold that the NT is reliable [and so] distance themselves from any notion that the NT is just another book like all the others...they take it [specifically, the NT, but probably also the whole Bible] to be the source of religious truth above all other sources, the norm or guide to religious truth above all norms and guides. All others are subordinate to scripture and are to be tested by scripture".*[78]

This somewhat pejorative statement, set alongside the use of the term 'suspicion' (as opposed to 'trust'; Davis does not, here, use the term 'suspicion'), would seem to imply a 'good guys' (those who trust) versus 'bad guys' (those who are suspicious and, by further implication, hold a very 'low' view of the Bible) scenario in Biblical studies; although one hopes that these implications are unintended. Yet it is not altogether clear that those allegedly 'suspicious' interpreters of the Biblical text understand the Bible as being "just a book like all others". For myself, the Bible is both a collection of writings unsurpassed as a record of God's revelation in Christ and, also, normative (although not exhaustive) for "religious truth".

Earlier in his essay Davis terms those who take a position different to his own "NT critics": a surprising designation as one might reasonably have thought of him (as a published NT scholar) in the same way: someone who reads and makes exegetical judgements concerning the biblical texts (because that – despite his implicit denial - is what he is himself doing). But it is clear that he is using all these customary terms both pejoratively and also quite negatively. Yet he states that he himself recognises that *"the Bible contains discrepancies and inconsistencies that I am not able to harmonize sensibly"*.[79] An honest statement, to be sure: but one which raises a number of questions about how he might (for example) reconcile such "discrepancies and inconsistencies" with 'divine supervision' of the text. Furthermore, what has been described by some as 'suspicion' (a term capable of enormous negativity, particularly in a faith context: 'you mean you are suspicious of God?') is actually nothing of the kind: it is merely the scholarly process in which one doesn't just take things for granted, but interrogates such evidence as we have and seeks, honestly, to reach the best conclusion, without pre-judging what that conclusion should be. In other words, if it is 'suspicion', it is both a positive and a wise form of suspicion: perhaps similar to the advice parents give their teenaged children prior to an evening out with friends.

There is a multitude of complex issues raised by Davis' claims, although far too many to rehearse in this study. For example:

"At first sight, fundamentalism is a Bible-believing point of view: 'we are those who believe the Bible'. But this is a more ambiguous position than appears at first sight. It could mean either of two very different things. It could mean: 'we believe the Bible, because the Bible says the things we believe'. Or it could mean: 'we believe the Bible and will follow its guidance, even if it seems to lead far away from the things that we now believe'. I suspect that the former is closer to the normal fundamentalist position. But that former point of view can easily turn into its negative counterpart: 'unless the Bible says the things we believe, then we can't believe it and won't believe it'. The core of the fundamentalist position is the rejection of alternative interpretations, not in every point but in the 'essentials'. But...it is in the 'essentials' that the Bible itself suggests or even demands alternative lines of interpretation."[80]

Even if Davis is not himself an absolute inerrantist (despite asserting the 'infallibility' of the Bible, he does so with some qualifications), the logic of his kind of thinking ultimately leads to a form of 'biblical inerrancy' in which it is believed that the Bible, because it is given by God, is without any fault or error in its teaching:[81] no mistakes and no contradictions, and certainly no confusing linguistic riddles (unless they are obviously such – like Jesus' parables[82]). This approach inevitably impacts on Christian doctrines: if they are 'biblically based' then they must be true (which is why, at the Reformation, Protestant scholars emphasised that the only acceptable doctrines were those which could be clearly found in the Bible). The 4th Evangelist wrote (1: 14) that "the Word became flesh and lived among us..." and, therefore, that is precisely what happened, although how it occurred was, at least to a degree, up for debate; that it occurred was not; it was accepted simply on the basis that 'the Bible says so'. Such a view of Scripture comes close to 'bibliolatry': treating the Bible almost as being itself worthy of worship, not least because it sets the Bible on a pedestal where it is above contradiction, and so never to be questioned.

Nevertheless, even inerrantists are not normally absolute literalists (could there be any such today, for they would presumably have to accept the whole biblical flat earth cosmology?), thus the Chicago Statement on Biblical Inerrancy (Oct 1978) affirmed the *"necessity of interpreting the Bible according to its literal or normal sense"* whilst explaining that this means *"the grammatical historical sense"* and that *"interpretation according to the literal sense will take account of all figures of speech and literary forms found in the text"*. Most recognise that non-literal language is used in the Bible (such as the parables) and that there is no need to go hunting the historical 'Good Samaritan' in the way that some still seek to find the remains of Noah's Ark. Nevertheless, unless the biblical passage is clearly poetic, allegorical (etc.), any statements should be taken literally as expressions of absolute truth. Yet, to take an example already considered: if God did provide an inerrant text, then the writings of Paul would not conflict (as they clearly do) with the accounts about Paul provided by Luke in Acts.

Although they recognise that the Bible does contain some non-literal language yet, due to their conviction that the Bible is God's 'Revelation' (as opposed to being a record or vehicle of that revelation), and because they understand that revelation to have been transmitted in the form of propositions and instructions, such 'inerrantists' at least imply, if not state outright, that God 'speaks' directly to them through the, in the main literal, written word ('the Word of the Lord' – 'what God says': again, often expressed in assertion: 'the Bible says...'). To clarify this distinction: when non-literal language is used in the Biblical text that will be obvious; but if the language appears to be literal (in the form of a straightforward statement or the assertion of a fact such as a special event or a miraculous deed), it is precisely that. Thus the dual assertion that creation took six days and that God created light on the first day is not seen to be at all contradictory even though, without the Sun (created on the 4th day) there could be neither the measurement of days (measured by the Earth's revolution around the Sun), nor the existence of light (the single light source within our solar system). Somewhat paradoxically this may lead some inerrantists to engage in a degree of rationalisation by explaining that the 'days' were not 24 hours in length and-or that God provided a separate light source before the creation of the Sun; some, furthermore, wishing to keep at least a little in step with modern science, might suggest that 'days' refer to geological aeons. Discussing this kind of fundamentalist biblical interpretation, Elizabeth Johnson comments:

> "As a result, adherents of creation science or intelligent design judge evolution to be absolutely contradictory to the revealed word

of God in scripture. Whatever scientists have discovered can be otherwise explained. That a literal approach is not the only way to read the biblical text is roundly ignored."[83]

Leaving aside the foolishness of ignoring the outcomes of modern scholarship: not only Biblical but particularly scientific, there is a multitude of very simple and straightforward examples which demonstrate just how wrong-headed is a fundamentalist-literalist approach to the Bible, and particularly the NT. Consider the following:

1. how did Judas die? suicide by hanging (Mt 27: 5) or falling down and bursting (Acts 1: 18)?
2. who was at the tomb on Easter morning? one young man in white (Mk 16: 5), two men in 'dazzling clothes' (Lk 24: 4), or a 'flying' angel who removed the stone from Jesus' tomb (Mt 28: 2 – 5)?
3. was the site of the resurrection appearances Galilee (Mk/ Mt) or Jerusalem (Lk/Jn) – some 60+ miles apart?
4. where did the Holy Family go after Jesus' birth? back to Nazareth after 40 days (Lk 2: 39) or to Egypt some two years later, only after which to Nazareth, apparently for the first time (Mt 2: 19 – 23)?
5. did Jesus baptise? yes – **Jn** 3: 22; no – **Jn** 4: 2;
6. when was Jesus crucified? after Passover (Synoptics have the Last Supper as the Passover meal) or before Passover (Jn 18: 28; 19: 14)?
7. when did Jesus 'cleanse' the Temple? at the beginning of his ministry (Jn 2: 13 – 22) or in his last week, after the Palm Sunday entry into Jerusalem (all Synoptics)?
8. was the woman whom Jesus commended for her faith Syro-Phoenician (Mk 7: 24) or Canaanite (Mt 15: 22)?
9. compare Matthew's genealogy of Jesus (Mt 1: 1 - 16) with Luke's (Lk 3: 23 - 38); to be more specific e.g. Mt 1: 5

links Salmon the father of Boaz to Rahab, the prostitute from Jericho, even though Rahab predates Salmon by at least a century and neither Israel's Scriptures nor later Jewish literature gives any indication that they formed a pair; and naming Joram the father of Uzziah (1: 8), Mt's genealogy omits three kings and a queen and jumps some 60 years; despite what Mt 1: 11 states, Jechoniah is Josiah's grandson, and so a generation is missing i.e. the genealogy-form is obviously artificial, put together for the theological purpose of showing how Jesus arose via the great heroes of the Jewish faith as related in the Jewish Scriptures but which, in so doing, literally contradicts the information supplied by those very scriptures;

10. when did the disciples receive the Holy Spirit? at Pentecost – 50 days after Easter (Acts 2: 1 - 4) or on Easter Day itself (Jn 20: 22)?

11. on the Damascus Road did Saul's companions hear the voice of the Risen Lord but "saw no-one" (**Acts** 9: 7); or was it the other way round: seeing the light, but not hearing the voice (**Acts** 22: 9)?

12. was Paul authorised in his mission by the Church at Antioch (Acts 15: 22ff) or 'by no human authority' (Galatians 1: 1 – see also 1: 21 – 22, 2: 2 etc.)?

13. did God choose Peter or Paul for the mission to the Gentiles (Acts 15: 7 or Gal 2: 8)?

14. did the dispute in Antioch take place after the council in Jerusalem (Gal 2: 11 – 21) or before it (Acts 15: 1 – 2)?

15. Luke, writing in Acts 8 – 9, describes Saul persecuting the Church and, in particular, travelling to Damascus with letters from the high priest authorising him to bring Christians 'in chains' to Jerusalem; but the high priest (nor the chief priests [9: 14; 26: 12] nor elders [22: 5]) had no authority to make arrests in Damascus, which was in the Roman province of Syria, not Judaea – "*It looks*

*very much as if **Luke has exaggerated** the effects of Paul's persecution of Christians, in order to emphasise his dramatic change of heart"*;[84]

16. compare and contrast the accounts of Jesus' ascension, both written by the same author, in Lk 24: 50 – end and Acts 1: 6 – 11: why do they differ to such a degree?

None of the above examples is a 'figure of speech': all deal with alleged literal, "normal" or historical 'facts' (although many are clearly no such thing); and yet each comparator clearly differs from, or even contradicts, its opposite number (and the argument, for example, that Jesus cleansed the Temple twice is hardly compelling – nor is that, as with the words from the Cross, what the individual Gospels actually tell us). Similar examples are plentiful in the OT as well: were animals created before humans or vice versa? (Gen 1: 24 – 27; Gen 2: 4b – 21). It cannot be 'both-and' ('God created some animals before humans' – again: that is not what it says), and I am often amazed at the extent to which self-designated 'Bible-believing Christians' manipulate the Biblical text in order to try and prove their point: as we have seen in the conflation of the two birth narratives and the often blind refusal to see just how different and contradictory they are. There are many other examples, at once both obvious and trivial, to which we might point: as the Bible relates only the 'creation' of Adam and Eve, and the subsequent birth of Cain and Abel, where did 'Mrs Cain' come from (Gen 4: 17[85]) and why did Cain build a "city" just for himself, 'Mrs Cain' and baby Enoch (and where did Enoch's wife come from...)? As in one of Spencer Tracy's immortal lines in 'Inherit the Wind': God must have done some "morecreating in the next county" unknown to the Biblical authors. More substantial examples include the obvious fact that the author of 1 & 2 Chronicles thoroughly rewrote and reinterpreted the traditions found in Samuel and Kings, and that the content of Exodus and Numbers was completely reshaped in

Deuteronomy. If God had really 'superintended the writing of the texts' and had done so in an efficient manner, then why were these rewrites necessary?

The most obvious answer is that the rewriting and re-editing was the work of later authors (also amending many of the Prophetic oracles[86]) who were somehow dissatisfied with what they had found – perhaps the theological, political or ideological agendas – of the earlier texts, just as Luke and Matthew were to redact, reshape and supplement the material in Mark's Gospel. As for the historicity of the OT: renowned British scholar, Philip Davies, having surveyed the debate over what became known as 'Biblical Archaeology' (the specifically Christian attempt to find archaeological 'proof' for the Biblical narrative, leading to the twin claim (i) that the Bible is historically true and (ii) that archaeology had 'proven the Bible right'[87]), writes:

*"**Neither statement is true**, however much some wish it to be. Scholarly and popular views of the history of 'ancient Israel' are still strongly divergent...[For example] the Exodus, though a central episode of biblical history, has never been amenable to plausible archaeological confirmation...**[The Biblical story] can no longer be relied upon as a secure framework for any kind of history**...We can no longer simply discuss 'what really happened' in the history of 'ancient Israel'. We are now aware that we need to consider what we mean by a 'history' and what we count as 'Israel'...[Davies concludes: the overriding principle is that] biblical texts betray the history of the [relatively late] period of their production...[although this]does not in itself rule out the historicity of any particular biblical event or figure...it does insist that unless we have evidence other than a biblical story [i.e. archaeological or external literary evidence], we cannot accept any claim for historicity, because in themselves, the narratives do not prove anything about their contents; what they do constitute is evidence of themselves, as stories once told, and the historian's first*

question is: why was this story told, and what does this story tell us about its writers and hearers or readers? "[88]

Yet for those who share Stephen Davis' *a priori* claim, no amount of argument will encourage them to reconsider their view of the Bible, because it is a 'faith' position immune (or thought to be immune) to rational argument: just like a blik.

"I have heard fundamentalists say, 'Show me one mistake in the Bible and I will throw out the whole thing'...[but] the truth of the Christian message hinges not on the inerrancy of Scripture or on our ability to harmonise the four Gospels but on the resurrection of Jesus. And the historical reliability of the Gospels does not hinge on the inerrancy of Scripture or on proof that no mistake of any kind can be detected in them".[89]

As a result of such beliefs, stories clearly not intended to be so interpreted (like the six-day creation of Genesis 1, the writing of which greatly post-dates the Adamic saga of Gen. 2 and 3), are often taken literally and the Gospel accounts of Jesus' resurrection are understood to be literal descriptions of a corpse 'coming to life again' (purely 'physical'): a view not supported, as Biblical scholar Morna Hooker notes,[90] by the broader biblical witness, particularly that of Paul. Then, again, did God really 'come down' to the earthly Garden of Eden in order to enjoy the evening breeze (Gen 3: 8), or are we here presented with a very anthropomorphised God (in 'human shape') within the context of an ancient myth: a made-up 'symbol-story' which seeks to express truth in non-literal and often dramatic ways?

As a result of this obsession with literality, many Christians tend not to recognise, even as a possibility, that God's revelation may be more historical (via events) or experiential (via people) than it is (at all) propositional (ideas and assertions); nor that God, valuing human freedom, may wish to inspire (encourage, 'nudge', release insights) authors of the scriptural text in a rather more nuanced and subtle manner than as Davis describes it: 'supervising' the writing process so that the writers only write what God desires to be written. That is why, taking again those two current controversies within the world-wide Church: attitudes to women and to homosexuality, the fundamentally different ways in which Scripture is understood are almost bound to drive Christians into opposing camps: one set who wish to take what is said literally as God's mandate for all time, and others who wish to use critical tools in order to interpret what is being written: judging, for example, the positions taken by some Biblical authors to be a reflection of their own cultural norms and prejudices, or perhaps privileging the 'larger picture' over the detail, so that the imperative to love and faithfulness in relationships 'trumps' any specific prohibition of particular kinds of sexual activity.

This alternative non-propositional, non-inerrant under-standing, both of the nature of Revelation and the nature and purpose of the Bible, views the Scriptures as entirely human constructions, reflecting the faith and beliefs of those who wrote them (this is the meaning of 'God-breathed': the authors were people of faith inspired by and writing to and for that faith, guided by an always 'light-touch' Holy Spirit[91]), but also as writings which have 'captured' and recorded, yet neither exhaustively nor infallibly, the experience of the first followers of Jesus, who was himself the Revelation of God.

For example, the 'experience' of Jesus' resurrection, being itself (presumably) numinous and mysterious, was transmitted orally via the tradition (that which is 'handed down' – the same Greek word is used to describe how Jesus was 'handed over' for crucifixion) and was written down, firstly by Paul (who also included a brief reference to his own experience of the Risen Christ), and considerably later (40 – 70 years after Jesus' death) by the Evangelists, none of whom were witnesses to that original revelation (the so-called 'Resurrection appearances'). Whatever the actual nature of the experience of the Risen Christ for those who originally had it, the way in which it was transmitted underwent a process during which it was gradually and necessarily rendered more comprehensible to those who hadn't themselves experienced it. The so-called resurrection 'appearances' became increasingly reified (Lat. *res*: 'thing', so 'thingified'[92]), perhaps because that was the most straightforward and the most understandable way of expressing a fundamentally inexpressible experience, and-or because that was the manner in which those Jews who believed in resurrection expected it to come about, and probably for whom the greatest problem was that it was the resurrection of an individual, rather than that of the whole people. What was originally an experience (at least according to Paul's own account[93] and by its very nature as relating to a post-mortem state) of an entirely spiritual 'event', 'hardened' into much more of a semi-physical event (Paul seems to have been unaware of the empty tomb tradition which may well have emerged as an aetiology for the resurrection appearances), albeit with some strange ambiguities and contradictions (so Jesus' resurrection body could both not be touched and touched: Jn 20: 17, 27).

In other words, we should take care to realise that there is not only a distinction to be made between literal and non-literal language but, as signalled earlier, another which must be made between an actual experience and the way in which that experience is transmitted to and received by others. It is even possible that the original experience (if numinous) is such that it cannot easily be shared with others. It is extraordinarily puzzling that Paul himself never actually describes his experience of the Risen Lord in any detail, but says only that he had one, offering no clue as to its nature: light (as in Acts), person (as in the Gospel accounts), or anything else. One might have thought that this first-hand experience of a 'resurrection appearance' – something that Paul claims was in the same category as the experiences of others and which *on that basis* gave him the right to be named an Apostle[94] – would be so important, exciting and life-enhancing that he would want to tell people all about it: 'what I saw/heard was this'. Paul is the only eye-witness in Scripture to the Risen Christ, and yet he tells us virtually nothing about what is surely the greatest of God's acts.

Indeed, in all his correspondence with the churches, he mentions it only in 1 Corinthians and Galatians. Why is that? Perhaps it was just too personal? Or the experience was so profound and of such a kind that it was impossible to describe to others? To take a somewhat different example: although the Bible often shows God speaking to people in an apparently normal way, we may imagine that divine communication is rather more subtle than that, and that the only reason the Biblical authors use ordinary language to describe it is because that is the only language we have. When, for example, God tells Moses his name: 'I am' (Ex 3: 14),[95] we may imagine that the insight, however it was originally communicated and received, and the ideas which were later built on it, are the outcomes of a human mind reflecting on and seeking to communicate a particular experience of the Divine. The only alternative is to believe (as some certainly do) that Moses (and many others among the prophets) had straightforward conversations with God, exactly the same as with anyone else,[96] perhaps hearing a voice echoing from the clouds, rather than discerning the communication of God's will through some kind of extra-sensory (beyond our senses) 'ineffable' spiritual experience. It is the very human language of the Bible used in very human ways which enables these important spiritual experiences and insights to be expressed in a more comprehensible manner: if the language were other than human, we could not understand it.

Precisely the same kind of distinction is true for the development of Christology: that between the reality in and of itself, and the way in which that reality is understood, represented or expressed, although not, in this case, an event to be transmitted. This 'truth' about Christ is not open to our knowledge and understanding in the same way that an event may be, not least because a person is always more complex than an event. So our Christology is better represented as the way in which we come to understand a person - Jesus Christ – and any attempt to do so requires careful and appropriate expression so as to open up something of the truth about the reality that was (and is) Jesus Christ. However, the way in which our understanding is expressed is not in or of itself 'the Truth', and to think that it is, is to make a fundamental mistake about the nature of the language and concepts being used. Rather it is our best effort (using the language and ideas available at the time) at shedding some light on that truth which, actually for any person (let alone Jesus), is fundamentally mysterious (in the best sense of that word). Who can fully understand another person? Who can fully understand God? To state that Jesus Christ is 'of the same substance' as Father God is an expression of our faith and his significance for us, and not itself an unchallengeable truth or 'fact'. It is what we choose (or not) to believe; it is a way of trying to understand that relationship which existed between Jesus and his Father God and, like any model, it will be more or less helpful. That is why the expression of the Resurrection in the Biblical texts is so opaque; that is why we need to distinguish carefully the experience itself from the way in which it is portrayed. There will always be a 'reality' gap between the two; just as there is a similar gap between scripture and what it seeks to capture in the stories it tells and the language it uses. There is no univocal identity between the two.

The fundamental mistake in Christology (what we have to say about Christ) or Theology (what we have to say about God), just as it is for our understanding of Scripture, is when what we assume, or what we come to believe, is itself thought to be the 'actuality' or 'reality': that what is described is what there is. This is the inevitable outcome of placing all our eggs in the 'literal basket', particularly well exemplified by the conceptual 'mess' we often find ourselves in when thinking of the Trinity (God as Committee). The truth is not so much that Christ is this, or Christ is that, but (i) God is beyond anything we can conceive and even our best ways of expressing what we believe about him are mere shadows of the truth (or may even be downright wrong); (ii) that Jesus' relationship with God is properly known and understood only by Jesus and God, although we are invited to share in that relationship. All we can do is find ways of presenting and expressing those insights which are not, in themselves, 'The Truth', but are ways in and through which we can begin to understand something of what the reality is, and be helped in our faith by that understanding. Once, for whatever reason, those ways become redundant (my claim is that the classic doctrinal formulations fall into this category), they fail to do their job and should be replaced by alternatives which might have more of a chance when contextualised in a culture that is not so ancient and so foreign.

The True Nature of Revelation

We have so far examined two distinctions which we need to make when considering the text of the Bible: that between literal and non-literal language (the ability to 'play the correct language game') and that between an event or person which is the subject of our enquiry, and the manner in which our understanding of that is expressed in literary or verbal form. In purely theological terms, undergirding both is a third and more fundamental distinction: that between (i) the 'primordial' or 'classic' (original) revelation and (ii) the later transmission or verbal expression of that revelation: they are not the same thing. The Bible is not itself Revelation, and the fundamental error made by inerrantists and other 'conservative' ('Bible-believing') Christians is to make that assumption which, as we have seen, gets them into all kinds of (ir)rational fixes. The Revelation (which was actual, but not directly to us, and cannot be accessed directly by us) is somehow 'contained within', and is then transmitted via the Scriptures (the medium of Revelation) to later generations who are, thereby, enabled to share in that revelation, and only then, having responded to it, make it their own.

For Macquarrie revelation is the

> "...primary source of theology...what is disclosed in revelation is then dimension of the holy...it is as if the holy breaks in and the movement is from beyond man [sic] toward man...Because of its gift-like character, revelation is of a different order from our ordinary matter-of-fact knowing of the world...A community of faith...usually traces its history back to what may be called a 'classic' or 'primordial' revelation. This classic revelation, a definite disclosure experience of the holy granted to the founder or founders of the community becomes as it were the paradigm for experiences of the holy in that community...Yet only because the primordial revelation is continually renewed in present experience can it be revelation for us, and not just fossilised revelation...".[97]

On the other hand:

> "**Scripture is not itself revelation**, but it is one important way (not the only one) by which the community of faith keeps open its access to that primordial revelation on which the community has been founded. The scriptures do not indeed automatically lay this revelation before us but, in conjunction with a present experience of the holy in the community of faith, the scriptures come alive, so to speak, and renew for us the disclosure of the holy which was the content of the primordial revelation. This power of bringing again or re-presenting the disclosure of the primordial revelation so that it speaks to us in our present experience is what is meant when

we talk of the 'inspiration' of scripture. Such inspiration does not lie in the words (it is not 'verbal inspiration'), but belongs to the scriptures only as they are set in the context of the whole life of faith in the community".[98]

Understood this way, the 'content' of Revelation does not consist of assertions, rules and regulations (although the latter may be implied: if God is love, then clearly love is paramount in human relationships), but consists of nothing other than God himself: God-in-Christ reveals God ("the dimension of the Holy"). Scripture provides the record of the impact of that revelation, in the manner Christians affirm: God's self-revelation came in and through and was mediated by the life of Christ. Revelation is a person and not a book; but it is the book which is able to mediate the personal and classic-primordial revelation to those beyond that first generation who didn't actually experience it first-hand. To take this view is hardly to regard scripture as being like "any other book": it is the precious record (the only one we have) of how God came to us in Christ; it is still, despite approaching it with some degree of critical 'suspicion' (for surely the alternative is to base its interpretation not on evidence, but rather on one's subjective blik: 'what I choose to believe'?) genuinely (to use Davis' words) *"the source of religious truth above all other sources, the norm or guide to religious truth above all norms and guides"*; at least, for Christians: those of other Faiths will have their own equally valued sources and there really is no need for any competition between them.

What is Revealed is God; Jesus Christ is not himself the content of the Revelation: rather, acting on behalf of God, Jesus Christ is the vehicle (the Revealer) of the Christian Revelation, just as Scripture is the vehicle for further transmitting that Primordial Revelation to those people and places which were not direct recipients of it: that Revelation was of God and it was Revealed in and through Christ. It is the continued use of scripture both liturgically and privately which enables the original revelation, which occurred at a particular point in time and space, to be available both worldwide (not simply in that place) and throughout the ages (not simply at that time), via the community which the Revelation established – the Church. There is no reason (except an excessive bibliolatry) to suppose that God's revelation doesn't continue in some fashion (most likely fallible) through the Church as 'the extension of the Incarnation', and possibly elsewhere as well. This latter, continuing revelation is not the primordial one, but is built on the basis of that primordial revelation, which it apprehends and develops. Furthermore, the revelation is not glaringly obvious (certainly not so obvious as a list of instructions); neither is it automatically laid before us: it requires appropriation, and then interpretation. Some may not recognise it, and thus reject it; for others it provides the meaning for their lives.

Those who focus God's revelation entirely on and in the Bible itself, would not accept this latter analysis: for them the Reformation cry 'sola scriptura' is all. Scripture is revelation; revelation is scripture; and if that is the case, then – guided by the Holy Spirit - it must necessarily be 'true' (Jn 16: 13) and, more to the point, true in that form; literally correct in every detail. Any who can't see that must be blind fools. For those who take this view, any act of 'interpretation' is actually unnecessary: what you read is the whole meaning, clear and uncluttered; only those who cannot see what is staring them in the face need or search for 'interpretation': 'you want to interpret it; I just read it as it is' (I have been told this on more than one occasion). Such a view fails to recognise that to make the judgement that 'scripture is revelation' is itself an act of interpretation.

But there is a much more important issue than whether or not certain Biblical narratives correctly represent 'what happened', which applies particularly, but hardly exclusively, to some of the earlier stories to be found in the Jewish Scriptures, venerated by Christians as the 'Old Testament' and so as presenting 'God's Truth'. If the earlier 'test' is an historical one, this latter is a moral one. How are we meant to treat those stories which appear to show God acting immorally? As we have already noted, there are several occasions when God is shown to be blatantly blood thirsty, instructing his people to maim and kill indiscriminately (cf. the Books of Joshua and Judges), and the Book of Revelation is hardly for the faint-hearted.[99] But perhaps even worse are those narratives which themselves form a central part of the Hebrew religious tradition, some of which continue to be taught to primary school children as 'great Bible stories' by teachers who have clearly given no consideration to their moral implications. We will briefly consider just two:

Noah's Ark: God's original creation, judged as "very good" at its inception, has failed; people (and apparently, by implication, also "the animals and creeping things and the birds of the air"; Gen 6: 7) have become 'wicked', 'evil', 'corrupt' and 'violent' (Gen 6: 5, 11 – 12); so God resolves to end it all and start again; as noted above, God, being God, could do so in the same manner as he had created – by his Spoken Word ('let there *not* be...'); but no: he decides to drown everyone except Noah and his family (it would be interesting to know just how the fish and other sea creatures died: an obvious and rational question);

The Exodus – the great 'salvation event' of the Jews, the centre point around which the Jewish Scriptures 'orbit': begins with promise as God commissions Moses to go and ask Pharaoh (nicely?) to 'let my people go'; but we immediately find the sting in the tail: God already knows that Pharaoh will refuse (Ex 3: 19) and so while God appears ready to 'perform wonders' in order to convince him, it soon becomes clear he actually has no intention of allowing the 'wonders' to have their apparently desired effect, because he tells Moses that he will 'harden Pharaoh's heart' (Ex 4: 21); so, one might ask: what actually is the purpose of the great wonders, except to allow 'God' to show off? the plagues then get progressively worse causing great pain and suffering amongst the ordinary people of Egypt, culminating in the death of the (totally innocent) Egyptian first-born, and all this whilst God himself[100] actively prevents Pharaoh from granting Moses' requests – presumably because if Pharaoh did so, the plagues would have to stop, and the overall effect would be spoiled! God is presented here as the 'cat' playing with the 'mouse'.

If weirdness may be considered yet another reasonable criterion for not accepting such stories as 'God's (literal) Truth', then what are we to make of the, probably little noticed, insertion in the Moses saga of Ex 4: 24 – 26,[101] in which it would appear that God actually tries to kill Moses, but is tricked out of doing so by Moses' wife, who circumcises her son and touches Moses' feet with the foreskin: "So he (God?) let him (Moses?) alone"; because he was put off by his feet being touched by a foreskin; and how can God be tricked?[102] Furthermore, why would God want to kill Moses who was on his way to do God's bidding?[103] How can any Christian treat such utterly immoral and, indeed, foolish tales as representative of the way that God acts? Surely, such people must ask: is there not another way of understanding these stories? And, of course, there are many such ways.

Having cleared the ground in such a way as to demonstrate that language is a complex phenomenon and ancient Scriptural language particularly so, both requiring and repaying careful interpretation; and further that so-called 'biblical history' is quite different both in intention and methodology from the modern 'critical' and evidence-based discipline (*"Most indications suggest that the biblical texts do not...convey a high quality of historical knowledge about the events they describe."*[104]), we are now in a better position to lay some biblical foundations which might not just permit, but even demand the production of a reformulated Christology.

Notes

1. Macquarrie J 'Principles' pp. 118 ff;
2. An analogy is a literary device which recognises similarities between the features of two things so that one may illuminate the meaning of the other, particularly when the characteristics of the one are better understood than those of the other; technically there are two **analogates** which may in many respects differ widely from each other; the **prime analogate** possesses the characteristic (the **analogue**) predicated of it in a 'formal' manner i.e. in a 'univocal' (proper/actual) sense; the **secondary analogate** has predicated of it a 'like' characteristic which is relative or derivative or 'virtual';
3. Gilbert Ryle (1900 – 1976): (1957) 'The Revolution in Philosophy' p. 8;
4. Written whilst Wittgenstein served as an Austrian soldier during the First World War and completed as an Italian POW; published in1921 (first Eng.Tr. Ogden CK & Ramsey FP, 1922);
5. Wittgenstein L (1958 ed. ET Anscombe GEM) 'Philosophical Investigations' para. 124;
6. ibid. para 8;
7. ibid. para. 38;
8. Explored in his posthumously published 'Philosophical Investigations' (1953);
9. Wittgenstein actually uses this latter term only five times in 'Philosophical Investigations';
10. A scholarly debate was conducted in the 1950s via the pages of the Oxford journal 'University' in the form of successive parables told by three philosophers (reprinted in a famous and significant book regarding the impact of the so-called verification debate on religious language: 'New Essays in Philosophical Theology' [1955]): the parables are: 'The Two Explorers' (orig. John Wisdom, 1944; Antony Flew 1950);

'The Lunatic with a Blik about Dons' (Richard Hare, 1951); 'The Resistance Fighter and the Stranger' (Basil Mitchell, 1951); because Flew begins by focusing on the notion of falsification (what does it take for any assertion to be rejected because evidence seems to demonstrate that it is wrong), this is sometimes called the 'falsification debate'; Flew complained that religious people never seem willing to say what would count against their beliefs, not even the painful death of a loved child (how can a loving God allow this to happen? '...oh well, it must be because...' i.e. what human experience would it take to deny God?); even if we accept that a religious belief is difficult to verify/prove, surely it ought to be open to falsification - you ought to be able to say what would/could/might count against it; as a result, explained Flew, those religious claims which do not allow anything to count against them are simply nonsense; Hare and Mitchell (and later, Hick in his parable of the 'The Road to the Celestial City' to be found in his [1957] 'Faith and Knowledge', where he suggests that verification may reasonably be eschatological: after death) took up the challenge in most interesting and enlightening ways; Richard Hare's particular contribution was to use the term 'blik' to express the unverifiable and unfalsifiable ways people 'view' the world, but which still make a great difference to the way they live their lives i.e. their beliefs may seem odd to some, but cannot be dismissed as 'nonsense';

11. The 'Sea of Faith' Network is named from a TV Series and accompanying book 'The Sea of Faith' (1984), which followed the seminal 'Taking Leave of God' (1980), both by Don Cupitt who, until his retirement was Dean of Emmanuel College Cambridge; Cupitt's position is quite difficult to pin down (not least because it seems to change subtly with each, virtually annual, book), but he has occasionally described

himself as a 'Christian Buddhist' (Therevada Buddhism, as opposed to Mahayana Buddhism, is atheistic);

12. Displaying such subtlety as to make them quite indignant when they are compared to Richard Dawkins et al; the philosopher Jeffrey Stout memorably called non-realism 'atheism in drag'!

13. 'God in Us: A Case for Christian Humanism' (1993), p. 25;

14. 'The Thoughtful Guide to Faith' (2004), pp. 15 – 17;

15. Here, 'God' represents our various conceptions of the Divine, which may be more or less true; God (without the inverted commas) is what God is – the Reality which is, in an important sense, beyond our ability to conceive;

16. "...non-realist faith is not Christian faith at all...To the extent that this language denotes a conscious taking leave of the historic church and its faith, Cupitt and fellow Anglican members of the Sea of Faith who subscribe to these views should have the courage of their convictions, leave the Church of England, and establish a new 'church'. If instead they think that they are reforming the church by jettisoning the content of the faith whilst retaining its form, those Bishops who refuse to ordain or to license members of Sea of Faith must be judged to have upheld the discipline and guarded the faith of the church": Andrew Moore (2003) 'Realism and Christian Faith: God, Grammar and Meaning' pp. 112 – 113;

17. A situation similar to the presence of Gnostics (those docetic Christians who believed that salvation came via knowledge: *gnosis*) in the early Church: "One of the striking features of Christian Gnosticism is that it appears to have operated principally from within existing Christian churches, that Gnostics considered themselves to be the spiritual elite of these churches, who could confess the creeds of other Christians, read the Scriptures of other Christians, partake of baptism and Eucharist with other Christians, but who

also believed that they had a deeper, more spiritual understanding of these creeds, Scripture and sacraments. This may well be why proto-orthodox church fathers found them so insidious and difficult to deal with...Gnostics were not 'out there' forming their own communities. The Gnostics were 'in here', with us, in our midst. And you couldn't tell one simply by looking" Foster P. (ed. 2008) 'The Non-Canonical Gospels' p. 126;

18. A 2014 'YouGov' survey of Anglican priests found that 83% of clergy questioned believed in "a personal God" (so, presumably, 17% do not); 2% said they were not sure if God were any more than a "human construct"; 3% said they believed in "some kind of spirit or life force"; reported in 'ThirdWay' (Dec '14/Jan '15) p. 5; the article went on to claim that "Clergy were significantly more likely to hold unorthodox beliefs they older they were and the longer they had been in ministry"; the Revd David Patterson (a retired priest) was reported as saying that "there is no conflict in preaching while being unable to believe in a personal God" and that, within his congregation, he would "take the line that how you feel about God is not in the least dependent on whether you think God exists or not. I preach using God's terminology, but never with the suggestion that God actually exists...Once you have accepted that religion is a human creation, then it is like art and literature and things like that. They are an extremely valuable way to understand yourself";

19. The OED defines 'theory' (Gk *theoria*) as "a supposition or system of ideas explaining something" or "a speculative view" or "the sphere of abstract knowledge or speculative thought" or "the exposition of the principles of a science etc." – all of which imply a view, speculative or otherwise, which explains in univocal/literal terms how something works; a theory is either completely/partially right or wrong

e.g. theories of evolution, gravitation, relativity etc. etc.; there is a univocal (1 to 1) relationship/correlation between theory and 'fact' or 'reality'; they are denotative; a '**model**' is a "representation", a "simplified description of a system" – in other words not a precise 'factual description': "One of the functions of models in science is to suggest theories which correlate patterns in observational data [however] one of the functions of models in religion...is to suggest beliefs which correlate patterns in human experience... religious models are analogical...[they are also] extensible and unitary...Ultimate interpretive models...are organising images which restructure one's perception of the world... [and] help to integrate the interpretation of diverse areas of experience" (Barbour I, 1974, 'Myths, Models and Paradigms' pp. 49 – 50);

20. However, predicted outcomes have changed and are still debated, in particular Heisenberg's failed unified field theory; some physicists now say that Einstein's relativity may have limits and will someday have to be revised; that is the nature of theories;

21. It was as late as the 1980s that the theory that planets existed only in our solar system was proven wrong; we are now aware of the existence of millions of planets orbiting stars, some apparently quite Earthlike hence reinforcing the possibility that life is to be found elsewhere in the universe;

22. Since the beginning of the 20th Century some 50 heresy trials and similar disciplinary actions (both informal and formal) have been held; as noted, Anthony Freeman was removed from his post by the Bishop of Chichester in 1994; other recent cases include Andrew Furlong (Church of Ireland, 2002), Thorkild Grosboll (Church of Denmark, 2003 – 2006) and Jon Sobrino (RC, 2007);

23. A God who can suffer or change; as opposed to the traditional idea of an impassible God who could do neither;

24. There were seven essayists; 'Church Times' review article by David Edwards, 1/7/77, p. 11, 13; the Leader article in the same edition was headed: "Sowing fresh seeds of doubt" (p. 10), thus underscoring the calumny that any who engage in new theological exploration must inevitably be 'doubters': true believers never touch new ideas!

25. It is difficult to judge which was the worse book: only Maurice Wiles, among the contributors to 'Myth' bothered to explain what a myth was, whilst choosing 'truth' as an antonym for myth indicates that the essayists of the latter volume didn't themselves understand the nature of myth; 1977 was obviously the year for tilting at theological windmills;

26. 'Church Times' review article again by David Edwards, 19/8/77, p. 9; one can see from the review's publication date how swiftly the riposte was rushed into print;

27. 'Global Anglican Future Conference'; in January 2016 "GAFCON Primates travelled to England **in the hope that godly faith and order could be restored through renewed obedience to the Bible**": Joint Statement by the Chairman of GAFCON The Most Revd Dr Eliud Wabukala and General Secretary The Most Revd Dr Peter Jensen; www. gafcon.org/january-2016/ accessed 2/5/16; we may note that the referent for "renewed obedience" is the Bible, not God;

28. Anonymised quotation from letters to Crossan cited (including the upper case words) in Crossan JD & Watts RG (1996) 'Who is Jesus?' p. 8;

29. ibid. p. 9;

30. ibid. p. 134;

31. Enns P (2016) 'The Sin of Certainty' p. 3;

32. ibid. pp. 3 – 4;

33. ibid. p. 9;

34. An entirely appropriate liturgical and theological acclamation, and properly expressive of the resurrection

hope, so long as we understand that Jesus is not 'alive' in the usual common usage of the word; occasionally the phrase 'more alive than ever before' is used to convey the difference;

35. We explore the existential dimension in Chapter 7;

36. As we have already noted: John Hick has proposed ('Faith and Knowledge', 1957) the notion of 'eschatological verification' expressed through his parable: 'the Journey to the Celestial City' pp. 176ff.; that there are some things which are unverifiable in this life, but may in principle be verifiable after death (such as the existence of God); two men are on a journey, one believes that it leads to the Celestial City, the other believes it is going nowhere in particular, but is happy to 'be along for the ride'; "...when they turn the last corner it will be apparent that one of them has been right all the time and the other wrong" p. 177; of course, if there is no God then there is unlikely (but not certainly so) to be a post-mortem state!

37. Boyd GA (2013) 'Benefit of the Doubt: Breaking the Idol of Certainty' pp. 14, 16;

38. Whilst *'ousia'* is normally translated as 'substance' (*'homoousios'* 'the same substance' at Nicaea), the terms, in Christian discourse, have been used interchangeably with 'being' (or 'Being'), as in the modern version of the Nicene Creed: "...of one Being with the Father..." and using both terms together in the BCP version: "...being of one substance with the Father...";

39. Macquarrie 'Principles' pp. 199 – 200;

40. Historians may well take seriously the public perception of an 'Angel (or Angels) of Mons' who was thought to have protected outnumbered British troops in Aug 1914, and seek to understand how such a perception arose; but none is likely to take the idea itself seriously as a historical 'fact' explaining the British victory;

41. Although the precise motives for Gavrilo Princip killing the Archduke might be disputed, his responsibility for doing so would not, because the evidence is so strong;

42. Diski J (2010) 'The Sixties' p. 1;

43. For example, why did Matthew alter Mark's account of the Syrophoenician woman so extensively (as he does again with e.g. the Caesarea Philippi pericope, where Luke follows Mark quite closely, but Matthew adds clearly important ecclesiological discussion Mt 16: 17 - 19), when he hardly changed anything at all in his retelling of the call of the first disciples (Mk 1: 16 – 20; Mt 4: 18 – 22) or the basic version (Matthew inserts his account of Peter trying to emulate Jesus within the Marcan framework) of the story of Jesus walking on water (Mk 6: 45 – 52; Mt 14: 22 – 33)? it is understandable that Matthew or Luke might wish to add detail to Mark when the latter's account is quite bare e.g. the way Matthew and Luke augment Mark's account of the Temptations of Jesus (Mk 1: 12 – 13; Mt 4:: 1 – 11; Lk 4: 1 – 3), although they do so slightly differently; just as Luke adds an important dimension, not to be found in either Mark or Matthew, into his account of Jesus' visit to the Nazareth synagogue (Lk 4: 16 – 30); in fact, it is also noteworthy that there are some occasions when Mark's account is the more extensive (e.g. Mark's account of the healing of the paralytic 2: 1 – 12) showing that both Matthew and Luke were prepared to edit down as well as up;

44. See e.g. Evans CA (2014) 'From Jesus to Church' (henceforth 'From');

45. That idea is anathema to many Christians, who take the view that Jesus must always be right and any apparent change of mind is obviously something he was planning to do all along; despite the fact that in the OT even God himself is sometimes portrayed as changing his mind e.g. Exodus 32: 14; Jonah 3: 10;

46. Evans CA 'From' p. 18;

47. Although Jesus was crucified by the Romans, and under Roman authority, the four Evangelists go to great lengths to blame the Jewish leaders and a (Jewish) crowd stirred up by them, and not the Romans themselves; history suggests that Pilate was a strong and ruthless (and surprisingly long-lasting) Governor/Prefect of Judaea (that kind of strength was needed due to sporadic unrest), and that he would have needed no encouragement to execute someone who presented (or even seemed to present) a political challenge; nevertheless, the Evangelists present a Pilate who was not only reluctant to kill Jesus, but who seemed to express sympathy for and interest in him; so in **Mark** 15: 2 Pilate goes so far as to ask Jesus whether he really is King of the Jews (the title had officially died with Herod the Great in 4 BCE, but revived by Emperor Claudius for Herod Agrippa I in 41 CE), and further, in v. 9, asks the crowds (referencing the historically doubtful tradition of releasing a prisoner at Passover time), whether he should release 'the King of the Jews' or the criminal, Barabbas (implying that Pilate thought the choice a 'no-brainer'); Mk 15: 15 informs us that the only reason Pilate eventually acquiesced in Jesus' execution was to "satisfy the crowd" which in reality, had he wished, could easily have been dispersed by the troops, numerically enhanced as they would have been at the potentially troublesome Passover time; Pilate even placed an inscription on the cross naming Jesus 'King of the Jews' (which, had the Emperor known, would have been enough to award Pilate himself the death penalty); **Luke** amplifies this same tendency by having Pilate say explicitly that he found no basis for any accusation against Jesus (Lk 23: 4, 14 - 15) and, in offering the choice with Barabbas, Luke has Pilate actually "wanting to release Jesus" (v. 20), and "a third time" asking "what evil has he done" (v. 22);

furthermore, the whole Lucan narrative from Jesus being "handed over" to the crucifixion itself (25: 15 – 38) might be thought to imply that it was someone other than the Romans to whom Jesus was handed over and who led him to crucifixion, as soldiers are mentioned only once (v. 36); **Matthew**, too, shares this approach, emphasising further that Pilate realised that the Jewish authorities had only brought Jesus to him "out of jealousy" (27: 18) and adding the brief pericope about Pilate's wife (v. 19) and her troubled dream about this (again) "innocent man"; and after Pilate 'washes his hands' of the whole business, Matthew again emphasises the culpability of the whole Jewish people who voluntarily take on the sole responsibility (together with their children) for Jesus' death (v. 25); in the **Johannine** narrative (18: 28 – 38), there is an extended conversation between Jesus and an obviously interested (and, in Mark's view – 15:5, even 'amazed') Pilate, during which Pilate tries to make the Jewish authorities deal with the matter themselves and then, after examining Jesus, finding "no case against him" (18: 38, repeated 19: 4 and 6); Pilate then only agrees to execute Jesus because he was afraid (19: 8), and, after trying to release him, finally succumbs to the 'blackmail' threat that releasing Jesus would 'set him against the Emperor' (19: 12); even at the end, Pilate asks "the Jews" whether he should crucify their King (19: 15); so **the whole thrust of the Gospel narrative is to exonerate Pilate from any responsibility** for Jesus' death and **place that on the Jews** – both leaders and people (and, incidentally, providing some rationale for the various periods of anti-Semitism in Christian history, on the basis that the Jews, not the Romans, were 'Christ-killers'); so even though there are aspects of the Christian narrative seeking to subvert imperial claims (Christ, not the Emperor is the real Saviour), yet still, in a world in which the Romans ruled with an iron fist, and particularly after the abortive Jewish War, it was felt important by the emerging Christian Church not to antagonise the Romans too much by blaming them for Jesus' death, when the Jews (as ever?) made a convenient scapegoat; furthermore, we might also discern a more positive 'PR' motive: seeking to assure the Roman authorities that, as even Pilate recognised, there was and is nothing to fear about Jesus and his followers, as all are 'innocent' of any crime against the Roman State;

48. Paul never makes this claim for himself; in Phil 3: 5 he describes himself simply as a "Hebrew born of Hebrews", a Benjaminite and a Pharisee;

49. It has often been argued by scholars that a discrete passion narrative was the first substantial oral, or possibly even the first written, narrative to be formulated about Jesus, and that narrative was used first by Mark (Mark's Gospel has been described as a Passion Narrative with an extended introduction, as the story of the final week in Jerusalem takes up almost a third of the Gospel), which was then made available to Luke and Matthew either via Mark or separately, as with John (debate continues as to whether the Fourth Evangelist knew any of the Synoptics);

50. A genuine historical question relates to the date of 'Palm Sunday': the waving of palm leaves is primarily associated with the harvest Festival of Sukkot (Booths/Tabernacles) which takes place in September-October; did Jesus' entry into Jerusalem occur 7 – 8 months rather than just 5 days before the Crucifixion? on the face of it, it seems likely that any 'plot' to arrest Jesus would take rather more than a few days to hatch, and we might sensibly conclude that the story of 'Holy Week' is a purely liturgical construction (and entered the Gospel tradition as such);

51. Placed in the 4th Gospel in the more unlikely position at the beginning of Jesus' ministry;

52. Dutcher-Walls P (2014) 'Reading the Historical Books' pp. 108 – 109; the processes of ancient historical writing are outlined pp. 106 – 130;

53. The very notion of the Sun standing still in the sky would require the Sun to be moving around the Earth, or for the Earth to stop moving in its orbit around the Sun; presumably if the moon 'stood still' (or varied in any way from its normal orbit) – and it is difficult, if not impossible, to imagine how such events might occur - there would be tidal waves and various other widespread catastrophes due to its gravitational pull; it is unlikely today that any other than the most extreme fundamentalists (on the grounds that God can do anything – particularly the otherwise impossible) would think this account a literal description of 'what occurred';

54. As we saw above, when considering memories of Jesus, whilst it is not impossible that some of Jesus' words, and perhaps particularly the stories he told (more easily remembered than individual sayings?), may have been remembered and passed on with a fair degree of accuracy, we do need to bear in mind the strong possibility that some, perhaps many, were either changed in the transmission, or else were invented and put on Jesus' lips by the Evangelists, as was a common practice the ancient 'biographies'; it seems very unlikely that the long discourses found in the 4th Gospel (written some 60+ years or so after Jesus' life) are authentically the words of Jesus, not least because they are so different in both style and content from the witness of the other three Gospels, and also in more practical terms, because there were no recording devices available in those days!

55. The only common saying (and common only to Mk [15: 34] and Mt [27: 46]) is 'why have you forsaken me?'; Lk has three sayings: 'Father forgive' (23: 34), 'Today…in paradise'

(23: 43) and 'Into your hands...' (23: 36); John has 'Son... Mother', 'Thirsty', and 'Finished' (19: 26 – 30); if Jesus really said all these things from the Cross, why were the Evangelists so selective in which quotations they used? the simple explanation is that Mt copied Mk, and that, in any case, all the sayings were the invention of the Evangelists writing 40 – 60 years after the event but seeking to make various theological points;

56. There is a continuing scholarly dispute as to how far, if at all, the 'we' passages of Acts (beginning at 16: 10 – 18, then 20: 4 – 21: 19, 27: 1 – 28: 30) represent a genuine eye-witness account, or whether they are a literary device (perhaps to add a degree of verisimilitude to the account);

57. "...we cannot expect Luke to be a historian in exactly the modern sense of the word: that would be both anachronistic and unrealistic, since Luke did not have access to the same kinds of documentation and resources as are available today, and the cultural expressions of written history then were somewhat different" Horrell DG op cit p. 13; and rather more definite: "How much reliance can we place on Luke's account of Paul's middle years. A moment's thought will make us realise that we ought to hesitate before accepting even that as the framework for a reconstruction of Paul's life...because] at times...Luke's account seems to conflict with Paul's, or is difficult to reconcile with it... Whom do we trust when Paul and Acts conflict? Usually, one is clearly on safer grounds with Paul himself, rather than with a secondary source": Hooker MD (2003) 'Paul' pp. 9 – 10, 18 – 19;

58. 'The Gospels are Reliable as Historically Factual Accounts' in Moreland JP et al (eds) (2013) 'Debating Christian Theism' pp. 417 – 429;

59. ibid. p. 426

60. "He has an insane blik about dons; we have a sane one. It

is important to realise that we have a sane one, not no blik at all; for there must be two sides to every argument – if he has a wrong blik, then those who are right about dons must have a right one". Essay B by RM Hare in Chapter VI 'Theology and Falsification': Flew A & MacIntyre A (eds. 1955) 'New Essays in Philosophical Theology' p. 100;

61. ibid pp. 99 – 100;
62. ibid pp 100 – 101;
63. ibid. p. 100;
64. ibid. p. 100;
65. ibid. p. 101;
66. ibid. pp. 101 – 102;
67. Essay on 'The Historical Jesus' (in 'Evangelical Faith and the Challenge of Historical Criticism' eds. Hays & Ansberry, pp. 158 – 181) in which Daling and Hays comment: "...we appreciate, if only instinctively, that tinkering with *(sic)* the historical Jesus will much more immediately affect the rest of Christian theology [and that such] sensitivity might tempt one towards instinctive withdrawal from historical Jesus scholarship altogether; there is, after all, a lot at stake with Jesus";
68. Davis himself is well aware of the kind of arguments against his position, because he examines them in the essay cited, when arguing the historical accuracy of the Gospels: Moreland et al pp. 418 – 421;
69. Boone KC (1989) 'The Bible Tells Them So: The Discourse of Protestant Fundamentalism' p. 25;
70. ibid. p. 25;
71. Boyd GA op cit p. 29;
72. Brynteson P op cit p. 2;
73. All four quotations cited ibid pp. 2 – 3;
74. www.eauk.org/connect/about-us/basis-of-faith.cfm accessed 4/6/16;
75. Moreland JP et al op cit p. 427;

76. First Vatican Council, Dogmatic Constitution on the Church 'Pastor Aeternus', 4th Session, July 1870, Chap 4, para 9;

77. Moreland et al op cit p. 417 ;

78. ibid. p. 427;

79. ibid. p. 417;

80. Barr J op cit pp. 176 – 177;

81. A slightly weaker version asserts that it is only the original scriptural manuscripts which do not affirm anything that is contrary to fact but, of course, as we do not have access to any autograph texts how can it possibly be judged that they are inerrant?

82. In Mk 4: 10 – 12 (together with the Matthaean and Lukan parallels), following the retelling of the parable of the Sower, the implication of what Jesus says is that parables are told to befuddle and confuse, not to clarify; Matthew makes the point quite explicitly: **"The reason I speak to them** in parables is that seeing they do not perceive, and hearing they do not listen, not do they understand" (v. 13); this is a quasi-citation of Isaiah 6: 9, although the original reference is not to a parable, but is a warning, at Isaiah's commissioning as a prophet, that people will not listen to him; the Evangelists are probably referencing the same kind of situation: people won't listen to Jesus, however simple he makes his message; but it is absolutely clear from a study of the parables themselves that, so far as their use is concerned, the opposite is true – that parables are a teaching aid, intended to enhance understanding, not obfuscate, by the telling of quite simple, homely stories; why else would Jesus use them? e.g. his response to the question: 'who is my neighbour?' is to tell the Parable of the Good Samaritan, presumably with the intention of providing an answer to the question, not making it more difficult to understand;

83. Johnson EA (2014) 'Ask the Beasts: Darwin and the God of Love' p. 7;

84. Hooker op cit p. 23;

85. In Gen 5: 4 we read that Adam had other sons and daughters; are we to believe that Cain married a sister?

86. "...as part of [the movement from oral words to written words, and written to collected] the oracles may have undergone a process of redaction, which involved the material being supplemented or adapted in some way, perhaps to clarify the prophet's message, to bring it up to date, or to apply it to a new context...The final stage of composition involved bringing the various collections together and shaping the material into the form which we now have today [which may have been significantly after the lifetime of the prophet]": Chalmers A (2015) 'Interpreting the Prophets' pp. 27, 29;

87. e.g. Werner Keller 'The Bible as History' first published in 1955, has had a second edition (with Joachim Rohork – Keller died in 1980) published in 2015;

88. Davies PR (2015) 'The History of Ancient Israel: A Guide for the Perplexed' pp. 4, 5, 12, 13, 141;

89. Evans CA (2007) 'Fabricating Jesus' p. 31;

90. "[Paul] emphasises the difference between the 'body' that belongs to the present and that which belongs to the resurrected life...[and noting that 'body' connotes 'more than flesh': the 'whole person'] in this present life, we know people through their physical bodies; in the resurrection life, we have to think of them as having spiritual bodies. So Paul begins a series of contrasts between the present physical body (which like a seed, is put into the ground, apparently dead) and the future, spiritual body...This physical body derives from Adam...but the spiritual comes from Christ...Some of the Corinthians had perhaps been deriding Paul's teaching on the resurrection, supposing that he was talking literally about the resurrection of physical bodies. Paul dismisses this idea as absurd – flesh

and blood cannot inherit the Kingdom of God…[but this] teaching about future resurrection bodies of Christians has an interesting implication for his understanding of Christ's own resurrection. Since Paul's whole argument for our resurrection is founded on Christ's resurrection, and his conviction that, in Christ, Christians share in his resurrection and will be conformed to his image…we see that Christ's own resurrection body must have been spiritual, not physical…Christ himself at his resurrection must have put on what is imperishable instead of flesh and blood. Paul could not have stressed more firmly than he does the importance of belief in Christ's resurrection, and this resurrection can certainly be described as a bodily resurrection; but it is a spiritual body, not a physical one, that Paul has in mind"; Hooker op cit pp. 155 – 157;

91. Jn 3: 8;

92. made (more) physical - as in Luke's description of the 'dove' (Spirit) at Jesus' baptism : cp. Lk 3: 22 ("..in bodily form") with Mk 1: 10 & Mt 3: 16 ("…like a dove" i.e. a straightforward simile);

93. Paul, whose eyewitness 'take' (1 Cor 15: 8; 9:1; Gal 1: 15; cf. Acts 9: 3 – 9; 22: 6 - 11; 26: 12 - 18) on the Risen Christ which seems – at least according to Luke in Acts - to fall into the vision/audition category – similar to the experiences of Ananias and Peter, is significantly different from that found in the non-eyewitness Gospel narratives, yet he categorises it as the **same kind of experience** ("…last of all…") as that of the other Apostles; there are several aspects of Luke's accounts that are not confirmed by Paul: what the Risen Christ said (Acts 9: 4); whether or not Paul was struck blind (Acts 9: 8 – 9; though cf. Gal 4: 15); Paul himself never mentions Ananias (Acts 9: 10 – 17); Paul simply tells that he had an experience of the Risen Christ, and that it happened near Damascus, and that he was commissioned to proclaim

the Gospel among the Gentiles; furthermore, the 'visionary' element of the experience, at least as narrated by Luke, doesn't actually entail a vision of the Risen Christ *per se* – it is a light and (as the auditionary element) a voice; Saul's companions apparently heard the voice but "saw no-one" (9: 7); or was it the other way round: seeing the light, but not hearing the voice (22: 9 - and just how do we explain Luke's contradiction)? nevertheless, Paul himself insists that "he appeared also to me", so raising the inevitable question: did Paul actually 'see' a person or was it a light which he interpreted in personal terms? or is the light Luke's way (and not Paul's) of describing the experience? one thing is clear (although often ignored, perhaps because it is incompatible with and inconvenient for relating a consistent narrative): Luke himself describes two quite different kinds of resurrection appearance: (Gospel) a recognisable person, and (Acts) a light and voice; to explain the difference as that between a pre- and post-ascension appearance rather begs the question: firstly, as Luke is the only writer to narrate an ascension 'event' in any case (just an allusion in Jn) and, secondly, because the question as to whether there was a **further change** in the nature of Jesus' resurrection body after the ascension (or at the conclusion of the resurrection appearances, if we prefer to put it that way) is never actually dealt with in Scripture;

94. 1 Cor 15: 3 – 8;

95. The privileged revelation to Moses: 'I Am Who I Am'- Heb: *hyh* or *hwh* is 'to be' - may be understood to reflect the nature of God (in the ancient world a person's name was thought to have immense power because it embraced or somehow 'contained' the true person) insofar as the authors understood it – again, it was an expression of their human understanding, set out in human language, and not itself 'the Truth'; whatever the actual etymology,

the Hebrew became associated with Yahweh [*Yhwh*]; but *hyh* also connotes 'to become' (a more dynamic concept – or even 'I cause to be'?): so God is not simply the 'one who is', he is also the 'one who causes to be' i.e. Creator; in other words, the tradition employed a terms because it was suitably expressive (as with '*Logos*' Word or '*Sophia*' Wisdom);

96. This is how the Biblical text presents it e.g. Ex 34: 29 – end, although making sure that something else – here, Moses putting a veil over his face – shows it to be unusual or special; yet again, Ex 33: 11 has Moses and God speaking 'as friends', "face to face", but does God have a face? in fact, just a few verses later (vv. 17 – end) God explicitly refuses to show Moses his face, but allows him to see his back! such language is, of course, *anthropomorphic*: it presents God in human form, seeking to convey the view that Moses and God were very close – in a way similar to the closeness of God and Jesus?

97. Macquarrie 'Principles' pp. 7 - 91

98. ibid. p. 9;

99. e.g. the outcomes of the seven trumpets in 8: 6 – 11: 19;

100. Pharaoh's heart 'hardens' or 'is hardened' (either generally or by his own will) after each plague, although only after Plagues 6 (boils), 8 (locusts) and 9 (darkness) is it explicitly said that God is responsible;

101. As set out in the final Biblical version, the insertion is confusing, not least due to the number of unidentified 'he's: in 4: 18 Moses asks his father-in-law's permission to go to Egypt, and that permission is granted; in v. 19 God tells Moses that it is safe to return to Egypt because his enemies were dead (exactly what the angel said to Joseph in Mt 2: 20); in v. 20 Moses and his family begin their journey; we then (21 – 23) have God repeating his instructions to Moses, but now introducing the twin notions that the people

Israel is God's first-born son, and then telling Moses to threaten Pharaoh with the death of his own first-born son (anticipating the final plague); we then have the insertion (24 – 26) with the ambiguous 'he's: "the Lord met him [presumably Moses, as he was the one to whom God had been speaking in the previous verse?] and tried to kill him"; the focus them suddenly moves to Aaron (v. 27) who meets Moses before he arrives in Egypt;

102. Houston (Houston W 'Exodus' in Barton J & Muddiman J (eds) (2001) 'The Oxford Bible Commentary') suggests that the reference to Moses' feet is most likely a euphemism for Moses' penis and so one explanation for the pericope is that it provides a "symbol legitimising this marriage between the leader of Israel and a foreign woman, which may have been a scandal to some of the first readers of Exodus in the Second Temple period" (p. 72);

103. "Many scholars have regarded the piece as an old legend in which the attacker was a demon, possibly intended to explain the origin of the practice of the circumcision of infants. Maybe, but this does not explain what it means in this context": ibid. p. 72;

104. Davies PR op cit pp. 22 – 23.

Chapter 4

The Biblical Foundations

The Gospel witness

It is (virtually) a truism that the Synoptic Gospels present a portrait of Christ significantly different from (some would judge: considerably at variance with) the Johannine portrait. In the former, Christ points unerringly towards his heavenly Father as the source of meaning and focus of worship, but says very little about himself; whereas the Johannine Christ speaks a great deal about himself, even appearing to claim a divine – whatever else we might want to call it, it is certainly not a human - nature ("... before Abraham was, I am" Jn 8: 58). It would seem, historically, that the critical turning point was when (whenever that was, but presumably quite early on in the development of Christology) **the Proclaimer became the Proclaimed; the Revealer became the Revealed**.

Had Jesus' followers continued, as one might expect of disciples of a religious, philosophical or political leader, to proclaim his message[1] about the Kingdom of God in the more Synoptic fashion (this is not to say that the Synoptics were not part of the transformed message – they were, and that was their whole *raison d'etre* – but at least they bore witness to the original message as well[2]), rather than convert that message into a proclamation about Jesus himself, one more firmly using the Johannine mode of expression (where talk of the Kingdom becomes talk of eternal life, and the focus shifts rather more from Father/God to Son/Word/God), then the Church would probably have developed quite a different kind of Christology: one which might have been more faithful to the reality which was the historical person of Jesus.

The Church has always found it difficult to square the

assertion of Jesus' humanity with his divinity, yet preachers continue to tie themselves up in knots over it, when the solution might actually be quite simple: Jesus never claimed to be divine and the Church's designation of him as such was just one possible way of expressing their understanding of his relationship with the Father. While it was the Johannine portrait rather than that of the Synoptics which came to dominate Christological thinking in those first foundational and formative centuries,[3] if the Synoptic portrait (probably based on material much earlier and closer to Jesus' time, but certainly without such deeply explicit theologising on the part of the Synoptic Evangelists) is the more authentic and more true to the historical reality, then in making the appropriate conceptual readjustments we might even conclude that the historical Jesus himself, as a devout Jew, would have been appalled to be described as God or divine (somehow identical to God, or at least sharing the divine nature) and would have rejected the notion outright.

In Mark (the earliest Gospel, on which Matthew and Luke based their own texts) Jesus' reply to the rich (young) man is: "Why do you call me good? No one is good but God alone" (Mk 10: 18), thus making an explicit distinction between himself and God: 'we are not the same; God is greater' (a view actually made explicit in Jn 14: 28: "The Father is greater than I"; although constantly mitigated by other statements, nevertheless showing that even the 4th Evangelist may have had access to this particular part of the tradition, and was faithful to it even though he himself held a much more elevated view of Jesus). Matthew (but not Luke, 18: 19) changes this to "Why do you ask me about what is good? There is only one who is good" (Mt 19: 17) in order to make the original contrast much more ambiguous. It seems likely, therefore, that by the time Matthew wrote (the 80s?) the Church's evaluation of Jesus' 'person' was already not only significantly greater than (it would appear) his own self-understanding had been, but also somewhat 'higher' than Mark's (as indicated by a Gospel 'trajectory' which ranges from no interest whatsoever in Jesus' origins [Mk], via virginal conception [Mt/Lk], to the pre-existent Logos [Jn]).

Although it may seem counterintuitive to many Christians, nurtured on a liturgical and devotional diet which leans heavily on, indeed assumes both implicitly and explicitly, the classic formulations of doctrine, and which even uses the same language (such as the *'homoousios'* of the Nicene Creed), the Biblical witness (excepting perhaps – and even here only to a degree - the later NT writings) presents Jesus fairly straightforwardly as a 'man sent by God' (as John the Baptist was described in Jn 1: 6, although Jesus was "greater" than him) in order to carry out God's purposes. Representative examples of such descriptions may particularly be found in the speeches made about Jesus in the Acts of the Apostles (written by Luke possibly in the 80s), because Acts tells not the story of Jesus, but the story of those whose purpose was to proclaim Jesus. As such it is a good indicator of what was believed around 50 years after the crucifixion, if not before that, albeit representative of what CH Dodd[4] termed the "apostolic preaching" as distinct from that of Paul.

In Peter's Pentecost speech (whether one believes these speeches represent Peter's actual words or that they are, in line with ancient historiography, the compositions of the author), Jesus was "attested...*by God*...with deeds of power...that *God did* through him" (Acts 2: 22); further, the Jesus handed over to death was a "man" whose death was known by God and whom God raised (vv. 23 – 24). Although some may claim that the distinction being made here is between Jesus' divinity and his humanity (these things happened to Jesus only 'in his humanity') that is not only technically heretical (because it 'confounds the person' by making a division between Christ's humanity and divinity), but it is not the plain sense of the text: there is nothing here to suggest that Luke was making any intra-personal ontological distinctions about Jesus – that is an anachronistic interpretation. Clearly Luke believed that there was something particularly special about Jesus (as implied by his birth narrative; but John the Baptist's birth was also special[5]) but there is nothing in Luke's writings to suggest that meant that Jesus was more than a human being, albeit one exalted by God at his resurrection/ascension.[6] The most that is said of Jesus in this passage (and although this is a significant designation in itself, again it requires no divine interpretation) is that God made Jesus "both Lord and Messiah": Jesus is given the status of "Lord" by God (as his vicegerent) and (at the risk of being repetitive, we recall that) 'Messiah' is a purely human designation.

At Solomon's Portico, Peter describes Jesus as God's servant (3: 13; also in 4: 30 although a variant reading attests to "child": Gk. *pais* can mean either); indeed, he is "Holy and Righteous" and also "the Author [or Pioneer] of life" (one who brings God's new life to others through his mediation of the divine will; there is no need to regard this as a literal as opposed to a metaphorical description): high designations, but entirely capable of non-divine interpretations. Before the Council, Peter describes Jesus as the 'rejected stone' (4: 11 cf. Ps 118: 22) before going on (at least by implication) to describe Jesus as a "mortal" (4: 12) – 'there is no other mortal name [name of a mortal]...' Before the High Priest, Peter and the apostles describe Jesus as "Leader and Saviour" (5: 31) having been "exalted" to that status by God; 'exaltation' (raising in rank) yet again does not require the ascription of ontological divinity: God presumably can raise up a mortal being to high (exalted) rank without that person being divinised (Elijah was allegedly taken bodily into heaven as, according to the much later affirmation of the RCC, so was Mary the mother of Jesus)? The concept of divinisation is Romano-Greek, not Jewish.

In Stephen's great speech Jesus actually receives only a minor mention, when he is referred to as the "Righteous One" (7: 52) and "Son of Man" (7: 56: standing at the right hand of God – the highest place of honour, but evidently not God himself unless, again, it is anachronistically read in a Trinitarian context; even then it falls inevitably into tritheism: 'gods standing beside each other'). Philip, on the other hand, only identifies Jesus as 2nd Isaiah's (in context human, both individual and corporate) 'suffering servant' (8: 34ff).

In Peter's speech to Cornelius, although Jesus is certainly described as 'Lord of all', once again this designation does not in itself require an ascription of ontological divinity (neither does the Philippians 'hymn' [2: 6 – 11: scholars continue to debate whether Paul is using words produced by others – a pre-existing song of praise] where Jesus is given the 'name above every name'). Jesus, certainly raised by God and exalted, is presented here primarily as the one who carried the "message [God] sent to the people..." (Acts 10: 36): Jesus is the one whom God chose (and "anointed ...with the Holy Spirit and with power") to be his messenger and, as a result, "God was with him" (v. 38). It would have been a simple matter for Peter (and/or for Luke) to say (if either ever believed that): 'Jesus is Lord because Jesus is God/divine';[7] rather Peter/Luke says: "God was *with* him" together with the universal proclamation of the NT: "God raised him" (vv. 38, 40 – never 'Jesus raised himself'): plainly subject, verb, and (different) object.

We may also note Paul at Psidian Antioch (13: 16 – end): Jesus is foretold by the prophets, killed and raised by God, "no more to return to corruption" (v. 34), which would have been his natural state; it is "through **this man**" that sins are forgiven. Further Paul in Thessalonica (17: 1 – 9): Jesus is Messiah and King; Paul in Athens (17: 16 – end): Jesus is a "man...appointed" by God. Paul in Corinth (18: 1 – 17): Jesus is the Messiah. Paul in Ephesus (19): the main focus here is the contrast between the baptism of (the man) John and that of (presumably the man) Jesus, and also the power of Jesus' (and implicitly Paul's) name to expel evil spirits. Again, Jesus is a man empowered by God; (20: 17 – end): Jesus is the "Lord" who authorised Paul to continue his own ministry: "to testify to the good news of God's grace" (v. 24); Jesus is the one who proclaimed God – but not himself God.

In Paul's great defence of himself to the Roman authorities (21: 37 – 22: 29) Jesus is only mentioned as the one who commissioned Paul; in his speech before Felix (24: 1 – end) Jesus is not mentioned at all until in a latter hearing (vv. 24 – 26) when reference is made to "faith in Christ Jesus". Faith may, of course, be applied to a human person (or, indeed, placed in a machine) as much to God, as it essentially connotes trust (we may remind ourselves that the predominant usage of *pistis* in Paul was 'trust' and not 'belief'): so we have faith in God, but we also have faith in those whom God has sent to us. There is a clear distinction made in Acts 20: 21 when Paul (Luke) says: "...as I testified to both Jews and Greeks about repentance towards God and faith towards our Lord Jesus": two distinct attitudes (repentance and faith) expressed towards two distinct people (God and Christ). Then before Agrippa (26: 1 - end), Paul's main theme is a God who "raises the dead" (v. 8), Paul's own conversion, and Jesus designated again as Messiah (v. 23). Finally in Rome (28: 23 – end), Paul "testifies about the kingdom of God" and tries to "convince them about Jesus", although we are not told precisely what it was he sought to convince them about Jesus; but to the end of his life these were his twin themes: the kingdom of God and the Lord Jesus Christ (28: 30 – 31): not the Kingdom of the Lord Jesus Christ.

Clearly for Luke (at least), read through a pre-Conciliar lens and with the plain sense of the text taken seriously, Jesus was a very special man (and, as with other special men throughout the Hebrew scriptures, the outcome of a 'God-assisted' birth) anointed, sent and accredited, and even ultimately exalted by God, but still very much a man, subject to pain and death (although raised from death, this is never seen as a 'natural' outcome for Jesus: the Resurrection is always attested in the NT as a great act of God). Most importantly, Jesus is presented as distinct from God – there is no attempt by Luke to identify Jesus either with or as God (and, as noted, it is difficult to imagine traditional Jews like Peter doing so). It may be argued that Luke (and others) didn't have the language or concepts to express what they really believed, and those came later; but to say that begs the question: if they didn't have the language or concepts, how can we possibly know what they believed?

Whatever the first few generations of Christians believed about Jesus (and if we read what they wrote without imposing our own preconceptions and beliefs, we can find that out reasonably well), as time went on, the Church's Christology gradually became 'higher' and 'higher' and the 'Christ of Faith' - what came to be believed about Christ - began to overshadow and, to a degree, replace the 'Jesus of History'. Theologians had to work harder and harder to find ways of ascribing divinity to Christ, not least due to the need to differentiate between him and the Father not only in order to protect monotheism, but also to protect his genuine humanity. Were they successful? The end result was a doctrine of the Incarnation which still struggles to hold divinity and humanity in tension without falling into either docetism or adoptionism, together with a doctrine of the Trinity which teeters either on the brink of tritheism or an equally human-denying modalism, as it tries to hold to its monotheistic roots, on which, somewhat ironically, the historical Jesus was himself nurtured and which he unambiguously proclaimed (e.g. Mk 12: 28 – 30).

When we come to consider the NT (particularly the Gospel) evidence in a properly critical, judicious and open-minded manner (rather than trying to make it fit *a priori* beliefs and assertions), we find that nowhere in the Synoptics does Jesus call himself divine, and even if Jesus accepted the messianic title (which is not at all certain), that itself neither denoted or connoted divinity in any way. The crucial (and 'critical' in the proper sense) question – one seldom asked - is this: if Jesus didn't claim to be divine, why do we feel the need to claim divinity on his behalf?

There are several possibilities. We might seek to argue that the Chalcedonian formula is a revealed mystery that we must believe without understanding it - but if that is so, why should we believe that, rather than any other claim made about Jesus (e.g. that of the Aetherius Society, that Jesus lives on Venus)? More significantly, we might assert divinity in Christ as a way of expressing his existential importance and significance for us: his effect on our lives (and thus on our relationship with God) is 'God-shaped' or 'God-driven' (using the concept of symbol, we might say that Christ re-presents [presents again] God to us; he is God-for-us; it is as-if-he-were God). Finally, if we take seriously the importance of what has been termed God's 'prevenient grace' (God always 'comes before' us), then we see that the initiative in every aspect of the Christ-event (the Incarnation) is always God's: this, itself, may be sufficient reason for calling Christ 'divine', as his work is God's work and not his own; what he says and does is 'of God' and that in itself permits us to refer to Jesus as divine, provided we do not understand that designation as (somehow) literal.

The late Bishop John Robinson (of 'Honest to God' fame), having argued that Christ *"is God about his decisive work. What he does God does"*, went on to make a distinction between him being *"not just a man doing human things divinely, like any saint or seer, but a man doing divine things humanly."*[8] However, it is not immediately apparent just what kind of distinction Robinson is seeking to make beyond the claim that Jesus was greater than saints and seers, although, surely, these too may also be thought to have been doing 'divine things humanly' (rather than 'human things divinely', whatever either of these phrases – beyond being rhetorically felicitous - actually means)? If we are meant to understand that the difference lies in 'God being in Christ...' in a very special (ontological/metaphysical) way, one in which God does not engage in with others (saints, seers or prophets), then the claim is being made that Christ is, *a priori*, different from the remainder of humanity – and that carries with it its own problems, not least the meaning of the continued assertion that he was genuinely, fully and truly human.

This is the very kind of claim that many Christians make without recognising the conceptual dangers of doing so. What exactly – as in Graham Kendrick's popular hymn 'Meekness and Majesty' – is the 'Man who is God'? This hymn, presenting Jesus with the words: "This is your God..." provides a very good example of 4th Century Apollinarianism and is thus a reminder of the ever present danger of falling into heresy and of the numerous occasions on which Christian attempts to spell out the meaning of Christ during those first five centuries did so. Without doubt, the historical Jesus of Nazareth (and, of course, the Risen Christ, however that experience is to be understood[9]) clearly impacted so profoundly on people, that many came to think of him as 'no ordinary man'. But it is not immediately obvious that being 'no ordinary man' leads inevitably to the conclusion that such an extraordinary man must be ontologically divine: there have been plenty of extra-ordinary men *and* women, throughout history and today, who have, by their lives, deeds and words, 'raised the bar' of humanity, but (like other alleged miracle workers) have not been deemed divine. Yet still, few Christians would even want to say that Jesus was (for example) 'another prophet' – although that itself is a high and demanding vocation, and is clearly how some did think of him.

New Testament Models of Jesus

Jesus of Nazareth, Prophet of God
Designation as prophet is hardly inappropriate. Jesus is described

as being like "one of the ancient prophets",[10] specifically Elijah
redivivus (Mk 6: 15 &//s) and, as previously noted, the act of
healing the widow of Nain's son recalls Elijah's raising of the
widow of Zarephath's son (1 Kings 17: 17 - 24) which, together
with the feeding of the 5000 and the healing of a blind man,
results in Jesus being named a prophet (Lk 7: 16; Jn 6: 14, 9: 17),
as did his teaching (Jn 7: 40). He was welcomed as a prophet
at the 'Palm Sunday' entry into Jerusalem (Mt 21: 11), and the
chief priests didn't arrest him on the specific grounds that the
crowds "regarded him as a prophet" (Mt 21: 46), as did the two
disciples on the Emmaus road (Lk 24: 19), and even Peter, when
speaking in Solomon's portico (Acts 3: 22). Although such an
identification is implicitly denied in Mk 8: 27 – 30 (&//s) and
possibly also in Jesus' own description of the Baptist as "more
than a prophet" (Mt 11: 9 – if John, who was both 'less powerful'
and not worthy to carry his sandals [Mt 3: 11] was 'more than
a prophet', what did that make Jesus himself?[11]), that did not
prevent the reporting of an alternative tradition that has Jesus
at least implicitly identifying himself as a prophet when rejected
at Nazareth (Mk 6: 4 &//s), when he sets his face towards
Jerusalem (because prophets can only be killed in Jerusalem: Lk
13: 33 – 34), and possibly also in other teachings (Mt 10: 41). The
'woes' to the Scribes and Pharisees, whom Jesus condemns for
attacking the prophets, even contains an allusion to crucifixion
(Mt 23: 34) perhaps showing (within its *sitz im leben*) that the
early Church also used 'prophet' as a designation for Jesus (the
one who was crucified), although this was obviously not their
only designation. It is entirely possible that the references to
'prophet' embedded in the tradition reflect the understanding of
those who actually knew Jesus and that, by the time the gospels
came to be written, such historical traditions have had various
and increasing layers of more complex Christological reflection
imposed upon them.

What are the characteristics of a prophet of God?

*"Fundamentally, [an OT] prophet was an **intermediary**; he or she was called to stand between the divine and human realms. Like Israel's priests, the prophets occupied the liminal zone between God and the people; they were members both of the nation of Israel and of the divine council. The prophets' intermediary status is perhaps best illustrated by their role as **communicators of the divine will**. On the one hand, the prophets could be **commissioned directly by God** to speak a word of judgement or salvation to the people. On the other hand, they could be **sought out** by people who required divine guidance for a specific issue or problem or divine intervention in a time of crisis".*[12]

When we consider these prophetic criteria it is easy to recognise that Jesus meets most, if not all, of them; we should, perhaps, change 'prophet as metaphor' into 'prophet as fact':

1. Jesus was (however understood) 'commissioned' ("accredited" Acts 2: 22) by God; he operated with God's authority;
2. the Church has, from the earliest days, understood him to be an intermediary with God; this is the whole basis of atonement theology as well as the Church's prayer 'through Jesus Christ our Lord';
3. Jesus clearly sought to communicate God's will, particularly God's 'Kingdom project' ('Your Kingdom come...') or (John) the path to eternal life;
4. people sought Jesus out for teaching and healing;
5. like many of the OT prophets, Jesus had to deal with religious and political opposition, and like some of the prophets he was eventually killed by them;
6. *"As First Testament [OT] prophets undermine the idea that God wants people to offer sacrifices, Jesus undermines the idea that there is any point in rules about purity (Mk 7: 1 – 23). Like a First Testament prophet, he can push people to accept*

more radical standards from within the Torah than the Torah sometime allows – for instance, in forgoing the right to divorce your wife (Mk 10)".[13]

We may reasonably conclude that there is sufficient evidence that, however Jesus later came to be understood, there existed an historical tradition which suggests that Jesus of Nazareth had been thought of (or may even have thought of himself) in terms of prophethood and that, in Jesus' own view (as a faithful prophet), 'only God was good'.

The Suffering Servant

It is often suggested that Jesus' own concept of self-identity was specifically modelled on the Second Isaiah's (to distinguish the writer of Isaiah 40 – 55 from the 8th Century Isaiah of Jerusalem whose prophecies are to be found in Isaiah 1 – 39) 'suffering servant': the 'man of sorrows and acquainted with grief' (Isaiah 53: 3: AV and as in Handel's 'Messiah'; NRSV - "He was despised and rejected by others; a man of suffering and acquainted with infirmity" understood, by many, including Handel's librettist, as a type or even prediction of the Passion). Yet, in context,

*"Isaiah 53 is not a prophecy of the Messiah but a portrait of how Yahweh's **servant-prophet** becomes the means of Israel's being put right with God, of Israel's personal renewal, and of the nations' coming to acknowledge Yahweh. But one can see how the chapter came to help people understand Jesus' significance".*[14]

Whether or not Jesus understood himself in such terms, generations of Christians have done so on his behalf, and that identification, if not messianic, is at least that of a prophet (Goldingay argues that the 'suffering servant' was – as a partial identity at least[15] - the Second Isaiah himself) and one, at that, with both the message and the means of redemption which can obviously be delivered by God's agent on his behalf (one of the cardinal issues for the development of the Christian doctrine[s] of atonement is that, for Jesus to bring atonement and salvation, he must himself be divine; but he must also be human in order to redeem human beings – for either, it is reasonable to ask 'why?').

The most direct self-ascription of Jesus witnessed in the Gospel tradition is actually based in the thought of (so-called) 'Third Isaiah' (Chaps 56 – 66) when, in Lk 4: 16 – 19, Jesus reads from the scroll of Isaiah (specifically 61: 1 – 2, but combined in Luke's version with 49: 8). Third Isaiah does not call himself God's servant (as does 2nd Isaiah) but

> "...he does describe himself as one upon whom Yahweh's spirit has come...and as one Yahweh has **anointed**...and he has a **commission** like that of Yahweh's servant in that his task is to bring good news to the lowly and freedom to prisoners",[16]

and the fact that Jesus read from this section of Isaiah (or was so portrayed by the Evangelist) would suggest a very clear view of his vocation (either of Jesus himself or of the tradition about him). Indeed, when the disciples of the Baptist are sent to ask Jesus whether he is "the one who is to come..." (Lk 7: 19), they are told: "Go and tell John what you have seen and heard: the blind receive their sight, the lame walk, the lepers are cleansed, the deaf hear, the dead are raised, the poor have the good news brought to them" (Lk 7: 22) thus both confirming and extending the link with Isaiah (cf. Isaiah 35: 5 – 6: "Then the eyes of the blind shall be opened and the ears of the deaf unstopped; then the lame shall leap like a deer, and the tongue of the speechless sing for joy"). Further, in Lk 21: 22 Jesus (or Luke) evokes Isaiah in his prophecy about the destruction of the temple, where the siege of Jerusalem represents the 'days of vengeance/vindication' (cf. Isaiah 34: 8; 62: 2): the fulfilment of both God's threats and his promises. Again, Jesus is identified (and identifies himself?)

with the prophetic tradition (specifically that of Isaiah) through which he is imbued with God's spirit, anointed, and receives a commission. But, again, not himself divine.

Priest of the Most High God

In many religious traditions the priest is understood to be some kind of intermediary or mediator with God on behalf of the people, having been chosen by God for that role. In the Christian tradition, a priest or minister is one discerned to have received a 'call', a vocation, from God, in essence similar to that of some of the prophets e.g. Isaiah 6: 1 – 8; Jeremiah 1: 4 – 5 (even chosen from the womb, although perhaps God chooses all whom he calls from the womb?). Some ministries are actually deemed to be prophetic in their focus: in 1 Cor 12: 28 second in rank (?) after apostles. Generally, in the Gospels, 'priest' refers to Jewish religious officials to whom, for example, the cleansed leper has to show himself in order to be readmitted to the community. The exception is its use in Hebrews – here, Jesus himself is the priest, in particular a high priest, presumably understood as a direct contrast to the very politicised office (as it had become) of the Jewish High Priest (who shared responsibility, in the eyes of the Evangelists, for Jesus' death), and one appointed "according to the order of Melchizedek" (5: 6, 7: 17) who himself had been "priest of the Most High God" (7: 1 cf. Gen 14: 18 - 20). For the author of Hebrews, Jesus is (again) 'more than' a priest (the contrast is made in Hebs 10: 11 – 14). Nevertheless, the association with Melchizedek would suggest a representative role *par excellence*, and whilst Jesus is presented as being above all other priests, he is still 'the Priest of God' who performs his ministry on behalf of God, opening up God's sanctuary (10: 19 - 20) by his self-sacrifice and presiding (as high priests are called to do) over "the house of God" (10: 21). But, like the Messiah, the priest is not God, nor thought of as divine in any way.

'King Jesus'[17]

The Synoptic Christ brought a simple message: 'the Kingdom of God/Heaven'[18] is near (Mk 1: 15 – Jesus; Mt 3: 2 – the Baptist), or is even already here (Mk 10: 29, Lk 17: 21). The Gk. *basileia* may be translated either as 'kingdom' or 'kingship': an area being ruled or the authority exercised by that rule (this latter meaning particularly in the Book of Revelation e.g. "royal rule" and "authority" in 17: 12). Of course, the meanings are complementary, and the concept of God's Kingdom is thus capable of multiple interpretations: God rules now, so let us make it both real and visible in our lives; or a more an eschatological concept (Lk 13: 20, 14: 15): God's rule will be made real (and in Christian interpretation over the centuries) as a future event, either on (a renewed) Earth or in Heaven. As we have seen, it was when the focus moved from Jesus' proclamation to Jesus the proclaimer, that the message about the Kingdom became a message about Jesus, who was thus seen as the personification of the Kingdom (the Kingdom comes in the person of Christ). As Luke puts it directly: it is Jesus' kingdom inherited from "his father David" (thus far apparently a political entity), but that kingdom will be never-ending (Lk 1: 31 – 33): an eschatological concept.

That is why there is also plenty of evidence in the Gospels that Jesus himself was often thought of as (some kind of) 'King' *per se*, in which the 'earthly' and the 'heavenly', the present and the future, were to become inextricably mixed:

'King': the OT basis of Mt's understanding of the 'Palm Sunday' entry into Jerusalem (Mt 21: 5: the OT reference is Zechariah 9: 9 which might portray a messianic-type leader, although the word itself is not used; cf. Jn 12: 15); reflecting the aim of the crowds after the miraculous feeding (Jn 6: 15); Pilate's question and Jesus' reply (Jn 18: 37); Pilate to the crowds and their reply (Jn 19: 15);

1. 'King of the Jews': for whom the Magi searched (Mt 2: 2); Pilate's question (Mk 15:2 & //s); Pilate to the crowds (Mk 15: 9, 12; but in Jn 18: 39 implied); the jeers of the crowds (Mk 15: 18, 32 & //s); Pilate's sign on the cross (Mk 15: 26 & //s);
2. 'King of Israel': "scribes and elders" mocking Jesus (Mt 27: 42); Philip (Jn 1: 49); John's 'Palm Sunday' (12: 13);
3. 'Messiah, a King': accusation put to Pilate (Lk 23: 2), presumably recalling a military 'Davidic' messiah.

In context, even when 'king' is used without any explicit referent, it would seem to mean 'King of the Jews' or 'King of Israel' (this latter, by then, somewhat anachronistic), and these titles connote more of a political than spiritual entity (which is why Herod was worried that he had a rival in the 'new-born King'). It would seem likely that, however the Evangelists portray the motives for Jesus' crucifixion (which seems to entail the 'whitewashing' of Pilate), the accusation that Jesus was seeking to be king in a political sense (Jn 6: 15 portrays the crowds seeking to make him king which would have been, in Roman eyes, and in the eyes of their puppet, Tetrarch Herod Antipas [4BC – AD39], an act of subversion) may well lie at the basis of the Roman crucifixion – why else would the Romans be interested in what, for them, would simply have been an itinerant Jewish preacher? He must have been perceived as some kind of political threat, however small. The Johannine Christ points out the misunderstanding to Pilate: this was no political concept (18: 36), although even an eschatological concept may have present political implications (hence the Baptist preaching, amongst others, to soldiers).

If 'kingship' didn't refer to a political entity as such (although, within the Jewish Scriptures, particularly the Psalms [e.g. 8, 19, 47, 67, 76, 97, 98, 100] God is often portrayed as the ruler not only of the whole Earth, thus with some territorial connotations, but also the Universe), what was it? 'Not of this world' would seem to imply an other-worldly (spiritual; so Jesus 'waged' war on evil spirits) and/or an eschatological event: 'at the End', God will reign; at the culmination of all things, God's rule will prevail (an idea replicated in the OT notion of 'the Day of the Lord' which, in developing Christian thought is gradually transmuted into the 'Second Coming of Christ').

As a result, an alternative understanding developed that, far from Jesus being the proclaimer of the Kingdom, it was Jesus who ushered in the Kingdom of God in his own person: he was the proper King of God's Kingdom (as in the pre-Advent Festival of 'Christ the King'). But before we jump to the conclusion that this is evidence that Jesus was already (at least at the time of the writing of the Gospels, if not before) considered 'to be God', we must be clear that Jesus is never portrayed as saying anything like: 'it is *my* kingdom': indeed, Jesus teaches his disciples to pray to the Father: "*Your* kingdom come..." (Lk 11: 2). More plausible is the idea that God appointed his 'agent(s)' who, by virtue of that 'appointment' were able to share in the divine kingship, and have royal authority over and to his people. An alternative, albeit linked, idea is that the coming of Jesus as 'precursor agent' shows that God is preparing to act decisively, and in a royal (authoritative) fashion. Various texts claim that Jesus acted with a special (royal?) authority: Jesus taught with authority (Mk 1: 22 &//s), Jesus forgave with authority (Mk 2: 10 &//s) and cast out demons with that same authority (Mk 3: 15 &//s). Indeed, his enemies frequently questioned that authority (Mk 11: 28, 29, 33 &//s) although, interestingly, Jesus refused to tell them precisely where his authority originated (Mk 11: 33), with the Evangelist implying that Jesus was almost teasing them ('you won't answer my question, so I won't answer yours'). The possibility exists that the real reason for this coyness is that Mark hadn't quite worked out precisely what he believed the link to be between God and Jesus, and so he was 'hedging his bets' by being a little 'mysterious'.

In this sense, Jesus not only announced, but also 'embodied' the Kingdom of God; Jesus was God's appointed king who ruled on his behalf (hence the emphasis on the Davidic link), and who expressed God's royal authority in his words and deeds. A second century Greek papyrus asks: "What is a king?", and answers: "One who is equal to God".[19] This notion may provide a philosophical basis for some of the claims made about Jesus within a broadly Hellenistic-Roman culture. Around the time that the 4th Gospel (in which Thomas confesses: "My Lord and my God" 20: 28) was being written, Emperor Domitian (81 – 96CE) was being addressed as *dominus et deus'*: 'Lord and God'. One of the implicit aims of the Evangelists was to present Jesus as the 'real' Son of God over against such imperial claims. The understanding of the 'divine' (either representative or actual) nature of a King in the ancient world (where in some cultures – including that of the Roman Empire in which Jesus lived and in which the Church grew - the King/Emperor was actually deified[20]) may have encouraged, or at least supported, the notion that 'King Jesus' must also be divine: that if he had God's authority then he must share God's identity, failing to recognise that was not a necessary corollary. Such an interpretation is superfluous. As we shall see, it was quite normal in the ancient world for the identity of God/King and agent to be blurred. The agent spoke 'as if' he were the Master: he was (if not literally, then as close to literal as could be) 'his master's voice'.

Apostle

A particularly intriguing designation appears only once in the NT, again in Hebrews (3: 1) where Jesus is actually called an 'apostle', a term most commonly used to describe Jesus' disciples, post-resurrection (most references are to be found in Acts), who were 'sent out' to proclaim the Gospel (although the term is occasionally used of disciples pre-resurrection, once in Matthew [10: 2], twice in Mark [3: 14, 6: 30] and five times in Luke [6: 13,

9: 10, 11: 49, not itself a direct reference to Jesus' disciples and alongside use of 'prophets', 17: 5, and 22: 14]). In what sense could Jesus be called 'apostle'? It may be helpful to bear in mind that the Hebrew equivalent to *apostellein* ('to send out') is *shaliach*, a description of the Jewish legal institution whereby representative envoys were sent out with full negotiatory powers to use on behalf of those who sent them (a rabbinic saying held that 'the one whom a man sends is the equivalent of himself') thus supporting the interpretation that Jesus was essentially God's representative or vicegerent – it was 'as if' the person in authority were there himself (the vicegerent symbolised the King). So the apostle was an 'envoy' (the marginal translation in the NEB of Hebrews 3: 1) or 'fully authorised representative' sent by the overriding authority: a designation which makes particularly good sense when allied with the many occasions in the Fourth Gospel when Jesus refers to "the One who sent me". It was this authority which was passed on to those more commonly understood as apostles: "...as the Father has sent me, so I send you" (Jn 20: 21b).

Prophet, Servant, Priest, King and Apostle...and more?

Such designations of Jesus have an important role to play in Christian piety. John Newton's popular hymn: 'How Sweet the Name of Jesus Sounds'[21] seems to pack as many as possible into one verse: "Jesus, my Shepherd, Husband (Brother/Guardian/Saviour[22]), Friend, My Prophet, Priest and King; My Lord, my Life, my Way, my End...". But the designations are clearly connotative and allusive rather than denotative and definitive. 'Shepherd', an OT metaphor for God (e.g. Pss 23: 1; 80: 1) is, in the NT, similarly applied to Christ (Jn 10), suggesting 'one who cares for' – from which we derive our word 'pastoral'. Similarly, the use of 'life' and 'way' draw our minds to the Johannine Christ's words (Jn 14: 6) where such terms are open to a wide range of interpretation, just as 'End' may recall the '[Alpha and] Omega' of the Book of Revelation (22: 13). It would clearly be wrong to assume (not least, because many people who lead or care for others may be called 'the shepherd of the sheep') that because 'shepherd' is used both of God and of Jesus, there must, thereby, be an ontological identity or unity between them; it could simply designate a unity of function – Jesus is faithfully 'shepherding' God's flock, unlike those false shepherds of Israel (Ezek 34: 1 – 10), who had been commissioned by God, but neglected their duties. So while God himself is the true Shepherd (vv. 11 – 16), he delegates his work to his agents: "I will set over them one shepherd, my servant David, and he shall feed them and be their shepherd" (v. 23), although they continue to be God's sheep: "You are my sheep, the sheep of my pasture, and I am your God, says the Lord God" (v. 31).

Such terms may take on profound and rich meanings when used theologically:

> "Christ the **king**, who wins his victory over the enslaving forces, is also Christ the **prophet** who gives us the 'example' of obedience, but still more he is the **priest** who utterly gives himself as sacrificial victim and thereby brings right into human history the reconciling activity of God in a new and decisive manner".[23]

In each case, these terms are employed as metaphors in order to shed light on 'Christ's Work', they are not meant to be taken literally (so, for example, Jesus was never a Jewish priest) although, as suggested above, perhaps 'Jesus as Prophet' should be. Some of the designations may have originated in the tradition as those originally applied to the historical Jesus for, as we have seen, he was understood (certainly in the pre-Gospel tradition as well as after) using a variety of designations, particularly that of a 'prophet' and, perhaps even more particularly, a prophet in the mould of Isaiah's 'suffering servant'. Such traditions were faithfully gathered and preserved, although not particularly focused on, by the Evangelists. By the time they came to record them, their own developing Christologies required that these various traditions were both affirmed (as a minimalist description: 'this is the least we can say') but also denied ('this is not a sufficient designation'): "*The categories of prophet and messiah are not wrong, but they fail to do full justice to [Jesus'] identity*".[24]

Although the Church came to the conclusion that Jesus was more (much more) than a prophet or whatever other title has been used of him (and it is the 'more' that has proven most difficult to express and explain), there is a clear indication in the NT documents that the various designations are not, in themselves, totally inappropriate. Nevertheless, we do need to remember that a prophet (and priest, king and apostle - just like the Messiah) was always human, never divine: God's representative, not God.

This inevitably leads us to the question: if Jesus was 'more than a prophet' (and we recall that this was apparently Jesus' own view of the Baptist: Lk 7: 26) what is 'the more' (presumably more than John the Baptist's being 'more than a prophet'), and how is it best characterised? As we have seen, the common Christological default position has been (and, for many Christians, continues to be) that 'the more' was his divinity – it is that which sets him apart from (mere) prophets. Yet the evidence is strong (I would say conclusive) not only that Jesus himself never claimed to be divine, but also that that the ascription of divinity (in the sense of sharing God's being) to Jesus is a (much) later development and, in terms of the Gospel tradition, it is sourced rather more from John than from the Synoptics, where claims that Jesus was divine (as opposed to being exceptionally special) are arguably not to be found at all. Furthermore, I have already claimed that the very notion of a 'man who is God' is incoherent and that it drives us irresistibly and inevitably into the docetic heresy, thus undermining any realistic hope of continuing to believe and proclaim that Jesus was truly human. We shall explore this argument further in the form of two linked case studies.

Case Study 1: Richard Hays' Christ as "the embodiment of the God of Israel"

Richard Hays[25] argues that all four Gospels, most directly John, but even the more restrained and theologically nuanced Mark, portray a Jesus who is *"the embodiment of the God of Israel"*.[26] Of course, the word 'embody' does not need to be understood literally: an actor may embody the essence of the character she is playing; the painting may truly embody (in the sense of accurately expressing or revealing) the qualities of its subject; a son may embody the characteristics of his father ('isn't he like his dad?'[27]); 'to embody' can mean to express, to personify or to exemplify some quality, idea or even another person in some concrete fashion: thus the footballer embodies (in his words and actions) all kinds of good sporting qualities, or a polymath such as da Vinci may embody (have within himself) a great variety of different kinds of expertise. However, it appears, not least because he recognises that his claim *"runs against the grain of much NT scholarship"*, that 'embodiment' for Hays means that God was somehow literally "in Christ" (is there then a difference between 'em-bodying' and 'en-fleshing': the latter, as with the *Logos,* understood to 'inhabit' Jesus in a broadly literal manner?): this is no simple representation, but the real thing.

The two particularly interesting theses he advances are:

1. a 'high' Christology is to be found not only in John but in all four gospels;
2. that this Christology developed, not particularly due to the impact of Greek philosophical ideas on a quasi-Jewish faith (a process which was to become much more significant later on), but can be read (albeit indirectly) both reasonably and properly from the Jewish scriptures themselves, and was thus interpreted by all the Evangelists

as confirming this 'embodiment' of God in Jesus.[28]

Hays very fairly accepts that Mark's language is equivocal on the Christological issue in that he

"...offers us no conceptual solution to the problem [of just how Jesus shares God's identity]. Rather, [Mark's] narrative holds these elements in taut suspension. His central character, Jesus, seems to be at the same time...both the God of Israel and a human being not simply identical with the God of Israel",

and he helpfully lists those elements of Mark which do not posit such an identity between Jesus and God:[29]

1. the Son of Man will (only!) sit at the right hand of the throne of God (12: 35 – 37; 14: 62): *"this is a position of extraordinary honour and power, to be sure, but is exalted proximity quite the same thing as simple identity with the God of Israel?";*
2. *"Jesus declares his own ignorance about the time of the end, in contrast to the knowledge of the Father (13: 32)";*
3. *"...several passages identify Jesus as the 'Son' (1: 11; 9: 7; 12: 6) and distinguish his role from that of the Father (8: 38; 11: 25; 14: 36). This Father/Son language binds Jesus in the closest possible relationship with God, whose glory and authority Jesus shares, while maintaining some distinction of roles and persons";*
4. at Gethsemane Jesus *"subordinates himself to the will of the Father",* playing *"the role of Israel rather than the role of God";* does the concept of 'playing a role' imply a modalist model of God and a docetic view of Christ?
5. the cry of dereliction from the cross *"once again draws on the language of the Psalms to express not only a distinction between Jesus and God but also a stark separation".*

Yet despite what seems to be fairly clear evidence from a prime source that there were important distinctions being made between God and Jesus (as one might expect from adherents of a monotheistic faith) up to the time that Mark came to be written, it is certainly not the case for Hays (who actually cites that evidence) that

> "...the more one focuses on the synoptic tradition and locates Jesus within a monotheistic Jewish/OT context, the more improbable it would be to identify him as divine".

Rather, he believes,

> "...it is precisely through drawing on OT images that all four Gospels portray the identity of Jesus as mysteriously fused with the identity of God".[30]

Hays does recognise that his claim will *"force us to rethink what we mean when we say the word 'God'"*, and this issue will be pursued further below.

We will now take as an example, and critically evaluate, some of what Hays has to say specifically about **Matthew and his use of the OT**. Firstly, he claims that Matthew (8: 23 – 27)

> "...more strongly [than Mark] hints at Jesus' divine status in the word ['Lord'] the disciples use to address him when they wake up in the midst of the storm"[31] [i.e. they worshipped him as God]: "it is difficult to imagine a clearer illustration of Matthew's didactic remoulding of the tradition. Whereas Mark's enigmatic story summons readers to awe-filled meditation on the mystery of Jesus' identity, Matthew reimagines the water-crossing as a clear parable of Jesus' relation to the church: the worship of the disciples anticipates and represents the worship eventually given to the

Risen Lord...there is only One who can command the wind and storm, only One who can stride across the waves...The worship of the disciples acknowledges and declares Jesus' identity with the one God of Israel, present in the midst of his people".[32]

Two points immediately stand out: firstly, does calling Jesus 'Lord' (*kurios*) automatically imply that they 'worshipped him' as divine? Mark uses the term only 6 times for the 'earthly' Jesus, but never unambiguously: 1: 3 (citing Malachi 3: 1 and Isaiah 40: 3); 5: 19 (is Jesus here referring to God or to himself? a partial citation of Ps 66: 16); 7: 28 (used by the Syrophoenician woman; most likely an honorific 'Sir'); 11:3 (apparently a self-reference of Jesus, but the exact meaning is unclear); 12: 36-7 (as 2: 28, a citation of Ps 110: 1 where it is not actually David speaking to the Messiah, but God speaking to the King). But no one in Mk's narrative, nor the narrator himself, actually calls Jesus 'Lord' directly. In contrast, Mt applies the term 34 times and the disciples regularly use the title of Jesus (compare parallels Mk 9: 5//Mt 17: 4), and only unbelievers use (the lesser?) 'teacher'. The use of 'Lord' in the gospel accounts varies considerably in its meaning, often connoting 'Sir'. Of course, 'Yahweh' is 'the Lord' (also *kurios* in later editions of the LXX, after YHWH was deemed too holy to use, so e.g. Mark's quotation of Isaiah in 1: 3 has YHWH rendered *kurios*), but are we really meant to suppose that the disciples (either historically or even in the view of the Evangelists) were calling Jesus 'Yahweh'? To imagine Jews calling a man 'Yahweh' is (almost?[33]) beyond belief.

Then at the conclusion of the pericope Matthew has the disciples saying: "What sort of man is this, that even the winds and the sea obey him?". Some might wish to claim that this was an obviously rhetorical question; that they knew precisely what kind of man this was: it was a man who was (also) God! But rather more straightforwardly, (within the story, whatever the nature of any event) it may represent genuine puzzlement on the part of the disciples – a kind of 'Wow! What's going on here?' for certainly puzzlement and confusion fit well with disciples who are portrayed as so frequently misunderstanding what was 'going on'. But here, again, we have to differentiate (which Hays fails to do) between two quite different *'sitze im leben'*: what (if anything) actually happened on the lake sometime in the late 20s, and how did Matthew expect his story to be understood?

Indeed, Hays' suggestion that Matthew was 'hinting at' the divine status of Jesus (even if that was what Matthew did) tells us very little: we may reasonably ask why Matthew (and Mark before him) felt the need to 'hint' at all about such an important matter. If one or both genuinely believed that Jesus 'embodied God', why not say so directly and unambiguously? Furthermore, we may reasonably enquire as to what they might have thought the concept of 'embodying God' actually meant. Does it express ontological identity between Jesus and God, as the Church later came to believe, or did they understand Jesus to be acting on behalf of God, with God's authority (and power) and in so doing expressing, exemplifying, or otherwise personifying divine characteristics in his life? Hays recognises that the language and concepts by which Jesus' 'divinity' might be more precisely articulated were not available until the 3rd or 4th Centuries, and that before that time, such 'truths' had to be expressed more in story than in philosophical form; but, how then, if these ways of understanding were so elusive, should we think that the later way of putting it must be correct (or, rather, the most effective way of expressing Jesus' relationship with God)?

It may be that the story-christology is actually saying something rather different and fits more with the actuality of the Jesus-event and the crucial Christological question: how the man from Nazareth related to God. Even Hays' reference to 'parable' with regard to the story of Jesus stilling the storm (or walking on water), by which we are invited to think of the stories as 'recapitulating' the ideas (expressed most vividly in the Psalms) associated with the Creator God taming the chaos[34] at creation, doesn't seem to have alerted him to the possibility that a perfectly reasonable (and probably more natural) interpretation of this story is not that 'Jesus was the One who commands with wind and storm/strides the waves', but that in his life, Jesus was the agent of the great Creator God ('the One who commands...') and that is what is meant by the notion (however expressed) of 'embodiment'. Hays seems to move directly from parabolic to literal language saying, in effect: 'the story is a parable, but it also describes what really happened', when, in fact, a parable is a made-up story in and through which the story-teller seeks to communicate a point. It may or may not communicate that point successfully, but to enquire whether it is true is the same as trying to find the 'historical Good Samaritan'.

Secondly, Hays' conclusion from the above is that

> *"Matthew is identifying [Jesus] as nothing less than the embodied presence of Israel's God, the one to whom alone worship is due, the one who jealously forbids the worship of any idols, images, or other gods [and goes on to claim that] the clinching argument for this reading is to be found in the story of the devil's temptation of Jesus in the wilderness".*

Here, according to Hays, the rejection of the devil in Jesus' citation of Deut 6: 13 (via LXX in Mt 4: 9 - 10) means that

> *"...readers have little choice but to interpret Jesus' acceptance of worship (proskunesis) from other characters as an implicit acknowledgement of his divine identity".*[35]

Readers clearly have a number of alternative, and probably far more valid, choices. In Matthew's temptation stories, the devil begins: "If you are the Son of God..." (4: 3, 6), in the context of OT theology, a completely human designation,[36] not: 'If you are

God' (without a doctrine of the Trinity as its conceptual structure 'Son of God' could not possibly mean 'God', and certainly does not mean 'God' in the OT). Jesus' response is to state that God's word is just as important, if not more important, than physical food (restated in John 6: 49 – 51), and that it is wrong to test God's protection of his 'Son'. Furthermore, in the example on which Hays focuses, it is the devil who seeks worship, not Jesus: to which Jesus replies that only God (not himself) who should be worshipped. There is nothing whatsoever here to support Hays' twin contentions either that Jesus accepts worship, nor that the disciples offered it.

A third example of Hays' rather tendentious argument is based on the story of Jesus' dispute over the Sabbath, where in Mt 12: 6 there is the assertion by Jesus that "something greater than the Temple is here" (not found in Mark's version of the pericope):

> "...we are not told precisely what the 'something greater' might be, but the inference lies readily at hand that it must be Jesus himself. What could be greater than the Temple other than the one to whom it is dedicated, the one who is worshipped in it? Matthew's argument is in effect this: if Jesus is 'God with us', then his presence sanctifies the labours of those who seek to serve him, even on the Sabbath. Indeed, if Jesus is 'God with us' then his personal presence now takes the place of the Temple where the presence of God was formerly thought to dwell".[37]

Perhaps a simpler interpretation of this story (and this particular text) is not so much that God now dwells (literally?) in a man instead of (literally?) in a building (which in Matthew's day, has been destroyed), but that faith in Jesus has succeeded or even superseded the life and worship of Second Temple Judaism (which seems to sum up the whole thrust of Matthew's Gospel)? This doesn't require any ontological interpretation of 'God with us', which in turn reminds us of a pretty obvious – but often ignored - question: why did the angel instruct Joseph to name the child 'Jesus' ['the Lord saves'] rather than 'Emmanuel', if there was a prophecy that God's messiah (or whatever) would be given the latter name? Or to put the question another way: if Jesus was named as instructed by the angel, why does Matthew cite a prophecy in which he should [Mt 1: 23 "...and they *shall* name him..."] have been called Emmanuel, but wasn't?

One final example confirms Hays' propensity to interpret his chosen texts far too literally (and simplistically) and then proceed to build huge theological edifices upon them: when he refers to the teaching on "church discipline" in 18: 1 – 35 as coming directly from Jesus. Many commentators would understand the more obvious *sitz im leben* of this teaching to be the Church of Matthew's day, not least because, in Jesus' day, there was no 'Christian' Church. Unsurprisingly, the matter is not this straightforward: as we have already seen, having asked the question 'did Jesus intend to found a church?', Craig Evans argues that Jesus did not intend to found "*an organisation and a people that stand outside of Israel*", but rather he wanted a "*community of disciples committed to the restoration of Israel and the conversion and instruction of the Gentiles*",[38] in which case 'the church' would refer to scattered groups who had responded to Jesus' message, perhaps linked to or similar to local synagogues. What eventually emerged became separate from Judaism; the other model would have continued to be part of Judaism, at least in some manner ("*Regrettably, Christian exegesis sometimes confuses Israel with the church*"[39]). Whatever the origin of this section of Matthew on the Church, Hays claims that Jesus' accompanying "extraordinary promise" to be a continuing presence in the community ("When two or three are gathered in my name..." 18: 20) should be understood in precisely the same way as found in the post-temple Mishnah concerning Torah, where the Shekinah – the Divine Presence - is with those who are studying Torah together. Jesus then is that same divine presence. But again, Hays fails to see that just as the Torah was thought to mediate the divine presence (and was not, in itself, thought to be divine) so we might also understand Jesus as mediating the divine presence without, himself, being divine.

It is absolutely clear that the first Christians, the vast majority having been nurtured in Judaism, who came to believe that Jesus was the promised messiah (or even more than that), and who, initially at least, continued to live and worship as Jews, searched their Scriptures in order to find 'evidence' that Jesus' coming had been foretold, particularly by the prophets (even more than in the Torah, which orthodox Jews – clearly 'Christians' were unorthodox – valued the more). This even though the overwhelming emphasis of these prophets was to 'forth-tell' (announce) rather than 'fore-tell' (predict). But, as one scholar of the OT prophets warns moderns who share this kind of thinking:

> "The tendency to jump straight from Old Testament 'predictions' to their New Testament fulfilment means that little consideration is usually paid to the significance of the prophetic message for its original audience, the ancient Israelites. We thus fail to hear the prophetic word as it was intended – as the word of God addressed to a specific situation in the life of God's people".[40]

The great prophets (even those who wrote apocalyptic material) spoke to the present, not the future.

Matthew, a particularly good example of this tendency to search for 'proof-texts' about Jesus in the Jewish Scriptures, even flagged up some of his alleged findings by use of the formula: "['such-and-such'] was spoken by the Lord through the prophet", or similar. But whilst Hays seem prepared to accept that this was an entirely valid exegetical exercise, many might see it more in terms of wish fulfilment – looking for evidence with the firm belief that it is there to be found, and thus being prepared to stretch whatever can be made to fit one's *a priori* beliefs and principles. In the five cases cited by Matthew in his nativity story, four are stretched far beyond their original referent, whilst the fifth (the 'Nazarene/Nazorean', 2: 23) can't actually be found anywhere in the OT in this form (perhaps Matthew had in mind some reference to 'Nazirites'?[41]). In 2: 15, where Hosea 11: 1 is cited, Matthew uses the verse to demonstrate how it had been 'predicted' that Jesus would go to and return from Egypt (something which, historically, must be very doubtful and which entirely contradicts Luke's itinerary), it is abundantly clear that Hosea is referring to the past Exodus event. For his part, Matthew is making the theological point to his Jewish hearers and readers that Jesus is the new Moses (just as he does by having the infant – by then, not a baby - Jesus, like the young Moses, threatened with death and hidden). Whilst some may argue that because scripture is 'inspired' (whatever might be meant by that description) it may thereby contain not only an obvious (contemporary) referent, but also (future) ones hidden unless accessed through the eyes of faith, such a claim, like that which has God superintending the writing of the Bible, borders on the literally 'non-sensical', because anyone can assert that anything means what they want it to mean without feeling any obligation to provide evidence or a rationale for their belief.

Such an approach to the Jewish scriptures wasn't limited to the first 'Jewish-Christians', but has been continuous in Christian practice through the centuries, and particularly the exegetical interests of the Patristic period where the Church Fathers

"...approached the Jewish Scriptures, usually in their Greek or Latin versions, as puzzles or mysteries to be resolved under the guiding authority of the 'paschal mystery', that is, the saving significance of Jesus' life, death and resurrection. This master narrative served as the key that would open up the many mysteries of the Old Testament. They regarded the Old Testament as a book of divine promises fulfilled in and through Jesus. Or they viewed *it as shadows cleared and illuminated through the incarnation of Jesus, the Word of God. Their approach was neatly summarised by Augustine's dictum that 'the New Testament lies hidden in the Old, and the Old is made manifest in the New'. The Fathers gave a thoroughgoing Christological interpretation to the Old Testament, and their influence remains strong today..."* [42]

For all these Christian commentators, no doubt arising out of their genuine belief that God must have revealed the coming of Jesus, the exegetical exercise in which they were engaged was right, honest and entirely valid: if Jesus had been designated by God, or somehow was God (and it is the 'somehow' which is problematic), then his presence must surely be detectable in the Jewish scriptures: all you need do is 'seek and you shall find'. The more cautious interpreter, however, may feel that such an approach is going rather further than is either reasonable or appropriate.

Case Study 2: The implications for Christology of a physical Virginal Conception

No one, having read their accounts of how Mary came to conceive Jesus (Mt 1: 18 – end; Lk 1: 26 - 56), can deny that both Matthew and Luke exhibit a relatively 'high' Christology: one which introduces a more supernatural, if not precisely 'divine', element into the Synoptic picture of Christ which is arguably absent, or perhaps just less obvious, in Mark. Nevertheless neither Matthew's nor Luke's Christology is as highly developed as that represented by John's pre-existent *Logos* and his portrayal of a Christ who glides 'divinely' through human history offering sophisticated theological insights which are in stark contrast to the simple, homely aphorisms and parables found in the Synoptics. And none is as high as Hays claims.

For Matthew, Jesus is the progeny of an unusual, 'Spirit-led', but otherwise undefined pregnancy-event. In 1: 18 Mary is "found to be with child *from the Holy Spirit*", and the same description is offered as an explanation to the worried Joseph. This contrasts with Luke's more direct, but still somewhat ambiguous, description of Mary being 'overshadowed' by "the power of the Most High" (Lk 1: 32), which hints at a more specific "operation of the Holy Ghost", as this particular activity of the Spirit is described in the BCP's Proper Preface for Christmas. This 'operation' has often been portrayed in art using symbolic representations of the Spirit: as in Fra Angelico's (Madrid) 'Annunciation' and Carlo Crivelli's 'The Virgin Annunciate' (both early – mid 15th Century) in which a beam of light shines from heaven onto Mary; or Jean Hey's 'Annunciation' (mid-15th Century) in which a dove hovers over her head; or the early 17th Century anonymous Mexican 'Annunciation' and Rubens' version (c. 1628) which, among many other examples, have both light and dove. All gently nuanced, and certainly nothing whatsoever of a sexual nature.

What meanings are such references to the action of the Holy Spirit meant to convey? That this was a straightforward act of human conception, yet one so important as to require the use of 'Spirit-language' in order to emphasise its special nature; or that this was a direct divine intervention overriding or altering natural processes of human conception? Before any be tempted to respond: 'obviously the latter'; the distinction is entirely valid because, however one reads the story, its essence is very down to earth: a girl became pregnant – and it really is not at all obvious that the Evangelists' accounts require us to understand Jesus' conception as a unique divine intervention in an otherwise natural process. Conception is ultimately a matter of human biology and, unless we are wedded to the view that 'God can do anything', how that process works must be taken seriously.

As to 'what actually happened', Matthew is more suggestive than explicit: Mary, he wrote, was "found to be with child". The reader may feel slightly teased: 'just who is the father?' All that Matthew tells us is that it definitely wasn't Joseph. Just what is Matthew hinting (for he is certainly not for telling): that Mary was made pregnant by some other man; perhaps someone God was using to implement his will (although this raises more questions than answers)?[43] Or did Matthew really understand Mary's pregnancy to be the direct result of a divine fiat? If this latter is the case, then Christian exclusivists (those who claim that Christianity is superior to every other Faith because it alone was directly established by God, and therefore it alone can offer salvation) will find they cannot have it theologically both ways: believing God to be, by whatever method, the biological father of the man Jesus ('biological' in that he was the cause of Mary's very real pregnancy), whilst at the same time arguing that their Faith is far more sophisticated than others'; particularly, no doubt, those of primitives who posited physical intercourse across the divine and human realms. Yet although such ideas were particularly prevalent within a Graeco-Roman culture where the gods were thought by many, if not the more sophisticated, to sire demi-gods and heroes via mortal women (and vice-versa), and in which early Christianity came to be nurtured (with the sophisticated philosophy if not the gods), a direct divinely created pregnancy hardly sits well within a Jewish context. The fact that Matthew is quite coy on the detail *might* suggest that he wished to avoid such a crassly simplistic conclusion. We may compare the evident desire of the authors of Genesis 1 to remodel, in a more subtle and theologically sophisticated fashion, the anthropomorphic picture of the Creator God found in Genesis 2.

Yet many modern Christians continue to propose modified versions of this scenario, such as: 'God didn't actually take human form and have sex with Mary; but he did will Mary to be pregnant, and so it happened without any involvement of a human male'. Yet at some point, however 'spiritual' (in this context implying non-material) God's role is, it has eventually to cross over into the physical. Put bluntly: presumably God would have to provide a replacement for the male sperm. Parthenogenesis does not occur in human beings and, if it ever did, the child would be female.[44] In other words, whatever the explanation, particularly if it is still claimed that Jesus was really human, and docetic instincts have been genuinely curbed, it must take account of the 'mechanical' dimension of conception, and not just rely on a somewhat simplistic form of theology: Mary became pregnant because God said so. Failing that we are left with a magical as opposed to miraculous event: as with water into wine, the divine simply causes something to happen by a 'clicking of the fingers': which is exactly how a Newtonian interventionist God is thought, by those Christians who still hold onto that antiquated idea, to operate. Doesn't putting it like this expose the foolishness of a literal interpretation of the story which, when taken to its logical conclusion, has God apparently acting (albeit in a much less crude manner) rather like Zeus? That, despite putting his faith in Isaiah 7: 14, would surely have been beyond the pale for Matthew.

Is it not possible, therefore, that Matthew, as a good Jew nurtured in his Holy Scriptures, had in mind something more akin to the recurring stories in the OT (just as with Elisabeth, mother of the Baptist, in Luke) of barren women being divinely enabled to give birth (just how did three consecutive generations of the same family happen to marry barren women, together with Abimelech's wife and his female slaves [Gen 20: 17]: this apparent epidemic of barrenness points more to theology than it does to gynaecology not least because, in Abimelech's case, we are told that God caused it [20: 18])?[45] Here the emphasis (within the context of these ancient sagas) is on God curing the barrenness: there is never any suggestion that the biological fathers were not Abraham, Isaac and the other previously disappointed husbands. Of course, neither is there any suggestion that Mary, like Elizabeth and the others, was barren. Yet, again, theology must trump gynaecology. It is sometimes implied that OT women who were barren were also fairly old, thus emphasising the miracle that they were enabled to give birth (so, for example, Sarah dies aged 127 before her son Isaac is married aged 40: Gen 23: 1, 25: 20; Isaac was 60 when Rebecca gave birth: Gen 25: 26). Mary may just have been entering or emerging from puberty; certainly the later tradition emphasises her youth. The point is particularly strongly made by both Luke and Matthew that Mary is not yet married: legally binding betrothals were arranged, as in some cultures today, possibly when the boy or girl, or both, were still children; traditionally the young Mary was thought to have been betrothed to the much older Joseph.[46] Matthew's narrative might indicate an unusually young age for child-bearing or, even more simply, signifies that Jesus was particularly special. The straightforward meaning in all these stories is that the children arising from both extremities: old age and youth, were particularly blessed (i.e. unlikely) gifts from God ("...from the Holy Spirit"). Of course, all this is pure speculation on my part: the result of reflection on the meaning of the relevant texts, and how they might relate to each other: and I have to say, truthfully, that not even I am entirely convinced by my argument. Although I do think there is something to be usefully pursued in the twin issues of God and barrenness specifically, and God and conception generally.

Bearing that last point in mind, an even more straightforward explanation was offered many years ago by the popular, prolific, and certainly very orthodox Bible commentator, William Barclay. He wrote:

> "The Jews had a saying that in the birth of every child there were three partners, the father, the mother and the Spirit of God. They believed that no child could ever be born without the Spirit, and it may well be that the New Testament stories of the birth of Jesus

are lovely, poetical ways of saying that even if He had a human
father, the Holy Spirit of God was operative in His birth in the most
unique and special way".[47]

Leaving aside the difficult concept of uniqueness, which we will
discuss further below, Barclay appears to be acknowledging
that the doctrine of the virginal conception must be understood
theologically, and the way he explains that makes good sense:
God is involved in every new life; but most especially in the
life of Jesus. But as with every other birth (and particularly the
births from those who had previously been barren), he did not
make Mary pregnant.

I mentioned in the introduction the impact that Leslie
Weatherhead had on my thinking as a theologically naïve and
somewhat unbiddable Christian teenager (our 'youth curate'
who was eventually raised to the *Episcope* might be prepared
to comment). In 'The Christian Agnostic' (I found the title
attractively mischievous and compelling) Weatherhead offered
a theory[48] based on his correspondence with a researcher (GA
Wainwright) into the Near/Middle Eastern concept of 'sacred
marriage'. In brief: a king or high priest, acting on behalf of the
divine, had ritual sexual relations with a specially chosen virgin,
and the child which resulted was regarded as a 'son of God',
a 'divine king', or even an 'incarnate god'. He further pointed
out that the words: "...you have found favour with God" (Lk
1: 30) are *"almost identical"*[49] to the words Herodotus uses of the
Divine Bride at Babylon.Weatherhead then goes on to consider
the role of Zechariah (the Baptist's father) who, so Luke tells us,
was duty priest at the Jerusalem temple (Lk 1: 9) and in whose
house Mary stayed for three months (apparently the same time
period the Mesopotamian virgin bride had to remain in the
sacred precincts) immediately following the Annunciation.
Why, he asks, did Mary go there "with haste" (Lk 1: 39); what
needed to be done so quickly (implied answer – she had to

become pregnant in order to fulfil God's will)? Furthermore, what role does Elizabeth's pregnancy have in the story other than to demonstrate that, though old, Zechariah was still potent *"and could fulfil his priestly duty"*?[50] The reader will see where this is leading:[51] Zechariah, the priest of God, working on God's behalf, was Jesus' biological father and he impregnated Mary as a sacred act. This, the argument goes, is what Luke implied not only by having the angel's message to Mary be about a future event ("The Holy Spirit *will* come upon you, and the power of the Most High *will* overshadow you..." 1: 35), but it also provides a rationale for his inclusion of the otherwise quasi-relevant story about Elizabeth; about which Matthew has nothing whatsoever to say (as already noted, the differences between the two nativity stories are massive and cannot be conflated; it is obvious to me that they are independently created and, as a result, totally different stories).

Perhaps my particular interpretation (focusing on barrenness) and-or the many others offered by those unwilling to interpret the accounts of Jesus' conception literally are coherent (a reasonable way of interpreting the texts); perhaps they are even authentic (precisely what the Evangelists intended to imply); they may be neither. The first is always a matter of opinion; the second is potentially a question of fact – was that the point Matthew or Luke was seeking to make or did he have some other in mind? It is even possible that neither Matthew nor Luke were quite sure either of what had happened or how to express their particular interpretations of Isaiah 7: 14 (or whatever else Luke had found in the tradition) in story form. After all, although he points out specifically that Mary and Joseph did not engage in sex until after the birth of Jesus (Mt 1: 25),[52] Matthew nevertheless includes Joseph in his genealogy of Jesus (Mt 1: 16). These claims are contradictory only if the story is thought to be historical; otherwise each element has its own theological point to make: (i) that Jesus' conception didn't depend on "the will of the flesh or of the will of man" (as John put it: 1: 13), but (ii) that he came from the line of David (which would have entailed a biological, 'fleshly' link, probably through the father). We can only have a limited idea (either that which an author chooses to make clear or where there is some other reasonable indicator of implied meaning) of what was going through any Biblical writer's mind as they tell their stories, simply because we only have the words they have left us; and those, like all words, require interpretation. We should, therefore, exercise considerable caution when claiming to offer precise interpretations of ancient religious (or any other) texts.

Of course, in Luke, Mary explicitly confesses her virginity: 1: 34 – 35: "How can this be...?". This, however, may be the result of Luke's tendency to reify spiritual matters, perhaps to make them easier to understand. As we discussed above, the relatively late development of an empty tomb tradition was a means of making the resurrection 'appearances' of Jesus comprehensible: 'if they really experienced Jesus, then his body must have left the tomb' (*post hoc ergo propter hoc*[53]). An entirely spiritual presence is, as many centuries of emphasising a bodily (physical) resurrection have demonstrated, a difficult concept to express in understandable terms. That is, no doubt, one of the reasons why many Christians are still convinced that the 'truth of the Resurrection' depends absolutely on it being an entirely physical, historical phenomenon; yet, as we have seen, that is not the most obvious way of reading the relevant NT texts.

In his account of Jesus' baptism Luke converts the Holy Spirit which was, for Mark, only "like a dove" (a simile) and only seen by Jesus (Mk 1: 10; also Mt 3: 16), into an implied publicly visible solid dove: "in bodily form" (Lk 3: 22; cp. Jn 1: 32 in which the dove visibly perches on Jesus). Furthermore, in his accounts of the Ascension (and only Luke provides any such account) we find, firstly in the Gospel version, that Jesus, still in post-resurrection 'bodily' form, somewhat vaguely 'withdraws' from the disciples and is then "carried up into heaven" (Lk 24: 51, method undefined: reflecting the general idea that God's abode was above the skies and so, in order to get there, there had to be a literally upward trajectory, as in 2 Kings 2: 11 where Elijah "ascended in a whirlwind into heaven" in a chariot of fire). In Luke's second and longer account (Acts 1: 6 – 11), in which he offers a little more detail, (possibly because he has had more time to reflect on how best to express an experience which was not his own) Jesus, at first in full physical sight of the disciples, is then (again apparently literally: there is no indication otherwise) "lifted up and a cloud took him out of their sight" (v. 9). Although any of these descriptions might easily be interpreted in a spiritual and linguistically non-univocal manner (similes, metaphors and the like), as with the 'empty tomb' tradition, Luke (who trumps Mark's single young messenger by having two, not simply in white robes, but in dazzling robes; not to be outdone, Matthew converts them into a single angel, "[whose] appearance [was] like lightening and his clothing white as snow", who descends from heaven, removes the stone from the tomb and sits on it) chooses to make them more straightforwardly physical: the Spirit is not just 'like a dove', it *is* a dove (or rather, is in the 'bodily' form of a dove); the Ascension doesn't just mark the point – which was bound to come sometime - at which the disciples no longer have direct access to Jesus' particularly close spiritual 'risen' presence: it becomes the 1st Century equivalent of Star Trek's immortal: 'Beam me up. Scotty!' (a line, by the way, which Captain Kirk never actually uttered).

It seems unlikely that Luke knew Matthew, or one might expect at least some of Matthew's Nativity to have found its way into his (a mention of the Magi, perhaps), but it is entirely possible that he knew of the particular tradition, which Matthew may have either received or created, in which Jesus's conception is referenced by Isaiah 7: 14. It may be that Luke then latched onto the word 'virgin' and took the concept to its apparently logical, physical conclusion (again, as with the 'empty tomb' tradition):'if the prophecy was about a virgin giving birth, then Mary must literally have been a virgin; so, in my account, that is what she must make absolutely clear to the angel'. Luke, in his story of the boy Jesus left at the Temple, is often interpreted by preachers as making a distinction between Joseph and Jesus' 'real' Father (Luke 2: 49). Yet any Jew might have referred to the Temple as "my Father's house" and to God as Father; the concept of the Fatherhood of God wasn't invented by Jesus (e.g. Deut 32: 6; Jer 31: 9; Is 64: 8).

How did the Evangelists understand the concept of a virginal conception? Despite Hays' optimism on such matters, we just don't know; all we can do is draw inferences from the textual evidence in front of us and accept the possibility that we may be quite wrong in our interpretation. I confess that I find the 'Zechariah solution' quite neat, but ultimately unconvincing; not least because it raises all kinds of impossible-to-answer historical questions: how did it come to be? Did Zechariah conceive – pardon the pun – the plan and 'sell it' to Mary, or was it vice versa? Did he actually rape Mary, a young vulnerable guest in his home? (Before anyone claims that would be impossible for a priest of God, let us not forget historical and ongoing contemporary cases of clerical child abuse). This is yet another demonstration of just how hard it is to draw history from Biblical narratives, simply because the evidence is so sparse: or is no evidence at all.

We also need to recognise the impact on our thinking of the ways in which Christian writers over the centuries have embraced, even captured and so bolstered the story in order to promote other theological agendas: for example, the notion (owing much to Augustine) that Jesus had to have been born without a human father because, ever since 'the Fall', 'original sin' had been transmitted to future generations via the male; only if Jesus were conceived without that taint could he be free from sin, which (they aver) he had to be in order to be our

Saviour. For Catholic Christians in particular, this had a knock-on effect of also requiring the Immaculate Conception of Mary herself, ultimately defined by Pope Pius IX in 1854: a belief complementary to that of Mary being a perpetual virgin (which, as we have seen, if we take the Biblical accounts seriously is simply not true). Is it any wonder that the Church, since quite early days and reflected in its various Calendars, has embraced virginity as something inherently 'saintly' (and conversely appeared to promote the view that sex is inherently sinful)? So doctrine continues to be built upon doctrine. The danger is: should the original ever be undermined, the whole edifice falls. If, historically, there was no 'Fall' (if the story of Adam and Eve is understood for what it is: a myth), then the doctrine of Original Sin is either lost completely (because based squarely on a non-event, it becomes meaningless) or, at the very least, requires substantial reinterpretation.

When we consider the issues in these terms, there is no requirement to think that Jesus did not have a human father and, as I have already asked: if he did not, how can he be like us? Just in case a reader were tempted to say: 'Denying the physicality of the virginal conception (they might add: 'and of the Resurrection') is just a very modern reductionist fad', then s/he may be surprised to learn that some 80 years ago the CE's Doctrine Commission published a report in which it was stated: *"There are some among us who hold that a full belief in the historical incarnation is more consistent with the supposition that Our Lord's birth took place under the normal conditions of human generation"*.[54] We may note that this is not a negative: 'some find the doctrine difficult to believe' type of comment, but a positive affirmation: 'The Doctrine of the Incarnation is potentially harmed by believing in a literal virginal conception'.

A somewhat basic theological question (although, as so often with such basic questions, one seldom asked) inevitably follows: 'why was a miraculous birth thought to be necessary for Jesus?' Or to put the same question in God-shaped terms: 'why did God feel the need for it to happen like this; why couldn't 'the Incarnation' have been effected through a purely natural birth – surely God had that power?...after all, the natural laws of the universe, and everything that flows from them, originated with the Creator'. If the answer were to be given: 'because Jesus is actually God's son and that requires the father's (Father's) involvement in the birth' then that again both begs the Christological question, and proposes an unnecessarily literal interpretation of the meaning of the term 'Son of God': one not to be found in the Jewish Scriptures, and one which inevitably impacts on the use of Father-Son language in Trinitarian discourse. Are we to understand that the Eternal **Son**, the Second Person of the Trinity, became, at a point in history 2000 years ago, the 'biological' **son** of the Father? If we do think that, how can we possibly protect the essential unity of the Godhead? Such an idea would irreparably 'divide the substance' because we would be compelled to imagine that one Person of the Trinity 'gave birth' to another Person of the Trinity, presumably twice: in both the divine and earthly realms? This is presumably why the Fathers used the helpfully opaque concept 'begotten' (*gennao*; and 'procession' for the Holy Spirit, for the origin of the eternal Spirit creates the same dilemma: how can anything eternal have an origin?) to express how 'the Son' related to 'the Father'. In any case, as we discussed in Chapter 2, that is not a required interpretation of *gennao*. If there is one God, as we proclaim, then the crude picture of God making Mary pregnant in order to give birth to the Incarnate Son, is both nonsensical and profoundly misleading: indeed, it has misled Christians for almost two millennia.

The historical bottom line is this: we simply have no idea who Jesus' father was; but we have no real reason to think (despite Matthew's blunt denial) that it wasn't Joseph, either within or outside marriage (it happens). Both Mt 13: 55: "Is not this the carpenter's son...?" and Lk 4: 22 "Is this not Joseph's son?" may reflect the original – pre-virginal conception – tradition that Jesus was the biological son of Joseph and Mary. Luke's prior reference in 3: 23: "as was thought", is clearly designed as a corrective to fit in with the means of conception he has earlier described. Even the 4th Evangelist is happy to write, without further comment, that "[The Jews] were saying, 'Is this not Jesus, the son of Joseph..." (6: 42); and in his response Jesus doesn't even bother to contradict what they had claimed. Furthermore, Philip tells Nathanael that they had found "Jesus, son of Joseph from Nazareth" (Jn 1: 45; leading to the famous comment "Can anything good come out of Nazareth?"). It would seem that John, with his Logos-Christology, is either unaware of any tradition of a virginal conception, or is simply disinterested in it.

Did both (or either) Matthew and Luke believe in a physical virginal conception? Unless we are determined to answer in the affirmative, whatever the evidence (it is a requirement of our blik), then the most obvious answer is that it is difficult to be sure. But even if they (or one of them) did, that doesn't mean that we have to do so: the language they use, and the way they deploy it, does not require us to take it literally. Both 'nativities' are capable of a non-literal interpretation and, in any case, we should remember that all language about God is necessarily non-literal. In fact, it makes much more sense and the results are much more profound when understanding the accounts of the virginal conception as theological language, the primary focus of which is God: the stories make it clear that God was intimately involved in the Christ event from the very beginning (and in John's much more sophisticated theology, the very beginning is exactly that). Indeed, one theologian has argued that the doctrine of the virginal conception actually undermines the doctrines of Chalcedon, a view in line with the above quotation from the CE's 1938 Doctrine Report:

"In thinking about Jesus as truly divine, focus on the virgin birth as the mode of incarnation has had two main unfortunate consequences. One is the tendency to speak of the incarnation as though it refers to the inception of Jesus' life rather than its totality. Once Jesus' conception and birth are seen as a normal aspect of his being and having a personal body rather than entailing an extraordinary divine intrusion, the emphasis can fall where it should in talking of incarnation. Incarnation stands for the way in which the triune God relates to creaturely humanity in and through the entirety of the life of the particular human personal body of Jesus of Nazareth, which culminates in his death and resurrection and which is also part of the larger story of God's interaction with Israel. To speak of Jesus' divinity, then, is to claim that in and through this entire human life, not in special moments or events within it, God has chosen to identify Godself. The personal identity of Jesus in his humanity now decisively defines how God is most aptly characterised...The second unfortunate consequence of the focus on the virgin birth as the mode of incarnation is the tendency of some to hold that one of the major indicators of that divinity is precisely that Jesus was miraculously conceived without a human male. But this is to introduce confusion...It is the fully human personal body, Jesus of Nazareth, and not a hybrid or semi-divine figure, in whom the divine Word is incarnate...It is worth noting that, according to the rules of Chalcedonian Christology, this is to confuse the two 'natures'...The birth of Jesus initiated by God without a human father but with a human mother confuses the categories of divine and human by identifying the divine aspect of Jesus with his conception in space and time and makes the exception to what was confessed about his full humanity. It replaces an aspect of normal human existence for Jesus with a divine property...What Chalcedon talks of as a hypostatic union is not one that has a particular location in Jesus' psyche or in some temporal event in his life. The virgin birth inevitably ends up making his conception precisely such a point of confusion between the two natures, Arguably, therefore,

declining to understand that conception literally enables one to do better justice to the intent of Chalcedon".[55]

We could put the matter much more simply: conception is, by its very nature, a private affair. How can anyone, other than the mother, know for certain how she became pregnant (some mothers don't know even that)? In Mary's case we have no direct evidence, one way or another, regarding how she became pregnant. The first Evangelist, Mark, shows absolutely no interest in the matter; the two Evangelists who do (and who have used Mark as their main source, suggesting either the existence of another source or that either one or the other created the tradition themselves) are writing some 80 years after the alleged event. Neither claims that Mary or any family member told them about the manner of Jesus' conception, although when I was at school taking an A Level course in Biblical Studies, it was almost a cliché found in textbooks and some of the academically less rigorous commentaries that Mary was Luke's source and Joseph Matthew's, although there isn't the slightest evidence for that. This idea was based entirely on the observation that Luke tells the story of Jesus' birth from Mary's perspective, whilst Matthew tells it from Joseph's.

However we decide to interpret the higher Christology represented by Matthew's and Luke's accounts of a conception that deserves or even requires the adjective 'virginal', it is still a considerable leap from the idea that God was somehow specially involved in Jesus' birth to the claim that this can only be explained by positing ontological identity between Jesus and the 'God of Israel'. As we have seen, there are enormous difficulties squaring any literal interpretation of the accounts of Jesus' conception with his true humanity. There is something essentially and probably irredeemably docetic in the doctrine. If Jesus truly was the outcome of a conception which did not involve a male parent then he was in a very real sense only quasi-human: and that is not what the historic creeds claim. Indeed, as Lincoln argues (in my view successfully), a literal interpretation of the doctrine breaks a cardinal Christological rule by confusing the divine and human natures and, in so doing, undermines Chalcedon. Hays may well be right to interpret Matthew's understanding of 'the Incarnation' (the term actually derives from the Johannine model: 'en-fleshed') as Jesus 'embodying' God, just as for Paul "God was *in* Christ..." (2 Cor 5: 19); but just what is meant by the concept of embodiment or of being "in Christ", particularly within the context of a monotheistic faith, he somewhat anachronistically assumes rather than argues. It could equally well, and taking seriously the importance of monotheism to the first Christians, be better interpreted both metaphorically (as we have seen above) and functionally (as we shall discuss below): Jesus is given the authority to stand in the place of God, as were many others in the Jewish Scriptures, and in carrying out that vocation 'embodies', expresses, personifies, exemplifies the very characteristics of his Father God.

What we may validly learn from the Old Testament

We have seen how the first Christians, the vast majority Jews, pored over their Scriptures in order to find clues about, and even what they considered to be direct predictions of, the coming of the Messiah. So, for example, Jesus had to have been born in Bethlehem (even though he is always 'Jesus of Nazareth', never 'Jesus of Bethlehem') not only because it was 'Royal David's City' (the carol which has 'little town' is the more accurate), but because it had been explicitly foretold by the prophet Micah (5: 2). We have also seen how some of their 'discoveries' (of the presence of Jesus in the OT) tended to stretch the original meaning of a prophecy or a verse from a Psalm to breaking point by altering the original meaning entirely (as with Hosea's "... out of Egypt..." which clearly refers to the Exodus, not to the perambulations of the infant Jesus). The claim is sometimes made that OT texts can validly have several different meanings and apply to multiple situations, perhaps hidden from those who wrote them, is simply special pleading: there is no shred of objective evidence for the view. It is yet another form of the 'God superintended the writing...'-blik.

Some have even suggested that there are elements of the Jesus-story, particularly the passion narratives, which may have been constructed from, and so created by, those very Scriptures (e.g. Jn 19: 24 from Ps 22: 18; Jn 19: 36 from Ps 34: 20), perhaps for liturgical purposes. In other words, before there existed any of the texts we now recognise as the NT documents, explicitly Christian worship – as opposed to the normal Jewish worship in which these 'Christian' Jews also engaged (Acts 2: 46 – 47) - exclusively used the Jewish scriptures (the only ones they had) and, in using them, gave particular emphasis to those texts which were thought to have prophesied the coming of Jesus. Frequent repeated use of those texts may have merged with, or even created, traditions about Jesus. That was perfectly understandable: if it is believed that such-and-such a text was about Jesus, then it is a short step to incorporate it into pericopae being formed and passed on about him. For example, if Psalm 22: 18 was thought to refer to Jesus, then it must have been the case that, at the crucifixion, the soldiers cast lots and divided his clothes among themselves. 'If it says so in scripture, then it must have happened.'

Our modern lectionaries engage in the same kind of process by linking OT and NT texts within an overarching theme (led by the content of the Gospel reading), perhaps implying to some that such matches are original and authentic when, in fact, the pairing is simply the outcome of that same concern: to show that the Jewish Scriptures witnessed to Jesus (something that many if not most Jews would vehemently deny); or at least to use the OT reading either as background material (entirely appropriate) or to demonstrate similarities (less appropriate when those similarities are either forced or when there is no attempt to clarify the relationship between the two readings, something that is left to the preacher to do: accurately or not[56]). In the Revised Common Lectionary of 1992, based on the 1969 Roman Lectionary modified and developed in an ecumenical context, there is a separate OT 'Track 2' specifically geared to do that job: just how successfully it does so is a matter of opinion.

It is a purely a matter of judgement as to whether a particular OT text is a genuine 'prophecy' (prediction) of some (distant) future event (a 'fore-telling'; many commentators consider the OT prophets to have been mainly 'forth-tellers': proclaiming God's message to the people and events of the time[57]), or whether the later account of, or reference to, that future event has itself arisen from the OT text: for example, just the combination of Ps 22 and Isaiah 52: 13 – 53: 12 alone encapsulates much of the main thematic structure together with some of the detail of the Passion. As with any matter of judgement, people will disagree. That is why it is important to examine the criteria each put forward in support of their argument such as, in my view, the pretty obvious way (I won't go so far as to claim 'very obvious' as I recognise that it is not at all obvious to those who take a different view on what is implied by the 'authority of scripture'), due to clear disparities between context or misunderstandings due to translation, in which Matthew's (and John's) 'such-and-such happened in order...' is an artificial 'explanation-after-the-event' literary device, even if the Evangelists didn't see it that way: they too had their bliks. Most often there is no argument offered for the view that the OT 'predicted' the coming of Jesus. Such a position represents, we might say, a sub-blik arising from the primary blik: the conviction that the Bible was divinely 'supervised' or otherwise produced by God's direct fiat. The debate, then, becomes pointless simply because it is no debate at all: there is no battle of arguments in which one side's view is modified or even defeated by the other.

Leaving such controversies to one side, I should now like to offer a positive exploration of what the Jewish Scriptures, validly interpreted (using exegesis: reading from them what we judge them to be saying; rather than eisegesis: reading into them what we want them to say), can inform us about how the particular conceptual route taken by the Christological pathway from human messiah (prophet or whatever) to Second Person of the Trinity, or what Hays calls the "embodiment of the God of Israel" in the man Jesus, came to be taken.

Firstly, the tendency for the **distinction between the identity of God and that of his agents to be blurred** (e.g. in Judges 6: 11 – 15 the angel speaks to Gideon, and suddenly the speaker is God himself cf. Abraham [Gen 22: 11 – 12], Hagar [Gen 16: 7 – 13] and Moses [Ex 3: 2 – 3: 7]. In Ex 23: 20 God promises to send an angel and adds that God's name will be with him etc.). If Jesus was the 'anointed one' (or in any other way chosen by God) then he was certainly God's agent (commissioned to act on God's behalf). When the 'human being' in Daniel 7 is given (by God) "dominion and glory and kingship", those things that are God's by right, we can begin to understand how, in taking on the characteristics and 'rights' of the divine, the identity of the "one like a human being coming with the clouds of heaven" (understood by the early Church to be Christ, so e.g. 1 Thess 4: 16 - 17) came to be merged with the identity of God. Put at its most simplest, the thinking went: 'if Jesus had God's authority (etc.) it stands to reason that he must be God'. As we have already seen, that is not necessarily the case at all (the secondary agent can carry the authority of the primary) and the issue is, again, helpfully clarified by Goldingay in his discussion of Isaiah as 'messenger':

"There is a solemnity about being addressed by someone who comes with the Great King's authority and speaks with the 'I' of the great

king, as if he were the great king (cf. Is 36: 4, 14, 16). That is how the prophet speaks as Yahweh's messenger, as if he were the Great King. He brings the great king's presence; he speaks performatively... To the scene opening up before him, Isaiah ben Amoz brings an angle of vision that differs from the one Jeremiah or Ezekiel would bring to it. Revelation comes via a human person. When an envoy relates Sennacherib's message to Hezekiah, he may sometimes pass on his king's actual words, but he also engages in dialogue with Hezekiah's staff and continues to speak as if relating the king's own words. He has the authority to speak on his king's behalf in the way that seems appropriate in the context. Even when he himself devises the words, he can use the 'I' of his king. His words have the king's authority. They are the king's words, even though he formulates them. Something similar is true of Isaiah ben Amoz".[58]

Jesus, who has perhaps chosen the prophet Isaiah (without knowing or needing to critically differentiate between three or more of them) as his role model, is, then, one who operates under the direct authority of God, but so much so that it appears to those who meet him 'as if' he were God. As Goldingay puts it of Isaiah: "*...as the prophet who represents Yahweh, he gets treated in the same way as people treat Yahweh (Is 28: 7 – 10)*"[59] in this case, badly.

Similarly, the tendency for some of **God's own characteristics to take on a virtually independent existence,** particularly 'Wisdom' in the OT and even more so in the 'Inter-Testamental' writings, but also, to an increasing degree in Christian thought, the 'Word' – particularly as the 4th Evangelist identified the Word both with God (1: 1) and with Jesus (1: 14), as well as (possibly) using the so-called 'I am' sayings to perform the same function.[60] Again, one can imagine that if these *divine characteristics* have work to do within the created order they must become *somehow* identified with it. The notion of angels (particularly in the way they are understood by some people today, such as the idea of guardian angels) who seem to move freely between the divine and mundane realms (e.g. Lk 2: 13 – 15) provides one model and, presumably, no-one would claim that angels are 'uncreated'? Similarly, the expression of a divine Word who 'came down from heaven', did his work, and then returned 'from whence he came' (Acts 1: 11): an essentially mythic trajectory (which is not the same as saying that the story of Jesus is a myth; rather that in its overall form it exhibits some mythic elements). Indeed, in a similar way, even a city (in this case, Jerusalem) can take on an independent metaphysical existence beyond its normal (natural) referents:

> *"In Isaiah, Jerusalem-Zion (like 'servant') is a tensive symbol, capable of having more than one referent...[able to] refer to that corporate personality as a metaphysical entity that in some sense exists independently of its population..."*[61]

The notion of particular characteristics existing apart from their bearer is quite normal in linguistic usage, such as with metonymy where, for example, 'crown' (what is worn) comes to refer to the monarch (who wears it) or the institution of the monarchy (in which it is worn). It only becomes a conceptual problem, as with some Christological assertions, when taken literally. Do we even need to remind ourselves that HM Queen Elizabeth is not literally a crown?

A third enlightening factor relates to another theological tendency to be found within the Jewish Scriptures, as explicated by Stephen Herring.[62] Broadly speaking, in the ancient Near East (Mesopotamia, Assyria and, to a degree, also in Israel) certain images ('image' used in the technical sense as the deity's cultic representation) were understood to be, in some sense, **manifestations of the divine presence and power** and, particularly in Mesopotamian culture, the distinction we have so far made between ontology and functionalism was not so clear-cut – rather than being different, they were seen as two sides of the same coin. Just as the king exercised divine agency in ruling on behalf of the gods, representing them to the people, and maintaining cosmic order through rites and ceremonies (and so was, in that sense, 'divine'), so the priest was also understood as an image of the god Marduk, and both king and priest, albeit in and through their distinct roles, manifested divine identity, power and agency: *"in a sense, they acted as the proxy to the divine, and embodied and represented the divinity to the rest of creation and society"*.[63] Similarly, argues Herring, Israel had a long history of using divine imagery, with specifically anthropomorphic examples being dedicated to Yahweh in the earliest cultic settings. Furthermore, the Biblical authors were heavily influenced by the ideological environment of the Babylonian Exile and adapted, for their own purposes, the Mesopotamian notion of humanity as imaging the Divine.

It is in the Priestly redaction of Gen 1: 26 - 27 that we find its ultimate expression (as the last great creative act) in humanity made "in our image...so God created humankind in his image, in the image of God he created them...", just as Adam's son Seth was born "in his likeness, according to his image" (Gen 5: 3), implying the closest of connections leading virtually to a form of identity: the son is also, in a sense, the father, as the line carries on through the generations and the initial identity is maintained, as it is sociologically and anthropologically (in some cultures) through continued and valued use of the family name, and biologically (universally) through genetics. This is yet another example of merging identities: Christologically, with the 'Son of God' being identified (at least to some extent) with his Father. But, as we have seen, Jesus was certainly not the only one to be designated God's son; in the OT the term was used of any deemed to have a special relationship with God, but particularly:

1. Exodus 4: 22: [the people of] **Israel** is called "my firstborn

son"; as in Jeremiah 31: 9, 20

2. Psalm 89: 26 – 28: **David** says to God: "You are my Father...", to which God replies (again): "I will make him the firstborn [son], the highest of the kings of the earth"; 2 Sam 7: 14 again of David: "I will be a father to him, and he shall be **a** son [of God] to me" (note 'a' son, rather than 'the' son: there could be many sons).

Furthermore, the kingly/priestly models outlined above also came to be applied to humanity in general: just as kings ruled over the people, so humanity was given dominion over creation (Gen 1: 28 – 30), representing God to the other orders of that creation in the same kind of way. Hence (again, in some way and in the broader sense) all humanity consists sons and daughters of God[64] (see further below).

Moving to what is probably the Priestly editing of the Book of Exodus, we find Moses (recalling that the Evangelist, Matthew, in particular, implicitly presented Jesus as 'another Moses' by, for example, modelling the 'Sermon on the Mount' on the five Books of Moses) also embodying the divine image, but here in a specific and individual rather than a corporate sense, most explicitly as he descends from Sinai with his face shining[65] because "he had been talking with God" (Ex 35: 29). After which he felt the need to put a veil on his face (except when speaking to God), presumably because his 'divine' radiance was just too much to bear? In other words, despite the clear understanding that there were two 'persons' present together: God and Moses, there was a somewhat crudely described sharing of identity (to the extent that Moses' face shone) when Moses was acting as God's mouth-piece. Indeed, the earlier representation of the divine presence (the cloud/pillar of fire) was always absent when Moses was on the mountain (because that was where God was too), and it was in that context that the people felt the need to 'plug the gap' with the Golden Calf which they even worship (Ex 32) – they needed Yahweh (or something beyond themselves) with them as a presence and as a focus of their worship, just a Christians find God's presence (in Christ) in and through the Eucharistic 'body and blood' although, properly interpreted, this is no idol (not least because it is understood to be a 'Dominical' sacrament).

Furthermore, we find that within the context of his campaign against cultic images, the prophet Ezekiel (36 – 37), himself infused with God's Spirit, becomes a model for Israel's endowment with the Spirit. In other words, it was not just wood or stone that 'hosted' or 'embodied' the divine Presence, but humanity. We may infer from these examples that there was, in elements of OT theology, the notion not only that humanity in general could reflect the divine image and embody the Presence, but that particular individuals manifested the divine presence and, like some of the prophets, exercise divine power.

Summing up what the OT can authentically tell us (as opposed to that which we choose to read into it) which can support our Christological thinking, we find:

1. a tendency for the distinction between the identity of God and that of his agents to be blurred: this is a potentially rich insight for aiding our understanding as to **how the relationship between Jesus and God came ultimately to be expressed;**

2. a tendency for some of God's own characteristics to take on a virtually independent existence: particularly **the way in which *Logos* came to be understood as an 'aspect of God' which could 'take on human flesh';**

3. that certain images, and particularly people, were understood to be manifestations or symbols of the divine presence and power: this will help us understand **how a human being could be thought to embody the divine presence, without the need to think of such a person as**

divine.

Even if one cannot agree (wholly or in part) with Hays' judgement that (i) Jesus' divinity can be read so easily from the OT, although there are clear examples God's identity being associated or even merged with that of others, and in which humankind in general, but also particular people, may mediate the divine presence and exercise divine power, or that (ii) all the Evangelists exhibit a (relatively) high Christology, it is quite reasonable to view Jesus as an individual (and why, *a priori*, should he be thought to be the only one?) who 'embodied' God's presence and action in the world, although not (so I am arguing) as a person who was ontologically God – except insofar (as in the above examples) that God's 'being' (essence) was expressed in and through a human person and human actions. In other words, the OT doesn't require us to imagine that Jesus was God in any 'literal' sense (although, if we accept that we can only use non-literal language about God, then it is difficult to explicate exactly what 'literal' means in this context) and actually encourages us not to do so; even though that is how the Conciliar Fathers may well have understood it. The Jewish scriptures support the notion that God has expressed himself in and through genuinely 'human' beings such as the prophets and, as we have seen, 'prophet' was one of the genuine designations attached to Jesus in his day.

This discussion returns us to one crucial issue: the 'Chalcedonian Definition', the Nicene Creed, the Athanasian Creed (and other such statements of faith) may well have been understood by their creators to have been a univocal expression of some 'fact' about God and/or Jesus but, in the light of our modern understanding of linguistic diversity and subtlety, we should not feel obliged to follow them down that particular linguistic path. Rather, we may take what they wrote and see it not only more simply, but more accurately, as the way that Christians in those days expressed their conviction that 'God was in Christ...'. To deny that the way they expressed those 'truths' makes less or even no sense today, is not to deny the validity of their fundamental assertions: that there was an extraordinary 'connection' between Jesus of Nazareth and the God of Israel, and that connection has made an existential difference to millions of lives, then and now. We shall explore that important, even fundamental, Christological claim in the next chapter.

Notes

1. As did the Buddha's disciples, although later on the same transference of emphasis from message to messenger occurred;

2. It is noteworthy that in Peter's Pentecost speech (no doubt constructed by Luke – in which, incidentally, Jesus is described as "a **man accredited** by God" Acts 2: 22) there is no mention whatsoever of Jesus' teaching, although in 28:23 Paul seeks to 'explain' the Kingdom of God (as well as proclaiming Christ);

3. Even the Fourth Gospel has texts which would support a purely human-functionalist interpretation: "...the Son can **do** nothing on his own, but only what he sees the Father **doing**; for whatever the Father **does**, the Son **does** likewise" (5:19; see also 7: 16, 8: 28, 40 and 14: 28); so equally "The Father and I are one" could be a reference to function or activity ('I am one with my Father in and through doing his work'): exactly that same kind of unity which Christ himself sought with his disciples (17: 11); it makes a significance difference, when considering these sayings, as to whether they are the *ipsissima verba* of Jesus or express the theological views of the author of the 4th Gospel; if Jesus never actually said: 'The Father and I are one' (etc.), and that is simply the view of 'John' (for whom Jesus is the 'Word made flesh' – a claim never actually made by Jesus, even in the 4th Gospel) then to build a huge theological edifice on it is surely a mistaken

enterprise? perhaps an accurate summary of John's position is that he presents Jesus's relationship with God in **both ontological and functional categories** in order to express his undoubted understanding that Jesus' relationship with his Father was very special (the same function as the stories of the 'virginal conception' in Mt & Lk, of which John seems to know nothing);

4. 'The Apostolic Preaching and Its Development' (1936);

5. Although there is no direct reference to Elizabeth being 'overshadowed', like Mary, by the Holy Spirit/"power of the Most High", there are hints of an unusual conception (Lk 1: 18) and yet no direct claim that it was Zechariah who made her pregnant (1: 21 – 25); there is no "the man knew his wife" as found in Gen 4: 1 etc.;

6. Luke is the only Evangelist to write of the Ascension as a distinct 'event' (although the stories in the Gospel and Acts differ in important respects), but here, in Peter's speech (vv. 32 – 33), the resurrection and the ascension seem to be merged into a single action;

7. If there is only one God then there is (by definition) only one divine 'entity' – 'lesser divinities' (as in other ancient mythologies) would be ruled out; so if Christ is divine, then something like the doctrine of the Trinity is required – something not conceptually available in the 1st Century; there are therefore only two theological positions to explain the NT witness: either there is a Trinity, but that had to await the 4th C. for explication and, until then, the NT authors had to use other kinds of language, such as allusions or types, to express that truth; or Jesus was not ontologically divine but stood in the line of God's servants throughout the ages;

8. Robinson J 'Honest to Christ Today' in 'The Roots of a Radical' (1980) p. 60;

9. Even the resurrection and ascension traditions do not automatically 'prove' or even assume that Jesus was divine:

both the Old and New Testaments describe various instances of people returning from death to life (e.g. 1 Kings 17: 22; Jn 11: 43 – 44; Acts 20: 9 – 10 etc.); equally, stories of people being taken up to heaven clearly represent not deification, but rather signify a divine blessing e.g. Enoch (Gen 5: 24) and Elijah (2 Kings 2: 1 – 14); in the wider Roman world, Jesus may well have been identified, by any who wanted to bother, alongside Romulus, Heracles and Augustus as those taken directly into heaven (and then deified – in the case of Emperors by a vote in the Senate);

10. Lk 9: 19; like Moses (Acts 3: 22 – 23) or Elijah (Jn 1: 21); the story of the Transfiguration (Mk 9: 2 – 8 & //s) places Jesus directly alongside and in conversation with these two of the greatest OT Prophets, with no direct suggestion that they weren't of equal rank; indeed, Peter wanted to make "dwellings" for each of them: for Luke (9: 31) all "appeared in glory";

11. Clearly the Evangelists believed that Jesus was greater than John; the latter was the forerunner; he had to decrease whilst Christ increased (Jn 3: 30), yet it is also clear that followers of the Baptist continued to revere him well into the future and this may explain why the Evangelists emphasise the utter distinction between the Baptist and Christ: "John's rewriting of the Synoptic material [in the 90s] ...may have been due in part to a desire to counteract an excessive veneration of the Baptist. In Ephesus there were persons who knew only of the baptism of John...and it is possible that they made exaggerated claims for their master" CK Barrett op cit p. 171;

12. Chalmers A op cit p. 32;

13. Goldingay J (2015) 'Do We Need the New Testament' (henceforth 'New Testament') p. 36;

14. Goldingay J (2014) 'The Theology of the Book of Isaiah'(henceforth 'Isaiah') p.72;

15. The Servant is presented as both individual and corporate (Israel);
16. Goldingay 'Isaiah' p. 77;
17. cf. 'King Jesus hath a garden': Traditional Dutch Carol (1633) 'Heer Jesus heft een hofken';
18. Matthew mainly, but not always, uses 'Heaven' e.g. 19: 23 – 24 where both phrases are used, showing that they both mean the same thing: 'heaven' stands for 'God' cf. 1 Macc. 4: 10 (Just as 'Crown' stands for 'Queen');
19. 'Heidelberg Papyrus Collection, Inv. 1716 Verso' cited by Smith DL (2015) 'Into the World of the New Testament: Greco-Roman and Jewish Texts and Contexts' p. 35;
20. So Julius Caesar was understood by some to have been divine during his lifetime, addressed as 'Jupiter Julius' and had a temple consecrated to him; this designation became much more popular after his death, perhaps indicating some reticence to calling a living person divine; so his successor, Augustus (Emperor at the time of Jesus' birth), although called *divi filius* ('son of a god') during his life, was not declared *divus* until after his death, when it was declared that he had ascended into heaven (just as Romulus, legendary founder of Rome, had done, without [like Enoch and Elijah and, according to Josephus [Antiquities 4.326], Moses as well) actually dying , but taken in much greater style than that of Augustus, and who even returned to give instruction to those who followed him); subsequent Roman Emperors took varying views of their 'divine status';
21. 'Olney Hymns' 1779;
22. Variants found;
23. Macquarrie 'Principles' p, 321;
24. Hays RB (2015) 'Reading Backwards' p. 19;
25. 'Reading Backwards';
26. ibid. p. 107;
27. The story has been told (although I cannot source it) of

the school nativity play in which the last 'King' forgets his lines and, being told by the teacher to 'say something! say anything!', utters this immortal phrase: a wonderful basis for a Christmas Day sermon, one which requires positing no ontological identity: 'Christ, in his commitment to his Father's will and self-giving love exemplified divine qualities to the world...';

28. Hays doesn't explicitly acknowledge that all four Evangelists (as did all the NT authors) wrote in Greek and used the LXX as their scriptural source (and that the Fourth Evangelist, in particular, seems to have been dependent to some extent at least on a Greek philosophical understanding of 'Logos') as a result of which all the NT writers must, to a degree, have 'imbibed' Greek concepts simply through using the language;

29. Hays op cit. p. 27;

30. ibid. p. 108;

31. ibid. p. 43;

32. ibid. p. 44;

33. Kaiser CB (2014) 'Seeing the Lord's Glory: Kyriocentric Visions and the Dilemma of Early Christology' argues (p. 9) that "the first disciples experienced a manifestation of YHWH in a glorious anthropic...form and...recognised the face and voice of their teacher [Jesus]": just as the performance of certain OT vision texts is reflected in certain apocalyptic, rabbinic and mystical writings, so the early Christians performed visions of YHWH in their worship i.e. visions initially focused on God became visions "refocused...on Jesus" (p. 130); as a result traditional OT devotional language hitherto used solely for YHWH was applied both to God and to Jesus, creating a dilemma which could only be solved by positing identity between them – so it was these kinds of religious experiences which generated early Christology (as well, so he claims, as generating the

resurrection narratives); as we have noted 'Lord', in the NT, has a wide range of meaning: Jesus is frequently called 'Lord' in the Gospels (e.g. Mt. 15: 25), but so is God (e.g. Mt. 1: 20), and although 'Lord' and 'God' are often associated (e.g. Mk. 12: 29 "...the Lord our God"; Lk 10: 27 "...the Lord your God"), the designation 'Lord God' (in the OT: YHWH Elohim) is relatively rare (e.g. Lk. 1: 32; 1: 68; but most usage in the Book of Revelation 1: 8; 4: 8; 18: 8 etc.); recalling its use in the liturgical 'Gloria', in the rest of the NT Jesus is still frequently called 'Lord' (e.g. 1 Cor 1: 2) but Jesus (as Lord) and God (as Lord) are firmly demarcated (e.g. 2 Cor 1: 2; Gal. 1: 3; 1 Thess 1: 1; Rev. 11: 15 etc.); only in Jn 20: 28 is Jesus called both 'Lord' and 'God', and that designation is open to a breadth of interpretation;

34. We consider chaos theory as theology, below;

35. Hays op cit p. 45;

36. *huios tou theou*: "*it might be thought that the term...would represent a cut-and-dried case that Jesus was thought to be divine, but even here the evidence is rather ambiguous: in itself the* **term did not imply divinity**; *although it usually denoted someone who was* **an agent of God**" (Ludlow M [2009] 'The Early Church' p. 9); the phrase was widely used in the ancient world to refer to someone close to/favoured by the gods; in the OT it referred to 'all men' (e.g. Deut 14: 1) and also to kings/righteous/angels; in Lk 3: 38 Adam, and thus all humanity, are children (sons) of God; frequent use in Paul of the idea of Jesus as God's son, but the actual title is used only 3 times with an emphasis on resurrection and exaltation; it was a key Christological title for Mk, yet (within the narrative) known only to Jesus himself, to God, and to the demons: no disciple ever uses it, and only the (foreign) Centurion openly confesses it; it was only in the shadow of the Cross that (Mark's) Jesus acknowledges himself to be Son of God, although it is not at all obvious what meaning should be

attached to the term (nor can we know with any certainty whether the historical Jesus ever actually used it);

37. Hays op cit p. 45;

38. Evans CA 'From' p. 18;

39. ibid. p. 33;

40. Chalmers op cit pp. 158 – 159;

41. In the OT, Heb. *'nazir'* ('consecrated', 'separated') is one, such as Samson (see particularly Judges 13: 2 – 5) and Samuel (1 Sam 1: 11), who takes a vow of service to God (cf. Numbers 6: 1 – 21) and who would abstain from certain foods and drink, not cut their hair, and avoid ritual impurity (like contact with dead bodies); the prophet Amos criticises Israel for making God's chosen Nazirites drink wine (Amos 2: 11 – 12); we may understand the concept of the Nazirite as another form of divine agency i.e. working on behalf of God – which is presumably why Matthew makes this reference; interestingly, the two great OT nazirites, Samson and Samuel, were both born of previously barren mothers (as many of Israel's heroes, including John Baptist) and had their vows taken by their mothers; it seems clear that Matthew is emphasising not simply that Jesus is another Moses, but is yet another chosen by God to do his work, even if such an interpretation is ignored by many Christians who wish Jesus to be absolutely unique;

42. Brettler MZ et al (2012) 'The Bible and the Believer: how to read the Bible critically and religiously' p. 12;

43. We shall explore this possibility further below; but over the years a variety of other suggestions have been offered, including one in which Mary has been raped by a Roman soldier, thus promoting Jesus' direct identification with the pain, shame and the awful social consequences of such events; in this scenario Joseph becomes the heroic figure who saves her from all that;

44. Parthenogenesis occurs naturally in many plants, some

invertebrate animal species and a few vertebrates; parthenogenetic offspring in species that use either the XY or the X0 sex-determination system have two X chromosomes and are female; there are no known cases of naturally occurring mammalian parthenogenesis in the wild and if it occurred the progeny would have two X chromosomes;ighHigh

45. The main characters are Sarah (Abraham), Rebecca (Isaac), Rachel (Jacob), and Hannah (Elkanah: parents of Samuel); almost every great man issued from a mother who had been previously barren, thus indicating that they were God's particular gift; how much of a theological clue is provided by the fact that Mary's Song (the 'Magnificat' Lk 1: 46 - 55) is clearly modelled on Hannah's Song /Prayer in 1 Samuel 2: 1 – 10?

46. The idea that Joseph was an old man, found in Christmas carols such as the Cherry Tree Carol (in some versions Joseph is jealous that the child in Mary's womb in not his, and when Mary asks him to pick her some cherries he refuses: "let him gather cherries, Mary, who got thee with child"; the foetal Christ then orders the branches to lower so his mother can pick the fruit) and in popular imagination, has no basis in canonical scripture; it may well have been conceived and nurtured to make him appear less likely to be Jesus' father;

47. Barclay W (1957) 'The Gospel of Luke' p. 7;

48. Weatherhead op cit. pp. 73 – 75;

49. ibid. p. 74;

50. ibid. p. 74

51. For the full argument to be appreciated, Weatherhead needs to be read; I recall being quite impressed with this 'solution' when I first read it all those years ago, although perhaps I should note that Weatherhead himself never directly makes the claim that Zechariah was Jesus' father (calling it 'speculation'): perhaps even in the theological ferment of

the 60s he felt that was going just a little too far; presumably he valued the possibility sufficiently to refer to it;

52. The later belief that Mary was a perpetual virgin is clearly contradicted here and by the references in the Gospels to Jesus' brothers and sisters e.g. Mk 3: 31 – 35, claimed by some diehards who cannot cope theologically with the notion that Mary (or Jesus for that matter) could ever have sex, to have been his cousins or Joseph's children from a previous marriage – neither idea referenced in scripture;

53. 'after this, therefore because of this';

54. 'Doctrine in the Church of England' (1938) p. 82;

55. Lincoln A 'Born of a Virgin? Reconstructing Jesus in the Bible, Tradition and Theology' (2013) pp. 279 – 281;

56. As we have already seen, the story of the healing of the widow of Nain's son seems to have been a recapitulation of an original story about Elijah relocated into the Jesus narrative in order to make the theological point that Jesus was a great prophet and healer like Elijah (or in other scenarios, like Moses; or, in the story of the Transfiguration, both); in Year C (the Year of Luke), Proper 5, Lk 7: 11 – 17 is paired with 1 Kings 17: 17 – 24, but that pairing could be understood in a variety of ways, no doubt led by the preacher, successfully or not, depending on their knowledge and skill in dealing with the texts; similarly for Year C, Pentecost: pairing Acts 2: 1 – 21 (the Pentecost story) with Genesis 11: 1 – 9 (the Tower of Babel) might be considered inspired, even if not intended (in that Genesis may have been chosen to partner Acts on the comparatively trivial ground that each story is about language: many of the pairings seem to do with apparent similarities), in that one way of interpreting the Pentecost story is as a reversal of Babel: at Babel language divided, at Pentecost it united; depending on the rationale offered this might suggest that the Pentecost story in which the disciples received the Holy Spirit shares the mythic genre with the

more obviously aetiological Babel story (only Luke tells the story of Pentecost and we have already considered examples of his tendency towards reification, albeit slightly modified here: "a sound *like*..." and "tongues *as of*...", although stating that "a tongue [actually] rested on each of them" Acts 2: 2 - 3) – after all, did not the disciples receive the Holy Spirit on the first Easter Day (Jn 20: 22)?

57. Chalmers op cit pp. 5 – 7;

58. Goldingay 'Isaiah' p. 92;

59. ibid. p. 93;

60. We may note the view of CK Barrett: "[Jesus] pronounces *ego eimi*, not to identify himself with God in any exclusive and final sense, but to draw attention to himself as the one in whom God is encountered and known" 'The Gospel According to St John' p. 98;

61. Goldingay 'Isaiah' p. 110;

62. 'Divine Substitution: Humanity as the Manifestation of Deity in the Hebrew Bible and the Ancient Near East' (2013);

63. Burdett MS 'The Image of God and Human Uniqueness: Challenges from the Biological and Information Sciences' in 'The Expository Times', Vol. 127(1), 2015, p. 4;

64. The actual term 'Sons of God' appears to have had a more specialist, arguably mythic, referent in the OT: regarding Gen 6:2, 4 (NEB "sons of the gods") several of the early Christian Fathers (e.g. Justin Martyr, Eusebius, Clement of Alexandria, Origen) identified them with fallen angels; for Davidson R (1973) 'The Cambridge Bible Commentary on the New English Bible; Genesis 1 – 11' this issue is clear: "Attempts have been made to explain *the sons of the gods* as nobility or royalty or the true worshippers of God [but] by all Old Testament analogy *the sons of the gods* can only mean one thing, divine beings. In Job 1: 6 and 2: 1 the same phrase is translated by the NEB *the members of the court of heaven*" (p. 69), and in NRSV "heavenly beings" as also in Job 38: 7 and

Ps 29: 1;

65. Is there a direct link here with the Synoptic tradition of Jesus' transfiguration? (i) the context is again a "high mountain" (associated particularly with the presence of God); (ii) Moses and Elijah were there; (iii) the nature of Jesus' transfiguration is (for all) "dazzling white clothes" (Mk 9: 3, Mt 17: 2; Lk 9: 29) and, further, in Mt "his face shone like the sun", illustrating Mt's tendency to present Jesus as the new Moses; Luke also has (9: 29) "the appearance of his face changed"; (iv) in Lk's account (9: 31) Moses and Elijah also "appeared in glory" (shining?).

Chapter 5

The Impact of a very Human Christ

A Man who mediates the Divine Presence

In the light of Jesus' apparently extraordinary impact, we still need to factor in a crucial and distinctive element to explain why the Church, quite early on, felt that prophethood, apostleship, priesthood and even messiahship, were not sufficient categories to designate Jesus and 'hinted' at (or more) something approaching divinity, perhaps a process which involved the three theological tendencies identified in the previous chapter. But if it wasn't ontological divinity, then what was this 'more'?

Perhaps it might be expressed as **the very clear experience of many (but certainly not all) who met Jesus was that, in meeting him, they had somehow been met by, or otherwise experienced, the presence and demands of the Divine, the Absolute, the Mysterium** with whom he had the closest possible relationship. Yet not even generating this kind of religious experience (the evocation of the Divine) requires us to conclude that Jesus himself must (literally) be God; only that he is one who, in and through his openness to God, and specifically his obedience to the will of God and his willingness to put self last, even to the point of death, has been a **vehicle** through whom God is evoked and experienced by others.[1] We might, therefore, say of Jesus that he was 'God or Spirit-filled' or 'God–expressing'. Macquarrie[2] terms the Second Person of the Trinity 'Expressive Being': Being is expressed, or expresses itself, via its *Logos*, in a (human) being in a similar way to that in which others have also be God-filled; or that Jesus was peculiarly open to the presence of God; or that he was particularly transparent to God (or whatever phraseology best suits). Keith Ward puts it admirably:

*"Jesus is presented in the Gospels as a man who is uniquely close to – so close as to be **in some sense** identical with – God. So we might ask, how close can a human be to God? Jacob Neusner tells of how in ancient Judaism outstanding rabbis were sometimes said to be 'embodiments of Torah'. They lived in such obedience to the law of God that they seemed to embody it in themselves. It does seem possible for a person to have such an intimate knowledge of God that they could be said to share in the knowledge of God (obviously in a way and to a degree possible for human minds). It is possible for them to have such love for God that they might feel no separation between themselves and God but rather a unity of heart and mind; many mystics speak in such a way. And it is possible for them to be so completely obedient to God that they could be said to become channels of divine action, justice and compassion in the world. So there could exist a human being who shares in the knowledge of God, is united in love to God, and is a channel of God's love for the world. It is possible that it is God's intended destiny for every human being that they should be in such an intimate relationship with God, and perhaps that is what Paradise is".*[3]

Here, Ward appears to want to protect the humanity of Jesus from theological erosion in that he sets out a very reasonable and compelling model of someone 'close to God' who is 'so obedient' as to be a 'channel of divine action', and is so in a manner that demonstrates the possibility that such is the potential of us all. Further, Jesus 'embodied' God (Hays also used this term) in the same (or a similar) way that great rabbis embodied Torah: living *"in such obedience to the law of God that they seemed to embody it in themselves"* (recalling that the Torah was sometimes understood to mediate the divine presence): Jesus lived his life for God in such a way that it seemed to some as if it were a divine life, because that life was a vehicle for God's presence.

Was Jesus unique?

Yet although Ward's is a model that, against any criteria, is broadly functionalist (a 'channel of divine action'), he still wants to affirm *"the absolute ontological **uniqueness** of Jesus among all human persons"* for *"only by a unique divine initiative could this be possible"*: 'this' being "living by the full and unimpeded power of the Spirit", thus qualifying any apparent functionalism he has previously described. The Spirit can only have 'unimpeded power' (whatever that means in the context of his argument for human freedom and autonomy) in a human life, if that human life has been specially 'created' by God, because such a person

"...must be distinguished from the idea of a man who simply shows love and wisdom in a spectacular way by his own power...[because] the absolute moral purity and inspired wisdom of Jesus is [implied 'only'] realised by specific divine action...".[4]

'Ordinary' humanity, therefore (even perhaps extraordinary humanity), is incapable of 'embodying God' prior to 'Paradise' (where, presumably, such embodiment would not be required). Ward doesn't explain why he believes this to be the case, not does he explain how this doesn't compromise "the true humanity of Jesus" which he appears to believe it essential to maintain.

Clearly it is important, if we are using the term 'unique' of Jesus (or anyone else for that matter) to understand and be clear about the sense in which we are deploying it. The term 'unique', particularly in this context, always begs the question of meaning which, in this case, is not as straightforward as it might, at first, seem. A simple dictionary search of a word derived from the Latin *unicus* ('single, sole, alone of its kind'), actually throws up two meanings: not only '**distinctive**' (more directly related to the Latin in the sense of 'there being only one'), but also '**superior**' or 'being better than others' (with the related sense of '*standing alone or apart* in comparison with others', as in an often used phrase: 'second to none').

Is Jesus a 'one-off' type of human being: the only one and so 'different in kind' from the rest of humanity? Here ultimate discontinuity is implied; and this would seem to be the sense of uniqueness used by Ward when he says of Jesus: *only by a unique divine initiative could this [Jesus' ontological uniqueness] be possible*". Or is he superior (morally, spiritually?) to the rest of humanity of which he is genuinely part ('different in degree' i.e. some element of continuity[5])? Is he unparalleled in an objective sense (the difference can be demonstrated) or in the value-judgements made about him? More to the point, what kind of criteria could we propose to demonstrate either application? There is no direct evidence available to us that Jesus was a unique ('alone of its kind') specimen of the species *homo sapiens* within the human genus *homo* (and it is difficult to conceive of what such evidence might consist), in which case, presumably, he wouldn't actually be *homo sapiens,* or if we are to be precise, *homo sapiens sapiens* (the term which differentiates modern human subspecies from *homo sapiens idaltu*: an extinct subspecies of *homo sapiens*) at all, but would be a new subspecies, perhaps *homo sapiens spiritualis.* Nor do we have sufficient information to know beyond doubt that he was the singular epitome of moral and/or spiritual virtue,[6] although that might be what we choose to believe. As we have seen, we have relatively little information about Jesus' historical life available to us and, as a result, Jesus' allegedly perfect morality cannot be objectively proven 'beyond reasonable doubt', even if the NT authors, who were writing from faith, were both explicit and unanimous about that – which they were not. Should, then, Jesus' 'uniqueness' be understood (in either sense) to refer to his position among humanity in the same way as it is often (certainly traditionally) claimed that humanity is different from and also superior to other animals? What are the issues?

If Christ is "ontologically unique" (in that he was *fully united to God from the first moment of his earthly existence"*), where does that leave his genuine humanity? Can such a person still be counted human 'like us'? If one takes any group (here, humanity) and say of it that all its members are of the same group, except that one particular example is 'ontologically unique', in what way is that exception still a full member of that group? Furthermore, we might reasonably ask: what does the concept of 'ontological uniqueness' mean: unique in one's 'being', but what, precisely, is that? Whatever it is, to use the language of Nicaea: if Christ's 'being' is unique, then clearly it does not 'share' or have the 'same being' as other members of the group: humanity (as affirmed in the Athanasian Creed; *"...Man, of the Substance of his Mother..."*.) Nevertheless (so asserts Nicaea) Christ's 'being' does share the same 'being' of one who is not a member of that group (human 'beings') but of a different group (of 'divine being[s]'?). But however much the writers of the Athanasian Creed claim that Christ shares the nature of both humanity and divinity, by averring that Christ was

> *"**God, of the Substance of the Father**, begotten before the worlds: and **Man, of the Substance of his Mother**, born in the world. Perfect God, and Perfect Man: of a reasonable soul and human flesh subsisting; **Equal to the Father, as touching his Godhead: and inferior to the Father, as touching his Manhood**. Who although he be God and Man: yet he is not two, but one Christ..."*

how actually can this (apparent contradiction) be? God is creator, not creature: if, to revisit the Arian controversy, Christ is deemed not to be a creature (but *homoousios* with the Father and, later, the Second Person of a Triune God), then he cannot (virtually by definition) be a creature; for how can the Creator (and as Divine *Logos* Christ is also 'Creator': Jn 1: 3) also be a creature? Put simply: if Christ is not a creature, he cannot be human – or at least, not human as we are, because we are 'all-creature'. If he is a 'creature' he cannot be 'God'. Just to say that Christ is 'all-creature' with added divinity is close to being incoherent, because we cannot explain what it means and, as I have argued, all attempts to do so have failed.

It is also clear from the above that the main problem with claiming 'ontological uniqueness' is that if someone's 'being' (again, whatever that is thought to mean) is unique (different) then it is literally 'a one-off', 'incomparable' (etc.), which inevitably means (as in the use of *homoousios*) we are seeking not only to compare the literally incomparable (the divine-man) with something comparable (humanity), but also compare something which we don't know or understand (God's *ousia*) with something else we don't know or understand (the *ousia* of Christ) *because it is incomparable*: the result is muddle and confusion. Yet this is how Ward wishes to explicate the life and person of Jesus Christ.

Further, for Ward, this *"perfected **life**, a life beyond evil and grounded in perfect love, is not only possible, but it is a positive hope for many religious believers"*. To put this another way: the Incarnation provides, *"**by a special act of divine power**, an example of a perfected life in human history, as a sign of the promise and reality of its final destiny"*.[7] But why should such a process require a "unique divine initiative" or "a special act of divine power"? Why can't it be the 'natural' outcome of the way God works within his creation (as suggested above: a normal pregnancy)? Furthermore, why should it be thought a quasi-eschatological "positive hope" or "sign of a promise..."?: could not God work to raise up such a person who functions on his behalf on more than one historical occasion and, more to the point, if this state of closeness to God is really God's intention for the whole of humanity, might he not be striving constantly to achieve this, through the operation of the Spirit, in all of us, now and in the future? In which case this would not be a "unique divine initiative" and Christ would not be "ontologically unique"; but it would still be a divine initiative of which Christ was the (or an) outcome and possibly also (but not necessarily) the first-fruits. I suppose, in the end, another question is deceptively simple: why should Christians be so concerned that, in a universe of wonders, the Incarnation should be thought of as a unique event? Why is any form of 'uniqueness' (as difference) required at all as a descriptor of Jesus?

What of general human uniqueness, and how might our understanding of that affect our understanding of the alleged uniqueness of Christ: indeed, does the one support the other? The classic theological basis for the claim that human beings are unique (different and superior) amongst animals is based on the notion that we have been created in 'the image of God'. In the previously cited article Michael Burdett outlines four interpretations of what that can mean:[8]

1. **functional**: as noted above, the 'royal-functional' model in which royalty reflected the divine presence is extended to the whole of humanity which thus has dominion over creation *"as a consequence of being in the image of God"*. On this understanding *"[the whole of] humanity...is unique because it has been tasked with ruling over, caring for and shepherding the rest of creation"*. This supports the notion that humanity in general, but also in particular, can represent (re-present) God to his creation;

2. **substantive** ("the most dominant [interpretation] in Christian history"): here the image of God refers to *"some quality or faculty that is inherent in the human being"*, characteristically 'reason' (or intelligence): *"this has often meant that humans are unique because they are either rational when others are not, or that their intellectual powers are unique to such a degree that they are qualitatively distinct amongst the rest of creation"*. There would appear to be no claims in the NT that Jesus was either intellectually or rationally

superior to other people, except insofar that he seemed to have insights into the Jewish Scriptures (and into human beings) that were distinctive and (occasionally – Jesus appears to have been, in many ways, a thoroughly orthodox Jew) somewhat different from those, like the scribes, who had been traditionally trained. In this sense, perhaps, Jesus might be understood to have been a 'maverick' teacher (sometimes called 'Rabbi'), but not, so far as we know, a trained scholar; more to the point, neither did the Synoptic Christ have access to divine secrets (Mk 13: 32);

3. **relational** (particularly dominant in the 20th C.): the *"unique relationship humanity has with God"* or *"our ability to have robust relationships with other persons"*. Again, recognising that Jesus clearly had an utterly close relationship with Father God, are we to understand that relationship was different in kind, rather than in degree (e.g. more intense, radically closer), to the relationship that others have with their 'Father in Heaven'? What would be the evidence for that?

4. **dynamic**: *"...not something completely given to humanity at the beginning of creation but is instead completely gained through history and in conformity to Christ"*: only Christ is *"the full measure of the image of God"*. However, as attractively pious as this claim might seem to some, it is not actually what Genesis claims: in 1: 27 God created (implied: all) humanity in his image, and there is no indication that this image is given partially (and if Christ is thought to be the only person ever to have had this image fully, then clearly God's intention only came to pass relatively late in the history of humanity). Indeed, everything was "very good": 1: 31 implies 'the best it could be', presumably with humanity truly reflecting God's image, at least, until the Fall (if such an 'event' ever

occurred; I would sooner say that being in the image of God doesn't prevent humanity from 'screwing-up'; there is certainly nothing in the Genesis account which tells us that 'the Fall' – not a term ever used – somehow removed the image of God from humanity). Although, in Burdett's view, this conception is *"more flexible in terms of human uniqueness than others"* I would argue that it actually 'kidnaps' the concept for its own Christological purposes and, in so doing, changes its meaning significantly: from a general ascription (as it originated) to a much more limited one that, having been modelled in Christ, can only be fully and properly realised eschatologically. Not all human beings may act in such a way that reflects God's image, but this is rather different from saying, in effect, that no-one can do so except through Christ. This not only undermines the concept completely, but it also effectively confuses two issues: the 'nature of humanity' with the 'nature of a redeemed/transformed humanity', although Burdett allows for the possibility that it might still retain part of its original meaning: *"we could say that human uniqueness is related to **our special ability to transform and to grow**, often in distinctly moral and spiritual ways, towards Christ [nevertheless, adding]...who is himself the full image of God"*.[9] Did only Christ have the 'fullness' of the *imago dei*, whereas the rest of the human race has had it only partially (if at all), so that Christ is unique against this criterion i.e. Jesus is superior to the rest of humanity? Did evolution take a further step (only) in Jesus i.e. Jesus is different from the rest of humanity (perhaps a new type of human being)?

If humanity stands at the pinnacle of creation (unique – in both senses - amongst other animals) does Jesus, against the same criteria (either different or superior, or both different and superior), stand at the pinnacle of humanity and is thus genuinely unique (among humans)? Current scientific thinking suggests that although there may be pockets of continuing human evolution (e.g. people indigenous to areas such as Nepal who, over the centuries, have found their haemoglobin adjusting to living at heights where oxygen supply is relatively low), in general, due to technological advances through which we have been able to control much of our environment, human evolution has slowed considerably, (although many scientists believe that should there be a cataclysm of some kind, either humanity as a species will be wiped out, or human evolution will 'wake up' and begin again to cope with and adjust to whatever has been brought about by cataclysmic change). If Jesus is thought to have been (something like) the next (or even final) point in human evolution, then for this to be the case, he would need to be the fore-runner of others like him (although in the tradition, despite Dan Brown's 'Da Vinci Code', he was biologically the last of his line: some Christians find it impossible to imagine that Jesus had sex, simply because, in one strand of Christian thought, sex is sinful). Alternatively, Jesus would be an aberration. But perhaps this is how some Christians prefer to see him, believing that thinking of Jesus as too much 'like us' is impious?

Further, in the context of exobiology (the exploration of life beyond Planet Earth in a universe which appears to demonstrate convergent evolution) *"...the proposal that life has emerged only once, or that it has reached intelligence only once, may be difficult to uphold and, with it, the assumption that human beings are unique in this way...We have less and less reason...to suppose that human life is unique-as-better [i.e. superior]: that it outranks every other form of life 'by reason of superior excellence', by means of a perceiving intelligence"*.[10] How might the claim that humanity is not unique affect our understanding of the alleged uniqueness of Jesus (as a human being)? The only conclusion would seem to be that amongst a non-unique humanity Jesus was different in kind: he is the only unique 'being' (of whatever kind) in the universe: in which case, he was not ' human as we are'.

The classic definition of humanity (probably since Aristotle) has been that of 'a rational (and intelligent) animal', and that allegedly distinguishes us from other animals, although only so far as we know, for the concept of human uniqueness, in the sense of being superior to (although related to: continuous with) the rest of the animal kingdom, may be more difficult to sustain today than in the past (as we discover more about animal intelligence[11]):

> *"There is no question but that many other living creatures experience emotion, enjoy sophisticated levels of knowing and communicating, and act with a certain purpose. In this regard human beings belong on a spectrum with others in the community of life".*[12]

However, no animal has yet shown a degree of intelligence to match that of human beings[13] and we may reasonably judge that human beings are unique in some important ways:

> *"...human beings find themselves uniquely emplaced on the planet. Bodily earthlings who like all living creatures interact with their environment as they are born, wax, and die, they are yet able mentally to transcend any particular time and place. They ask questions, dream of what comes next, wonder about the meaning of the whole. Able to act with deliberate intentionality, they choose goals beyond biological survival and reproduction and act to achieve them. They make art in visual, aural, tactile, and literary mediums. And can they ever innovate and invent! A highly ethical animal, they can consider principles of right and wrong, weigh what they ought to do, and choose one path over another in the face of temptation. They can interact as an agent with other similarly free, existential agents and hold each other accountable. They can love with deep emotion, self-giving, and spiritual exhilaration, and hate just as strongly.*

They can even love an enemy...The point is, the human species is a singularity."[14]

In this case, the use of 'unique' denoting difference may also be maintained *vis a vis* animals, for although human beings are part of the animal kingdom, they may be thought to stand distinct from it due to the many areas not only of superiority, but also (although related) difference e.g. language skills, technological abilities etc. – "*...both senses of uniqueness are in play here*".[15]

For Aquinas, humanity was distinct (different) in being created in the image and likeness of God, although he allowed that other animals may share in this to a degree (having a *vestigium* of God's likeness), and that human beings bear God's image (generally, but not in every respect) less perfectly than angels (there is no sense here of humanity only having the *imago dei* partially, just less perfectly – whatever that may mean). Presumably, angels are different from human beings and if Jesus is, as the author of Hebrews puts it: "superior to angels" (1: 4, 5 – 9), then he is clearly far above humanity and again, logically (because angels are not human), not human at all. So we arrive at the same doctrinal sticking point: just how can Jesus be ontologically human and ontologically divine at the same time, and just how is Jesus unique (apart from being the only divine-human, to speak of which begs the question): is he unique by difference or superiority – or perhaps both? And the continuing dilemma: what then of his genuine humanity?

Ward argues:

"[For] virtually all human beings, earthly life is a journey from alienation towards unity with the divine being. Suppose, however, that there is a person not born in such alienation, a person whose will is turned to God in love and trust from the first. This would be a person who was never egotistic or overwhelmed by self-centred passion; who was always mindful and self-controlled, compassionate

and loving; and who experienced a constant sense of the presence
of God and the power of the Spirit prompting and inspiring their
thoughts and feelings".[16]

Ward may well be right that such a person is very rare, but in
actually saying that "virtually all human beings" are not like
this, he implies that some (not just one, or else he would have
needed to have written: 'all human beings but this one...') may
be, and so 'uniqueness' is, at a stroke, destroyed by Ward's
own 'pen'– in fact, Ward, only a little later on, suggests that
Gautama Buddha may have been one such, thus undermining
his own claim for Christ's uniqueness (could Christ and the
Buddha both be unique?). It is entirely possible (particularly
bearing in mind his previous remarks about human potential)
that Jesus has been one of a number of non-egotists (etc.) who
have served God faithfully and self-sacrificially, although what
possible empirical evidence could we have for the existence of
anyone (including Jesus, if it comes to that) who was **"always**
mindful and self-controlled" (and so on)? All these criteria relate
to qualities which are internal to the person, although they may
show themselves in external action. But to identify one or even
more such people accurately would ultimately require a 'God's-
eye-view', not least because, as with Jesus' 30-year life, we know
relatively little about them, and we certainly cannot know the
inner thoughts and motivations of anyone unless they tell us –
and Jesus was famously silent in that, unlike some other seminal
beings, he wrote nothing. In other words, Ward's claim, being
non-demonstrable, is simply a statement of what he believes.
Indeed, he goes on to suggest that *"such a person would not need*
repentance or faith in the sense of contrition for wrongdoing and
commitment to a God who is not fully known and felt", to which,
again, we may respond: 'how do you know?'

The basis issue, yet again, is this: if Jesus were so truly
different from the rest of humanity (in that he was so good

and knew God so well that he, alone, had need neither for repentance or faith) then what kind of human being would he have been (and here some may be tempted to invoke the old theological 'solution' that Christ avoided 'original sin', thus begging multiple questions) bearing in mind, as Macquarrie points out, that a "basic characteristic" of human existence is our finitude (together with what he defines, continuing to creatively redeploy existentialist terminology, as the "polarities": extremes often held in tension, of human existence: possibility/facticity, responsibility/impotence, anxiety/hope[17]) which, whilst not itself 'sin', is nevertheless related to that important Christian concept:[18]

"To be finite is to live in risk and uncertainty, and that this is our life is clear to us from everyday experiences in which we have to commit ourselves to policies of action without complete knowledge of all the relevant circumstances and still less of all the consequences that will flow from the action".[19]

If Jesus is deemed to have been 'Perfect Man' (presumably finite) and 'Perfect God' (who is infinite) then did his human nature exist only in his biological construction and not in any other aspect of his human existence, or was he finite as are we: in which case how can he also be divine?

In conclusion, it is probably best to avoid using the term 'unique' of Christ altogether,[20] even when we are clear as to the meaning we are ascribing to the term, as being an unhelpful and potentially misleading way of describing the Jesus-event: firstly because everyone is, to a degree, unique in a sense which transcends both meanings (we are all different in so many ways – no one, not even our twin, is the same as us; no-one is better at everything than everyone else.). Secondly, because we do not have the evidence on which to base such a comparative judgement: we might believe it but we cannot demonstrate it. Put simply: how do we know that God has not raised up others like Jesus who have led God-centred lives and done God's will: all of whom have been entirely human? But thirdly – and this, theologically, is the crucial issue: if Jesus is unique in the sense of being not only superior (different in degree) but also different from us in kind, in what sense is he still ' human as we are'?

In which case, we should not be reluctant to affirm that it was through the **very human Christ**, a full and genuine humanity without any 'divine' accretions or additions, that God has chosen to meet us: why should this be thought strange, or even impossible? There is no separate or new *'homo sapiens spiritualis'* because we are all, at least potentially, members of the (sub)species *'homo sapiens spiritualis'*: humankind as God has always intended it to be from the time he 'in-spired' (the mythical) Adam. Perhaps, in limiting the descriptor to 'sapiens' ('wise' – wisdom/*sophia* is one of the divine characteristics), anthropologists have simply failed to recognise or understand the essential spiritual nature of humanity. Humanity without spirituality is not humanity; or, put another way: the spiritual dimension is an innate and essential characteristic of what being a 'human being' means. To be human is to be spiritual; to be spiritual is (so far as we are aware: there may be other spiritual beings) to be human. Spirituality is both of the essence and, at the same time, the entelechy of the human condition. Jesus was effective as God's servant not through the possession of some kind of divine 'substance', but entirely through his humanity and, more to the point, because that very human life fulfilled the criteria for humanity as it was meant to be which, sadly, many of its members, over history and today, fail to meet. Why? It is all to do with how we grow and mature as spiritual persons.

One might characterise the process in terms which would probably, and quite reasonably, invoke the criticism: simplistic. But sometimes simplicity has its advantages. When we are born, and during our first months and possibly for some years afterwards, we are essentially and probably instinctively self-centred: we act as if and, worse, we may even come to believe that the whole universe revolves around us and our needs: it has been created just for our benefit. Babies and toddlers scream for attention when they are hungry, wet or just generally looking for comfort and gratification. As many parents have found to their cost, 'spoiling' the child has gone too far when that child comes to believe, and continues to believe even into adulthood, that s/he is the most important thing in the world: both entitled and owed; when the constant inner refrain is 'me, me, me' and, as far as anything or anyone else is concerned, "I don't care". Through a more balanced and sensitive process of being enabled to grow, not merely physically, but emotionally and morally as well, we come to learn that our little universes contain other people who also have needs: some, perhaps, even greater than our own. Greater maturity may even lead us to prioritise the needs of others, as we come to understand, either in religious or non-religious terms, that our vocation is "not to be served, but to serve..." (Mark 10: 45). We reject self-centredness in favour of other-centredness or, in Christian terms, God-centredness: for God intends us to become like him (to be icons of his likeness) and 'let-be': just as he did and continues to do through the ongoing act of creation. The process of becoming self-sacrificial rather than self-centred entails developing our spirituality through the realities, the joys and the sorrows, of ordinary life. It may also entail the extraordinary step of taking up our cross and following Jesus: whatever that means for us and the situations in which we live.

Sadly it is also possible that we never achieve that which we have been called to be and to do. Our spiritual growth is somehow truncated. Instead of enabling others, we use them to further our own selfish desires: in short, we treat people as commodities, only to be regarded in so far as they maximise our pleasures.

Or it may be that, having achieved such growth at some stage in our lives, as we approach old age the heart turns in upon itself (as medieval writers termed it: *cor incurvatum in se*) and we finally succumb and revert to that original 'babyish' condition. That is when we blur or even lose the image and likeness of God. It is tempting to say (sounding appropriately pious) that the 'spiritual' state is supernatural, whilst that original state is 'natural' (perhaps due to our 'fallen' and 'perverted' condition, as some Christians would claim); but that would be to miss the point entirely. It is not a question of natural versus supernatural (and that mistake may lie behind the thinking of those who need Christ to be ontologically divine); it is rather a question of human potential, and our success or failure in achieving that. Jesus exemplified such achievement: in and through his life the image of God was realised. He was (continuing the myth) the Second Adam: the one who 'got it right'. As we shall consider shortly: he might reasonably be described as a spiritual prodigy endowed with divine charisms: but still one who was truly human. But before reaching that point in our discussion we need to be able to understand something of the nature of spirituality, what it may mean to be human (both 'being' and 'becoming') and the connections between them. So we will take a 'time out' from the overall argument in order to explore these concepts further.

Excursus: *Homo Sapiens Spiritualis*

The Heb. *ruach* and Gk. *pneuma* share overlapping meanings: breath, breeze, wind, and spirit which, across the Biblical texts, connote the mysterious and creative power of God: invisible, but with tangible results (just as we 'see' the wind moving the branches of a tree). God's *ruach* hovers over the waters at the beginning of creation; God breathes "the breath of life" (*ruach*) into Adam's nostrils so he becomes a "living creature", one endowed with God's image and likeness (a reasonable, though not original, link between Genesis 2 and Genesis 1). This is true 'in-spiration': the in-breathing of God which creates and which nurtures the development of human life. The Evangelists use *pneuma* variously for the (Holy) Spirit, the Spirit of God (as at Jesus' baptism), the 'poor in spirit' (Mt 5: 3), the 'human' spirit (Mt 26: 41) and unclean spirits (Mt 10: 1). In several places in the Letters it means the 'spirit of man' as opposed to either *psyche*[21] or *soma* ('soul and body' cf. 1 Thess 5: 23). An interesting conjunction is made by Paul when he writes of being "absent in body [*somati*]" but "present in spirit [*pneumati*]." (1 Cor 5: 3). So *pneuma* seems to relate particularly to the non-material dimension of a living person, but it also has meanings which go beyond *ruach*.

The former is often opposed to *sarx* (flesh) in a way that is not the case with the Hebrew equivalent *basar*. In the OT 'flesh' simply refers to human material weakness in contrast to the greatness of the Spirit God; but in the NT 'flesh' takes on a much stronger moral dimension, as well as referring to the physical body (e.g. Mt 16: 17 and 19: 5; Jn 1: 14; Lk 24: 39). In Jn 3: 6 flesh is directly contrasted with spirit, although there is also a certain amount of ambiguity here, such as in Jn 6: 51 – 56 where the people misunderstand Jesus' words (and John compounds the misunderstanding with his Eucharistic references). 'Flesh' also suggests something potentially sinful (e.g. Rom 7: 5, 18. Gal 3: 3):

> *"Thereafter [from Pentecost] the Christian is to live no longer as* **sarx** *(nor even as* **psyche***) but as* **pneuma***, in the very specific sense of living according to the Holy Spirit of God in Jesus. It is to be stressed that 'flesh' and 'spirit' are not opposed here in a dualistic sense of body and soul; their opposition in early Christian thought as expressions of human non-response or response to God's Spirit continues to assume the Hebrew view of the human being as indivisibly body and spirit".*[22]

The Biblical image of 'spirit' suggests something that is essentially creative, life-giving and life-enhancing. This Spirit is like the wind (Jn 3: 8; Acts 2: 2): it blows where it wills; it is elusive, impossible to tie down; even mischievous and playful (as in the Hindu tradition where the Sanskrit *'lila'* reflects the playfulness of God in establishing the cosmos). She comes from God and finds her home at the core of humanity. When Jesus 'inspired' his disciples for their future work, the Fourth Evangelist has him breathe on them so they (again?) receive the Holy Spirit (Jn 20: 22; this is the Johannine 'Pentecost'), that originating Spirit of creation.

Hebrew also has the concept of *nephesh,* sometimes translated as 'soul', but the more accurate translation being 'personality', or even 'vitality'. This is because the Hebrew mind has no concept of a separate 'body and soul':[23] a human being is holistic. So, for example, in Genesis 2 whereas the AV and RV describe the *adam* as becoming a 'living soul', the RSV properly changes 'soul' to 'being', just as the NEB changes it to 'creature'. God makes an *adam* from the *adamah* (ground dust) which he invests (by breathing his *ruach* into it) with his own *nephesh,* his own vitality, and Adam thus becomes a living *nephesh:*

"Men and women were created a complete unity thought of as entirely alive or entirely dead. It is the nephesh that dies. After death they went down into Sheol – the pit – where they spent their time in a shadowy state of non-experience. The dead are still a nephesh, but a nephesh that has lost its substance and strength. That is why proper burial was so important in order that the entity of the nephesh might be maintained even in death. But for the Hebrews real life was confined to the earth".[24]

Nephesh, then, refers to the inner being of a person but, although it emanates from the *ruach* of God, it is not immortal (Num 23: 10). In some OT references *nephesh* is seen as a kind of shadow version of the body which, whilst escaping the body at death, eventually fades away. Whilst *ruach* and *nephesh* have close connections, the former connotes much more in the way of energy and activity, the life-breath of God, or the life-force within humanity. *Nephesh* suggests something rather more physical: it may even be captured (Ez 13: 18). In the LXX *ruach* became *pneuma, nephesh* became *psyche.*

As we are aware, much Biblical imagery is evocative rather than precisely descriptive: it connotes rather than denotes: well suited to a subject which is, by its very nature, elusive. Such images as it offers of spirit are, like that subject, always just beyond our grasp. 'Spirit' is 'incomprehensible' (a reasonable, if not precise, rendering of the Lat. *immensus* in the Athanasian Creed), meaning *not* that we cannot understand it at all, but that it is always greater than our concept of it: like something you catch out of the corner of your eye which then slips away as you turn your head to follow it. That's why we have problems when we try to translate these images into concepts and definitions: no concept or definition of spirit is entirely adequate to the reality (not least, we remind ourselves, because no language can embrace the divine). The imagery of 'spirit' hints that there is depth, complexity and richness to reality that are not exhausted by the visible and material: we are more than just physical bodies; our environment is more than just an aimless physical process. Yet although different, the material and the spiritual are not opposed (as the Gnostics thought); rather they are fully integrated. That is one of the central messages of the Incarnation: the Word became flesh: he didn't just pretend. Jesus was genuinely human.

This imagery also affirms that the Spirit is not static; it is, in Judaeo-Christian terms, a dynamic, formative and life-giving power. It is not just there in the background; it is, we might say, more invasive than pervasive. It is less like the air we breathe and more like the delicate micro-manoeuvrings of a surgeon: always working to bring good out of every situation. 'Spirit' (it has been suggested[25]) may technically be a noun, but it exhibits the characteristics of a verb: 'spirit', even without the 'to', is a 'doing word'. It points to the mysterious affinity that binds mankind to God. God is other than us, but he has shared his creative Spirit with us: that aspect of God which is active and present in the world; a dynamic reality shaping lives and histories; closer even than our very breath. So the Spirit which is God's is also, in a similarly mysterious way, ours: "You made him a little lower than the heavenly beings and crowned him with glory and honour" (Psalm 8: 5). Here the Psalmist is full of awe and wonder – words often associated with spirituality or spiritual awareness: yet whilst awe and wonder are aspects of spiritual awareness, they are not ends in themselves. We will be affected by a raging sea which is beautiful, but which also destroys; the stars at night which cannot be counted; or a profound musical experience which may move us to tears. But these are merely pointers towards the real wonder of existence – *that* we are at all, rather than not; and *what* the true nature of our being (in the sense of what it means 'to be') and - we might also say, because this is the terminology used at Nicaea – Being (as in 'of one Being with...') is, and how the two are connected. So the great lesson we have to learn is not just how to perceive the effects of the Spirit of God working *outside* us, but also the effects of the Spirit working *within* us. It is only that insight – the capacity to have it and the courage to employ it - which gives us any hope of beginning to find some clue to the nature of the divine Spirit, and so, by derivation, our own.

Unfortunately, the Spirit working in us is more often obscured than recognised; put in chains rather than unleashed. This is because much of humanity tends to focus attention on, even lust after, the merely physical and transient: that which gratifies the senses, but does little else for us. But the potential to get it right is always there, and it is that potential which teachers and those who minister in our churches are called upon to identify and nurture. Children and congregants must be taught to see beyond the merely surface and superficial, for one particularly important aspect of spirituality is being able to see beneath the surface: in depth. Why particularly teachers? Because ever since the 1944 Education Act, schools have been responsible for promoting pupils' 'spiritual development' (now an aspect of SMSC: spiritual, moral, social and cultural development), although it is really only since the beginning of regular school inspections in the 1990s that schools have come to take this requirement seriously; not least because many teachers (as others involved in education) hadn't the faintest idea what it meant. Conversely, there is always a danger of using the word 'spiritual' to mean whatever we want it to mean: it then becomes devoid of meaning, and impossible to speak coherently about. I dread the module on Spirituality taken by my curate-training groups because it is so easy to waste time trying to define it; paradoxically, it wastes even more time if we do not.

Certain aspects of human life have traditionally been associated with the notion of spirituality: religion/worship; relationships; experiences which take us beyond ourselves; creativity, art and music; mystery; prayer, silence and meditation; the transcendent, the ultimate and the eternal. These are all positive and potentially productive ways of expressing our common humanity. But there are also less positive ones: a 'hot-house' religious experience reserved for the few preoccupied by their own inward condition; some kind of personal piety sometimes involving unctuous self-pride and a 'holier-than-thou' attitude. It is quite understandable why schools, particularly those which are not Faith schools, may be frightened off by a concept they find hard to understand and even harder to relate to the lives of their pupils who, often like their teachers, confuse spirituality and religion, and equally often reject both. So teachers may light a candle in the school assembly and hope for the best, hoping that children will surely 'catch' spirituality and another box can be ticked.

Andrew Wright, one of the most creative and stimulating academics researching spirituality and religion in education, tells us that what is needed is *"a pedagogy capable of addressing both the universality of humanity's spiritual aspirations and the actuality of distinct spiritual traditions"*.[26] This helpfully underlines the fact that there is a universal spirituality (and should that be any surprise for those who believe in a Creator God?): a spiritual yearning in humankind which is not limited to particular religious traditions, although it is often mediated and organised through them (we might actually define 'religion' as one way in which we organise our spirituality). After all, the windy-spirit blows where she wills, and we mustn't think that we, as Christians, either have a monopoly on her or that we can control her. The entire creation is the domain of the Spirit, as is the whole of time and history, and is a central ingredient of all Faith traditions.

> *"Spirituality is the relationship of the individual, within community and tradition, to that which is – or is perceived to be – of ultimate concern, ultimate value, and ultimate truth, as appropriated through an informed, sensitive and reflective striving for spiritual wisdom."*[27]

Intrinsic to the human condition, human spirituality expresses itself in different contexts and with different foci, some of which may be religious, but others may not. The aspiration to spirituality is an intrinsic part of being human; indeed, without it we cannot be human.

As mysterious as the Spirit may be, her basic intentions for us may be quite straightforward: *"to do with becoming a person* [we might say: a human being] *in the fullest sense"*.[28] God's Spirit is seeking to make humans human; as we were always meant to be until other things (call it fallenness, disobedience, selfishness or whatever) got in the way:

> *"Man (sic) 'stands out' from all other creatures on earth and has the possibility of exience* [Macquarrie's own term for 'going out' to be distinguished from 'existence'/'ex-sisting': 'standing out'], *of going out and transcending himself into a fuller form of life. This possibility was his from the moment that breath or spirit was breathed into him by God, bestowing on him the divine image and the possibility of closeness to God and participation in the divine life."*[29]

In other words, spiritual development (development in the Spirit) is fundamentally about how we grow into - how we grasp and use - our personhood: how we come to attain true fullness of life and become truly human.

This invites us, if not to reject, at least to complement the traditional expression: human 'being' with that of human 'becoming': a far richer and more dynamic concept. The meaning of Being (evidently related to 'being'[30] as expressed in Macquarrie's claim that [Holy] Being becomes manifest in and mediated through [the] beings[31]) and that of Becoming (the upper cases denoting the technical manner in which the words are being deployed as, for example, in the Nicene Creed's 'of one Being with the Father') has fascinated philosophers from Plato onwards, although Plato interpreted 'Becoming' rather more narrowly as the world of sense-experience, as opposed to the 'Real' and timeless world of forms: so, for him, 'Becoming' was something essentially unreal. But our 'becoming' is very real. Commenting on the journey towards what he terms a 'Religion of Being', Don Cupitt remarks:

> *"To get into Being, to attune ourselves to Being, to learn to respond to Being, we need to free ourselves...from a series of distinctions that*

together have had the effect of alienating ourselves from Being...Of these distinctions, the most important is that between Being and Becoming."[32]

He thus does away with the distinction altogether by joining (in his language "eliding") the words together thus: 'Be(com)ing', so that the link between Being and Becoming is maintained and strengthened. The Nicene Fathers claimed that Christ shared the Father's Being but understood this in an exclusive sense: *only* Christ shared the Father's Being; *homoousios* was what made him special. If we take a rather broader understanding of Being (the subject matter of ontology) and link that understanding with God (as we have seen Macquarrie do), then it is entirely reasonable (without descending into Pantheism) to understand the Creator God as sharing his Being with ('pouring himself into') the whole of his creation: after all, we call ourselves (and even potential aliens; but not yet animals) 'beings', perhaps simply implying that 'we are' or we exist. In fact, both the nature and experience of our own existence will be crucial to our Christological journey, for this is ontology from the inside. Just how our being is shared with Being continues to be a matter of philosophical speculation, and it is not necessary for this particular journey to indulge in such.

I now want to make the same kind of case for the lower case 'being' and 'becoming' as has been made for the upper case forms. In so doing, we need to hold in our minds that our 'being' is not only related to whatever it is we call 'Being' (or 'Holy Being'), but that our 'becoming' is also related to (let's just say for the moment) the 'Becoming' of 'Being'. Some philosophers (following Heidegger's thinking in 'Being and Time' [1927]) have asserted, against purely a static notion of Being, that Being has a history; or, in Cupitt's intriguing phrase: *"Being is its own becoming..."*.[33] However we seek to interpret the link between 'Being' and 'being', or that between Being and God, it is perfectly clear from the Biblical account that God has a history (ignoring the technicalities of what we somewhat opaquely call 'eternity', and how that might relate to time; but certainly not the popular conception that God somehow pops in and out of eternity because, as in anything to do with God, the reality is likely to be much more subtle):

> *"Being has itself a history, over and above the history of our apprehension of Being. Perhaps indeed we must speak of a history of Being, if we allow for a genuine transcendence of Being and anything like an act of grace or revelation. But on the other hand, history belongs to Being, not Being to history"*[34]

It is clear that what Macquarrie has said about Being must also apply to God. If God does not 'have a history': if God is a purely static transcendent power, then God couldn't reveal himself or be "gracious to us and bless us" (Ps 67: 1) within a historical context. Particularly in the OT, God is the God of history: God 'does' and 'says' things in a variety of historical locations (Abraham and the Patriarchs, Moses, the Prophets and so on) one following another along the threads of time. But the God who said to Moses "I am who I am" (Ex 3:14) unfortunately became rooted in Christian theology (through privileging the Greek over the Hebrew conception) as unchangeable and impassible. In protest at this particular theological dead-end, the so-called Process Theologians amongst others have argued that 'becoming' must take precedence over 'being', for only then can our concept of God as the 'I AM' be dynamic. This is a God who acts and a God who cares; after all, you cannot love passively. God, so we claim as Christians, and despite the continuing contaminate of Docetism (the result of emphasising ontological divinity), has revealed himself in the historical life of the man Jesus of Nazareth. What else is this but some kind of historical development in the 'life of God'? In this sense, God's

Being Becomes.

So must ours: whilst 'being' and 'becoming' are not identical, they are necessarily linked: we must become what we are to be. But what we now are is the given: the baseline, we might say, for what we are to become. The distinction between being and becoming is therefore less absolute: the latter must always be included in the former. Nevertheless, making some kind of distinction between 'being' (being human or a human being) and '(a human) becoming', or at least drawing out their distinctive features, can be theologically productive. We tend to refer to ourselves as 'human beings' (sometimes, just as 'beings') quite casually, without acknowledging the real potency and force of this notion of 'being', and its potential for 'becoming'. If we are not careful the notion of *'human being'* can connote either completion (the 'being' has now 'become') or a condition of stasis (as with Classical Theism). We have made it; we are at the pinnacle of creation; there is no need for change because there is nowhere else for us to go.

This is why at least a nod towards the notion of 'human becoming' enables us to have a much richer understanding of ourselves and our potential: in fact, much more than a nod because our being must include becoming in order for us to be spiritual beings (or becomings). This identifies the importance of a process of development in our humanity (generally and individually) or, utilising a multi-religious concept: a road of pilgrimage along which we are travelling, in the hope of growing towards our destination. Macquarrie, as we shall see, has developed an exciting Christology whereby 'christhood' is proposed as the end-point, or the peak, of humanity. In his language, 'Becoming' turns towards and moves into Being at the point of Christhood. We shall explore this idea further in Chapter 6.

As well as speaking of 'human being', we also speak of 'human nature'. For the Greeks, *'physis'*, *'nature'* connoted emergence and development. As Macquarrie notes, the word

> *"...has to do with being born, arising, and etymologically it comes from the same root as 'genesis'. Heidegger thinks that the Latin word 'natura' was a poor translation of the Greek 'physis', and that in general the Romans obscured the Greek philosophical vocabulary when they translated it. The Greek 'physis' is, in turn, the noun corresponding to the verb 'phuein', which is one of the words that serves to express the idea of 'being'...however, in a special way... as to include 'becoming' as well as 'being' in what [Heidegger] calls 'the restricted sense of inert duration'...Nature, then is the emergence of the beings..."*[35]

So it is our human nature to 'emerge' towards our potentiality. We are not there yet, whatever we may believe: there is still some way to go before we become what we are called (originally intended) to be. Just what this might mean has exercised the minds of philosophers, theologians and Sci-Fi writers (there is an important overlap between these vocations, and there are many prophets to be found among the latter) for decades. What will we yet become?

Leaving aside secular utopian ideas about the development of a super-humanity ('super' often only in terms of intelligence and technological achievement), we might say with rather more humility that, for us, what evolution is really about is becoming, like Christ, truly human: fulfilling the divine plan for us. Empowered by God's Spirit we realise (make real) the image of God which we already bear but which, for most of us, has not yet been fully developed. This is an essential point for our Christologies: God didn't become human through some miraculous conception; Jesus became completely human through his obedience to the will of the Father and through his self-sacrificial love for others. It is now we who need to become human like him, or as human as he was. 'True' humanity, therefore, is not something that Jesus possessed alongside a 'dollop' of 'true' divinity; true humanity is that which Jesus (and perhaps others) attained and to which most of us can only continue to aspire: true divinity (as we shall discuss further below) may arise from that. But it is not an add-on; it is, as we will find that Athanasius claimed, the essential purpose of the Incarnation.

It is the possession of the 'breath of God' that makes us human (or, perhaps, provides our human potential) and perhaps also provides the potential for true divinity (in others words, humanity and divinity are not necessarily opposites). It was the endowment with spirit that enabled humanity, made in the image and likeness of God, to be creative and responsible and to rise above lower levels of life, or those levels of life where consciousness (and hence, spirituality) is – so far as we know – less or even undeveloped. Some may point out that although animals are clearly 'living beings', God did not breathe his Spirit into them, only into Adam (Gen 2: 7); but that, again, is to take the evocative Biblical text far too literally. Clearly the authors were more focused on the very special nature and authority of humanity (Gen 1: 26) than they were (at least at that stage) on the rest of the created order. But just because God has breathed his life-giving Spirit into us, that doesn't need to suggest more than a 'kick-start': we are not yet fully-formed; just as babies need to grow physically, so we all need to grow spiritually. It is self-evident that we haven't achieved all that our humanity has to offer and to be: there is a still unfinished potential for human transcendence (which, again, we discuss further below). That is why to focus on the spiritual is to focus on the entelechy of our humanity.

When we talk of 'spirit' we are pointing to that dimension of being human that makes us more than mere physical organisms or just highly complicated animals, but which is still open to possibilities that have yet to be unfolded. That is just one reason why we shouldn't relate to other people as things in the world. That de-humanises them: it blocks or removes their 'breath'. We must relate to them as persons. But what is different between a person and a thing is not something that can simply be observed by the eye or measured by some device (as with the current debate about Artificial Intelligence): it is as subtle as that very life-giving Spirit which works within us. Yet it is also self-evident that there are, and have always been, those who are far from being what God intends humanity to be: whose 'spirituality' still has to be realised. They are certainly human in biological terms, but their humanity goes little further beyond that. That, presumably, is why evil people may sometimes be described as 'animals'. This isn't to insult animals; it a way of recognising the stifling, or even the loss, of the Spirit that is within them. God doesn't impose himself; if he is unwelcome he may well go elsewhere.

Furthermore, it is not just about singular personhood. An essential aspect of spirituality is that it transcends individuality; it thrives best in relationships. As theologian-educationalist John Hull has put it: *"spirituality exists not inside people, but between them"*.[36] So we should certainly not think of spirit as some kind of additional substance (that's where Spiritualists have got it entirely wrong); it is simply code for a depth of being and the depth of relationships that is not exhausted by the senses, nor is it conveyed by the merely physical:

> *"Spirituality stands at the junction where the deepest concerns of humanity, and the belief in transcendental values, come together in the movement toward ultimate fulfilment in life...Authentic spirituality takes into account the delicate balance of human growth and development, the wider concerns of society, and the multiplicity of ways that spiritualities are enfleshed in people's lives. Authentic spiritualities are positive human expressions of self-liberating transcendence that are directed towards the common*

good of humanity".[37]

Although I have suggested that discerning the activity of the Spirit in us and around us is not easy, it should not be beyond anyone's capacity to do so: providing they are willing to take notice. 'Spirit' has certain ways of identifying herself: a call sign (we might say). Perhaps it is no surprise that in modern anonymous societies increasingly starved of spirituality many Christians (and others in their own traditions) turn to the intense experiences of the Pentecostalist-type sects. However, the main tendency in the NT is to see the work of God's Spirit, and therefore the truly spiritual life, shown in the rather less sensational, but ethically far more important 'gifts' or 'fruits': love, joy, peace, patience, kindness, generosity/goodness, faithfulness, gentleness and self-control (Galatians 5: 22):

> "...although the NT retains vestiges of the idea that the Spirit is some quasi-magical force that operates subpersonally and irresistibly, the new conception of the Spirit arising out of the new revelation in Christ departs from the idea that his work is chiefly to be seen in occult happenings like interpreting dreams, predicting the future, or speaking with tongues, and looks for that work instead in the highest qualities of personal being".[38]

It is the reverse of these - the non-spiritual - that we so often see around us: hatred, despair, violence, impatience, unkindness, varieties of selfishness and evil, short-termism, coarseness, and a total inability to control oneself. The true gifts of the Spirit draw us out of ourselves (that is true 'ek-stasy') into a new way of living: from self-centredness to a new openness. The hemmed in and narrowly focused life is broken open and the spiritual person is born.

The Johannine Christ spoke of bringing abundant life: life in all its fullness (Jn 10: 10). That is not easy to translate either into a sermon or into a school curriculum; but it is that kind of outcome which ministers and teachers should be talking about and planning for: helping those for whom they care on the road to becoming more truly human or, in Christian language, fulfilling their vocation to express the image of the infinite God in their finite lives. Again, from the 4th Gospel: "What is born of flesh is flesh, and what is born of the spirit is spirit" (Jn 3: 6). The challenge is enable others to perceive those depths in our lives and in the lives of those around us: to turn away from the merely fleshly, surface and superficial. In this celebrity, fame and wealth obsessed age that is very difficult. But the more we go out beyond ourselves, the more open we are to God and to other people, the more our spiritual dimension is deepened and the freer we become. On the other hand the more we turn in on ourselves, the less spiritual, and so the less human we become, and the more captive to our baser (animalistic) instincts. Some, like those who murder or otherwise abuse their fellow humans, may be thought of not simply as evil, but as those who have given up on their own humanity. They have blotted out *their* spirit, and their actions have quenched the fire of the Spirit *in* them. But faith in a loving God who has generously given us his Spirit, gives us also the hope beyond hope that their condition is not terminal; that repentance, redemption and transformation is always possible, and that one day, even after death, they may finally recognise and respond to the call of God's Spirit within them (that is why those who are so sure there is no point in praying for the dead are placing limits around the love of God, which never gives up on us). Or, of course, they may not; they may remain 'spirit-blind': the eschatological consequences of that are presently, and may always be, beyond our ability to know.

The great paradox of spirit (and hence spirituality) is that by going out and spending ourselves, we not only realise our spiritual potential, but we grow stronger rather than weaker.

Again, for teachers, this is where spiritual development fits so well with social and moral development and, of course, with values education. This is because spirituality is not primarily about an internal, individual, value-free process as some seem to present it. Those who 'don't do God', often don't 'do' Spirit either. Many educationalists have criticised the vagueness with which 'spirituality' has sometimes been used in schools to obscure the fact that some values may be in conflict, and claim that it has promoted a self-indulgent and uncritical acceptance of individualistic values prioritising, for example, individual self-esteem over against those aspects of interrelatedness that are crucial to human development. Ultimately authentic spiritual development must be underpinned by judgements about what is and what is not worthwhile, which is why children must be enabled to challenge inauthentic and transient values. That is part of their spiritual education.

Perhaps the ultimate paradox is that of self-awareness. It is in our self-emptying (our self-kenosis) rather than in our self-assertiveness or self-promotion that we become most self-aware: aware in particular of what God has called us to be, and with the determination to follow that vocation wherever it leads (this is the Christian version; the same ideas might be expressed in different language by members of other Faiths, or of no Faith at all: but they will ultimately be referring to the same kind of idea: seeking to fulfil others and not just ourselves). Such self-awareness is not to be confused with self-confidence: some of the most confident people appear to have little, if any, true self-awareness. What they are aware of is not the self: it is a façade or a broken model of the self still enslaved to 'things' (that is why the Biblical authors warned so frequently about the love of money which diminishes all else: Mt 6: 21; 19: 21; 1 Tim 6: 10 etc.). The spiritually developed person (if I may put it that crudely) is aware of herself, her limitations and weaknesses, her worthwhile abilities, and especially her true nature as a child of

God, born in his image. With our *humanitas* linked (as we saw in my introduction) to God's *humilitas*, our groundedness (*humus*) is precisely what God values so much that he uses it to fulfil his plans for his whole creation (and, again, this can be expressed in non-religious terms such as being ecologically aware, working for those in need, and so on): particularly through Jesus Christ, the true human.

We need to be careful to avoid the simplistic notion that development and growth 'in the Spirit' involves a one-off and once-for-all evangelical conversion-type experience. Perhaps that is the case for some; but for most of us, becoming human is a continuing process of rebirth and renewal; perhaps a continuing struggle which, as I have suggested, even transcends death? It is all about our preparedness to live our lives letting others be: not in the sense of leaving them alone - quite the opposite - but in the sense of enabling; building up rather than pulling down; service and sacrifice. At its best, the church provides a growing point where the community building work of the Spirit of truth and value proceeds most intensely, as much through the whole community (the Body of Christ has many members but it is strongest as One Body) as through individuals. We ought to be able to see in our churches the flourishing of a true spirituality: that process of breaking open and bringing forth the new qualities of a true humanity. The Church should be an environment that supports the development of full personhood. Sometimes, sadly, the Church seems more concerned to diminish it through pursuing agendas and narrow concerns which arise out of its theological blind-spots, and so ends up imprisoning the Spirit, rather than opening itself up to God's agenda and his concerns. One of the CE's Eucharistic Prayers contains this petition:

*"Lord of all life, **help us work together** for that day when your kingdom comes and justice and mercy will be seen in all the earth."*[39]

The question all Christians need to ask is this: do we really try; are we not more concerned with recruiting new Sunday attenders to replace those who are leaving either by choice or by death?

Based on the above discussion, we can now, at least provisionally, characterise the phenomenon we call 'spirituality' and (hence) spiritual development and (thus) *Homo Sapiens Spiritualis* in the following terms:

1. a capacity for going out and beyond ourselves – the technical word is 'self-transcendence'; put into more straightforward language we might think of our ability (or not) to empathise, to love, to relate, to care, to be forgiving, to be unselfish; perhaps even to be sacrificial;
2. it is to do with the openness, freedom and creativity that enables us to shape ourselves in the world of which we are part (and to intelligently and ethically shape that world); in religious terms: to become what we are called to be; in more ordinary (secular) language: to fulfil the vast potential in us to be more truly human, and not just to live a truncated or spiritually impoverished humanity;
3. it is to do with the possibility for self-consciousness (not in the pejorative sense), self-criticism, understanding, responsibility, the pursuit of knowledge, the sense of beauty, the quest for the good, the formation of community, the outreach of love – all these ideas represent what we might call 'life in the spirit' or simply 'abundant life'.

This means:

1. for humanity: the process by which we are enabled/led out[40] to find and grow into our true humanity;
2. in religious terms: travelling the road to becoming what God has called us to become;

354

3. in more secular or humanistic terms: becoming the best person we have it in us to be;
4. for all: living life in its fullest and enabling others to do the same.

This is what the whole of humanity is called to be; as was Jesus in his spirit-filled and wholly human life. Once achieved (when God's Kingdom has come on earth as in heaven) then this will represent, if not the epitome of creation (who could possibly say?), then at least one of God's top priorities: a **true shared humanity** that goes out from itself and lets other be. We will use this literally wonderful idea (read again Psalm 8) to help further our discussion.

A True Shared Humanity?

Ward's continuing analysis is instructive and may cast light further down the Christological path than he imagined. Crucial to any reformulation of the "divine-human identity" (Ward argues) must be a more profound understanding of the **freedom and autonomy** of human personhood than the Conciliar Fathers possessed (which had led at least some of them to come up with the notion of the Logos assuming an impersonal, 'anhypostatic' human nature). Indeed, for many, the reality of freedom and autonomy is crucial to our humanity and personhood: unless we are free beings we cannot be responsible beings (the fundamental problem with those who argue a form of predestinarianism in which God has already resolved, before our birth, what essentially we are like and whether we 'deserve' heaven or hell – or if God has merely resolved our eschatological fate without regard to 'what we are like', then such an arbitrary and capricious god is not worthy of worship).

But our undoubted freedom and autonomy are not absolute. We have already encountered the insight that human existence is characterised by our finitude, and that among the 'polarities' (tensions) of that existence are the oppositions of possibility and facticity (we may have enormous potentialities, but those are always tempered by the various 'givens' and realities of our lives; our pre-existing 'situations' which are the result of our utter – and, for Sartre, horrendous - contingency) and between responsibility and impotence (we may wish to be responsible beings, but our relative lack of power may place considerable constraints around that wish or we may know what we ought to do, but not have the moral will to do it). Put briefly: we are as free as our life situations enable us to be: in some aspects of our lives our freedom and autonomy may be extremely limited by our heredity and environment (our intellect, our health, our location in history and geography, and so on). Nevertheless, despite all such constraints, most of us (particularly in the developed world) do have a tolerable level of personal freedom: we are able to take decisions which affect us and others; we are able to mould aspects of our lives according to our aspirations. We are, in short, able to take some degree of responsibility for our lives – to do good, or to do evil, and to accept (willingly or not) the outcomes of the choices we have made. That, we might say, is the essence of being a mature human being (which is why some societies set an age of criminal responsibility beyond which we have to pay for our crimes). Furthermore, the religious idea of some kind of eschatological 'judgement' (with reward or punishment) acknowledges that we may well have to face up to our 'sinful' acts of both commission and omission (e.g. Mt 25: 31 – 46 and expressly, in the Hindu tradition, through the process of re-birth).

Yet as we have already seen, for Ward, someone

"...who was never egotistic or overwhelmed by self-centred passion; who was always mindful and self-controlled, compassionate and loving; and who experienced a constant sense of the presence of God and the power of the Spirit prompting and inspiring their thoughts

and feelings...could only exist by an extraordinary and specific act
of God, exercised continuously throughout a whole human life",

albeit with a questioning caveat: *"Is such a person possible? The*
conception is not self-contradictory. It is theoretically possible".
Although this particular assertion may not be contradictory,
both the assumption and the traditional doctrine underlying it
surely are? If it is claimed that 'Jesus is (really) God' (or similar)
then, as noted above, it must logically be the case that he is
not human. Further, although there may well be many things
that are 'theoretically possible', the more important issue is:
what evidence do we have that this theoretical possibility is
what occurred in the real human life of the man from Nazareth
and, more to the point, do we need to accept that such human
'perfection' can only be brought about by God's special fiat? In
which case, again, this perfect person is not a fundamentally
'normal' person at all, but a (kind of) divine construct and, as
a result, we find ourselves falling towards, if not completely
immersed in Docetism.

Despite asserting that Jesus can only be 'perfect' through
God's 'direct action' (specific divine intervention in the process
not only of birth but the personal development which followed),
Ward still wishes to develop an argument about **human potential**:

> *"...thus a perfected life, a life beyond evil and grounded in perfect*
> *love, is not only possible, but it is a positive hope for many religious*
> *believers"*.

Yet this possibility, for Ward, can only come about because
Christ provided a 'unique' model based on a 'unique' divine
act, implying that this ultimate destiny for human beings, an
eschatological condition of which Christ was the only first-
fruits, is entirely the work of God and nothing whatsoever to do
with us. What space is left for human freedom and autonomy;

for our response to God? The logical outcome of such a view is that Christ is different from us in kind not because he was able, through his own free and autonomous life, nor through the relationship he formed with the Father, nor through God's prevenient grace, his 'prompting and guidance', to raise up our humanity, but because his origin was a special, exceptional event ("fully united to God from the first moment of his earthly existence" in a way in which the rest of us are not). In short, a unique miracle.

Yet Ward is also keen to dismiss some of the conclusions of the classical formulation of the doctrine (despite claiming that this was not what Chalcedon implied):

> "The idea is not that God 'turns into' a human being, or that God completely controls the thoughts and deeds of a human being... in the case of all human beings, God has a complete knowledge of all they feel and think. But the feelings and thoughts of most human beings often conflict with the will of God, and so God must preserve a certain distance from them...In the case of a grace-perfected life, however, there would be no alienating distance between God's nature and this human nature. One could rightly say that the acts of this human person accord perfectly with what God wills and with what God is. And this likeness is not accidental. It is essential, for it is prompted and guided by God".[41]

One might agree with all of this, and yet there is still the undeniable problem that for Ward, Jesus must somehow be a special case because he was a unique occurrence, a result of special 'intervention' from 'outside'. If that were the case, then, what (eschatological) hope is there for the rest of us, who have not been recipients of this 'special treatment' except that God will alone change us into what we are not: perfected humanity - presumably without our alleged freedom and autonomy having any role in that process either?

As we noted above, Ward's answer to this dilemma (which seeks both to have the cake of human freedom and autonomy, and also to eat it) is the concept of "**divine-human synergy**". Referencing the use of this term (meaning 'working together') in 2 Cor 6: 1, Ward explains that as God is personal, despite being infinite, it is entirely possible for him to "cooperate" with "finite" persons "and in the process both may be changed".[42] He helpfully argues that

> "...it is not that God has just one preordained plan which finite persons have to work out in a predetermined and precise way. God's plan is that persons should cooperatively work together to create new forms of goodness...[and] new values...that only a God who synergistically interacts with finite persons could bring about".[43]

Thus far, all this makes very good sense indeed: God working with free, albeit finite, beings and bringing good out of every possible situation (there may be some situations in which the prompting of the Spirit doesn't work). One might imagine God working in this way with all kinds of people in all kinds of situations, some of whom might not even be aware of the existence of their divine partner. But still Ward cannot be satisfied that God worked with Jesus in this manner (or even that Jesus was particularly open to God, perhaps more so than most, but potentially in the same way). He claims that Jesus is not only "*a truly human person, but he is not only a human person*".

What, then, is the more implied by the 'not only'? It is (by "a synergistic union")

> "...the earthly manifestation of God [in that] there is the deepest possible unity, original and dissoluble, between his humanity and the mind and will of God. In that sense, Jesus is God. But he is not God simpliciter. He is God insofar as God turns towards the world in compassion and takes form within the world – God as participant

in the world".[44]

So Ward has moved, in a backwards direction, from a viable description of 'synergy' as the way that God might interact with (the whole of?) his creation, to insisting that the way he does so with Jesus must (presumably *a priori*) be special/unique (etc.) without ever bothering to explain why that must be.

Jesus *"is God"* because (and in the sense that) there is *"the deepest possible unity...between his humanity and the mind and will of God"*. If this is, as it seems, to be another way of saying that Jesus' mind was, in fact, the mind of God, or even that Jesus' human mind was to any degree controlled by, or even operating alongside, the mind of God, then Ward has fallen headlong into the Apollinarian heresy, which understood Christ to a fusion of a divine Logos or mind and a creaturely body. For Apollinarius, there is no human mind in Christ – that is replaced by the *Logos* (as per Jn 1: 14), so the *Logos* was simply enfleshed (takes the place of the rational mind so that, in effect, there was a divine mind veiled by human flesh, resembling humanity but not *homoousios* with it) thus, to all intents and purposes, denying that Jesus was truly human. There was no true unification of Godhood and manhood, but rather the 'takeover' by one of the other. Even if we pursue the dyothelite route that there were, in Christ, two minds – divine and human - operating (somehow together), then just one of the problems that throws up is how those minds interact: does one (the divine) control the other (the human), or do they operate in some other way? Either way, the genuine humanity of Christ (and his autonomy and freedom) is severely compromised.

Ward goes on to suggest that

"...when Jesus prays to the Father, it is the human person, limited in power and knowledge, one finite being among others...who voices his human desires and intentions...it is not God as the eternal Word

*who prays to God as Father – which would be the case of the divine speaking to itself. It is the human person of Jesus, who is truly **in some sense** identical with God as participant, who prays to God as creator. We might say that one aspect of the earthly manifestation of God prays to the cosmic reality of God as infinite creator".*[45]

Certainly, we might say that, but does it make any sense? Ward himself adds: *"At first sight, this may not seem to make sense"*, to which I would add: 'neither at second nor subsequent sights as well'. If we seek to unpack this a little, Ward seems to be suggesting that God (as the Divine Word) is, in Jesus, operating within a human life (thus implying at least some form of dyothelitism based on each 'nature' having a will or mind) but that (implied 'obviously') the divine mind doesn't speak to itself – rather, it is the human mind that (operating alongside the divine mind?) which prays (to the divine mind within it, or to the divine "cosmic reality" presumably outside of it?).

Today we are more likely to associate mind with personhood (whereas for the Fathers, mind was primarily associated with a 'nature') and so if there are two minds within me, then there are two agents who may not think, know, or will (think and decide) the same things (analogous to multiple personalities disorder, which we tend to think of as two discrete 'persons' in one body). Ward denies this and seeks to defend his proposal by an argument based on the distinction between brain states and mental states and what he terms 'double-aspect identity theory':

"'…whatever it is' that unites both divine and human natures in Jesus forms one unitary reality, but within that unity two separate aspects can be distinguished – the finite and the human, the infinite and divine.[46]

This (he believes) allows him to argue that
"There is only one mind and will in God…and that Jesus is a

*real human creative subject of action, whose unity with God is synergistic or one of total cooperation...[Thus] in Jesus there is a real and **unique** unity of the divine mind and a human mind, but that should not be conceived as the mind...of the eternal Word subsuming, or taking over, the human mind. On this interpretation, the Word is not a 'mind' in the relevant sense of a distinct and separate subject of creative action and unique experience. Between the uncreated mind of the threefold God and the finite mind of Jesus there is in one way a complete ontological disparity, a difference in kind. They do not compete for the same ontological space, as the personalities of human schizophrenics may. In Jesus there is a compound unity of a human subject who expresses the eternal thought of God and the divine subject who exists in three forms of being and who wills Jesus' divine life and thought to express the eternal Word".[47]*

All the words Ward deploys above in his explication of Christ's nature drive me to the conclusion that, essentially, Jesus was not like us: how can Jesus be described as a "real human" when his mind forms a "real and unique unity" with the mind of God? My own inclination is to apply Occam's razor to this erudite analysis, most simply on the basis of a question I have previously asked: 'just how do you know?', but also because I cannot comprehend how anyone can argue for some form of non-functional (ontological?) identity between Jesus and Father God (which Ward appears to be defending), whilst also declaring there to be an "ontological disparity" between them. We really cannot have it both ways: either Christ was 'truly human' (like us) or he wasn't; surely a human being who is (consists of) both a human and a divine 'subject' (by which I assume Ward means a centre of consciousness) is not like us, but is, at the very least, some kind of aberration?

Ward concludes this chapter on 'The Idea of Incarnation' by returning to where he began: to an, at least, quasi-functionalist description of Jesus. Asking: "Does this make Jesus divine?", he answers his own question by stating that Jesus was neither omnipotent nor omniscient (apparent characteristics of divinity – so, in that sense, Jesus is not actually divine at all although I assume that some would argue something like 'the human part of Jesus was not divine, but his divine aspect obviously was'), but that he was

> "...the realisation of the divine ideal [?], but also the one through whom God acts decisively...both the revelation of the goal of union with God and the one who establishes the definitive Way to such a union",[48]

so suggesting not only that Jesus was the agent of God ("the one through whom God acts"), but also the first-fruits of a process which is intended to embrace the whole of humanity (which he both reveals and establishes). Clearly (albeit in Ward's view, unique) different in degree, but not in kind. For why could not both of these functions (action and revelation) be carried out by a genuinely, fully human being? Why do we require such theological sophistication (or sophistry?) in order to understand how Jesus acted on God's behalf and, in so doing, revealed God's nature and intentions to the world? Why must Jesus be ontologically unique (and Ward really needs to explain, having also claimed that Jesus and God are ontologically 'disparate' where, precisely, that leaves the question of Jesus' nature) and why must Jesus' life only be the outcome of "a unique divine initiative"?[49] Joining these two claims together may seem to suggest that Jesus was actually neither human nor divine, but something entirely different. But how could we possibly know what that was?

Different in Degree

We are led inexorably by this discussion to one particular theological principle which has already arisen several times but which, if we are to take Jesus' humanity with utter seriousness, we must accept as a given: that **Jesus was not different from us in kind, but (merely?) in degree**. Indeed, how could he be totally different from us if, as a human being, he is part of the created order (this was always one of the prime difficulties of the 'two natures' model, as it was to a degree in the Arian controversy, where even Arius was clearly unwilling to have a genuinely human Christ – the God-man, even if not *homoousios* with the Father, must be different from the rest of humanity). This is why the Fathers of Nicaea (and after) felt the need to propose a Christ who was uncreated, yet still really human. But how could that be? Human beings are, by definition, creatures: was it just Jesus' 'divinity' that was uncreated? If so, what exactly does that mean?

The essential theological problem, recalling the particular concern of the Fathers that 'what is not assumed cannot be redeemed', is this: if Christ was not part of the created order (this was the Arian heresy, for which – in view of the Christological convolutions which followed – we may now have at least some sympathy) and was a totally different kind of 'being', then there is a very real sense in which he is fundamentally (and soteriologically) irrelevant to us and our needs (that is also the logical outcome of belief in a literal virginal conception which would make him very different from the rest of us). Positing a divine person who 'puts on' or 'assumes' human flesh (and, again, what does that mean?) doesn't solve the problem. If any Christian feels obliged to maintain that Jesus was different in kind (rather than in degree) then the problems raised by that assertion need to be addressed – if that is possible: for how can we comment at all on a person who is fundamentally different in kind from the rest of us? It would be like a visitor from outer space, perhaps of the Star Trek 'dragon'-type (the Gorn), inviting us to comment on their beauty.

Furthermore, if Christ was different from us in kind, then presumably whilst Chalcedon need not be reinterpreted, it must still be explained – then it can either be accepted as true or dismissed as meaningless (in which case, it cannot be true, because 'non-sense' can be neither true nor false). Whatever, it seems absolutely clear that a traditional Christology finds it difficult, if not impossible, to 'protect' Jesus' humanity (as heretics down the ages will testify) and, as a result, much that is said about Jesus in the Churches, which still use traditional language and concepts, is essentially and perhaps inevitably docetic.

The dilemma is clear: a Christ different in kind can never be a truly human Incarnation of God; it may be a quasi-divine epiphany, but that is somewhat different. But a Christ who is different in degree may be; it depends entirely on how we interpret the concept of 'Incarnation', and how a human being might be part of that. Presumably, if Jesus is truly 'one of us' then the potential 'incarnate one' – one who expresses the nature of God in and through their humanity - might have been someone else? Indeed, despite Brian Hebblethwaite,[49] it is logically possible that there has been more than one Incarnation: who (apart from God) is to say otherwise?

Notes

1. Have there been others? see Macquarrie J (1995) 'The Mediators';
2. Macquarrie 'Principles' pp. 199 – 200 "The energy of primordial Being [the Father] is poured out through expressive Being and gives rise to the world of particular beings…Being mediates itself to us through the beings";
3. Ward K (2015) 'Christ and the Cosmos: A Reformulation of Trinitarian Doctrine' p. 73;
4. ibid p. 74;

5. Davison actually reverses these concepts: uniqueness as "... 'standing apart' [superior] as something better, stresses discontinuity [whilst]...uniqueness as distinctiveness ['one of a kind'] encompasses elements of continuity": Davison A 'Human Uniqueness: Standing Alone?' in 'The Expository Times', Vol. 127(1), 2015p. 12; I argue below that to be 'one of a kind' is to be 'the only one' and hence discontinuous with (outside) a group; however, one may be unique in a 'superior' sense whilst remaining continuous with (a member of) a particular group;

6. It is intriguing that in one of the non-canonical Gospels ('The Infancy Gospel of Thomas') Jesus is presented as quite bad-tempered and immoral as when (3: 1 – 3) one of his young friends annoys him, Jesus causes him to be "completely withered"; his friend's parents complain to Joseph: "What kind of child do you have who does such things?"; on a second occasion another child (who accidentally bangs Jesus' shoulder) is struck dead! (4: 1 – 2); Joseph tries telling Jesus off and, in response, Jesus blinds his accusers; Joseph then "grabbed [Jesus'] ear, and yanked it hard", to which Jesus responds in a quite non-filial manner (slightly reminiscent of Lk 2: 49?): "It is enough for you to seek and not find; you have not acted at all wisely. Do you not know that I am yours? Do not grieve me" (5: 1 – 3); the morality of such stories was not a prime concern of the (probably late 2nd Century writer) who simply wanted to demonstrate the awesome power of the child Jesus; quotations from Ehrman BD & Plese Z (Eds. & Trs. 2014) 'The Other Gospels: Accounts of Jesus from Outside the New Testament';

7. Ward op cit p. 76;
8. Burdett art. cit. pp. 4ff;
9. ibid. p. 5;
10. Davison art cit p. 15;
11. For example, experiments with what are considered to be

amongst the most intelligent birds (the crow family) have demonstrated the ability in these birds to recognise that, with a narrow phial of water, only half full, containing a worm floating at the top of the water level, the way to access the worm is to drop stones into the phial so that the water level rises (Archimedean birds?); further, some scientists have expressed the view that dolphins are currently at the same intelligence-level as humanity was 100,000 years ago; information accessed 12/10/15 from BBC TV programme 'The Search for Life: the Drake Equation' presented by Dallas Campbell;

12. Johnson EA op cit p. xiii;

13. Davison art cit. p. 15;

14. Johnson EA op cit p. 240;

15. Davison art cit p. 12;

16. Ward op cit p. 75;

17. 'Principles' pp. 59ff;

18. ibid pp. 264 ff;

19. ibid. pp. 50 – 51;

20. See discussion ibid. pp. 304ff; Macquarrie prefers the term 'definitive' in that he understands Jesus to have 'defined' God's nature;

21. *Psyche* was originally 'life' in Homer and the early poets, then it came to refer to a departed spirit or ghost in the Underworld; in Plato it is the immaterial and immortal soul - later the conscious self or personality, regarded in abstraction and actually distinguished from oneself; in both the LXX and the NT it refers to persons, portraying various aspects of the self – the mind, the spirit, the emotional life, and even feelings; it is able to experience pleasure; also used of the moral and intellectual self, the mind (but not the same as *nous*); psyche, like *anima* (though more often than *anima*), carries with it a definite idea of immortality; however, in the New Testament *psyche* does not have the more physical

connotations found in *nephesh*, and is variously translated as life (44 times), soul (33 times) and person (4 times); so *psyche* clearly suggests aspects of selfhood and a life that has ultimate value;

22. Noffke S article on 'Soul' in Sheldrake P (ed. 2005) 'The New SCM Dictionary of Christian Spirituality' p. 593;

23. This is a particularly important point because the common Christian belief in the 'soul', as something separate and separable from the physical body, owes its existence to Greek as opposed to Jewish thought; this is why the concept of resurrection fits far better (only?) with the Jewish model than it does with the Greek, and why so many Christians get muddled over what is to be believed about life after death: am I raised, or does my soul separate from my body? the answer for many is to come up with some kind of very bad synthesis of them both, which makes no sense at all;

24. Phillips A 'Being Human' in 'Theology' Vol 118(4) July/August 2015, p. 243;

25. I don't claim this as my original insight, but I have been unable to reference it;

26. Wright A. (2000) 'Spirituality and Education' p. 96;

27. ibid. p. 104;

28. Macquarrie J. (1972) 'Paths in Spirituality' (henceforth 'Paths') p. 41;

29. ibid. p 4;

30. For example, in Macquarrie's 'Principles' the language of 'being'/'holy being' may seem somewhat opaque, but is in line with Macquarrie's 'existential-ontological' analysis although for him this is no metaphysical or otherwise speculative question: "...we began by asking about ourselves, and it was the confrontation with the nothingness in our own existence that opened our eyes to the being which contrasts with nothing. So our question about being is not a theoretical question...it is an existential question in the sense

that it is asked by someone who is involved in the question of being" (p. 107); Macquarrie then **explains what being is not** (pp. 107 – 110) i.e. **not** *a* being, a property [that we have], a class [of things], a substance, nor is it 'the absolute'; he then seeks to clarify what 'being' may be **distinguished from**: becoming, appearance, or 'the ideal'; finally, he attacks the question of meaning itself: being is incomparable (like the *'mysterium'*) and a *"transcendens"* i.e. "nothing that is... nevertheless more beingful than anything that is" (p. 113); it is also "act" (perhaps 'energy'): but his preferred definition is "that which lets-be" and which, although "wholly other" (cf. Otto), makes itself present in and through particular beings, which themselves, therefore, "participate" in being; so "being 'is' [use of inverted commas to remind us that – really – being is "nothing that is"] the incomparable that lets-be and that is present and manifests itself in and through the beings" (p. 115); is Macquarrie saying that 'being' **is** God? not exactly: "'God' and 'being' are not synonyms" (neither, of course, does he believe it makes any sense to think of God as **a** being, super or otherwise, as classical theism has tended to do), and so he prefers (detailed argument on p. 115 – but basically because some people have interpreted 'being' as "indifferent or alien") the term "holy being" for God, for "in spite of admitted ambiguities, it makes sense to recognise the holiness of being, and to take up before it the faith-attitude of acceptance and commitment" – the remainder of his, now classic, 'Principles of Christian Theology', seeks to explain and illustrate this usage (and where he uses 'Being' as shorthand for Holy Being = God – although he warns us not to have a too static conception of Being [or, indeed, being], because "Being always includes becoming" [p. 122]); **to sum up**: 'being', an incomparable, transcendent 'energy' that undergirds everything that is (and causes it to be, because being 'lets-be'), expresses itself through the beings (particularly, human beings, and most dramatically and definitively in Christ, where **Holy Being** and **a being** come together), and when we approach 'it' in faith we become aware of 'its' holiness (again, a very similar analysis to that of Otto); so 'God' has an ontological meaning (denoting being) and an existential meaning insofar as we have faith/commitment towards 'it' (within the Christian tradition Holy Being is recognized, addressed and worshipped as the Triune God; other Faiths have their own terms of reference/symbols e.g. Brahman in Hinduism, Allah in Islam etc.);

31. 'Principles' pp. 199 – 200;
32. Cupitt D (1998) 'The Religion of Being' p. 26;
33. ibid. p.26;
34. 'Principles' p. 164;
35. ibid. pp. 222 – 223;
36. Hull JM 'The Ambiguity of the Spiritual' in Halstead JM & Taylor MJ (eds) (1996) 'Values in Education and Education in Values' p. 66;
37. Perrin DB (2007) 'Studying Christian Spirituality' pp. 22, 25;
38. 'Principles' p. 334;
39. Eucharistic Prayer E: CW p. 197;
40. 'Education' strictly derives from the supine of the Latin verb *educare*, which, linked to the idea of assisting at a birth, carries the meaning of 'bringing up' or 'rearing' a child, normally referring to the more limited idea of bodily nurture/support; however, the Latin *educere*, meaning 'to **lead out**', 'to **bring out**', can also carry the meaning 'to bring up' and may be thought to represent a richer and more creative understanding of the educational process;
41. Ward op cit pp. 76 – 77;
42. ibid. p. 77;
43. ibid. pp. 77 -78;
44. ibid. p. 78;
45. ibid. pp. 78 – 79;

46. ibid. p. 79;
47. ibid. pp. 80 – 81;
48. ibid p. 81;
49. ibid. p. 74
50. 'The Uniqueness of the Incarnation' in Goulder M (ed. 1979) 'Incarnation and Myth: The Debate Continued' pp. 189 – 191: '...only one man [sic] can actually *be* God to us, if God himself is one': why?

Chapter 6

The Incarnation as the Advent and Epiphany of God

Why Jesus?

Why, if anyone may have the potential to express God in their lives (presumably to varying degrees), was it Jesus who did so (as Christians believe) so definitively? Perhaps because

> "...this has in fact been the way things have turned out. The unique [special, definitive etc.] place of Jesus Christ is part of the givenness of history. Sceptics will say that this is just an accident, but those who believe that history has meaning and a goal will see the place of Jesus Christ as providential...[however] we cannot simply mean the individual, Jesus of Nazareth, in isolation, for no individual exists apart from social relations. Each must be seen in a social and historical setting. The Christ-event which is said to be the focus of Being certainly has its centre and origin in this particular person, Jesus Christ, but he is unintelligible apart from the whole complex of relationships which bind him to Israel, to the Church, to the entire human race, and it is this vast ongoing movement of spiritual transformation and renewal that has to be borne in mind when we consider the claim made for Christ".[1]

Once again, none of this requires us to think of the human Jesus himself as metaphysically/ontologically divine (and to put it as crudely as this has been defined by the Church as heretical, so reminding us that, despite the language used by many Christians, the truth is much more subtle) even though the Church, mightily influenced by the *Logos* doctrine of the 4th Gospel and the undergirding secular philosophies of the day, did eventually come to that kind of 'having one's cake and eating it' conclusion.

Yet to deny ontological divinity (however that is defined) to Jesus is not to deny that he was part of God's eternal plan for the redemption of his creation: perhaps not so much a detailed pre-formed strategy fuelled by divine foreknowledge, but more a vision to be worked at within the contingencies of a free creative process. We might put it like this: God, on his own initiative, works tirelessly through the normal processes of creation (including evolution) and, as a result, there arises a particular individual at a particular time and in a particular place who is able (through the quality of his character and of his own free choice) to 'deliver' God's mission. Perhaps this was one amongst many attempts at developing the right 'agent', some of whom might, through the freedom or frailty of the individuals concerned, have not reached the potential God willed for them. Even a fairly conservative Christian scholar concurs that God did not 'get it right' first time:

> "First [God] commissioned humanity to subdue and care for the world. **It didn't work**. So he tried destroying most of the world and starting again with one family. **It didn't work**. So he tried a third time with one family but separated them from the rest of the world in order to bless them so spectacularly that the entire world would pray to be blessed as they were blessed. This strategy **also didn't work,** and the descendants of Abraham and Sarah ended up back in the Babylonia from which they had come. **God tried a fourth time** by re-establishing the community centred on Jerusalem, though many people who had been scattered around the Mediterranean and Middle eastern worlds stayed in the place of their dispersion or spread further...So **God tried a fifth time** by sending his Son into the world. When this strategy again initially failed in particularly catastrophic fashion, God again transformed disaster into potential triumph. He turned the failure and his refusal to be beaten by it into a message that could go out to the entire world...".[2]

But God refused to be beaten by the various and repeated failures within his creation, and eventually he succeeded – but, presumably, he might not have done so at that particular time had the circumstances still not been entirely right. The Slovenian atheist philosopher, Slavoj Zizek, puts it like this (reflecting on the ideas of Jean-Pierre Dupuy): "*Christ was contingent, but once he is here he is [an] absolute necessity*".[3] In other words, this particular 'Christ event' didn't have to happen; it happened because Jesus freely accepted the work and will of God in and for his life and, had he not done so, then another similar event would eventually have occurred (the 'next attempt'), because it was the will of God that that be so. As Zizek explains: "*it happened contingently, but once it happens, it retroactively becomes necessary*".[4]

However, despite the need to reinterpret the classic doctrines, none of this kind of revised thinking should be understood to deny that 'the Word [or Wisdom] became flesh...'; it is, rather, to ask what such language regarding the en-fleshment (or 'embodiment') of these divine characteristics (existing almost independently) might mean. Instead of thinking that a metaphysical 'person' ('Son'), or some personal aspect of God ('Word', 'Wisdom'), was somehow implanted into a foetus (or at some other stage of Jesus' development), we are speaking rather of God being at work in the natural evolution of humanity which, journeying via the development of consciousness and intelligence (humanity eventually reaches the stage where it is able – although may not be willing - to dismiss irrational beliefs in favour of those tempered, at least to a degree, by our knowledge and understanding of the way the world works) culminating in its most spiritual (most open to the Divine) in the person of Jesus; and perhaps in others as well. As the one appointed by God from all eternity it is easy to understand how, in doing the work of God, Jesus came to be thought of as somehow sharing in the divine Being. That particular way of understanding Jesus' unity with God was due to the Hellenization of an early Jewish-Christian theology, morphing eventually into a purely Christian theology (in other words, an originally Jewish interpretation took second place), and was expressed using the concepts and language of ontology. But it didn't need to be put that way: in the OT the same kind of ideas were expressed in narrative, rather than in philosophical, forms.

Furthermore, Jesus, as he engaged in God's work, came to be seen to embody, or to be an embodiment of, divine characteristics. As we have seen, it is not necessary to express this idea in ontological categories. We might understand, for example, that in doing the work of God, Jesus truly expressed (as 'Word') and acted (as 'Wisdom') according to the divine nature – so much so, it was 'as if' he embodied (en-fleshed) these divine characteristics which, treated virtually as quasi-independent 'beings', could easily be seen to take human form: in this case as Jesus of Nazareth, who came to be thought of as the 'Word' (cf. John 1) and the 'Wisdom' of God (cf. 1 Cor 1: 24). Again, it makes a real difference as to whether we understand such ideas as narrative or philosophical theology. But the most directly relevant question is this: if Jesus was genuinely human, how did the process by which he becomes (let's say) 'invested' with God (or with God's Spirit, if preferred), or in which he transcends his humanity and even came to be understood to be 'God-Incarnate', occur? What precisely was the nexus of 'natural', albeit God-moved, events which led to Jesus Christ? In other words: how did the Incarnation happen in the real life of a real man?

How did (does) Incarnation 'work'?

The best way of developing a meaningful christology (talk of Christ) is to base it on a meaningful theology (talk of God): how we understand the nature of God will determine how we understand the nature of the Incarnation. It may well be that the predominantly Greek concept of the God of Classical Theism (a remote figure, hardly the dynamic God of History, who spoke to Moses 'as a friend', revealed in the OT) drove the Doctrine of the Incarnation into a theological *cul de sac*. What is the nature of God that led to a man being termed 'God-Incarnate', and what was the nature of that Incarnation if brought about by that kind of God?

Rather than using the model proposed by Classical Theism, connoting ideas such as an impassible God (who cannot feel or suffer), an interventionist God, an Incarnation inevitably different in kind, and all the other aspects of such a limited concept, we might consider employing the panentheistic notion of a God who both pervades the cosmos (who is immanent) as much as he is also beyond, or 'outside it' (who is transcendent):

> "...such a position [NIODA[5]] allows for divine presence without supernatural intervention in the natural world. God works in, with and under the material forms of nature in a sacramental presence that providentially guides but does not intervene in natural processes".[6]

This view of God and thus how God 'works' became increasingly persuasive as scientists have come to recognise the weakness of traditional Newtonian physics in which the universe is pictured as a machine with certain immutable laws (which an interventionist God – who 'owns' those laws - might occasionally bend or break as he performs his miracles), and about which predictions can be made. This is still a popular model for Christians because such a universe is easily visualised and can be thought to be totally reliable and determined by God's providential care (of course, it also raises further even more difficult questions: if God can intervene at will, why doesn't he wipe out cancer, or prevent earthquakes and tsunamis?). But the main problem with it is that, as a model, it is woefully inadequate, and in modern science (if not in general consciousness) has been properly sidelined.

We have seen above how two modern scientific theories: quantum and chaos, might impact on our understanding of how God works. This way of understanding things means that God's work in the Incarnation (as in the 'miraculous' in general?) doesn't break any laws of nature, because these so-called 'laws' are actually operating within unpredictable systems. In other words, whatever the nature of God in his God-self, and whether God is bound to operate within the 'chaotic' systems he has created, or whether he chooses to do so, God the creator has been, from the very beginning, intimately involved in the whole of his creation, its growth and development, and still is:

> "...God is dipolar [in process thought], consisting of a consequent or responsive nature – affected by experience of all other entities - and a primordial constant nature. God works as an agent at the subjective level, exercising power by **persuasion or lure** rather than coercion. Further, just as we exist, influencing and being influenced by others, so God has a genuine relationship with creation where he also is influenced...God is able to lure the physical while interacting with the 'spiritual'...thus God creates through an evolutionary process that includes chance, in order to give human beings the possibility of development, with the consequence of the risk of suffering".[7]

Despite the anti-intellectual and anti-scientific views of some Christians, particularly those who stubbornly cling to a literal 6 day creation, we may reasonably assume the basics of the modern scientific consensus: that our universe is over 13 billion years old, whilst Planet Earth is around four and a half billion years old; that the first great evolutionary step forward was from non-life to living single cell organisms, and from those very simple to incredibly complex multi-cellular organisms and, as noted above, that the most recent significant creative developments, over the past half million years or so, have been those of

Consciousness: being aware that we are;

Intelligence: the ability to understand ourselves and our environment and, to a degree, the technical ability to mould that environment; together with the ability to communicate with clarity our knowledge and understanding to and from others;

Moral Awareness: the ability to distinguish between good and evil, right and wrong;

Spiritual Development: the degree to which we are able to discern and evoke the Transcendent and, in so doing, realise our true humanity.

These advances have certainly taken place in human beings and, possibly (to a degree) in some other forms of life as well. It would also seem premature to assume that these evolutionary steps all derived from a single source (although they may have done): scientists have, for example, found microbes living in 'arsenic baths' – pools and swamps which contain a purely natural form of arsenic, but in such amounts as would destroy any 'normal' life – which appear to have a unique form of DNA, fundamentally separate in its structure from forms of life as we know them. Such examples might demonstrate separate strands of biogenesis (life-beginnings): that is, separate life-origins just on this one planet, implying the possibility of multiple sources for the origins of life not only here, but possibly elsewhere in the universe.

The panentheistic God doesn't intervene in the world (as does the God of classical theism) from 'outside', rather he is constantly working within the physical systems that he has established. We might say that God's Holy Spirit (i.e. God at work) is constantly striving, not so much to organise everything, as to seek to bring the best out of every natural process at every instant:

"...there is a divine kenosis in relation to creation, in that God is not the puppet-master pulling every string, but he allows people to be themselves, and to make themselves; and, indeed, the whole of creation, in appropriate ways, to be itself, and make itself".[8]

Because those processes have an innate freedom she (the Spirit[9]) doesn't, so-to-speak, 'force matters', but rather "providentially guides":

"The one God who creates is also Wisdom made flesh whose self-emptying incarnation into the vagaries of historical life and death reveals the depth of divine love. Could it not be the case that, rather than being uncharacteristic of God's ways, compassionate self-giving love for the liberation of others is what is most typical of God's ways, and therefore also distinguishes divine working in the natural world? In which case we can expect to see not the exercise of controlling power but of divine power as sovereign, cruciform love that empowers others...the one God who creates and redeems is also the sanctifying Spirit whose self-gift in grace brings healing to sinful hearts and broken situations without violating human freedom. Could it not be that since the Spirit's approach to human beings powerfully invites but never coerces human response, the best way to understand God's action in the evolution of the natural world is by analogy with how divine initiative relates to human freedom? Even when the offer of grace is rejected it is not withdrawn; the Spirit graciously continues to invite, prod, push, pull, lure the heart into loving relationship. But the freedom of the creature remains."[10]

We might illustrate this through the mystery of healing: why are some people (physically) made well and some not? Perhaps because whilst God is always and everywhere working to heal (and cure[11]), there may well be some processes which work with him, whilst others work against him (the particular body; the available medication and technology; the skill of the surgeon: all the physical actualities which God has 'let-be' and with which God must contend) and God will not "override free will" either of people or (however anthropomorphic the idea may seem) of nature itself. I have met many people who, following the unexpected or traumatic death of a loved one, particularly a child, say: 'I find comfort in that this is obviously what God wants... God has called her to himself'; or even, 'God has caused this to happen'. As a priest I can do no other than passively collude in such a view; as a theologian I want to say: 'You are completely wrong; God does not want this; it is just that for whatever reason, he cannot prevent it'. I write this on the 50th Anniversary of the Aberfan disaster (the collapse, in October 1966, of a colliery spoil tip in this Welsh village, killing 116 children and 28 adults): did God cause that to happen? Of course not: it was a human-created disaster waiting to happen (although, of course, there are also natural disasters for which, presumably, God has at least indirect responsibility). Has his Spirit been working in that community ever since? With the anniversary TV programmes showing the way the community of Aberfan and its families have coped with their great losses over 50 years, who can doubt it?[12] As to the tragic side of life: this is just the way things are in a world such as this, where geology shapes the very environment for life: disasters occur; people, even children and babies, die of congenital illness or disease. I might go on to reflect on the post-mortem outcomes in the light of resurrection faith, but not too far: we must not claim to know more than we can know. All we can do is have faith in the loving purposes of God.

The picture I am painting must all seem pretty chaotic. But the concept of chaos is not a modern discovery: it is to be found in a number of ancient cosmogonies (stories of the Beginning).[13] We might even understand the overcoming of chaos as a mythic way of representing God's 'victory' in creation (creation as an act could presumably go well or not: which is why the writer of Genesis 1 emphasised its success: "God saw everything that he had made, and indeed, it was very good" 1: 31). However, a contrast is often drawn between the cosmogonies of the ancient Middle East (which tell of battles between gods and monsters) and the more mature theology of the Priestly writers who constructed Genesis 1 (- 2: 4a: where God simply has to say: 'Let there be...', and it happens), recognising that Genesis 2: 4b – 3 is an older, cruder and more mythological attempt to express the same kind of ideas, alongside attempting to deal with other important questions as well. In a sparking, entertaining and insightful book of biblical theology[14] Gregory Mobley outlines the plot of the 'Enuma Elish': the Babylonian Creation story, in which the storm god Marduk battles with and defeats 'Mother Ocean' (Tiamat) and her eleven cronies (monsters all, who are imprisoned), and then makes an orderly (non-chaotic) world out of her dismembered body parts, leaving watchers to ensure that none of the defeated waters escape (to cause floods?). So although

> "...chaos threatens order, yet the ordered world was constructed when the liquid, chunky mash of chaos was poured into forms. Chaos is the raw material of creation."[15]

It has become an assumption in many Christian theologies of Creation that God created the world out of nothing ('ex nihilo'), but that is hardly what the Biblical creation stories tell us.[16] The older story, which focuses on Adam and Eve, reports that "In the day [note: singular] that the Lord God made the earth and the heavens, when no plant of the field was yet in the earth..." (Gen 2: 4b – 5), so leaving the question open. The much later Genesis 1 is more explicit: "In the beginning, when God created the heavens and the earth, the earth was a formless void and darkness covered the face of the deep [the 'abyss'], while a wind

from God swept over the face of the waters. Then God said..."
(Gen 1: 1 – 3a). The older story makes no comment at all on what
the earth was created from or with, whilst the later story is quite
clear that before God started his creative activity a 'formless'
and 'void' earth already existed, along with its waters. God
is presented here not so much as creating 'from scratch', but
bringing order to a pre-existing chaos.

However, we should realise that, as with the many human
ways of describing how things began (and how they might end),
the reality is likely to be rather more subtle and nuanced:

*"Creation in Genesis 1 is not so much about making things out
of nothing as it is about bringing definition and identity and
differentiation to nothingness. The chaos was not obliterated;
rather it was controlled, fenced in, held behind a firmament. Chaos
was organised into orderly structures; 'everything according to its
kind'."*[17]

Even in scientific terms, if it be thought that the Big Bang came
'*ex nihilo*', it is not altogether clear what that 'nothing' was (or
wasn't): 'nothingness' (like 'timelessness') is itself a mystery:

*"A philosopher might ask what 'begin' means and how 'when'
can be fixed before there was any time. He or she might take the
cosmologist back to what must lie behind the 'explosion' hypothesis
and ask from where and from when was there 'density' or 'hotness'
or 'explosiveness' or anything to explode...A member of a primitive
tribe might not understand the question 'when' for quite different
reasons from a philosopher or a modern novelist or a believer relying
on a sacred book or a cosmology, having no clock and no calendar
and no way of measuring the passage of time except in terms of the
broad rotation of the seasons."*[18]

Evans later adds to her discussion:

"What was the nature of this nothingness, if it was nothingness? Most creation accounts whether they are myths or attempts at philosophical or even scientific explanations, envisage some sort of 'stuff', a primordial matter, whether solid, liquid or gas. The Big Bang explosion seems to rely on there being 'something' to explode",[19] finally asking: *"If there was 'stuff', and the 'stuff' is therefore 'uncreated', was the Creator himself this first 'matter' or was he separate from it? If he was something different from the 'matter', was he always there, alongside it? Was anything else 'always there'? And what do 'there' and 'always' mean in a primordial context anyway?"*[20]

Christians would, no doubt, rebel against the idea of God (or God's substance, which we have already recognised as difficult to conceive, particularly that 'stuff' allegedly shared by Christ) being 'made' of the same 'stuff' as his creation although, as we have seen, such language shouldn't be taken literally. 'Creation out of nothing' signals nothing about the process, but that God is never dependent on anything else for and in his creative work:

"God creates by dint of the sheer loving dynamism welling up from the unfathomable plenitude of divine being...Matter is not a presupposition of divine creative activity but a result of it...'Out of nothing' affirms there is only one source of all that is, namely, infinite holy Mystery".[21]

Yet if we claim that God somehow operates 'within' his creation then clearly there must be some kind of intimate relationship between the two, which is why in rejecting pantheism (the idea that God and the universe are the same) as well as rejecting classical theism which posits an absolutely transcendent ('beyond' and 'separate from') divinity, we have embraced panentheism in order to do our best to express the nature of a

God who both transcends, and yet is at once immanent in and through, the created order. The idea, for example, that God 'pours himself into his creation' doesn't require us to conclude that creation must be made of God-stuff; rather that creation is, in a sense, God's personal gift: a gift in which he takes the risk of 'letting-be'. Yet many of the ancient cosmogonies have a creation somehow made up of the god(s) who brought it about and, despite our proper rejection of such crude designations, we should recognise that there are echoes of these cosmogonies in Genesis 1, even though those echoes are fairly subdued and, by now, pretty faded.

This is what Mobley terms the "Backstory of Creation": as we have already seen, the Priestly author clearly wants to distance himself from the mythological idea that creation is the result of a battle and its substance made up of various parts of the defeated 'monster', in favour of a more elevated and sophisticated theology in which God is above and beyond (transcends) his creation, and that all he has to do is speak and it is made:

> "God made a cosmos, a world that functions, hums and purrs, through some invention (such as light), but mainly through arrangement, structuring, and separation. God was the sculptor who discovered the form hidden in the block of stone".[22]

Nevertheless, those mythic ideas are still hovering in the background, and occasionally come to the surface in other Biblical writings:

> "Priestly theologians buried this story of creation through a competition between the Lord and the dragon of chaos below the surface of their measured prose in Genesis 1, but in the less-constrained discourse of biblical poetry the dragon breaks free."[23]

Thus we find rather more than just vague allusions to the dramatic stories in the Psalms (74: 14, 16 – 17; 89: 10 – 12) and even in Second Isaiah (51: 19): the heads of Leviathan were smashed; Rahab was crushed like a carcass and cut into pieces. Rahab/ Leviathan was the dragon of chaos. Why was chaos seen to be so significant, and why (referring back to the 'Enuma Elish') was it deemed to be so important that the chaos monsters are not destroyed, but rather imprisoned and (most greenly) recycled? It is because

"...*a healthy world consists of checked raw energy [and that] chaos cannot be erased because to do so would eliminate change, novelty, drama, or conflict. No sand, no pearl.*"[24]

It is clear, therefore, that the modern insights represented by 'chaos theory' are not at all foreign to theology, but are to be found to be implicit (and sometimes explicit) in the Hebrew scriptures. The world in which the Incarnation occurred, and the creatures (including human creatures) which inhabit it, have chaos as their default position. Creation and Incarnation represent the ways in which God brings order not only to nature 'red in tooth and claw' but also to the "unruly wills and affections of sinful men [passions of sinful humanity]".[25] We recall that Wilkinson quoted Polkinghorne's view that God may well

"...*work in the flexibility of these open systems as well as being the ground of law. God's particular activity is real, but it is hidden*".

The overcoming of chaos is not just something that God does 'at the beginning', but is an ongoing task: God's Spirit working constantly to bring good out of potential or real evil. This helps us to understand that the Christ didn't 'just happen' to come long (and God then, somewhat pragmatically, chose him – the Adoptionist heresy), but allows that God had been working towards that event throughout eternity, exercising some guidance over both process and outcome. It underlines that the Incarnation was God's initiative and would always come about, although the details of that event (who and when) were not pre-determined. In this sense, Incarnation may be understood to be part of the process by which creation is taken to its next (and perhaps ultimate) step: consciousness, intelligence, moral awareness, spirituality and then *theosis* (the concept of transcendent humanity which we will develop in the next chapter).

To sum up: rejecting the now rather dated (and more Greek than Biblical) idea that God is impassible: that nothing can affect or change him (surely, if God is love, then love – as Andrew Lloyd Weber famously asserted – 'changes everything', including both the lover and the beloved?), we recognise that God's relationship with his creation is in constant flux: a win here, a loss there, yet we can still have faith in God's ultimate providence that the whole of creation – currently groaning[26] – will reach the consummation that he plans (that is why, for Macquarrie, creation, providence, reconciliation and consummation, as they blend seamlessly into one another, are all of a piece: God's single unitary action[27]). Further, with a future that is fundamentally uncertain, then (perhaps literally) almost – but not absolutely - anything might happen: God's constant striving may bring the best results, or he may sometimes be stymied by human (or physical – what of earthquakes and tsunamis?) evil that he 'lets-be'.[28] But there will be those, like Jesus (or, indeed, any prodigious spiritual person) who are so open to his workings, whose wills are so in tune with (but not governed by) the divine will, that they are able to do that will actively and without concern for their own priorities. These are the people who have, for one reason or another, responded to the strivings of God, so much so in Jesus' case (so we believe) that they become, to other observers, almost 'Godlike' in the love and compassion[29] they display – for that is the very nature of God. Such people have made real

"...a free relationship between created and creator... those who believe they are in a relationship with God, yet are free to act; those who believe that they are loved and that their actions matter in the world"

and, furthermore, as Denis Edwards, revisiting the theology of Rahner, helpfully expresses it:

"...radical dependence on God and the genuine autonomy of the creature are directly and not inversely related...the closer creatures are to God, the more they can be truly themselves...Creaturely integrity is not diminished because a creature's existence is dependent on God but flourishes precisely in this independence. This is true not only in the divine relationship to human beings but also in God's interaction with all the dynamics of the natural world, including the emergence of our universe and the evolution of life on Earth".[30]

It may not often happen, but sometimes it does, that 'your will be done' becomes a reality. Yet

"...we need not suppose that every event that happens and every development that takes place is serving some serious purpose of God. In the profusion of living forms, the psalmist sees a kind of playfulness of the divine creativity [Ps 104: 24 – 25]...But all is not randomness and play, or we could make no sense of it. Randomness and play occur in a context of order".[31]

In other words, despite the randomness within the physical universe, and the beings it has produced, their freedom to choose right or wrong, their spiritualties mature or stunted, and where awful and often pointless things seem to happen, God is still ultimately in control – there is some order at the macro- (and possibly also at the micro-) level – ultimately his will **will** be done, whatever that takes! That, fundamentally, is the message of the Incarnation (the same as the message of Jesus): God's Kingdom will come.

The Nature of Christhood

So the man Jesus, appearing in history "in these last days" (Hebs 1: 2) and "like his brothers and sisters in every respect" (Hebs 2: 17) – absolutely and truly human - was the end result of a range of possibilities and events. However, these did not include any specific act of intervention such as making a woman pregnant, but they eventually met the requirements for the full implementation of God's plan or vision after so many years of human and particularly prophetic development. All this came about through a causal nexus of creative, evolutionary and entirely natural (God-established) relationships: physical, biological (particularly genetic) historical (including political/ economic), cultural and religious, to lead to one person (Jesus), or possibly more than one, who exemplified and modelled in and through his absolutely human life the essential character and nature of God (particularly his creative 'letting-be' which, if embraced, enables us to gain 'fullness of life' Jn 10: 10) working on behalf of and with the authority of his Heavenly Father.

Because of this he was indeed Immanuel – 'God with us' (although he was also Jesus – 'God saves'). It was **in this life** that, as Macquarrie put it (utilising an ontology with its potentially abstruse metaphysic mitigated by a more personal existentialism), humanity and divinity converged, and 'Being was revealed through and focused in a being'. God comes (his Advent) and is manifested (his Epiphany) in the man, Jesus, who was crucified:

"Christ's self-giving, his love or 'letting-be',[32] becomes complete *and absolute in the accepting of the cross. Self-hood passes into Christhood, the human Jesus becomes the Christ of faith, and there is the convergence of the human and divine 'natures' in the one person...Christ's most utter self-abasement is also his ascension, when we recognise that God is in Christ. This is the transfiguration, when the light of Being shines forth in this particular being... Jesus Christ may be properly understood as the focus of Being, the particular being in whom the advent and epiphany [of Being] take place, so that he is taken up into Being itself and we see in him the coming into one of deity and humanity, of creative Being and creaturely being. And what we see in Christ is the destiny that God has set before humanity; Christ is the first-fruits, but the Christian hope is that 'in Christ' God will bring all men to God-manhood".*[33]

Macquarrie agrees that that Christ should not be understood to have been different in kind from us, arguing that his 'ascension into divinity' is the destiny of all humankind and part of God's plan for the whole of creation.

It is instructive to consider more fully Macquarrie's understanding of the central issue of divinity-humanity: **'God-manhood'** as he terms it, which he situates within the broad title 'Christ' or, more specifically, the concept of '**christhood**': the motifs of which are "obedience" and "absolute self-giving".[34] We might, thereby, see more clearly how the language of Incarnation can be used to put some flesh on the more generalist bones of the work of a panentheistic God which I have attempted to outline above. Hopefully, we will then see how this act of reinterpretation can remain faithful both to the intentions of the Church Fathers and also to the rules of the Christological 'language game' they sought to establish, whilst also continuing to honour its apophatic horizon.

Historically we can trace how the title 'Christ' gradually changed its meaning from a simple translation (*Christos*) of (the very human concept of) 'messiah' to a title, indeed almost a name (Jesus Christ; Christ Jesus), of a Divine Lord. In other words, 'Christ' itself, beginning as a purely human designation of one chosen by God to carry out some task, and ending as an enduring title of the 'God-man', may be understood to connote something of the 'admixure' of divinity and humanity. More fundamentally, christhood is an aspect of 'selfhood': something existentially intrinsic to us and not just an 'add-on' (Jesus didn't become Christ; he always was Christ). Interestingly, Macquarrie locates 'Christhood' within a notion against which many Christians might rebel: the idea that Jesus, like (potentially) the rest of us, had a vocation: a call from God. This, he claims, is most clearly to be discerned in the story of Jesus' baptism:

> "The story has become one of vocation, and this is surely very relevant to the task of trying to explicate the person of Christ. A vocation makes sense only in the context of a process of growth and commitment. The incarnation, understood as the advent and epiphany (presence and manifestation) of Being in Jesus Christ, is not to be understood magically as something that happened 'automatically' in a moment, say at the moment of conception, or the moment of birth, or even at this moment of baptism. Just as we have argued that the self and selfhood are not things or properties conferred on the existent at the beginning, but are to be understood existentially as ways of being that are to be attained (or not attained) in the course of existence, it must now be asserted that the same is true of Christhood...A moment of vocation implies that there has been a growing sense of vocation; but furthermore, the decisive moment of commitment does not rule out (rather, it entails) a continued development of the sense of vocation, and an unfolding ambulando of a content which may not have been explicit in the moment of commitment itself...Jesus must have had his moment of vocation, that is to say, of decisive commitment to his career, and this moment must have been both preceded and followed by a developing understanding of all that his vocation implied...

Thus the story of the baptism, while it is meant to point to Jesus as the Christ, implies his full humanity, as one who responded to a call and commitment that would only fully unfold as he went along. This story justifies an existential rather than a supernatural approach to the question of the meaning of Christhood. It will be understood that the word 'supernatural' is used here in the bad sense of magical. It need hardly be said [but Macquarrie recognises that some of his critics will say it] that it is not being denied that Christhood is a work that God or Being, not man or any particular being, initiates and brings to perfection".[35]

In this reading of the Baptism story, we have presented to us a genuinely human Jesus who has accepted God's call to be his representative/expression/functionary/agent in a way similar to (but perhaps not the same as – although, if not, then what is the difference?) any other example of divine calling either in the Bible (e.g. Abraham, Moses,[36] Samuel, Isaiah, Jeremiah) or within the Church (even the humble vocation to priesthood), and surely also, within other Faiths, and even perhaps among those who have none who unknowingly work as vanguards of the Kingdom? Jesus gradually became aware that his Heavenly Father (his 'abba') had plans for his life that would transcend the family building business! It is of particular interest that Macquarrie uses the term 'magical' to dismiss any idea that Jesus' vocation was essentially different in kind to other vocations (just as I am accustomed to using the term to define and reject any *ex opere operato* understanding of the sacraments – not exact, but full of meaning!), although one issue that has now to be dealt with is the accusation that what I have so far described is a 'descent' into adoptionism; but that is easily done.

Macquarrie, although laying emphasis on Jesus' call from God rather than on a virginal conception which invested a foetus with divinity (or in which God 'inserted' a divine foetus), still affirms that whatever else the incarnation was, it was the work and the initiative of God:

> *"The doctrine of the virgin birth is meant to point to Christ's origin in God [and to Christ as] the one who has come from God and in whom God's advent and epiphany...have taken place"*.[37]

Jesus didn't just happen to be a 'good bloke' whom God chose and adopted, once he had demonstrated his 'good bloke' credentials. Jesus was indeed God's agent from all eternity (a reasonable interpretation of John's *Logos* model), because that is how God works. But not in a manner which might be thought of as 'magical', such as manipulating human evolution by personally making a woman pregnant (a story to be found, in various forms, in other Faiths). It is important to note, as argued above, that process doesn't require full pre-knowledge of events by God and neither does that truth require a literally divine conception. It was in and through Christ's genuine human life (and death) that God was manifested and was able to address us. But this life was not (so to speak) taken over by God (as in the pointless dyothelite debate as to how the mind of the Logos worked alongside the mind of the human Jesus), but was one that willingly and freely gave itself to God's salvific agenda. It is in this sense that Christ's work was actually God's work, and so 'divine work'.

Another important dimension of this process is contained within the Church's understanding of 'charisms': the notion that God 'gifts' us in various ways (1 Cor 12: 4 – 11), although the full implications of that seems to have been somewhat less explored than, say, the dramatic (and occasionally excessive) 'speaking in tongues'. There is no accompanying notion in Paul's writings that these gifts take over the recipient or that they are imposed upon us for, like any other gift, they can be either received or rejected (as some post-Christmas adverts offering 'unwanted Christmas gifts', or their religious equivalent in social baptism).

Those who receive particular gifts and are able to work with them and display them powerfully in their lives, may be termed 'charismatic', and whatever the gifts were with which his Heavenly Father endowed Jesus (the gift, for example, of a full, unmediated relationship with God; the ability to discern God's will and the courage to act on it), it was Jesus' 'spiritual charisma' to which some (again, not all) people responded when they came to recognise the presence of God in his life. Again, this does not, in itself, separate Jesus from other people: his spiritual gifts may have been particularly profound (just as Mozart's musical gifts were almost 'miraculous'), and although they were no different, in principle, from any other person's God-given 'charisms', they may be considered prodigious. They seem to have been such as to, in the context of the evolution of intelligent, conscious life, represent a further step 'upwards', towards a much more intense spiritual awareness in human evolution. Perhaps, as we considered above, Jesus (as other great spiritual 'athletes') was one of the first of a new sub species: humanity as we have the potential to be?[38] The label is not particularly important, but it does fit in with the notion that Christ was the first fruits of a new creation, which is the destiny of us all, as in the important, but often neglected, Eastern doctrine of *theosis*: human transcendence.

A Transcendent Anthropology

Western soteriological models (how we are 'saved') have tended on the whole to be 'objective'.[39] The process of salvation has been carried out (by Christ) for us, but without us and 'outside' us (*extra nos*). Christian scholars have variously discussed the 'classic/victory' model, the 'ransom' model, the 'satisfaction' and the 'penal substitution' models. In Eastern Christianity, however, salvation was often understood to have been wrought, not so much by Christ's 'work', but **through the very act of Incarnation** itself. Although many atonement models are based on the assumption that Christ **did something** for us (most specifically by/through his death on the Cross) and although that kind of thinking has tended to dominate our liturgies and hymnody, it has certainly not been the only Christian way of understanding how salvation has been 'won', nor was it the clear and unambiguous expression of the Biblical witness. For many Patristic writers it was Christ's union with humanity itself which redeems that humanity, and by which it is thereby sanctified, transformed and elevated:

"Our Lord Jesus Christ...did, through His transcendent love, become what we are, that He might bring us to be even what He is Himself" (Irenaeus);

"God lived on man's level, that man might be able to live on God's level" (Tertullian);

"The Word...became man just that you may learn from a man how it may be that man should become God" (Clement of Alexander);

"For he was made man that we might be made God" (Athanasius).

A similar theology is to be found in the Collect for the First Sunday after Christmas:

Almighty God, who wonderfully created us in your own image
 and yet more wonderfully restored us through your Son Jesus Christ:
 grant that, as he came to share in our humanity,
 so we may share the life of his divinity...[40]

The understanding that salvation is, in effect, deification or divinisation (*theosis*) may variously be defined as the restoration of divine image in humanity (or, if we remove the concept of the Fall as an 'event', the further development of that image), attaining the likeness of God, sharing in the divine life, deliverance from death and corruption, and *"union with [God] so far as is possible"*.[41]

It was not officially defined until the 6th Century, but it is ubiquitous in Patristic writings. Of course, such a concept, and the ways in which it has been expressed ('he became man that we might become God') should not be understood to mean that we really 'turn into' God (perhaps similar to the Hindu concept of individual absorption into the divine). We remain entirely human. Yet *"while there is no ontological change of humanity into deity there is a very real impartation of the divine life to the whole human being"*,[42] and

> *"...there is a real and genuine union of the believer with God, but it is not a literal fusion or confusion in which the integrity of human nature is compromised. Orthodoxy consistently rejects the idea that humans participate in the essence or nature of God* [there is no ontological identity]. *Rather, we remain distinctly human by nature but participate in God buy the divine energies or grace. At no point, even when deified, is our humanity diminished or destroyed"*.[43]

This outcome is due (using Biblical images) to Christ, the Second Adam, recovering through his obedience to the Father what was lost in and through the (sinful, disobedient) First Adam. The 'human-divine' Christ (deified as 'firstfruits') is the new (and 'sinless') Representative Man (the meaning of 'Adam'). However, this particular understanding of atonement tended to be restricted to the Eastern Church for most of the Christian centuries, and only in recent years has the Western Church come to appreciate its contribution to understanding of atonement, as the more forensic-legalistic models have become rendered more and more meaningless,[44] or even morally objectionable. How the Fathers dealt with this perspective, and how it was tied it into other soteriological models, has been usefully explored by Brian Daley[45] who argues that

> *"...the soteriology of the early church...most commonly understands*

redemption or salvation as being achieved in Jesus' identity rather than accomplished as his work; whereas Western soteriology since Anselm typically takes redemption as something Jesus has done for us by his actions, above all by his death in innocence on the cross...Patristic soteriology, both Eastern and Western, tends to see redemption as already achieved in that personal union of God and a man – a union beginning in Jesus, uniquely rooted in him, but ultimately involving every human being willing to accept this new identity of human divinity or divinized humanity as their own future".[46]

However, this did not mean that the Fathers dispensed entirely with other images and metaphors (cleansing, healing, sacrifice, ransom, defeat of death/devil etc.):

"...the same abundance of soteriological metaphor can be found, even within single works and single passages, that is found in the NT – sometimes in rather bewildering juxtaposition".[47]

Daley goes on to describe this usage in some detail claiming, in particular, that

"...for many Patristic authors, the most basic way in which Jesus gives new life and freedom to the human race is by revealing in human terms the transcendent reality of God, who is the underlying source of life"[48]

We might reasonably add 'revelation' (what Daley terms 'communication imagery') to our list of salvific images: for Athanasius

"...it is the Word's revelation of himself in human form that makes clear what Genesis meant in saying we are made in the image of God, and that restores that image to its full 'likeness' to the creative

Word on which the image is modelled".[49]

In this paradigm, therefore, it is not so much that Jesus has acted on our behalf or was even a kind of 'agent-mediator' between humanity and God; rather, salvation is

> "...first of all something Jesus brought about in his own person, and that our change of status or relationship with God, our restored health and well-being as creatures of God, has already begun in what has happened to Jesus...[this is because] for virtually the whole of the Patristic tradition, Eastern and Western, the final fulfilment of the human vocation is to have the full reality of God's image, in which we were originally created, restored within us through our identification with the Word of God – our original image...".[50]

In other words, salvation entails nothing less than the transformation of our human nature that

> "...begins during this life in the forgiveness of sin and human growth in holiness, and that will reach its fulfilment in the resurrection of the body".[51]

This also implies the equal transformation of a

> "...restored and revivified human community...people of mixed religious background and moral virtue...[furthermore] in the healing of all the ancient divisions that have polarised reality since the start of creation: divisions between created and uncreated, intelligible and sensible, heavenly and earthly, the pre-lapsarian and the post-lapsarian world, even male and female...all will be overcome in the renewal and reunification of creation, within itself and with God, that has now begun in the person of Christ".[52]

Over against much of the liturgical and hymnodic expression

of atonement (fuelling the general assumption of 'ordinary Christians'[53] that the Cross was the **only** instrument of atonement) this (alternative or primary?) focus on Incarnation *is* to be found in the Nicene Creed: *"For us **and for our salvation** he came down from heaven, was incarnate from the Holy Spirit..."*.[54] Furthermore, in the CE's Short Eucharistic Preface for Easter the reference (as one might expect at Easter) is to the Resurrection as the 'trigger' for salvation: "...**by his rising to life again** he has restored to us everlasting life"[55] Of course, salvation through the cross is also has its liturgical expression: in the Extended Eucharistic Preface for Easter, we find: "[*Jesus Christ has 'by the mystery of his passion'*] *restored in men and women the image of your glory*" (assuming that 'passion' simply means 'the Cross').[56] Similarly the Short Preface for Lent: "...where life was lost (i.e. on the "tree of shame"), there life has been restored".[57] The Short Preface for Maundy Thursday links Cross **and** Resurrection: "...we, **redeemed by his death** and **restored to life by his resurrection**...".[58] All these examples serve to show that liturgies do not focus entirely on the Cross as the means and process of atonement and often take a 'mix-and-match' approach. The whole point about models is that although they may *appear* to be contradictory, there is no such thing as a contradictory model – they are only more or less useful, helpful and properly expressive. As we have seen, theories are very different: a theory is right or wrong, and different theories may well contradict each other. Models are immune from such dangers and, as argued above, are to be commended.

For the late Roman Catholic theologian, Catherine LaCugna, *theosis*

"...*presupposes a real unity between divine and human; the Spirit through grace transforms the human being so that it becomes what God is...The Spirit deifies human beings, makes them holy, sets them free from sin, free from the condition of the 'biological hypostasis', conforms them to the person of Christ*".[59]

It is in and through Christ that

"...the visible icon of the invisible God [who] discloses what it means
to be fully personal, divine as well as human...[so] transforming
us so that 'we become by grace what God is by nature', namely,
persons in full communion with God and with every creature".[60]

Can, then, this notion of 'transcendent anthropology' (the raising
of humanity to divinity) be further elucidated? Indeed it can,
although a more extended quotation is required:

"It seems that we must assert that at the **limit of human existence**
(in the sense, that is to say, of the goal of human fulfilment) **Christ
manifests divine Being**, so that in him humanity and deity come
together. Thinking of this from the other [divine] side, it would
presumably be conceivable if, in this particular being of Jesus Christ,
expressive Being had perfectly expressed itself. If indeed Jesus Christ
is true God and true man, we seem driven to posit **a kind of open
space, as it were, where divine Being and human existence
come together**; or again, where creaturely being, which seeks to be
like God, has actually attained to the level of deity...[However] the
language [of Chalcedon etc.] was itself originally explicative and
interpretative, though to modern ears it sounds archaic and needs
reinterpretation. So far as it is still understood, it is usually taken
to mean some metaphysical analysis of the person of Christ, and so
to be defective in that existential dimension which is requisite to
any adequate Christology. But there can be little doubt that if we
could think ourselves sympathetically into the great Christological
controversies of the early Church, we would discover that behind
the seemingly abstruse language, issues of vital existential concern
were at stake...It seems to me that the key word for interpreting
[the Chalcedonian definition] is 'nature' (phusis – as in Christ
having two natures). If we take 'nature' to mean a fixed stock of

*characteristics which constitute anything as the kind of thing that it is, then we are up against grave difficulties...[But] as existent, man is always incomplete and on his way, so that if it is proper to talk of him having a 'nature', this must be conceived as open-ended. And furthermore, what could we mean by the 'nature' of God? If it is erroneous to talk of man's 'nature', at least in terms of a fixed stock of characteristics, it is presumptuous to talk of God's 'nature' in a similar sense [in that it] would be to claim to grasp God in a way that is incompatible with his transcendence and mystery...[But if we interpret 'nature' as] emerging, coming into light...[then] the Christological talk about the two natures not only makes sense, but makes very good sense indeed. For then human nature is to be understood as 'emerging'...[and] that all created things tend towards likeness to God, and in the case of man, as existing and not having a fixed essence, there is no end in sight along the road he can travel – 'it does not yet appear what we shall be'. Man's 'nature' is this emerging or coming to the light. So we can understand how it is that Christ has a complete human 'nature', and what was meant by saying that at the limit of existence, that is to say, at the furthest point along the road toward fulfilling or unfolding this 'nature' (existence), he manifest divine Being... for it is only personal being (or existence) that has the openness that would permit it to come into union with holy Being...For the principle of unity [of the two natures in one person] is Being; and the essence of Being, in turn, is letting-be. Personal being is superior to lower forms of creaturely being, and so more 'like to God' because of its capacity for letting-be. It is where this capacity for letting-be is raised to an absolute level that a particular person being could manifest holy Being, and so unite in one person the two natures, and at the same time be of one essence (substance) [homoousios] with the Father, the primordial letting-be...If we hold fast to the existential dimension in the understanding of christhood...so that we see christology as a kind of transcendent anthropology (as Rahner has done), with **christhood as the goal towards which created existence moves**, then the* *first point to be made is that we must be prepared to acknowledge a dynamic character in the incarnation, and that means some kind of development. We cannot think (this would be indeed mythological!) of the Logos being 'implanted' in Jesus at his conception...In seeing a parallel between anthropology and Christology, we have also seen a parallel between selfhood and christhood...[So] we may suppose that the incarnation is to be understood not as an instantaneous happening but as a process of coming together, and that Jesus progressively realised his christhood...Just as christhood (which may indeed be equated with the selfhood of Christ) is to be understood as coming about through a process of growth so the attributes of Christhood would not suddenly appear from nowhere, as it were, but would develop with christhood itself [the end result of which is 'sinlessness'[61]]...God is absolute letting-be, and letting-be is the ontological foundation of love. Letting-be is also self-giving or self-spending, so that God's creative work is a work of love and self-giving, into which he has put himself. In so far as created beings themselves manifest creativity, love and self-giving, they tend to be like God. This self-giving is supremely manifest in the particular being, Jesus Christ. Just as there is a self-emptying, or kenosis, of God as he pours out Being, so Christ empties himself into the life that is portrayed in the gospels".[62]*

It was in the life of Christ and through his self-sacrificial ('letting-be') obedience to the will of the Father that the entelechy of humanity is revealed in its capacity to replicate the nature of God's own creative 'letting-be'. This insight is by no means new: Aquinas argued that it is God's creative, immanent presence within his creation that enables creatures to constantly change (evolve) into something new – to transcend what they are, and become what they have it in them to be:

"The 'self' in self-transcendence means that the evolutionary capacity is truly intrinsic to creaturely reality. It comes from within the natural world...Just as God's creative act enables

creatures to exist, so the same creative presence of God enables the new to emerge from within the natural world itself, according to the natural world's own processes and laws. Emergence is a creaturely reality, but it exists only because of God's creative act. God's presence in self-bestowing love enables creatures to exist, to interact, and to evolve".[63]

Edwards then points out (although maintaining the traditional language understood in a traditional manner):

"Rahner links this pattern of self-transcendence to Christology, seeing Jesus Christ as both God's self-bestowal in the Word made flesh to the universe of creatures and, in his humanity, as the self-transcendence of the created universe to God"[64]

Such an idea can also be understood beyond its traditional expression, to be in line with the argument so far advanced: that Jesus Christ, fully human and 'naturally' evolved as such, was such in his gifted spiritual development as to be able to transcend his humanity and 'achieve' a divine-humanity. And (perhaps) so can we, without actually losing our humanity. As an Orthodox theologian has put it: *"Human nature at the contact of God does not disappear; on the contrary it becomes fully human"*.[65] Just as, we might add, Christ was fully human.

Incarnation Naturally

The meaning of the Incarnation may be understood, not as some kind of process whereby divinity is 'ontologically inserted' into or otherwise 'joined to' humanity, but by saying something like:

"...in the human life of Jesus, called the Christ, humanity – freed from its self-centredness – was able to self-transcend to such a degree that divinity shone through (is this not the theological message of the story of the Transfiguration?), expressed in the

commitment and deeds of the man who, in his life, realised (made real) and transformed (transfigured), and through the sacraments continues to enable us to develop, the full potential of humanity".

Jesus was entirely and absolutely like us in every respect: 'truly human' as the Church has always proclaimed. In this sense, his status as 'Son of God' (which, as we have seen, is a title applied in the OT as a completely human designation) is not a reference to a sonship which has come about via a supernatural conception (so that, in some sense, God is 'really' Jesus' father), but rather an honorific given to one chosen by God to do his will (like King David, who did not always succeed in his vocation). Those who seek to make a distinction between Christ's relationship with God and ours (at least that potential relationship), by pointing to NT texts in which we are (only) 'sons and daughters' by adoption,[66] have entirely missed the point. Indeed, even the biblical witness puts the relationship in more directly filial terms. What, for example, of Jn 1: 12, 13? Here, those who 'receive' Christ are given power actually to *"become children [tekna] of God"* and, furthermore, these are also (like Christ) *"born of the will"* of God.[67] CK Barrett comments:

"...the threefold negation (not of blood, nor of the will of the flesh, nor of the will of a husband) seemed to correspond exactly with the church's belief about the birth of Jesus...and [John declares that] the birth of Christians, being bloodless and rooted in God's will alone, followed the pattern of the birth of Christ himself".[68]

Once again, we need to recall the ever-present issue of the nature of the language being used:

"There is a parallelism between the Pauline idea of adoption and the Johannine of being born from above, both as far as the actual event and the succeeding state are concerned. Paul thinks in terms

of Roman law and of legal status, John in terms of the origin of new life...For both, the renewal means the beginning of faith in Jesus Christ...''[69]

In other words, 'birth' (as generally with *gennao*) is being used metaphorically both by Paul and by John, and therefore there is no ultimate distinction to be made between the Father/Son relationship of Jesus and our Father/Son (Daughter) relationship with God. It is not that he is the 'natural' child and we are (only) adopted (although in successful adoptions, no distinction is made between the adopted and natural children); as we saw in connection with our discussion of the divine image, we are all true sons and daughters, with Christ, of the same Heavenly Father.[70] If Jesus is genuinely human, then that is the most obvious way of understanding it.

On humanity in general, in the kind of language used by Paul (and perhaps we can see more clearly now that it is mistaken to take it literally), the Second Adam put right the faults of the first, and in so doing raised humanity to God-humanity (what Macquarrie, in a less politically correct time, termed 'God-manhood'), because this particular human was willing and able to express the very life of God and so was – yes, we can allow ourselves to use the word, even if we understand it rather differently from the Council Fathers – functionally, rather than ontologically, *homoousios* with the Father: one in intention, one in 'letting-be', one in healing and so on.

If Christ's life is continuous with ours, then we need to find some only-too-human ways of describing it. As we have already noted, one way that is both comprehensible, but also just a tad mysterious (as is only right with the things of God), is to use the associated notions of 'charism' and 'prodigy'. The word 'prodigy' may be defined as someone having extraordinary talent or ability, or even something wonderful or marvellous (the root idea behind the concept of 'miracle' originating in the

Lat. *prodigium* – a 'prophetic sign'). The term is often used of young people with 'prodigious' talent, say in music, chess or mathematics, (normally the kinds of activities that most of us find 'naturally' difficult) and the question may be asked: 'how did they come to be like this?', to which the answer may be offered (not necessarily with religious intent), that it is 'God-given'.[71] In normal parlance this phrase may just mean 'innate' or 'natural'. They are just like that. Presumably a scientific answer would look to heredity or 'something in the genes'; but again, that would be thought entirely natural. As we have seen, in theological terms (properly informed by scientific knowledge) whatever we are or whatever we may become, and however naturally we may understand that, doesn't preclude the action of God (or the Holy Spirit who is normally seen as 'God in action') working through the normal processes of creation and, in this way, some prodigious talent is properly a charism: 'God's gift'.

Mozart was 'granted' the sublime gift of music to such a degree that even trained musicians (let alone non-musicians) struggle to understand precisely how those abilities might be understood: how could he compose like that? How could he play like that? Jesus was granted the gift of – how might we describe it? – the closest awareness of Father God, the self-denying willingness to put God's agenda first, an innately true and unremitting compassion, the ability to evoke God ('to be God') for others, and so on. All of these qualities most Christians – even those actively seeking to be more Christlike – find difficult both to understand and to emulate (so Abelard's exemplar model is not the easy way out[72]). The point is this: most of us are not spiritual prodigies, for prodigies are not 'normal'. Nevertheless, it is theologically quite proper to understand that both Mozart and Jesus were granted their disparate gifts 'from all eternity' as these outcomes were always part of God's gracious plan to maximise good in all things and bring that good to an overarching consummation (Mozart is dead but his talent will live 'for ever'; Jesus is often acknowledged as the 'most influential man in history'). Such things may seem miraculous (and they are just that because they are amazing, wonderful etc., not because they are divine interventions, 'interferences' in the 'natural order'), but they – just like the Incarnation itself - are also perfectly natural. The mistake which some Christians share with atheists is in believing that the 'natural' automatically excludes God. Where the 'natural' and the 'supernatural' (whatever that is) come together, is probably too far above our spiritual pay grade for us to know.

Christ like us so we may become more Christlike?

It is only if Jesus' humanity is continuous with ours that our own lives can be understood to have the potential to be conformed to his. If there were a difference in kind, rather than degree, that would surely be impossible? That is why Jesus' 'divinity' needs to be understood in such a way that it is not entirely different (as we have sought to demonstrate, it logically would be) from what we already are; so offering a reasonable hope of our achieving what we have the potential to become. All this is expressed and made possible only through a genuine humanity, as opposed to one which is alleged to be genuine but which fails the most basic tests (finite/infinite etc.). Both by his teaching, and in this only-too-human life, Jesus expressed what Martyn Percy has (almost) called 'the madness of God': how God subverts our normal assumptions and behaviours through his generous 'letting-be', and in that subversion calls us to share in proclaiming and living lives of generous self-less love. Reflecting on the parable of the prodigal son, Percy explains that

> "...the justice of God is different [from our normal way of understanding 'what is right']. The parable of the prodigal plays with our sense of justice...Because the message of the parable is this: the love of God is so complete as to be almost unjust – and certainly

unfair. Indeed, the love of God might be a bit mad. You see, God loves people who don't deserve it. Not just the goody-goodies. He loves the lost; the hopeless; the squanderers and the reckless. God's love is mad; in human terms, at least".[73]

Jesus teaches that the first will be last and the last first (most unfair really – if I win the race I want the prize!), that God's Son (and those who follow him) came not to be served but to serve (something that even his closest friends had difficulty in understanding). The life he lived (so far as we can discern the 'facts' of that life through the traditions embedded in the Gospels) put that teaching into action: he ate and drank with 'sinners' both 'baptising' and 'eucharistising'[74] them in the process; he showed compassion and healed where he could; he invited people to become like a disenfranchised and vulnerable little child; he encouraged his followers to love and to forgive without limit (utterly mad!). Ultimately he gave himself up to the selfish and brutish powers of a humanity still unwilling (for whatever reason) to lift itself up 'by its bootstraps' so it might have a chance of coming to resemble the divine nature; and yet, miraculously, the potential remains. Perhaps it is this 'madness' which constitutes divinity: the utterly risky and reckless letting-be of a Creator God (and, in John, the *Logos* which became flesh is intimately associated with creation) who desires the other to become the best that they have it in them to be, recognising (as does every parent) that may not happen, but being prepared to cope with whatever situation arises, loving to the end: "greater love has no one than this, but to lay his life down for his friends...

...And you are my friends" (Jn 15: 13), called to follow where Jesus has led. We might (in fact, we often do) say that the Christian vocation is 'to be Christ to others': not (of course!) ontologically, but functionally, and in exactly the same way that we might claim that Christ was 'God to others'. So we are the presence of Christ in the world in the same way that Christ was the presence of God in the world:

"Christ has no body now but yours. No hands, no feet on earth but yours. Yours are the eyes through which he looks compassion on this world. Yours are the feet with which he walks to do good. Yours are the hands through which he blesses all the world. Yours are the hands, yours are the feet, yours are the eyes, you are his body. Christ has no body now on earth but yours."[75]

Those, for example, who work in hospitals have Christ's healing power in their hands, whether they, or the recipients, recognise it or not. In calling the Church 'the extension of the Incarnation', we might therefore understand its very mission not so much to fill pews (as so often mission – despite denials - is interpreted), but in being God's vehicle on earth by which the whole of humanity might be raised to divinity: raised in the likeness of Christ, expressed in and through its own Christ-like conduct. It is through the sacraments of the Church (God's gifts to be used, not some kind of 'magical' interventionist force) that this process is made tangible. Just as we perceive God in Christ, so we perceive the presence of Christ himself in the Eucharistic elements: they are Christ 'for us', and who needs the convoluted Reformation arguments about the interpretation of 'This is my Body' to understand what this means? The outcome of sacramental transformation is not so much about making humanity Christian as making Christians human: a transformation and conformation into true humanity (and so, in the sense we have argued, true divinity):

"The Church...is rightly called the 'body of Christ'...[because] within the Church, humanity is being conformed to Christhood, a transfiguration, resurrection, ascension is going on as the believers participate in the life of Christ, or in a couple of words, there is a 'new creation'";[76] [and again]: *"...however far this christhood is*

from the imperfect humanity that we see every day in ourselves, we nevertheless perceived that because humanity is not something fixed but stands in the openness of possibility, this very humanity is at its upper limit continuous with christhood".[77]

It is in this sense that we are able to comprehend more clearly just what the 4th Evangelist meant by calling Jesus the 'door' or 'gate' (Jn 10: 7 – 9): a door is not important in itself: it is merely the means by which we move from one room to another. Jesus may be understood as the gateway by which humanity and divinity come together as we go from one 'place' to another. A similar analogy may be recognised in the designation of the Pope as 'pontifex': the bridge-builder whose role is to take people, 'in the power of the Spirit and in union with Christ', from one side of the 'sinful divide' to the other. Indeed, it is through re-conceiving Christology in this way, we not only learn about Christ, but we also learn something equally important about our shared humanity. The mysteries of divinity and humanity may not be fully resolved (and may never be so) but at least they are more comprehensible than that entangled puzzle which is the *'Quicunque vult'*.

Notes

1. Macquarrie J 'Principles' p. 304;
2. Goldingay J 'New Testament' p. 18;
3. Interviewed by Simon Jones for 'Third Way' Vol 39, No. 7, Aug 2015, p. 21;
4. ibid: in Christian philosophy only God is necessary; everything else (the universe) is contingent;
5. Noninterventionist objective divine action;
6. Simmons EL op cit p. 49;
7. ibid. pp. 140, 174;
8. Polkinghorne J art. cit p. 25;
9. *'pneuma'* is actually a neuter noun, but in English 'neuter'

implies neither gender nor personal being: so why not 'make' 'her' female?

10. Johnson EA op cit p. 158;

11. Much depends on what is meant by 'healing' both within the Gospel texts, and also how Christians today understand what occurred when Jesus healed someone; many of Jesus' healing miracles were associated with exorcisms (the casting out of unclean or evil spirits) not least because many in the ancient world understood illness to be the result of attacks by such spirits: that is not our normal understanding of illness and healing in the modern world: most Christians, when ill, depend upon doctors and drugs rather than on exorcisms; so when Jesus is said to have 'healed the sick' does that automatically mean that he 'cured' their illness – 'made them physically well'? Eric Eve ([2009] 'The Healer from Nazareth: Jesus' Miracles in Historical Context') makes an important distinction between 'disease' and 'illness' on the one hand, and between 'healing' and 'curing' on the other: 'sickness' is the term which covers both 'disease' and 'illness', whilst 'disease' itself refers to "the organic (or mental/psychological) malfunction" (ibid. p. 52) i.e. some kind of physical or mental illness as we would understand it today, which would send us for medical intervention and which may or may not be 'cured'; 'illness' is "a more holistic concept...constituted by the sufferer's own understanding of his or her condition [and which is] shared with the sufferer's social group"; thus "whereas a disease is cured by biomedical intervention, and illness is healed when the sufferer (together with those connected with him or her) is satisfied that the problem has been dealt with" (ibid. pp. 52 – 53); so, for example, what is often described as *'lepra'* in the Gospels, translated as 'leprosy', is probably not that disease as we understand it today (Hansen's Disease) but a reference to any kind of skin problem which, in the

ancient world, would often exclude the sufferer from the community (for fear of contagion), and it may be the case that whatever happened to the actual skin condition (cure), Jesus' preparedness to touch the 'leper' was sufficient for him to be allowed back into the community, now being 'pure' rather than 'impure', and so 'healing' occurred; there are many other issues about Jesus as healer which go beyond the main concerns of this study e.g. the role of faith (either of the sick person or friends) in the efficacy of healing (Jesus often makes a direct link: Mk 10: 52; Lk 7: 50 etc.), or the somewhat mysterious failures or limitation of Jesus' 'healing powers' such as at Nazareth (Mk 6: 1 – 6a) which suggest that healing only 'works' if people believe in the healer etc.; for all these, and many other issues, see Eve's excellent discussion;

12. Reports state that a prime mover in the healing of the community was a clergyman ('Reverend Pendleton'); the Spirit no doubt uses her friends;

13. So, for example, the Greek author, Hesiod, tells how a semi-personified Chaos gave birth to the Earth, to an Underworld, and also to Eros (representing erotic love);

14. Mobley G (2012) 'The Return of the Chaos Monsters – and other Backstories of the Bible';

15. ibid. p. 19;

16. This Christian interpretation of the Jewish story may well have been influenced by Colossians 1: 16 and Hebrews 11: 3 (although neither explicitly say 'out of nothing'); contrast 2 Peter 3: 5 "...an earth was formed out of water and by means of water...";

17. Mobley op cit p. 34

18. Evans GR op cit pp. 18 – 19;

19. ibid. pp. 27 – 28;

20. ibid. p. 32;

21. Johnson EA op cit p. 216;

22. Mobley op cit p. 34;

23. ibid p. 16;

24. ibid p. 19;

25. Collect BCP 4 After Easter; CW 3 Before Lent;

26. Romans 8: 12 – 13;

27. 'Principles' pp. 268 – 269;

28. As Polkinghorne characterised it in the afore-mentioned *Church Times* article: "...the driving force of the amazing three-and-a-half-billion-year history of life on earth, from bacteria to you and me, has been a genetic mutation. But you cannot have genetic mutation, producing new forms of life to be selected and sifted through natural selection, without having the possibility also, of malignancy. So the fact that there is cancer in the world is not a sign that God is gratuitously incompetent, or uncaring, but that it is the necessary cost of a world in which we people are allowed to be ourselves"; art. cit. p. 25;

29. As Wilkinson notes: compassion "is not a mildly sentimental feeling; it means a stomach-churning experience, something that affects you right to the bottom of your being" op cit p. 85;

30. 'Creation Seen in the Light of Christ: A Theological Sketch' in Coloe ML (ed.) 'Creation is Groaning' (2013) p. 9;

31. 'Principles' p. 240;

32. Macquarrie's term for describing the essence of God's nature: ibid. p. 109;

33. ibid. pp. 302 – 303;

34. ibid. pp. 312 – 313;

35. ibid. pp. 283 – 284;

36. The author of Matthew's Gospel is constantly presenting, to his predominantly Jewish audience, Jesus as one like, or even superior to, Moses, who led Israel out of Egypt (the great salvation story of the OT, always paired with Easter readings in the Church's liturgy; so e.g. in Mt's birth

narrative Jesus (like Moses) flees and is hidden from an evil ruler [Mt 2: 13/Ex 1: 15 – 2: 10] and (like Moses) is brought out of Egypt [Mt 2: 15] (the Hosea reference [11: 1] points back to the Exodus [Hos 11: 2 - 4]) expressing the view that Jesus brings about, in his life, death and resurrection, a new 'salvific' Exodus;

37. 'Principles' p.281;

38. "We are not human beings having a spiritual experience. We are spiritual beings having a human experience": this aphorism is often attributed to Fr. Teilhard de Chardin, although some dispute that attribution, preferring instead to locate it with GI Gurdjieff; it is sometimes rendered "We are not human beings on a spiritual journey. We are spiritual beings on a human journey"; whatever the origin, it is a fine expression of the notion that human beings are essentially spiritual creatures and, that therefore, any apparent gulf between the divine and human requires much greater nuance;

39. The main 'subjective' model – Christ as exemplar – is often associated with Peter Abelard;

40. CW p. 381;

41. Dionysius the Pseudo-Areopagite 'The Ecclesiastical Hierarchy' 1.3; a more recent writer has defined it simply as 'Christification': Panayiotis Nellas 'Deification in Christ' (1987) p. 39;

42. RV Rakestraw 'Becoming like God: An Evangelical Doctrine of Theosis' in the 'Journal of Evangelical Theological Society' 40 (1997), p. 261;

43. DB Clendenin (1994) 'Eastern Orthodox Christianity: A Western Perspective' p. 130;

44. For details see JDA Bloor 'New Directions in Western Soteriology' in 'Theology' Vol 118(3) (2015) pp. 179 – 187;

45. '"He Himself Is Our Peace" (Ephesians 2: 14): Early Christian Views of Redemption in Christ' in Davis, Kendall

& O'Collins (2004) 'The Redemption' pp.149 – 174;

46. ibid. p. 151;

47. ibid. p. 154;

48. ibid. p. 154;

49. ibid. p. 155;

50. ibid. pp. 165 – 166;

51. ibid. p. 168;

52. ibid. pp. 169 – 171;

53. And possibly many 'ordinary clergy' as well i.e. any without a thorough, in-depth and up-to-date theological understanding – in my experience the task of achieving any degree of theological literacy throughout the Church should not be limited to the laity;

54. Although the Nicene Creed goes on to state: "**For our sake** he was crucified...", there is no indication that 'for our sake' is anything other than another way of putting "For us...", as in the previous sentence, in which the phrase: "and our salvation" is clearly an additional object related to the subject of the Incarnation; in other words, "...he came down from heaven" specifically "for us **and** [i.e. not only...but also] for our salvation"; but "..he was crucified..." [just/only] "for our sake" i.e. "for us" (undefined). Note that the Apostles' Creed doesn't mention salvation at all in connection with Christ (it may be understood to be implied by the words "the forgiveness of sins", but these are in the third section which relates to the work of the Holy Spirit);

55. CW p. 316;

56. CW p. 317;

57. CW p. 312;

58. CW p. 314;

59. 'God In Us' pp. 228, 297;

60. ibid. p. 1;

61. Macquarrie notes: "This is a confusing expression, for it is a double negative. Sin itself is a negative – a disorder and

a separation from God; sinlessness is in turn the negation of the negativity of sin. Thus 'sinlessness' means that the disorder is overcome, and that the separation from God is replaced by a coming together of God and man. In other words, sinlessness describes an aspect of christhood, and like christhood, it is gained in the deeds and decisions of life, and is certainly not a merely negative 'dreaming innocence'. Such sinlessness, when attained, may indeed separate from the ordinary mass of humanity, but just in the same way as Christhood separates from the ordinary mass of humanity – in both cases, humanity is brought to a higher level. It does not cease to be true manhood, but it becomes God-manhood, true manhood united with true Godhood... [It is through the exercise of self-giving love and obedience to God that] Christ **breaks out of the sin-bound human situation, and opens up the new life**, symbolised by the resurrection...Christ is the firstfruits, but the Christian hope is that 'in Christ' God will bring all men to God-manhood. 'Principles' pp. 301 – 303;

62. ibid. pp. 296 – 302;
63. Edwards D in Coloe op cit p. 11;
64. ibid. p. 11;
65. Meyendorff J (1969) 'Christ in Eastern Christian Thought' p. 65;
66. *huiothesia* lit. 'place as a son': Roms 8: 15, 23; 9: 4 (ref. to Israel); Gal 4: 5; Eph 1: 5;
67. A variant reading, not well supported, of 1: 13 changes the verb from plural to singular, probably to turn this sentence into a reference to the Incarnation;
68. 'The Gospel According to St John' (2nd ed. 1978) p. 164;
69. Cranfield CEB article on 'Birth' in Richardson A 'A Theological Wordbook of the Bible' p. 31;
70. As Jesus told Mary Magdalene: he was ascending to "**my** Father and **your** Father, to **my** God and **your** God" (Jn 20:

17);

71. Charles Marsh reports, in his biography of Dietrich Bonhoeffer ('Strange Glory', 2014, p. 8) that Bonhoeffer's mother, Paula, recognised her young son's "spiritual predilections", even as he grew up among strongly humanistic family influences, so suggesting that some are more 'naturally' open to 'the spiritual' than others;

72. Some of the sayings of Jesus are not only bewildering, but some of them seem alarmingly difficult to enact e.g. just from the first section of Matthew's Sermon on the Mount: must not break one of the Commandments (5: 19); not be angry (5: 22); not be lustful (5: 28); cut off your hand/foot if it causes you to sin (5: 30; repeated 18: 8); not to divorce (5: 32); don't resist evil (5: 39); love enemies (5: 44);and what is to be made of 'leaving your father unburied' (Mt 8: 21 – 22); Jesus the 'Prince of Peace' tells us he is not anything of the kind (Mt. 10: 34), and neither should followers of 'family values' get too attached to their families (Mt. 10: 35 – 36); we must prepare, like him, for crucifixion (Mt. 16: 24); we should sell all that we have and give the money raised to the poor (Mt. 19: 21) many commentators will point out that Jesus used hyperbole (camels and needles), which may well be true; nevertheless, many of his sayings are hard indeed;

73. 'Generous Liberalism: A Search for our Spiritual Soul' in 'Modern Believing: The Journal of Theological Liberalism' Vol 56 Issue 3 2015 pp. 262 – 263;

74. If, as some scholars have suggested (i) some early Christian communities baptised by feet-washing and (ii) the eucharist derives historically, not from the last supper but from Jesus' practice of what Crossan called 'open commensality' (table fellowship), then it might be appropriate to understand the Lord offering the 'dominical sacraments' in this manner 'in the flesh' in his traditional welcome to them and in the shared thankfulness for what they were receiving;

75. St Teresa of Avila (1515 – 1582);
76. 'Principles' p. 388;
77. ibid. p. 509.

Chapter 7

Proposals for Reformulating Christology

Setting the scene

Several theologians have sought to explain what it might mean to say that Jesus was different (only) in degree rather different than in kind from us: that he was not divine in the Chalcedonian/ontological sense, but that his divinity consisted in the way that God-the-Divine worked within and infused him. Here are two of the classic attempts:

Donald Baillie (then Professor of Systematic Theology at the University of St Andrews), in 'God Was in Christ: An Essay on Incarnation and Atonement' (1948), proposed that the Incarnation should be understood as a 'paradox of grace': the same kind of paradox as that suggested by St Paul (1 Cor 15: 10): "not I but the grace of God...within me". In other words, when (generally) we do God's will, whilst we act freely and responsibly, God's grace is at the very same time acting within us, (but without impairing our freedom. Baillie explains how Jesus' human life was authentically human, whilst God worked in and through that genuine human life:

> "...every good thing [a Christian] does, is somehow not wrought by himself, but by God...Never is human action more truly and fully personal, never does the agent feel more perfectly free, than in those moments of which he can say as a Christian that whatever good was in them was not his but God's".[1]

Furthermore

> "...this paradox in its fragmentary form in our own Christian lives is a reflection of that perfect union of God and man in the Incarnation

*on which our whole Christian life depends, and may therefore be our best clue to the understanding of...**that perfect life in which the paradox is complete and absolute,** that life of Jesus which, being the perfection of humanity, is also, and even in a deeper and prior sense, the very life of God Himself...If the paradox is a reality in our poor imperfect lives at all, so far as there is any good in them, does not the same or a similar paradox, taken at the perfect and absolute pitch, appear as the mystery of the Incarnation?".[2]*

Geoffrey Lampe (then Regius Professor of Divinity at Cambridge): in 'God as Spirit' (1977)[3] Lampe argued for a degree Christology of **'inspiration'**. Here, he urged, the Holy Spirit should be understood, not as a divine *hypostasis*, but simply as God *"active towards and in his creation"*.[4] The role of the spirit is to 'in-spire' ('breathe into'), and in the life of Jesus

"God indwelt and motivated the human spirit of Jesus in such a way that in him, uniquely, the relationship for which man is intended by his Creator was fully realised...".[5]

Indeed

"God has always been incarnate in his human creatures, forming their spirits from within and revealing himself in and through them".[6]

The Spirit of God, which is always operational within the human spirit, inspiring people to open themselves freely to the divine presence and respond in their lives to the divine purpose, did so most effectively (even, for Lampe, "uniquely") in the man Jesus. Indeed, he argued, the NT clearly sees Jesus as a 'spirit-filled' man whose life was a direct response of obedience to the divine Spirit. If, further, we take the assertion in Col 2: 19: "...in Christ, the Godhead in all its fullness dwells embodied": whilst this may seem to require an ontological interpretation, read against Ephesians 3: 19: "May you be filled with the very fullness of God", then a functional-inspirational interpretation may seem even more appropriate.

In both the above portrayals we are offered a Jesus who is totally human (thus removing the need to demonstrate his humanity), but one whose 'divinity' is a potential open also to all of us, via God's grace and-or inspiration (the Biblical witness is that Adam was nothing until in-breathed by the divine Spirit of God), although even these 'progressive', non-Chalcedonian theologians continue to use the language of 'perfection' and 'uniqueness'. There may be some Biblical warrant for this understanding (and reflected in the predominantly Eastern doctrine of *theosis*): in the confrontation detailed in Jn 10: 31ff, where Jesus is accused of blasphemy, might not his somewhat enigmatic answer ("...if those to whom the word of God came were called 'gods'...") be understood to suggest that 'divinity' is within the reach of all who receive God's word: hence, even the arch-orthodox Athanasius' dictum: "He became man that we might become God"?[7]

Proposal 1. Incarnation as function: a Functional Christology

A 'functional' incarnation may be characterised as **the union of divine and human action, as opposed to the union of divine and human 'being',** although it may be that an ontological unity of some kind may be understood as the intended *eschatos/* entelechy (of Christ and humanity: a scenario beyond our current understanding) or may still be an appropriate (if not *entirely* comprehensible or meaningful) way, suitably interpreted, of characterising how God lived in and through Jesus. By the very nature of divine Being it is probably impossible to know. Nevertheless, using functional categories does not, *a priori*, rule out the use of ontological categories, although it is clear, for example, that Jesus couldn't have been *both* different in degree *and* different in kind (which *homoousios* seems to require): we have a decision to make on that. Further, we need to be able to explain, if we can, exactly what is meant by ontological identity. Thus Lincoln (above), despite his insistence on the non-physical nature of the 'virginal conception', is keen to hold onto such ontological categories, arguing that

"Jesus is God precisely in the whole sequence of his historical human existence, where the humanity is not something appended to his divinity [as suggested by a virginal conception] but is precisely where the divinity is ontologically located".[8]

Indeed, Lincoln (like Ward) is also quite clear that Jesus was *"unlike other humans"*[9] (even without the virginal conception, he was different in kind). But, as we have argued above, this kind of 'having your cake and eating it' theology (Jesus did the work of God, but he did so because he was 'one with the Father' and thus unique) still offers a Christology which is full of contradictions (the most basic being: how can the divine be truly human?), which undermines the majority Gospel picture of Jesus, and which is (as I have argued) virtually incomprehensible.

But focusing now on a purely functional analysis of the divine-human union (which, also as argued, fits with the Biblical witness as well as being both theologically coherent and cohesive, and is able to complement modern scientific views about how the universe works) we may further propose the possibility that such 'unions' may occur whenever God's grace and Spirit is able to work effectively (better – is *permitted* to work effectively – as we do have free will) in the life of a person. In this sense, there may have been many 'incarnations' throughout human history (and in Faiths other than Christianity: philosophically, there is no *a priori* reason why that should not be so), in which case Jesus would certainly be different from the rest of humanity only in degree, thus protecting (where this study began) his absolutely genuine humanity which, arguably, the traditional formulations have signally failed to do. For Christians who feel an innate religious need for Christ to be ontologically 'unique' (both distinct and superior) as an *a priori* theological datum, none of the above would be satisfactory, and may be dismissed as irredeemably reductionist. I would argue that the interpretation of the 'divine Christ' I have so far proposed (surely no-one could accuse me of not taking the 'human Christ' seriously?) lies within the apophatic horizons of the Councils, utilising both the grammar and the vocabulary of traditional Christology, and has the added benefit of being perfectly comprehensible.

The kind of 'portrait' of Jesus which functional or degree interpretations might produce is described by **John Hick**, in this particular case, focusing on Jesus' charismatic and intense 'God-awareness':

*"I see Jesus as dominated, at least in the important moments of his life, by his **awareness of the overwhelming evident reality and presence of God** – the God of whom he learned from his Jewish tradition. He was aware of God as both limitlessly gracious and limitlessly demanding – both as the loving Heavenly Abba who welcomes home the prodigal son and also as the holy and righteous one who makes a total and absolute claim on human beings. So powerful was Jesus' awareness of the Heavenly Father in comparison with the awareness of those around him, including the official religious leaders of his time, that he must have been aware of a unique calling and responsibility to communicate the reality of God by proclaiming the imminent coming of the divine kingdom and the insistent divine claim upon each man, woman and child. He must have been conscious of a special role in God's dealings with the people of Israel in those last days before the kingdom came in power and glory. Inevitably he would, as God's voice to his contemporaries, have had a central position, in his own mind and*

in the minds of those who responded to him, within the crisis of the end time in which he and they believed themselves to be living".[10]

And by **Marcus Borg**, adding a little more contextual information:

*"Jesus was a peasant, which tells us about his social class. Clearly, he was brilliant. His use of language was remarkable and poetic, filled with images and stories. He had a metaphoric mind. He was not an ascetic; he was world affirming, with a zest for life. There was a socio-political passion to him – like a Gandhi or a Martin Luther King, he challenged the domination system of his day. **He was a religious ecstatic, a Jewish mystic, if you will, for whom God was an experiential reality.** As such, Jesus was also a healer. And there seems to have been a spiritual presence around him, like that reported of Saint Francis or the present Dalai Lama...As a figure of history, Jesus was an ambiguous figure – you could experience him and conclude that he was insane, as his family did, or that he was simply eccentric or that he was a dangerous threat – or you could conclude that he was filled with the Spirit of God...Jesus was a Spirit person...[one] who has frequent and vivid experiences of the sacred, of God, of the Spirit".*[11]

A functional Christology, thus, presents a genuinely human Jesus who had a perfectly normal birth, in that he had a biological father as well as a biological mother. The doctrine of the virginal conception may be understood (alongside the whole of the Gospel tradition) to represent the understanding that Jesus was special (and, for some, probably unique, but we have already explored the problems with that term) and to underline the fact (with which this current analysis agrees) that God was intimately involved in his life from beginning to end as, indeed, God is involved in the creation of all life. The difference is that, in Christ, God's plans were particularly effectual. Christ was God's willing agent, called to that task in the life experiences he had, and his acceptance of his vocation expressed in the 'inconvenient' (for the Church) baptism by John. From then onwards he operated with divine authority in such a radical way that he presented God's will to those he met in a challenging and life-changing manner. He can be understood as a spiritual prodigy with an absolutely clear and direct

> "...awareness of the overwhelming evident reality and presence of God... conscious of a special role in God's dealings with the people of Israel in those last days before the kingdom came in power and glory".

He may also have been

> "...a religious ecstatic, a Jewish mystic...for whom God was an experiential reality...Jesus was also a healer. And there seems to have been a spiritual presence around him..."

In short, Jesus was a Spirit-person, or a Spirit-filled person, one who expressed in and through his life, words and deeds, the nature of God. But he also lived his life in such a way that for some, it was 'as if' in meeting Jesus, they had 'met' God, or had encountered the demands of God in their lives: as John Robinson put it, Jesus was the "human face of God" ('Emmanuel' God 'to us' and 'for us'). It is this key idea: seeming 'as if' he were God, that we shall explicate in our second proposal.

To put the basic case for functionalism unambiguously: Jesus did not claim to be God and he was not God in any ontological sense; he was God's agent-functionary operating in a similar, if not the same manner as 'prophets, saints and seers' both before and after him, all of whom were also commissioned by God, and were engaged in God's continuous creative work of reconciliation and redemption. However, Jesus performed this work of God in such an outstanding, inspirational and historic manner that, as had happened before in tendencies reflected in the OT witness:

1. his identity and that of God were perceived to have merged; agent and master became one in the eyes of those receiving and accepting the benefits of that work; however, although the benefits of God's saving love were clearly the primary issue (whatever view one takes of Christ, that has always been understood as his purpose: the bringer of salvation: 'Jesus'/'Joshua' means 'God saves'), and the question of from whom or how salvation was 'delivered' might reasonably have taken second place; instead, it was to be the 'vehicle' rather than the 'source' of 'salvation' that took priority in the theological reflections of the Church (although the two issues were always inextricably bound together, for concern for soteriology was one of the great drivers of the debate about the Person of Christ): Christ, to all intents and purposes, replaced God; whilst I can't imagine a God of love, who gives of himself tirelessly and sacrificially in his 'letting-be', over-worries about that, it would be good for us to get the balance right: Christ's work was God's work, not because Christ was ontologically divine, but because he was about the saving work of his Father in which endeavour he and the Father were united in an apparently 'seamless' manner;

2. Christ operated, for those he met, as God's Word (he spoke on behalf of God; his words were God's words, even though he never used the prophetic formulae: "Thus says the Lord" e.g. Amos 2: 4, or "Hear this word that the Lord has spoken..." e.g. Amos 3: 1 etc.) and God's Wisdom (what he proclaimed was God's truth); yet, again, due to his extraordinary and prodigious charisma, these aspects and qualities of God, which had been understood as

virtually independent divine personifications, became – after considerable reflection by his followers - reified in his person; Christ 'the Word of God' who spoke on God's behalf became Christ 'the Word': the divine *'Logos'*, and eventually the Second Person of a Divine Trinity;

3. in and through Jesus' genuine and 'iconic' humanity, made in the image and likeness of God and the result of a nexus of entirely natural events in and through which God had been working creatively (at least) since 'the Beginning', he manifested God's presence and power to an extraordinary extent.

As we have seen, each of these three ways of 'being God' are to be found in the OT, and all provide entirely reasonable alternatives for expressing Christ's relationship with the Father. However we wish to express it, the very human Jesus clearly had the closest of relationships with his Father God and acted with his authority, on his behalf, in order to bring about his (God's, not Jesus') Kingdom. That kind of work may well deserve the appellation: 'divine', because it was in every sense a 'divine work' (it was God's work), although that concept should not be taken too literally (what, in any case, is 'literal divinity'?) because we then fall inevitably into the docetic heresy when the focus on Christ's work morphs into a focus on his person and, in the process, undermines his real humanity. Of course, recognising again that the expression is not the actuality, the reality of 'functionalism' may be expressed (and certainly has been) using a variety of linguistic tools, even including the language of ontology although, as we have seen and will develop further in the argument below, 'pure' ontology (ontology 'by itself') is a blunt and potentially misleading tool.

Proposal 2. Jesus the Symbol of God: a Symbolic

Christology

What does it mean to describe Jesus as a 'symbol of God'? Many Christians would understand it to be saying that Jesus 'just' represented (stood for or stood in for) God, in a purely functional manner; just as, for some, the bread and wine 'just' represent the Body and Blood of Christ in being a reminder (the weak form of *'anamnesis'*: remembrance) of the Last Supper. Indeed, some Christians would continue to argue that, even for Jesus himself, pointing to the bread and saying 'This is my Body', meant that the bread had 'just' a simple representative function: 'this bread here is only bread, but will stand for/in place of my Body in the future', rather than anything more esoteric as represented, for example, by the doctrine of transubstantiation. Others might understand the bread and the wine having a more metaphorical or even poetic role as in the CE's 'Common Worship', due to the theological breadth of the CE, necessarily ambiguous: "... that broken bread and wine outpoured *may be for us* the body and blood of your dear Son".[12] Here the broken bread 'stands for', simply represents (or represents simply) Christ's body (really) broken on the Cross, and the poured out wine his blood (really) shed. An easy metaphoric link is made between the two pairs without suggesting either that the bread *is* his body or the wine *is* his blood: they are those things only subjectively, "for us", but not objectively, 'really' (those Anglicans who believe in transubstantiation will ignore that nuance).

Those who take such a weak and limited view of symbol (as a purely functional form of representation or an alternative and reified form of metaphor) might then conclude that a 'mere symbol' is incapable of saying what needs to be said either about Jesus' relationship with God, or about Jesus himself; that it is not sufficiently 'strong' or 'powerful' a concept to capture the full and true meaning of the Incarnation. However, when it works effectively, there is no such thing as a 'mere symbol'. A symbol can be extraordinarily powerful both in theory and in practice, as we are probably aware if we think about the numerous examples we come across in our daily lives: for example, the Queen as symbolic Head of State (in contrast to many elected Presidents) has very little practical power, but nevertheless the loss of this symbol would have a far greater impact and consequence than the loss of those few actual powers she possesses. The symbol is innately important because of the importance of that which is symbolised, the value and worth of which becomes attached to that symbol.

To say that Jesus was a symbol of God actually takes us a step further from an unalloyed functionalism (a concept which, unmitigated, could embrace many different people who have 'worked for' God), in such a way as to make these two ways of doing Christology ideal partners. It also, linguistically, takes us far beyond a metaphor (which is why I regard Hick's 'Metaphor of God Incarnate' as unsatisfactory: it doesn't go far enough). Yet although a functional Christology and a symbolic Christology are actually distinct, they are closely related, and the link between them is that innocuous word: **'represent'**. As we have just seen, at a mundane level it denotes a 'stand-in': someone who goes somewhere or does something on another's behalf, such as the athlete who represents her school in a competition. Our concept of Christ as 'functionary' (an infelicitous term, but one which makes the point): 'one who works on behalf of', employs this kind of meaning. Jesus had been called by God to work on his behalf: to proclaim his message (like the prophetic: 'thus says the Lord', so 'the Kingdom of Heaven is at hand') and do whatever he is called upon to do, whatever the outcome. This is a straightforward representative function: 'I work for him' or 'I speak on his behalf'. In political terms, the ambassador provides a good example, not least when that ambassador has to go back to the political master to get further instructions: they are often not authorised to deal with absolutely everything. But sometimes they are so empowered.

As we saw with examples from the OT and the Ancient Near East, the royal or political representative function often went much further than just 'standing-in' for the king: it involved taking on, in a very real and practical sense, the fundamental and personal authority of the king to the extent of actually 'being' the king in and for that situation. If it were only ambassadorial (and not the real thing), then it still carried the greatest, even the ultimate, authority:

> "*There is a solemnity about being addressed by someone who comes with the Great King's authority and speaks with the 'I' of the great king, as if he were the great king (cf. Is 36: 4, 14, 16). That is how the prophet speaks as Yahweh's messenger, as if he were the Great King. He brings the great king's presence; he speaks performatively... He has the authority to speak on his king's behalf...Even when he himself devises the words, he can use the 'I' of his king. His words have the king's authority. They are the king's words, even though he formulates them*".[13]

The representative was, therefore, treated 'as if' he were the king because he re-presented ('presented again') the king directly to the people. The simple term 'represents' morphs easily into a more profound set of ideas wherein the distinction between the king and his representative becomes blurred; it is 'as if' the one were the other.

This is precisely how a symbol works. The symbol isn't the symbolizandum: Jesus is not God, but it is 'as if' to all intents and purposes and in a really powerful way, he were. As a result, it is easy to see how the two might be confused (which via the Conciliar pronouncements, they were: the only way the Fathers were able to conceive this relationship, due to the philosophies they were using, was ontological identity). As we shall see in the subsequent discussion, the more successfully a symbol works, the easier it is for this confusion to occur, and some balancing concepts become necessary. We shall therefore employ Macquarrie's existential-ontological method.

I have previously used language such as "extraordinary" and "prodigious" in order to recognise that Jesus, whilst not unique in kind (he was one of God's many 'agents'), was such a powerful and effective agent that the Church's reflection on his work led him to be thought of as (somehow) equal with God (Philippians 2: 6) and, later, ontologically divine. Whilst that conclusion goes too far, we do need another way of expressing that 'beyond the ordinary', 'ultra-effective' partnership, which may not be best achieved with a basic 'functionalism' (in other words, Proposal 1 provides us only with the basics). A 'functional Christology' makes the point that Jesus operated on God's behalf and any unity posited between them is best understood as unity of action rather unity of being. The concept of symbol takes us a step further by expressing the very clear idea that Jesus 're-presented' (presented again) God in his life *to such a degree* that it seemed to many 'as if' he were God, and so provides a category by which we can explore and express that 'more-than-just-an-agent' idea in entirely comprehensible language.

We need to recall the basic and vital idea that *the symbol is not the symbolizandum* (that which is symbolised); that is the mistake made by much classical and popular Christology ('Jesus is God') in positing a relationship of identity. The symbol presents as the symbolizandum, but *really* is not (this works in a similar manner to other linguistic devices: in the metaphor, the unfaithful husband really isn't a rat, although – at the risk of being unfair to rats – he may share those negative qualities associated with 'rattiness'). The way a symbol functions means that it attracts the meaning (and thus *to a degree* the identity), and hence the value, of the symbolizandum to itself in such a way that it is, 'for us' and in a real and immensely powerful way, the symbolizandum; and we treat it and respond to it accordingly.

Clearly, as we might expect, human language strains to express the reality of how God works in people and, in particular, how he worked in Jesus; but using a host of apostrophes we might say that the symbol 'is virtually', 'contains', and 'conveys' the symbolizandum 'properly' and 'precisely', and even 'really' (with suitable caveats). Because of this, recognising (and responding to) the symbol enables us to recognise (and respond to) the symbolizandum.

Let us consider what may appear at first to be a fairly mundane example: soldiers going into battle have often been willing to risk their lives for their country's flag either by carrying it (and so making themselves a target), or by seeking to regain it after it has been captured by the enemy. Simply to tell them that the flag is 'just a piece of cloth' would be to miss the point entirely. It is 'really', for them (in terms of its value, what it stands for, and where their loyalties lie), their country. Of course, it is not really their country: it is a piece of cloth. But in terms of how it is perceived and treated, and the context in which it is operating as a symbol, it 'is' 'really' their country. This is a particularly revealing example, because we can also recognise how a country's flag may attract enormous devotion and respect by some, but nothing much, or be understood to reflect a different set of values, by others. Much depends upon the context. The flag may be taken more seriously in this country by older than younger people; this generational issue will have been affected by the difference between those who actually experienced warfare or those raised in the aftermath of war, and those for whom warfare is purely a matter of history; or by political affiliations (nationalist or anti-nationalist). This may not be so much the case in (for example) the USA where children are explicitly trained in schools to honour the flag; how the flag is treated is a good litmus test (although not infallible) for the degree of patriotism one possesses. But the flag may have been taken out of its proper context and placed in one in which its meaning, and hence his power to attract, are diminished: an example of this is the way that the English flag of St George has been 'hijacked' by the extreme Right, who use it not to unite, but to divide. Finally, the flag may become an anti-symbol when, for example, it is set on fire by a nation's enemies; this may be seen as a proxy attack on that country (as with an actual attack on an ambassador), even though the flag-burning takes place in another country; as such it will create anger amongst those whose flag is burned that might even equate to the level of anger felt at a genuine attack.

This kind of ambiguity is evident in all symbols. Any symbol may be understood and valued in different ways by different people. It may exercise enormous power over some, and none at all over others. People may respond to the symbol positively, negatively, or with total disinterest. One symbol may be more effective in re-presenting the symbolizandum than another. Like any other kind of non-literal language, the symbol is not 'right or wrong', but more or less appropriate, or more or less helpful. If we agree that Jesus might reasonably be termed a 'symbol of God', then we can see clearly how that symbol 'worked' for some, but not others; how Jesus was often more misunderstood than understood (even by those who were his friends); how some understood him in one way, and some in other ways. For example, was Jesus the Messiah; if so, what kind of Messiah (political zealot or concerned only with transcendent matters)? Certainly some, like the Jewish leaders, saw him as impious or troublesome or iconoclastic (which led Matthew to defend him from that charge in 5: 17); others, like the Romans, saw a political agitator who required elimination. Others saw him as God's Son, 'the Son of Man', rabbi and healer. The Church came to see him as ontologically divine, specifically as the Second Person of a Trinitarian God; a view absolutely rejected by Jews and Muslims (for the latter Christ is a prophet, although not the greatest; although one can only wonder why a sense of competition should enter such discussions) for whom the idea of a Triune God is simple tritheism which, in its most simplistic expressions, it clearly is.

So symbols are always multi-faceted; they will evoke different responses, and they will often be understood in different ways. Even relatively simple universal symbols like water: whilst cleansing is an obvious characteristic, the use of water in religious libations is not always understood in the precisely the same way. In Christian baptism, water is not only used as a symbol for cleansing: it is also used to evoke the idea of drowning so that the person baptised may 'die' to the old life and rise to the new in Christ. It may also be seen (as water literally is) 'life-giving'. We can understand, therefore, why and how the concept of symbol is both very rich and particularly fecund.

As we have already noted, the concept of symbol and how it 'works' may be explicated, philosophically, by the deployment of the philosophies of 'existentialism' and 'ontology', and I shall now attempt to tease out how that 'works'. Existentialism and ontology may be regarded as the two sides of a single coin: they are both concerned with 'being'. Existentialism examines what it is 'to be' from the perspective of the individual existent (human) being; what is the nature and meaning of human existence? Ontology, on the other hand, enquires into what it means, in more general terms, 'to be', and the nature of 'being' (or Being) itself. We should note that philosophy provides an aid to understanding, helping us to shed light on and into sometimes potentially baffling concepts such as the nature of reality; it is not, itself, the answer to everything.

Existentialism is an anti-rationalist philosophical tendency and attitude to life concerned with the existence of the free individual living in (to many existentialists) an absurd or meaningless universe. Existentialists argue that philosophy must begin from the concrete situation of the individual in the world (rather than based in some esoteric *a priori* metaphysics) in which they find their existence and into which - to utilise Existentialist terminology – they have been 'thrown', without so much as a 'by your leave' (no one asked us if we wished to be born), and in which an 'authentic existence' is achieved only by living in the face of the reality of death (what Heidegger called 'Being-towards-Death'). We know (really) that we are going to die, despite the way many of us try to believe the contrary, and so live our lives avoiding the blunt fact. That, for existentialists, is an inauthentic way to live, and often leaves us alienated and fearful.

Many Existentialists are atheist, although both Heidegger and Sartre, in their different ways, have been accused of possessing a mystical streak. However, there is also a Christian form (or, perhaps, Christian forms) of existentialism which, though using the language and concepts of the existentialists, reinterprets their ideas in a more specifically Christian manner.[14] Macquarrie makes the important point (also quoting Sartre) about the 'elusiveness' of the concept and how it may no longer *"mean much at all"*, and that for the existentialist

"...there are always loose ends [because] our experience and our knowledge are always incomplete and fragmentary".[15]

Indeed, existentialism is not so much a philosophy, but a "style" or method of doing philosophy. That is why it can be (and has been) used and adapted so much by those that would hardly recognise themselves as philosophical bedfellows.

In the first chapter of his earlier book ('An Existentialist Theology' [AET]): Chapter 1: 'The Relation of the Philosophy of Existence to [Christian] Theology'), Macquarrie considers the relationship of the two, specifically via Bultmann's thought, concluding (with Bultmann) that the Bible itself set this precedent. Paul, in Romans, *"begins by describing the situation of man, and relates all his teaching to that"*[16] just as other Biblical authors "*did not make general statements, but confronted their readers with individual human beings in **existentiell** situations*".[17] Indeed, Macquarrie comments: where else could we ever begin, but with our own existence? Even with the teaching of Jesus "*it is not difficult to find elements...[which] invite comparison with the teaching of the existentialists.*"[18] Where are we to find God in what appears to be a broadly humanistic philosophy?

> "*It is true that this style of theology dwells on the human side of the faith relationship, and describes Christian existence in the world. However...the existentialist theologian believes that when one analyses human existence in depth, one uncovers experiences where God-language becomes appropriate. By its very nature, existentialism offers no 'proofs' of the existence of God, but it does push the analysis of human existence to those very limits of existence where faith arises.*"[19]

In other words, it is both reasonable and theologically permissible to press Existentialism into the service of elucidating our Christian concepts, properly recognising that "*a purely existential approach to theology is almost impossible*",[20] which is why he, and we, balance it (and *vice versa*[21]) with the philosophy of ontology.

How can existentialist ideas enable us to better understand how a symbol 'works'? Crucial to a symbol functioning is that people respond to it; if there is no response the symbol is not effective, and is thus pointless (so although others may well understand cognitively what it is, the symbol of the Cross will only be truly meaningful to Christians, for it will not convey the same 'affective' or 'effective' meaning to others). The use of the adjective 'existential' (in this context) makes the point that the symbol may touch the person most profoundly at the very point where their existence in the world gives them meaning. Or put another way: where they find meaning when reflecting on their existence. In short: the symbol is of utmost importance to those who regard it as belonging to them; it is essential ('of the essence') to them. However, all this is (so far) very subjective: it is based on *what people feel*. But they may be misguided; there may be nothing in the symbol which deserves this level of response (such as the current media obsession with the cult of celebrity, in which 'celebs' may be seen to symbolise 'achievement', 'the good life', the 'hero' etc.). On the other hand, it may be that the symbol is not properly recognised or properly understood. If, for example, we speak of God in terms of 'height' then it misses the point to say that God isn't actually 'up there', for the meaning of the symbol of height is that our response to God should be one of humility and reverence to one who is 'higher' (in the sense of greater) than us. The symbol must (although it will impact differently on different people) somehow 'ring bells' and, we might say, 'press the right buttons'. But even that is a relatively shallow way of putting it: the symbol must touch us at the 'depth of our being', at the level of what is most basic of and to us: perhaps that for which we may even be prepared to lay down our lives?

What we term an existentialist response is ultimately a response from 'where we are' at the centre-point of our lives to something which re-presents to us something we value ultimately and (probably) without qualification. The use of existentialist language and ideas helps us to express the view that the subject of the symbol has the greatest importance for us because it evokes (the most) deeply felt feelings and attitudes; that its meaning is not simply of interest, but is genuinely central to the way we live; that it has an unsurpassable impact on our existence. This reminds us that there is not only a significant mutuality between symbol and symbolizandum, there is a similar relationship between the symbol and the person using it. We might even say that the symbol has the ability to 'connect' us with the symbolizandum which, in other circumstances, may be rather less inaccessible: it offers us a direct connection with that we value most. In religious terms it helps us to evoke and discern God in and for our lives. The existential method, therefore, allows us to understand how a symbol so touches us (at the affective level of our feelings and moods and impulses) that we are compelled to respond to it (just as Ratty and Mole are affected by hearing the pan-pipes in 'The Wind and the Willows'). We may call that the 'subjective' element. The other side of the coin is the need to be equally clear about whatever it is about a symbol that creates that response (the 'objective' element): that is provided by the philosophy of being.

'**Ontology**' is the philosophy of being ('that which is') which connotes a greater sense of objectivity – looking outward - than existentialism (hence the notion that Jesus is 'really' God is at least implied, if not more, by the ontological category of *homoousios*). Some feel that existentialism, unmediated by ontology, is too subjective to be of much use (because it is about how we perceive our feelings, our lives, our situation, all or some of which could be mistaken about) and therefore needs to be balanced by an approach which takes account of the need to enlighten the nature of the being of the symbolizandum: that which is real, as opposed to that which we perceive to be real from our limited vantage point. Of course, as we have seen, the even greater danger is an ontology unmitigated by its existential element.

Ontology, therefore, provides what we might describe (using a similar kind of shorthand) as the objective aspect of the symbol. That it really 'contains' and 'conveys' something of the essence of the symbolizandum; not least, because if it didn't there would be nothing to which we could respond. Again, the symbol itself is not particularly worthy of response, only in the way and to the degree it enables us to 'touch' or 'reach out to' the symbolizandum. However, as a concept ontology is necessarily elusive and opaque:

"What is meant by the being of anything is supposed to be either

indefinable or self-evident. We do not pause to ask what we mean when we say that anything is. Yet, as Heidegger shows, it needs little thought to realise that the idea of being is obscure in the extreme, and since some understanding of being is assumed in every enquiry, that initial obscurity is bound to have its consequences in the ontical inquiry into which it is carried."[22]

Nevertheless, its use in terms of understanding a symbol is relatively straightforward, although we have to tolerate some element of imprecision: to connote that in some respect the symbol shares something of the 'being' of the symbolizandum. Writing of the relationship between the two philosophical methods, Macquarrie both warns and encourages:

"...existential interpretation...can never constitute a complete theological method, though it is certainly an indispensable element in any adequate theological method...so... our interpretation will be ontological in the sense that it will seek to elucidate from the symbolic material new and deeper understanding of Being. But here we must guard against the temptation of treating theology as if it were metaphysics and as if our aim were to provide just an intellectually satisfying account of God, the world, and man. With the rise of dogma in the early Church, concrete and existentially significant symbols tended to be edged out in favour of an abstract vocabulary of 'substance', 'nature' and the like. This kind of language does indeed serve to interpret and clarify the symbols, but then the dogmas come to be thought of as objective, neutrally descriptive truths."[23]

The classic formulations presented the being/substance or even nature of God as though it were a perfectly clear concept: some kind of 'God-stuff' (which Jesus shared). But as we have noted, the concept is so obscure that it has become (or was always) meaningless. Yet, no doubt God, however God may be thought 'to exist' (in a manner different from the created order), has some kind of essence (Macquarrie goes simply (!) for '[Holy] Being'; although what that may be is 'essentially' mysterious and indescribable in human language). The benefit of Macquarrie's 'existential-ontological' analysis is that it removes the need to think that our expression of the nature of God (and of Christ), like a theory, equates with the reality, and underlines the simple fact (which we have seen demonstrated throughout this enquiry) that our ordinary literal ('thingy') language cannot embrace the reality which is God, nor adequately describe how God functions within his creation. As Macquarrie warned: there is always a danger that we fail to recognise the essentially symbolic nature of religious language and see to reify our beliefs as *"objective, neutrally descriptive truths"*. When we take that problem seriously, we can begin to see how we can use these two philosophies of being (both the 'subjective' and the 'objective') to seek to understand just how we may effectively (but never exhaustively) express our beliefs about matters which are beyond our capacity to understand.

It is here that the concept of symbol comes into its own. Instead of a reified 'God-man', we have a man who served God and, who, in and through that service, was able to convey something of God's essence (whatever that may be) to many who met him. In understanding just how a symbol 'works' we can begin to understand something more about God, and also about Christ. God was 'in Christ', certainly, but not in any simplistic and literal manner. Rather 'God was in Christ' because the very human Christ was such an effective agent, that he conveyed the reality of God to many of those who came across him, and the many millions since then who have recognised 'God-in-Christ' as well.

If God is thought of (particularly in panentheism) not only as **transcendent** ('beyond') but also as **immanent** ('within'), God is therefore 'present' in his creation and his creation may well show some sign of that. The job of the symbol is to re-present and make manifest (be an 'epiphany') that which, otherwise, cannot immediately be apprehended by the senses. So in all beings there is a clue to the Being of God (however, we might seek to imagine that) and his relationship with us: he is Creator and we are what he has created. However we should try to avoid the conclusion that everything is a symbol of God. Certainly there are many different religious symbols, and perhaps everything has the *potential* to symbolise or otherwise disclose God. Nevertheless in our human history God may be understood to have revealed himself through particular symbols, or that some things do the job (of re-presentation) better than others (bread and wine rather than crisps and Coke). Presumably those symbols which are drawn from things mostly related to our human existence will be the most successful. Hence 'love': the supreme symbol of God (1 Jn 4: 8: "God is Love"). Ultimately, for Christians, the fullest re-presentation of the Being of God (or of 'Holy Being' in Macquarrie's terminology) is Jesus.

Macquarrie explains this twin 'philosophy of symbol' by taking 'light' as an example. The existential response is to be found in the

"...feelings and commitments which this symbol awakens in us, and which we may suppose are likewise feelings and commitments appropriate to the religious realities which light is taken to symbolise".

Similarly, the ontological dimension which *"[lights] up something of the mystery of these religious realities themselves"*.[24] So we can balance two aspects of what makes a symbol a symbol: that it evokes a response from us (perhaps most often 'feelings' – but those feelings may be of the greatest human importance: trust, loyalty, devotion, love and so on). But that response is not to the symbol *per se*, rather it is a response to what the symbol genuinely re-presents, which may be, in its innermost self, quite mysterious: what, for example, Otto termed the mystery that at once draws and overwhelms us but, at the same time, fills us with fear and foreboding. That mystery we call God.

Macquarrie makes the very helpful point that

"...*the power of a symbol to awaken an existential response must be related to its power to yield insight into some ontological reality*".[25]

The symbol itself (if it is effective – as we have seen, not all symbols will have the same impact) has the capacity to communicate or mediate to us some aspect of the reality of the symbolizandum which, otherwise, we would find difficult to discern. If Otto is correct that God can never be perceived directly, only evoked, then in religious faith we are dependent upon things like symbols, or music, or story, or mystical contemplation, or even other people, to have what limited apprehension and perception of, and insight into God, we are able to possess. In so far as we can comprehend all that which the symbol re-presents to us (which might be that which evokes in us something as apparently straightforward as loyalty to one's country), its essence or being (what it really is) is genuinely communicated to us by (although it doesn't actually belong to) the symbol – which might be something relatively simple, like a piece of cloth in the form of a flag; or even a human being. Macquarrie suggests that symbols "*drawn from nature*" (such as light, bread, wine, water etc.) lack

"...*a personal or existential dimension, even if it has possibilities for eliciting and existential response*".[26]

In other words, a symbol which is based on or in a person may have the potential to be the most effective.

Again, as we have seen, it is clearly easier to articulate the subjective (existential) working of symbols (because we do that from 'where we are') rather than the ontological element conveyed by them. Which is why many theologians feel the need to emphasise that 'objective' element of the symbol: to affirm that the symbol 'really' 'contains' (the inverted commas indicate that we are stretching ordinary language here) 'something' of the 'being' of the symbolizandum. If we focus only on the 'subjective' element, then ultimately there may be relatively little of the experience we will be able to share with others (as we discussed earlier, 'how was it for you?' becomes increasingly relative). This is the problem with some mystical writers: if we have not had that kind of experience ourselves, then it may be difficult to grasp precisely what they are seeking to convey about theirs. In a similar way, the 'resurrection experience' was difficult to communicate to those who hadn't experienced it at first hand. If we do not appropriately highlight the reality conveyed by the symbol, then those who complain (for example, of the bread and wine) that it is *merely* a symbol, are right.

In order to properly 're-present' the symbolizandum, the symbol must surely 'contain' (or at least 'transmit') something of the symbolizandum's 'being' within it (again, at the risk of becoming repetitive: whatever that means)? How? Presumably it might just be appropriate to say 'we don't know', but to do so is to risk rejection of the idea on the ground that we have no coherent way of explaining what we mean by it. That doesn't mean that we cannot recognise at least an element of divine mystery about it, but we do need to be able to provide at least some description of what we mean.

Taking a related example to which we have already referred might help clarify the issues before we seek to apply to concept to Jesus Christ. What of the **bread and wine** at Mass/Eucharist/ Holy Communion which 'become' the body and blood of Christ? Some Christians would say that it is not sufficient to call the Eucharistic elements 'symbols' because 'mere symbols' ('it's only a symbol') cannot convey the *depth of the change* which occurs when the bread and wine are consecrated and 'become' the body and blood of Christ. Such people do not recognise the power of symbol to genuinely 're-present'. Instead they seek other ways of explaining what 'happens' at the consecration. The development in the Middle Ages of the doctrine of **transubstantiation** (based on the Aristotelian philosophy of substance/accidents) sought to show how the bread and wine 'really' (in substance) changed into the body and blood: its *accidents* (shape, texture, taste, chemical composition) remain the same, but the *substance* (what it 'really' is) changes from that of bread and wine to that of the body and blood of Christ. The problem is that this doctrine only makes any sense (as with Nicaea and Chalcedon) if one accepts the philosophy (here, Aristotelian) on which it is based. Alternatively, a Protestant view might say that the bread and wine are 'mere memorials' of Christ and should not fall into a confusion caused by theological sophistry (hence the famous argument between Luther and Zwingli over the meaning of *'hoc est corpus meum'* – 'this is my body').

If, however, we hold a 'high' or 'strong' view of symbol, in which the symbol truly **re-presents** the symbolizandum, then we can see that following 'consecration' (the prayer of consecration/ the eucharistic prayer, over which Christians continue to dispute whether there is a 'moment' of consecration – either at the Words of Institution or alternatively the Epiclesis - or whether it is the prayer as a whole which is consecratory, as implied in the Anglican rubric over posture) the bread and wine is not trans*substant*iated, rather it is trans*sign*ified: the significance is changed (note the link with the word 'sign' – something which points to something else). Or perhaps we might say trans*valu*ated: the value or worth has changed. This is not merely playing with words (although for those with a 'low' or 'weak' view of symbol - probably the more extreme Protestants - are more likely to see it as such. For them the bread and wine act simply as a reminder of the body and blood of Christ; they would have no objection to returning the wine to the bottle if any is left because it is still 'just' wine). There is something very profound about the 'strong' symbol (recall the soldier who carries the flag to his death). What is it and what is the relationship of the symbol to the symbolizandum? (The answer to the first question depends on the answer to the second).

We may imagine that **relationship** on a linear basis:

1. **symbol/symbolizandum**

Here - as in the doctrine of transubstantiation, the symbol and the symbolizandum are virtually indistinguishable - the one *is* the other; the bread and wine *are* the body and blood. In this situation the symbol *literally ceases to be a symbol at all*; it is confused with the thing itself. In a sense this may seem to be idolatrous (although the doctrine of transubstantiation actually does seek to guard against this by stressing the 'accidental' - as opposed to 'substantial' - continuity with the bread) when that which re-presents God is actually worshipped in place of God (an idol is that which takes the place of God). Nevertheless, in practice, some religious folk are not sophisticated enough to make this distinction, and they fall into superstition, as in the middle ages the practice of carrying the 'host' (consecrated bread: *hostia* - the 'sacrificial victim') around on the body as a source of protection against evil. Or the situation (which I have witnessed) when an elderly Anglo-Catholic carrying the chalice, spilled some of the wine on the carpet and was distraught because he had spilled the blood of Christ.

2. **Symbol.....................................Symbolizandum**

Here symbol and the symbolizandum are so far apart that the symbol is 'weak'; it has no power to evoke a response because it is simply a 'reminder' of the symbolizandum (the 'low' view of the bread and wine). In fact it virtually becomes no more than a sign (something that points to something else). The difficulty of a 'low' view is that the symbol ceases to have much relevance at all: the wine is wine, and it 'simply' reminds us of Christ's blood. The Eucharist is a mere memorial of the Last Supper.

3.   symbol..............symbolizandum

Here symbol and symbolizandum are not the same, but they are properly balanced and closely related, so much so that one might understand that the symbol so evokes a response from the onlooker (the existential dimension) that it is *'as if'* the symbolizandum were itself present (the ontological dimension). This, properly judged, is the 'strong' or 'high' view of symbol in which although there is a clear distinction between symbol and symbolizandum (again: they are not the same), the symbol effectively conveys the significance, value and meaning of the symbolizandum. So the bread and wine are, to all intents and purposes ('as if') the body and blood of Christ, and are treated as such: those who receive them do so on their knees and in a prayerful manner; any left-over 'elements' are consumed with the greatest reverence. In this way the symbol effectively re-presents the symbolizandum.The ever-present danger here is a tendency to be tugged towards position 1 (above) as, for example, in the service of **Benediction** where the 'host' may be carried round the church in procession and people kneel as it passes. Is this going too far: has the symbol effectively become the symbolizandum, or is this just a strong and appropriate response to the symbol which has attracted the 'value' of the symbolizandum?

As we can see, there is a very delicate balance to be maintained. Sometimes the symbol is so weak that it is hardly worth using; it certainly cannot evoke much of a response. At other times it becomes so strong that it almost takes over from (or is seen to become) the symbolizandum (the bread and wine are the body and blood; Jesus is God). But an effective symbol should 'represent'; it should not 'pretend' to be the thing itself (just, as I have argued, Jesus didn't 'pretend' to be God). The symbol is a 'vehicle', a 'channel', a means of communication (hence its important role in religious language). The symbol should not be the object of worship; rather it should be the means by which worship may be directed at its true object: God. Sometimes there is (perhaps understandable) confusion about this among worshippers (as noted above: should prayer be addressed *to* Jesus or only *through* Jesus?).

In order to 're-present' the body and blood of Christ the meaning of the bread and wine must be transignified: their significance (value etc.) must change from relative unimportance to great importance. If we may somehow imagine God's 'being' (his essence) to be present not only within his whole creation (into which he has 'poured himself'), but particularly within Jesus Christ, then the fruits of creation: bread, wine (incidentally also 're-presenting' the partnership between God and man: "fruit of the earth and work of human hands"), are ideal vehicles by which to show (make manifest, as in 'epiphany') the coming ('advent') of God to the world 'in' Christ. But the bread and wine are also specifically linked to Jesus' actions at the Last Supper, and so, after consecration, they also 're-present' the very 'being' (meaning, value, significance) of Jesus. In this way the significance of the bread and wine changes because it takes on (is given by God - it is God who consecrates [makes/declares something to be special, sacred or holy], not the priest) aspects of the being of God-in-Christ; who in turn re-presents God's Being.

This discussion takes us to the verge of understanding how Jesus can be accurately described as a 'symbol of God'. As God's agent, he 're-presents' (presents again) God to the world. But he does so in such a profound and sublime way it is 'as if' God himself has come to us and (here the functionalist element) he is able to do so because in a very real (and not simply symbolic sense) the work he is doing is genuinely God's work.

So what is the all-important ontological dimension that can now provide a genuine connection between symbol (Christ) and symbolizandum (God)? How is the reality of the latter able to be communicated by the former? We have already considered the two most powerful criteria: firstly, the fundamentally intimate connection which exists between Creator and Creation, between the giver of life and that life which has been received (Ps 19: 1 – 4). The great Christian theological insight which came to supplant the old Greek conception, not least because the OT witness eventually came to be taken seriously on its own terms (not just because it allegedly 'predicted' Christ), is that God is immanent as well as transcendent – he is 'really' with us because he has 'poured himself' into the created order (whilst, of course, remaining distinct from it). Secondly, and arising from this, we saw how in the ancient Near East various images came to be utilised as manifestations of the divine presence, but by far the most effective were human beings, seen explicitly by the Priestly writer as made in the image and likeness of the Creator God himself. Jesus Christ, in his true humanity both part of the created order and made in the image of his Father God, brilliantly provided that manifestation. As for the existential dimension, we can see clearly how Jesus, in his 'divine' work and teachings, came to evoke undoubtedly disparate yet powerful responses, and radically changing the lives of literally billons of people over 2000 years. It was entirely because of the absolute and ultimate importance of the symbolizandum, that the symbol was able to evoke the greatest, most absolute, and indeed ultimate response and commitment. In other words, the life of Jesus is (effectively, in essence etc.) the life of God because God is most effectively re-presented in that life. Jesus Christ is 'God-for-us' because he re-presents God to us in such a way as to gain our willing commitment and devotion. The symbol works so well that, when looking at Christ we see God, because – to put it at its simplest

– we can't 'see the join'. As such, it is quite understandable why the Church, lacking alternatives, went for an ontological identity. But it was in emphasising this way of expressing the meaning of Christ (he is *homoousios* with the Father), without any mitigating and 'softening' existential element, that the Church's 'solution' to the meaning of Incarnation has always – despite strenuous denials – undermined Jesus' humanity.

Again, it is important to note the partnership of ontology and existentialism at work here in our use of the term 'symbol', particularly when using that term of Christ. The symbol doesn't just represent (stands in the place of, like the official at a meeting his boss couldn't attend): it re-presents – it actually presents to us something of the reality of that which it symbolises. As such, Jesus brings the reality of God – what God really is - into the midst of his people. It is not that God can't make it and sends Jesus instead! As I have put it before: when (some people) meet Jesus it is 'as if' they have been met by God, because Jesus is doing God's work in an absolutely effective manner: exhibiting love, compassion, a passion for justice and so on. These are just some of the 'divine attributes' to be found in the life of Jesus, and in this way Jesus is for us God's Word/Wisdom: terms which themselves connote God's identity, and which have already been understood as somehow 'independent' of God, and which have been expressed (made manifest) in a genuinely human life, not least because it doesn't require a divine life to express 'divinity'.

As has been said several times before: the corollary of this is the need to accept the possibility that Jesus was not the only symbol of God. There may have been and perhaps will be others. Some Christians find this very difficult to accept: Jesus is 'the only begotten Son of God' and there *are* no others. They may well be wrong: and what a loss that the others are, thereby, ignored. There is also a direct link to be made with myth: the 'symbol story'. If Jesus may be regarded as a symbol of God, then perhaps the metanarrative of the 'Christ event' may be regarded as mythological: the divine saviour who comes 'down' from heaven to earth, and then returns from whence he came. Each of these issues would require considerably more space to explore, so I will leave them as questions to be considered

So Jesus' 'divinity' (as we have seen, there is no reason why this term – part of the 'grammar' and vocabulary of Chalcedon – should not continue to be used) is to be found not in any alleged metaphysical content ('emptied' or otherwise), nor as the result of a 'real' hypostatic union, nor requiring a virginal conception (which can now be interpreted using theological rather than gynaecological language), but in and through his own devotion and a single-minded obedience to the Father. It was in this way that Jesus was God-for-us; God is genuinely (the ontological element) re-presented and expressed in and through this entirely human life. In both a functional and a symbolic Christology we may properly continue to use the terminology of 'divinity' of Christ: in the former he is divine in and through the divine work he does; in the latter he is divine in that he is able effectively to communicate, even 'be', the Divine to us: it is 'as if' he were God (the existential element) and so we treat this human symbol with the utter reverence that has properly become 'attached' to him, because the symbol has so effectively re-presented the symbolizandum: God has 'become' human, in that humanity has provided the medium for the mediation of divinity to us and its expression in and through us. Furthermore, the fact that the human symbol 'works' so well, offers us hope that we too may come to share the divine life: divinity is 'accessible' in and through Christ so that we may potentially achieve our own full humanity and our spiritual destiny. Thought of in this way, Christ's humanity may then be understood to be entirely genuine and not fatally undermined as it inevitably is, by a purely ontological Christology which invites us to understand him as an amalgam of irreconcilable metaphysical contradictions.

Can a functional-symbolic Christology still be Trinitarian?

At least, it may be argued: an ontological Christology in which there is a relationship of identity of being (substance) between God (Father) and Jesus Christ (Son) provides a solid foundation for the Doctrine of the Trinity. All we need to do is to add an ontologically identical Spirit, and we are there: Three 'Persons' in One God and One God in Three 'Persons'. Despite the fact that such a model (some might even call it a conundrum) produces its own dilemmas (is it tritheistic or modalist, and if neither, how do we explain it?), it is entirely reasonable to ask where an 'inspirational/functional/gracious/symbolic' Incarnational model leaves that central Christian doctrine of God. Does the attempt to protect Jesus' genuine humanity fundamentally undermine Trinitarianism? If there is no 'real' metaphysical 'Son'/'Second Person' (in other words, if we seek to interpret such language non-literally, with 'divinity' reflecting an identity of action rather than of pure being/substance), are we inevitably left with Unitarianism, or even some form of Binitarianism (Father/Spirit as opposed to Clement of Alexandria's Father/Son [a 'blessed Binity' as opposed to a 'blessed Trinity'[27]])? In order to respond to this understandable concern we need to consider three linked issues.

Firstly, modern theologians distinguish between the twin notions of an **economic or immanent Trinity**: the former denotes the Christian experience of God as Father, Son, Spirit (God reveals himself to us as Triune in the 'economy of salvation' i.e. through his saving work in Christ), whilst the latter denotes 'what God is in God's God-self' (put simply: God is really, ontologically, triune). Whilst some theologians believe that 'immanent equals economic' ('what you see is what you get': so-called 'Rahner's Rule'), other more cautious souls are not willing to go so far. They take seriously the possibility that whilst the immanent will always be reflected in the economic (i.e. 'Trinity' is not essentially untrue, because God's self-revelation would never be untruthful), the full truth is likely to be much more profound. Which is why Unitarians[28] are correct in what they affirm: the unity of the Godhead; but wrong in what they deny: that we genuinely meet God both in Jesus and in the ongoing work of God's Spirit. I shall spell out these distinctions and their implications in a little more detail.

A distinction can be made between 'what something is in itself' and 'the way we experience or perceive it': the Lat. *immanere* means 'to dwell or remain within', 'indwelling' or 'inherent', leading to the concept of the **properties of the thing itself**. 'Economy' (Gk *oikos* [household] and *nomos* [law]: how someone makes provision for their family) focuses on **how something presents itself to or affects us**. We may be enlightened by the 'Sun analogy': the heat of the Sun is both immanent (real in itself) and economic (as we experience it: hot, but not as hot as it really is); alternatively to say that the Sun 'rises and sets' provides an economic perspective only (the Sun as we experience it: it's the Earth that moves, not the Sun). So 'the economy of salvation' refers to how we experience God: not just God *per se*, but God-for-us; God's healing/salvific grace: God *ad extra*. Hence the '**economic Trinity**' designates the way God has revealed himself in creation and in salvation history as Father, Son and Holy Spirit. It recognises the possibility that God may not have revealed the fullness of his nature to us – there may be 'more to God than meets the eye' - after all: "*Scripture is in the language of finite humanity and, therefore, in one sense all biblical language is 'economic'*".[29]

On the other hand, the concept of the '**immanent Trinity**' is used to designate God[30] as God *really* is (God *ad intra*), presumably unknowable to us, except in as much as God has chosen to reveal his nature to us. In modern times:

> *"...liberal theologians in the wake of Immanuel Kant found it presumptuous to think they could speak speculatively or metaphysically about the secret life of the immanent Trinity. The inner dynamics of the divine being belong to the noumenal realm, whereas human cognition is strikingly limited to the phenomenal realm. Kant opened the nineteenth century by diking off the flow of Trinitarian speculation".*[31]

What Catherine LaCugna termed *"the defeat of the Trinity"*[32] because the separation of God-talk into *ad extra* and *ad intra* tended, in her view, to make much Trinitarian thought irrelevant to us. However,

> *"...if God is the reality that one comes to know by participating in this threefold economy, then knowing God is more like joining a party than it is facing an individual...the threefold economy...is the transcription of the music of God's immanent life into a form that can be played on economic instruments...the economy is the way in which the immanent life of God is given to my thought, my imagination, my life; and so each person is the way in which something of the immanent life of God is given to me – but of what it is that is given to me, I can only say that it is the unimaginable reality that truly shares itself with me in this way".*[33]

In other words, in Higton's view (put beautifully), the fullness of God in his immanence is not known to us, nor is it any of our business or concern.[34] We can only get hints via the 'economy'.

Others, however, have gone much further than Higton is prepared to go, arguing that the claim of the classic Councils that Father, Son and Holy Spirit are *homoousios* must itself be a claim about the inner reality of the Godhead: that *homoousios* requires an immanent (real/actual) Trinity. If the Son and Spirit are of the 'same substance' as the Father, then that must be what God is 'really' like (that, again, assumes that 'substance-language' is to be taken literally). The 4th century theologians and later (e.g. Aquinas) took (some form of) the social/immanent (or immanently social?) Trinity as a given ('modalism' had been consigned to the theological dustbin in the 3rd Century). Theologians came to assume that their reflections on the Trinity were, in effect, describing what God was truly like in his God-self, arguing that God's essential nature (love, truth etc.) must mean that what is revealed to us is what he actually is. This boldness, however, fails to take seriously that the *mysterium* may well be far beyond our ability to conceive.

In terms of the **historical development** of the doctrine of the Trinity, the earliest writers probably had an 'economic' understanding of the Trinity ('this is what our experience tells us about God': the concern was, as ever, with salvation i.e. the 'practical aspect' of God). But, as reflection developed, theologians began to ask if what they had experienced was actually the true nature of the Godhead (the immanent Trinity).

"This approach was finessed by the rational spirit of the Enlightenment, which produced the idea of God known today as classical theism. This is a solitary God viewed alone in 'himself' (the theistic God is always referred to in male terms) and arrived at primarily through philosophical inference. Transcendence is stressed to the virtual exclusion of immanence or indwelling, God and the world having to connect over a huge ontological chasm. And the Trinity itself is defeated". [35]

After a long period during which theologians had become accustomed to constructing doctrines of the immanent Trinity which had *"no connection with the economic Trinity"*,[36] 'Rahner's Rule' (the view that **economic is the immanent**) took centre-stage during the second half of the 20th Century. In Peters' view:

"By identifying the immanent with the economic relations, Rahner opens Barth's door a bit wider so that we might consider how the history of the incarnation as history becomes internal to the divine perichoresis itself. And along with the incarnate Son comes the world that he was destined to save, so that the whole of temporal creation enters into the eternity of God's self-relatedness".[37]

This sparked off what were probably the most energetic and creative Trinitarian debates since the days of the early Church, resulting in a variety of theological projects: a

"...substantial and ecclesially diverse body of work [which] succeeded in re-centring the whole burden of trinitarianism from 'God in himself' [i.e. immanent] *to 'God for us'* [i.e. economic] *and is probably the single greatest factor responsible for keeping the Trinity high on the agenda of creative theologians in recent decades".*[38]

However, there also followed a significant reaction to the turn to a type of immanence which effectively demolished the concept of the economic by denying any difference between the two concepts. It could be argued that the immanent will always 'trump' and overwhelm the economic, because what God actually is would always be more significant than how he 'appears' to be (if we know of what the Godhead consists, then we hardly need bother about focusing on precisely how he reveals himself, because what he reveals is the actuality) therefore any notion of an economic Trinity is effectively made irrelevant. Furthermore, if Rahner had been right to equate economic and immanent, then our understanding of the 'true nature' of God would inevitably be limited to human history (God is really only as he has revealed himself to us in history, and there is nothing more to say beyond that mundane context) and, hence, ultimately pantheistic (God is, in effect, identified with creation). However, many theologians have also criticised 'Rahner's Rule' because they fear that it meant surrendering the immanent Trinity (as opposed to surrendering the economic) so that all we can say about God is that he has revealed himself as triune, carrying the implication that his Godself might be quite different, but beyond our knowing. We should note that it does depend on how the identification of immanent and economic is (mis)understood:

> *"First, we can misunderstand the identification if we interpret the economic Trinity as merely a temporal manifestation of an eternal immanent Trinity. History, however, does make a difference, such that the incarnation means that God exists in the world in a new way...The second misinterpretation is to assume that the immanent Trinity first came into existence through the economic, that it did not exist until the incarnation. In our Trinitarian discussion, this occurs if we focus only on the economic history of salvation and neglect the understanding that God is also more than such a history and cannot be fully, even if importantly, described by such a history".*[39]

As a result of such discussion many theologians now urge that the advantages of affirming *both* an 'economic Trinity' *and* an 'immanent Trinity' must be taken seriously, and the concepts not simply merged; both are needed, even if we cannot resolve the question as to how, precisely, they relate:

> *"...a great number of theologians now see a distinction between the economic and immanent Trinity where they did not before, and are heavily invested in remaining committed to the economic trinity without lapsing into bare economic reductionism by surrendering the immanent Trinity altogether".*[40]

Once again, we see the advantages of a theological 'both-and' as opposed to an 'either-or': Horrell pleads for a 'tightening' of the relationship between economic and immanent:

> "Scripture's record of God's revelation in human history ('the economic Trinity') should inform and control how we think about the eternal relations of the Godhead ('the immanent Trinity')".[41]

Further, we may relate inner-Trinitarian relations to the relation of the Trinity with creation:

> "The immanent Trinity exists in simultaneous superposition with the economic Trinity and evolves within the entangled life of God with the creation".[42]

This is particularly important if, as we have argued above, Jesus is seen not as an intervention in creation, but fundamental to it: the outcome of how a panentheistic God operates.

In a helpful article,[43] Keith Ward draws attention to the **distinction between 'naïve realism' and 'critical realism'**, a distinction which can help us better understand the relationship between the immanent and the economic:

1. **naïve realism**, "*a reassuring and common-sense approach*",[44] has it that things generally appear to us as they are in reality (my laptop is a laptop and nothing else); and as we have seen, many theologians have assumed this to be the case with the doctrine of the Trinity. So it describes the reality of God: what God 'is really like'. It is 'reassuring' because it allows us to think that our doctrine is correct; it is 'common-sense' because (surely) 'what you see is what you get' (?); **but it is naïve** (certainly in terms of the mystery of God, if nothing else) in that it ignores plenty of human experience which suggests that what you see is not, actually, what you get: the example Ward gives is

that when we look at the night sky, the moon seems only a few inches across, but it is clearly not;

2. **'critical realism'**, on the other hand, asserts that although *"there is an existing objective reality that gives rise to our perceptions...it does not exist exactly as it appears to us. It appears reliably; it does not mislead us; it appears in ways appropriate to our sensory apparatus; but we should not think that we see it exactly as it is in itself".*[45]

As Ward points out, most of us operate on a day-to-day basis with "an unthinking mixture" of naïve and critical realism, but when we are "deliberately thinking carefully" we ought to be critical realists (we would not assume, for example, that when we 'cover up' the moon with our thumb, it means that the moon is smaller than our thumb; or that sticks really do bend when you immerse them in water). How does this impact on our understanding of the doctrine of the Trinity?

"It may be true that God really is threefold in being. **Yet it will always be true, also, that the way we understand this threefoldness will always be less than adequate.** *That entails that God in the divine nature itself will not be identical with the way we understand God, even though the terms we use of God may truly (but in a way we do not fully understand) apply to God. That entails that naïve realism about God is false. God is not in the divine being as we understand God to be. What we should also say, however, is that God is such that God genuinely, truly manifests the divine being to us in threefold form. This is an 'appearance', but not an illusion...***The appearance is a true indication of something beyond itself***...God has revealed the divine in Jesus. Given that is true, God really is threefold. This is how God truly and properly appears to us. All we need to remember is that we cannot conclude from this that God, even apart from such a revelation, really is just as God appeared in Jesus. All we are entitled to say is that God*

is such that God reveals the divine in Jesus in a threefold way. We are not entitled to say that God is not threefold apart from the revelation in Jesus. All we are entitled as Christians to say is that God is threefold in the divine revelation in Jesus. God is properly so. This is no illusion or mistake. But it does not entitle us to say much about the nature of God apart from this revelation...What a Christian is entitled to say, then, is that God is truly revealed in Jesus as Trinitarian. But we do not fully comprehend exactly what this means. We are certainly not entitled to say that God is exactly as we understand God. We need to be rather less arrogant than that".[46]

In short, we need to maintain a real distinction between the economic and the immanent Trinity, recognising that God is a *mysterium* not contained in or exhausted by our concepts. This means accepting honestly that the immanent Trinity (in principle, God's Triunity may not extend beyond the economy) will always be beyond our ability to know: despite Rahner, Horrell and many others, the economic Trinity is, theologically, all we have.

We have argued above that a divine unity based on action rather than on ontological identity provides us with a much more dynamic and realistic concept of the way in which God works generally within his creation, and specifically in Christ. If we apply that insight to an explicitly Trinitarian model of God (which is all we have: the only permissible Christian talk of God – the 'grammar' of Christian theology unlike, say, Muslim or Jewish theology - is Trinitarian) then we can see that it is actually Christ's 'work', rather more effectively than his 'being', which enables us to 'imagine' (create an image of) him as the Second Person of the Trinity. God is truly and adequately (but not exhaustively) revealed in Christ through their shared action rather than any shared ontological identity, and also because, as a symbol of God, Christ re-presents the symbolizandum both meaningfully (we can comprehend the revelation) and truthfully (the revelation is entirely truthful, insofar as it goes). A proper emphasis on the economic Trinity (recalling, yet again, the need for an 'apophatic horizon': God is essentially mysterious) enables us to imagine even more (even if we cannot fully understand it, it does make sense of the NT witness): not that the 'Second Person of the Trinity' is only a symbolic (non-literal) way of expressing the role of Christ in God's work (in the economy Christ, the agent of God, becomes truly united with God only through their joint action in the world), but that God, in raising Jesus from death as a signal of his vindication (however we understand the nature of that raising), has also 'raised him' into the divine being as the first fruits of *theosis*. This not-quite-literal statement (we cannot speak literally of God) would make Christ a very real part of the economic Trinity, although requiring us to maintain a justly humble degree of agnosticism over his connection to the (immanent) Godhead, of which we can say little or nothing: not least because even in the Bible there is no clear 'blueprint' provided. In the economy, therefore, the man Jesus is truly the Second Person of the Trinity, not as some kind of divine individual, but because in union with the Spirit (the Third Person: unless we fall into tritheism, shorthand for 'God at Work') he also did God's work and *in that action* symbolically shared, and re-presented, his Being (what God is) in and to the world creating thereby a genuinely mutual Trinitarian indwelling: insofar as we can understand that.

Secondly, talk of indwelling leads us to the ancient **notion of *perichoresis***. Early theologians were not only interested in developing the concept of a triune God *per se*, but were inevitably drawn into discussions about the nature of the posited **reciprocal relationships 'within'** the Trinity (how do 'the Three' interrelate?), based on this shared, albeit distinct, ontological identity. The verb *perichorein* (noun *perichoresis* - *peri*: around/ between; *choros*: dance – thus to 'dance between' - does Sydney

Carter's (1967) 'Lord of the Dance' hint at this?) was first used in Christology by Gregory Nazianzen (and later by Maximus the Confessor) to signify the 'communication of idioms' (i.e. how the human and divine 'properties' worked together) in the person of Christ. It was John the Damascene (in *De Fide Orthodoxa*) who began to use the term explicitly of the Trinity;[47] and from 7th – 8th Century, the idea became widely used in the East to refer to a mutual interpenetration or indwelling and interdependence 'within' the Trinity: "*...the archetype of the human community which is explicated in terms of interdependence, equality and mutual accountability, hospitality and inclusion.*"[48] The persons of the Trinity "*are fully open to each other, their actions ad extra are in common, they 'see with each other's eyes'*".[49] It wasn't until the Damascene's '*De Fide*' was translated into Latin in the 12th Century that the equivalent *circumincessio* came to be used in the West. But whatever language used, the concept itself helpfully reinforced unity whilst also making a radical differentiation between the 'persons' (Jn 14: 10 – 11). In contemporary theological reflection, the main reason for an appeal to *perichoresis* was in relation to the question of the location of the consciousness of God (shared among the three persons, but with a unified personality due to complete mutual indwelling):

"*...the triune life is marked by the most profound interpenetration. Yet it is precisely in this interpenetration that the Persons have their distinct being, and it is only through their unique individual identities that this interpenetration is possible. The unique subjectivities of each Person are formed through the unique form of intersubjectivity which pertains to them. Like all living things they are neither fully open nor fully closed systems. It is their radical openness to and for one another (in which Personal closure still retains a place) which constitutes their existence in this unique community*".[50]

As we can see, such discussions often tend to fall into the category of 'insightful bafflement' (how can we possibly speak about the consciousness of God at all except, perhaps, by analogy?), and need some considerable grounding in our understanding of the way that God works within his creation.[51] For example, although the Spirit came to be understood to proceed from/through the Father (and later the Son – *ex patre filioque*),

> *"...but also the Father is not Father except from/through the Son and the Spirit (ex filio spirituque). Similarly the Son is not Son except from/through the Spirit and the Father (ex spiritu patreque). In this way, the relations among the divine persons are not marked by a linear and hierarchical descent but by a circular and inclusive movement or dance (perichoresis)"*.[52]

For the RC scholar Emmanuel Durand:[53]

> *"The mutual immanence of the three Persons is understood as a consequence of their inseparability, because, since they are all in one another, the mention or presence of one of the three persons is accompanied by that of the two others as well. Such a perichoresis can be seen, on the one hand, in the intrinsic connection between generation [of the Son] and procession [of the Spirit], and on the other hand, in the effective reciprocity of the Trinitarian relations... [based on Jn 17: 21] Trinitarian perichoresis takes on a sense of a communion of love"*.[54]

In modern times, there are even attempts to explicate inner-Trinitarian relations using analogic concepts from science so, for example,

> *"...perichoresis evolves within the Trinitarian life of God as entangled superposition, relating Creator and creation in mutual interaction, supporting a panentheistic model of God"*.[55]

In the light of the earlier discussion of *theosis*, we might invoke the concept of *perichoresis* as one which embraces the Christian life as it seeks to follow Christ into that all-hopeful eschatological form of human transcendence (whatever that may 'look like') which is our potential destiny: we accept the invitation to join in the eternal 'dance of heaven' using Sydney Carter's words: *"Dance then...I am the Lord of the Dance said he...I will lead you all..."*. The late Anglican scholar, Maurice Wiles has, however, challenged the whole idea of *perichoresis* as over-speculative and not reflecting more broadly based patristic thinking. Perhaps, then, it can achieve rather more rooted in our functional/symbolic models rather than in an obscure and ultimately arid ontology? The human Christ, agent and symbol of God is, in his risen life, the true 'Lord of the Dance'; not the 'Man who is God', but the man who, through his selfless devotion to his Father's will, has expressed and so been drawn, both in his life and afterwards, into the very life of God, represented to us (in the economy) as Triune. Indeed, this is the specifically Christian witness: that the eternal work of the Father has, through the earthly work of the Son and the ongoing work of the Spirit, been taken further down the path to consummation: the dance goes on (provided we recognise that 'dance' here is a metaphor).

Which leads us finally and perhaps most crucially, for it is the issue which undergirds all the above, to the need to be constantly aware that **all our language about God is necessarily non-literal** (so Trinitarian/Christological language is equally necessarily non-literal, even though it is often understood differently) and this alone should give us pause when thinking that any of the traditional attempts to explore and explain what we understand about 'God-in-Christ' (such as that resulting from the classic Councils and which infuses our liturgies) are framed in simple/literal/univocal language.

We may feel, for example, that the kenotic insight that the divine Second Person of the Trinity emptied himself into the human Jesus is a helpful way of understanding the Christian experience (as it surely is, as well as being devotionally profound and spiritually uplifting: we, too, are called to empty ourselves...), but it is nowhere near any kind of literal description (such as the coal deliverer emptying his sack into the coal-hole). Rather, it is much closer to, for example, the notion that in a confessional, a sinner 'empties his heart' in penitence, or alternatively, in terms of the argument above, the emptying of God into his creation (including Jesus but not excluding the rest of humanity – and beyond), as opposed to the notion of one Divine 'person' (somehow literally) 'emptying himself' into a single human life. If we take seriously the fact of the vibrant diversity of language, together with the fact that no language can apprehend God, then we can see that all our doctrines, but particularly Trinity and Christology (essentially related), are more allusive than definitive, more connotative than denotative, more suggestive than providing final solutions. The notion of a truly human Christ being 'drawn into' the economy of the Trinity and engaging, not so much ontologically as dynamically, in the eternal dance of God, which is the single, unitive action of God in creation, providence, reconciliation (redemption) and consummation, is one that makes very good sense, and avoids (at least, to degree) the predominantly metaphysical speculation expressed in the now incomprehensible concepts and language of the Councils.

To sum up: the man Jesus was so infused by the Spirit and so obedient to the Father's will, that his humanity was 'raised' to divinity (as even Athanasius affirmed – the potential in every human being; but here, specifically referring to doing the 'divine' work of God i.e. what Jesus does, God does) and so ultimately incorporated within the divine life (the meaning of resurrection/ ascension?) that he (strongly symbolically) 'is God' for us. Such a designation of the Trinity is purely economic: we are not, for example, claiming that the immanent Godhead somehow shares our humanity (although some theologians want to argue that Jesus took his humanity 'into heaven' where he still bears the marks of the cross: hardly the kind of radical 'change' to which Paul alludes in 1 Cor 15: 35 – 57: would a raised Stephen Hawking still be in his wheelchair?). The truth is that God as God is 'wholly other' than his creation, yet despite this, because God is both Creator and Redeemer, and so intimately involved in his creation and its progress to the End, we may quite reasonably believe that the Godhead has, in Christ, embraced/raised up our humanity, and that he continues to do so.

The problem with this model (so some traditionalists may argue, although we need to recall that models are never right or wrong, only more or less helpful), is that we can no longer claim (if we ever wished to do so) that God is intrinsically ('immanently'), or has always been, Triune. To make such a claim is again above our theological pay grade. If God's Triunity is centred or predicated on the Christian experience ('in the economy') of Father, Son and Holy Spirit (as it clearly is, for this is where it originated), and if 'the Son' is a designation for Jesus-who-was-the-Christ, then obviously (again) we are only making claims for the economy and not for the immanent Godhead which is 'really' (in its reality) beyond our understanding, and thus a matter for sincere and honest agnosticism. For Hick,

> "...the kind of Trinitarian doctrine that is compatible with [a non-ontological Christology] is one in which the three 'Persons' are not persons in our modern sense of three centres of consciousness and will, but in the ancient sense in which a 'persona' is a role that someone plays...Thus the three 'persons' are three ways in which the one God is experienced as acting in relation to humankind – as creator, as transformer or redeemer, and as inner spirit".[56]

Although this may seem essentially modalist (but, again, what is the nature of even this kind of language), it may show the need for yet another heresy to undergo some appropriate rehabilitation, recognising that our language and concepts cannot adequately embrace the Godhead.

Neither is a functionalist position necessarily (although it can be if we are not careful) another version of the Adoptionist heresy, for I continue to assert that Jesus Christ had his origins (as do we all) in the redemptive plan of God which didn't simply follow, but was always part and parcel of God's single creative and redemptive action. Jesus didn't just 'happen along' and God then 'thought': "This is the man for the job; let's adopt him". The Incarnation, however it is to be understood, was always God's initiative, and not just 'accidental': we might say that the life of Christ was always in the mind and plan of God from the beginning (what/whenever that was). Indeed, for Macquarrie, Christology is necessarily paradoxical[57] and

"...*a closely related aspect of the paradox [is] the opposition between adoptionism and incarnationalism as two fundamental types of Christology. The terminology is not very satisfactory and there is bound to be a measure of anachronism in the usage, but it is convenient to use the term 'adoptionism' for the type of Christology which interprets the person of Christ as the raising of a human being to the level of deity, while 'incarnationalism' means the 'descent' of God into a truly human existence. As John Knox [in 'The Humanity and Divinity of Christ', 1967] has shown, the New Testament itself witnesses to a progression from adoptionism to incarnationalism. But the early preaching about the raising of the crucified Jesus to be Lord and Christ became more and more overshadowed by the fully incarnational theology, so that throughout most of the Church's history incarnationalism has had a completely dominant place in the Church's teaching, and adoptionism has been suspect as heresy. It can hardly be denied that the result was a loss of the sense of the true humanity of Christ and the rise of something like an unconscious Docetism...[But following modern attempts to rescue the humanity of Christ] now the danger is that the truths of incarnationalism may be lost or obscured, and in the last resort it is incarnationalism rather than adoptionism that offers the profounder interpretation. The two views are not finally opposed. Each requires and corrects the other, and either of them in isolation produces distortion...For how can a man be raised to deity unless God had already descended in humility into him? [Macquarrie then quotes his earlier comment that 'from first to last, this is the work of Being', and St Paul: "All this is from God, who through Christ reconciled us to himself" 2 Cor 5: 18]...But although we end with a full doctrine of incarnation, the paradox remains...".*[58]

It is this paradox with which theologians must continue to struggle (some, sadly, seeming not even to recognise that the doctrine of the Incarnation has a paradoxical nature) in affirming that (somehow) 'God was in Christ...'. If, for example, it is appropriate to denote Jesus Christ as (an existential/ontological) symbol of God, then perhaps it is also appropriate to denote 'Trinity' as a symbol or re-presentation or expression of God's interaction with his creation 'in the economy': in other words, we use the notion of Trinity as an expression of our Christian experience, rather than as any kind of description of God. Such ideas are representative of, express, and reflect the truth about God-in-Christ, but they are not the whole truth about the [immanent] Godhead which is quite beyond our ability to know. Nor, actually (echoing Higson), do we need to know. Whether such analyses are correct (or helpful) or not, in view of the philosophical and linguistic problems associated with the Chalcedonian 'Definition', the mere fact that other kinds of Christological understanding and expression are possible might suggest that we ought to be cautious in seeking to advance just one type as definitive and exclusive. Whatever else the Incarnation is, it is an aspect of the *mysterium* that is God. The single criterion by which we may judge which way of expressing the Incarnation is better, is not: 'which explanation is true?' but: 'which is most meaningful' (again, recalling that meaning must always precede truth claims). If it is not meaningful then it is nonsense, a waste of time and, furthermore, being neither true nor false, totally irrelevant.

So our functional and symbolic Christology can be as stoutly Trinitarian as anything that has gone before it (in fact, nothing can be 'stoutly' Trinitarian, just more or less enlightening) and, perhaps, rather more comprehensible (providing we recognise the dogma for what it is, rather than what it isn't): Jesus Christ is fully human formed as part of God eternal initiative and through the nexus of what we may genuinely call 'natural' events (including a natural conception and birth); he did God's salvific work and expressed God's 'Being' in and through a life of obedience and self-sacrifice, and so is properly a 'member' (language!) of a divine Trinity (understood, in true apophatic form, as economic). Yet our faith and our reflection upon its sources enables us to go even further (with due caution and theological modesty): having been raised and drawn into the great dance of liberation which, through the continuing activity of God's Spirit (which, after all, is God at work) and perhaps even the ongoing incarnational work of the Church, will ultimately embrace the whole of creation, of which Jesus Christ is both part and also the first fruits of its consummation. The unity of the Godhead is maintained (against the allegations of tri-theism) as well as its diversity (against the ravages of a humanity-denying modalism), and is to be found no longer in an unhelpful ontological identity (almost impossible to square with a genuine diversity), but rather in an shared salvific action which binds together Father, Son and Holy Spirit in a genuine human-divine partnership which, perhaps, was the purpose of creation in the first place.

Can Existentialism Rehabilitate the Traditional Conciliar Concepts?

As we saw above, one of the fundamental problems with the traditional mono-focus on ontology is that it leads to a Christ who might just as well be, like a butterfly, pinned to a board for closer examination. Without some existential element such a Christ is ultimately irrelevant to us: 'Jesus Christ is the Second Person of the Trinity, of the same substance of God the Father (and the Spirit), formed in a hypostatic union of two natures and, as such, has two minds/wills' may lead some to respond : 'so what: what has that to do with me?'. That is the inevitable outcome of a way of understanding a Christ who, having visited us and has now 'gone home' (the mythic trajectory), which has become both increasingly unbelievable and as remote as the former Greek view of God. As a result, this Christ struggles to be made relevant in and to the modern world. On the contrary, a 'non-Chalcedonian' (functional or symbolic) Christ is completely human, without doubt 'one of us', who has shared our human existence in a totally genuine manner (because his humanity is precisely the same humanity as we have, not a 'humanity' created by miraculous intervention) and without any incomprehensible metaphysical accretions. This Jesus is genuinely ours.

Neither should we forget that conciliar language is properly an interpretation rather than a 'fact' (the mistake made by generations of Christian theologians was believing the hypostatic union to be an indisputable fact: the 'Christ blueprint', the 'demonstrable theory'), and although (for example) a later Kenoticism accepted as an *a priori* datum that the Divine Son is an ontological reality, ontological language does not need to be interpreted literally: indeed, it is difficult to know, beyond our experience as human beings, what some literal form of 'being' – particularly Being - might look like. It may simply be, as Hick suggests, a helpful metaphor, and we shouldn't seek it to be more than that. But, as we have seen, such accretions were the result of the Church's attempt to understand 'what happened in the Jesus event' using the predominantly Greek language and concepts available to it at the time. Based entirely on the Jewish tradition, the results would probably have been very different: the Jewish Scriptures, for example, do not offer a philosophical (ontological) analysis of God, they present a personal (existentially relevant) and dynamic God active in history, and in a covenantal relationship with Israel, and with individuals within Israel (but one who also has the Persian King Cyrus as his messiah: Isaiah 45: 1).

Nevertheless, we saw, in our exploration of 'symbol', just how important it was that the symbol didn't mediate the ontological reality of the symbolizandum in a vacuum, but did so in such a manner that enables us to respond to it 'from the depths of our existence'. The 'pure' (objective) ontology needed to be mitigated by a genuinely personal (subjective) philosophical category: existentialism. If such a partnership is deemed to have been successful for symbol, is it not possible that this is the only problem which the classical formulations have: that the Jesus of the Councils just needs that additional element applied in order to rehabilitate those somewhat arid concepts? That Jesus Christ is not simply Jesus Christ (Second Person etc.) but 'Jesus Christ for us'? Perhaps if that were the case, then all the above 'flirtations' with functional and symbolic categories were unnecessary?

As we saw when considering how, in the ancient world, both the use of artefacts and human beings as 'manifestations' of God assumed the ontological and functional as two sides of one coin, can we now make a case for the ontological language of the Councils to take on an existential dimension, so that the traditional Christology ceases to be either 'dryly academic' and remote or irredeemably docetic? Christologies do not need to be understood using only one philosophical category; in fact, such a narrow focus diminishes the exercise. There is a richness in mixing and complementing what may be seen as quite disparate ideas with one another. Here, I revisit the traditional ontological concepts, and particularly the manner in which they were originally expressed, and we will see what may happen when we add a dash of existentialism to the recipe.

Despite defending the traditional use of the Chalcedonian/ ontological categories, **Christopher Schwoebel** (actually in his denial of the need) offers us the possibility engaging with a more existentialist methodology just to see where that takes us. I am sure that most Christians would agree that however we seek to define or otherwise identify the Person of Christ, it is how Christ impacts on us that is important for faith (what we might term his 'existential significance'). As argued above, an ontological analysis (if that is the category we decide to use) must also embrace or partner an existential analysis (and *vice versa*). However, Schwoebel writes (having quoted Bonhoeffer's question: 'Who is Jesus Christ for us Today?'):

"[Christology] is not a question about the ongoing relevance of Christ's message, nor a question about 'what' Jesus Christ might be for us, but a question about the [ontological] identity of Jesus who is confessed by Christians as the Christ in such an exclusive sense that the title-term 'Christ' has become a proper name in Christian worship, proclamation and discourse. The question, as Bonhoeffer phrases it, is an ontological question, a question about the being of the one whose identity is evoked by the name Jesus Christ. It is not a question about the function of Christ or a question about the ongoing effects of his work but a question that raises the crucial issue of being".[59]

I disagree: firstly, it certainly seems obvious to me that Bonhoeffer's question, in using the phrase *'for us'* (indeed, adding 'today'[60]), is thoroughly existential and so it will be useful to explore that philosophical concept a little further:

"What is analysed [in Existentialism] is human existence in its manifold modes of being, and the aim of this philosophy is that man should attain to self-understanding. But all the existentialists agree about the limitation of man's powers, and they agree that it belongs to the very essence of his existence that he must live without the comprehensive knowledge that was sought in metaphysics. Some philosophers do indeed develop an ontology, or philosophy of being, but nowadays this is usually claimed to rest on existential foundations and to be different from a metaphysic constructed by the speculative exercise of reason...[but] a philosophical theology beginning from the analysis of human existence finds within that existence itself the question of being...[so] an existential-ontological language, describing universal structures and experiences of the human existent, can serve as the interpretative parallel for the symbolic language of a particular revelation...If the existential-ontological language provides a frame of reference that will help us to locate and then understand the symbols, these concrete symbols will from their side enrich and vivify the relatively abstruse language of existence and being...[the ontological dimension, therefore] will seek to elucidate from the symbolic material new and deeper understanding of Being. But here we must guard against the temptation of treating theology as if it were metaphysics and as if our aim were to provide just an intellectually satisfying account of God, the world and man. With the rise of dogma in the early Church, concrete and existentially significant symbols tended to be edged out in favour of an abstract vocabulary of 'substance', 'nature', and the like. This kind of language does indeed serve to interpret and clarify the symbols, but then the dogmas came to be thought of as objective, neutrally descriptive truths...".[61]

Bonhoeffer's question is not simply 'what is the nature and meaning of Christ?', as if that nature and meaning existed somehow independently of anything else, that it is some kind of metaphysical truth (which was what much doctrinal development in the early Church seemed to assume), but what is the nature of Christ *and therefore* its meaning *for us*. After all, Bonhoeffer uses those two important words. In other words, the nature and the meaning of Christ's 'being' don't just – so to speak – 'stand alone', but have to be understood in the context of a responsive faith (the existential dimension).

Having said that, it is clear that there is always an ontological question (what is the nature of x?) which applies not only to the whole created order, but also to God (as in Macquarrie's distinction between being, beings, Being and Holy Being – God as Holy Being is not 'a being'; the various aspects of the created order take their 'being' from God and, as such, are 'beings'). But there is a huge difference between the use of the category of ontology as the primary (or even exclusive) Christological category (as in the classic metaphysical formulations) and asking the ontological question of Christ in the same kind of way we might ask it of anyone or anything else: which is logical if Christ is genuinely 'one of us'. Of course, for this to work, Christ does need to be 'one of us' in the fullest sense. If he is different in kind, then we are not merely lost christologically; we (as Christians) are probably lost existentially as well.

We should note in passing that adopting 'functionalism' as the primary category doesn't prevent us from (indeed, it requires) asking both ontological and existential questions about Christ, his nature *and* its impact on us: not only what 'God-in-Christ' means, but also – essentially - how that meaning impinges on our existence. When Jesus asks his disciples the question:[62] "who do people say that the Son of Man [I] is [am]?", he was told that some thought him to be (variously) 'John the Baptist, Elijah, Jeremiah or one of the prophets' (revivified). He then asks his disciples for their view, to which Peter replies: "You are the Messiah...", which Jesus acknowledges. But it is not at all obvious that any of the 'identities' offered by the disciples are meant to be understood ontologically (even 'Son of the living God') nor actually, for that matter, existentially. Indeed, it seems pretty clear that all the designations are *purely functional*, and that there is no great ontological mystery to be unravelled: the prophets and the Messiah ('anointed one') were those who worked and functioned 'on behalf' of God, and such roles are easily defined (and are defined in various places in the OT). In particular, there was certainly no understanding that they were (somehow) divine or otherwise not 'normally' human (even Elijah, whom the tradition has being bodily taken into heaven[63]). These were all people who had responded in their various ways to God's call: the response of human being to Divine (Holy) Being.

Nevertheless, implicit in the Caesarea Philippi narrative, as throughout the whole Gospel tradition (particularly evident in Matthew), is the at least implied existential question which takes 'discipleship' as its focus: it was *because* Peter was a committed follower of Jesus that he answered as he did (recognising what Jesus was, however imprecisely, but clearly with a developing awareness of his special character had led to his commitment), although even making that commitment (as today) *did/does not in itself* imply any particular understanding of *what kind of 'being'* Jesus had or was. Indeed, it is hard to imagine how any Jew of Jesus' day (or today) could have understood a man to be divine; again it must be stressed: 'Messiahship' did not imply divinity; it was a purely human designation.

Furthermore, we might also argue that the ascription of any particular ontological 'identity' to Christ (such as in Schwoebel's analysis) is, in any case, essentially a matter of faith: a thoroughly existential response. It is not the result of any *a posteriori* investigation or argument; it cannot be demonstrated by objective evidence. One cannot place Christ under some kind of metaphysical microscope and say: 'Ah, here is his divinity – take a look'. It is wholly an *a priori* designation: what someone chooses to believe and then adopts as a starting point for further discussion. In which case Schwoebel's whole argument is essentially circular and technically 'question-begging' (the conclusion is contained in the premise).

Unless one adopts a 'propositional' understanding of revelation: that God has used or even produced scripture in order to inform us directly of his nature (in the form of statements and propositions), the only thing we can say about Christ's person is that the Evangelists, Paul and others understood it in such-and-such a way, not least because, as we have seen, the language and concepts used in the NT are not the same as those later used by the Councils in their various pronouncements. We might wish to believe that one or more Biblical authors had a particular ontological understanding of Christ (such as that he was *homoousios*...), but, as they never use that kind of language that cannot be demonstrated. The closest we get to it is in the Johannine Prologue: '...the Word *was* God' (or 'what the Word was God was'); but its interpretation depends entirely on how we understand John's use of *Logos* or, more to the point: how John understood it. That inevitably must be a matter of opinion.

The NT shows us how people responded to Jesus (it has an existential focus) not 'what he was' (ontology); indeed, the whole of the NT is a witness to faith, and not (primarily) a theological thesis. Three further points are worth considering:

1. which comes first: is our response to Christ the outcome of the way we understand him, or do we understand him in a particular way because we have responded to his call?
2. which is the more important: to have an accurate understanding of Christ's ontological status, or to respond to his call?
3. is Christ only worthy of being followed if he is 'truly divine' in an ontological sense?

A further distinction worth noting is that between Christology 'done from above' and that 'done from below': the former takes Chalcedon as a given, so the process begins with the classic statements about the divinity of Christ (hypostatic union etc.) which are assumed to be 'the truth', and further reflection focuses on explaining how they can be true (an 'apologetic' motive). These 'high' Christologies

> "...*tend to assume the special, unique, divine nature of Christ and do not question it (that is why, even if they do not always seem it, they may be said to be 'from above'). They presuppose the results of the centuries of development up to Chalcedon and **do not feel the need to justify this basic presupposition again**. What they argue may not be fully 'orthodox' in the traditional sense, but it is bound up with elements of orthodox Christology in the same way as other variant Christologies were bound up with mainline Christology in the past".*[64]

On the other hand, Christologies from below make no *a priori* assumptions about Chalcedon, but start (properly) with the human 'Jesus of History' (making use of the findings of modern scholarship, particularly those concerning the interpretation of Biblical texts) and work from there to their conclusions – whatever they may be. Even if that means breaching traditional orthodoxy in some way: for example, in a multi-Faith environment refraining from claiming that Jesus is 'unique', and preferring terms such as 'definitive' or 'decisive'.[65] This is the approach we have, so far, taken. However, as Schwoebel helpfully points out:

> "*If it is true that the Word was made flesh, can we still separate 'above' and 'below' as alternative starting points? Is it not the point that the full reality of what is 'above' has been disclosed to us 'below' so that in Jesus Christ we have access to God the Father through the Spirit – on earth as it is in heaven? If it is true that Christ is the same, yesterday, today and forever, the one to whom*

the Father speaks eternally and who eternally responds to the Father in the communion of the Spirit, the 'Christus praesens' and the Jesus of history are not alternative starting-points but aspects of the comprehensive reality of the incarnate Son who now sits at the right hand of the Father. And if it is the point that the one who is exalted on high has no other history than that of the man Jesus, any account of the presence of Christ must refer to the Jesus of history and any reconstruction of the history of Jesus has to start with his presence to the Father and the Spirit and so from our present as it is shaped by that history".[66]

The basic problem is this: we may know what it is to be human (at least, to a point); but we don't know what it is to be God:

"That the incarnation is difficult, perhaps even impossible, for humans to understand, seems undeniable to me...[because] human understanding cannot comprehend how it is possible for God to have become human and...it is not possible for sinful humans to believe that it has occurred apart from divine assistance...apart from God's revelation, we lack a correct and deep understanding both about God and about human nature. We neither know God nor ourselves as we need to. Yet to know [that] 'the god-man' is a logical contradiction, we would have to have a fair degree of clarity about both concepts...".[67]

Evans' comments could be construed as a counsel of despair. Either it embraces a complete theological 'cop-out': we can understand nothing whatsoever about the Incarnation (in which case, we ought to keep quiet), or we have to place so much reliance on revelation (which inevitably has to be interpreted) that we could, in effect, say whatever we like, safe in the knowledge that we couldn't be contradicted. 'You might interpret God's revelation this way, whilst I... It's all just a matter of opinion'. Clearly either extreme is unacceptable, because we would have nothing meaningful (and hence 'truthful') to say to anyone, and Christian proclamation would be 'dead in the water'.

Accepting that the Incarnation is, at least to a degree, a mystery (not simply a puzzle: we cannot entirely comprehend how God works), nevertheless if 'it really happened' within our space-time existence then surely we ought to be able to understand and to say something about it? That is why it is so important to use every intellectual tool at our disposal. Not only the obvious: biblical and theological, but scientific as well. If Incarnation cannot be spoken of sensibly and reasonably in a modern world which is learning more and more about the vastness of space and the smallness of the basic building blocks of life, then it's probably best not to speak of it at all. Complacently treating it as something incomprehensible must inevitably mean that we can find neither meaning nor truth in the doctrine: and no Christian would wish to say that. We believe that (somehow) "God was in Christ" and, although we do not have the capacity, using human language and concepts which are inevitably limited, to say precisely how with any great degree of certainty and what the ontological implications of that are, nevertheless they are all we have, and we must use them with due care and humility. We need to be sure to set out the reasons why we put it this way rather than that, but ultimately recognising that none of us has a privileged insight into the Godhead. 'Ontology' is one philosophical attempt to enquire into the nature of reality; it is not an exact science, and should not be treated as such.

If there is a philosophical coin where one side represents 'ontology' and the other 'existentialism', then we are probably on safer grounds with the latter than we are with the former: at least it is based on our own very real experience of being human. In the meantime, we should do our best to ensure that whatever understanding we have of the Incarnation doesn't lead us either into a pious but ultimately irrelevant Docetism or any simplistic form of Adoptionism (even if Arianism is now a 'dead duck' in western theology[68]): each is still to be found within the Church. It seems hard to resist the conclusion that the ascription of a 'genuine' ontological divinity inevitably undermines Christ's true humanity and always descends into some form of Docetism. An ontology mediated (or mitigated) by some existential awareness – what Christ means for us – is a step in the right direction (after all, as we have seen, traditional Christological discussion was driven by the very relevant concern for salvation) but it is not sufficient. This is certainly not to suggest for a moment that those who formulated the classic 'definitions' of Christ had no 'existential interest' in what they were doing: they were devoted disciples, doing their best to express their faith in a living and redeeming Son with the language and concepts available to them. Nevertheless, what they came up with, particularly as set out in the words of the Athanasian Creed and the regularly recited Nicene Creed, was an objectified definition-like statement of the nature of the Divine, as though examining the Godhead through a high-powered telescope, without any explicit reference – beyond those to worship – to faith as a living response to and trust in God: although in the Nicene Creed the words are 'we believe in...', the clear intention is 'we believe that...'. Furthermore, the Athanasian Creed has quite a threatening preamble:

> "Whosoever will [Quicunque Vult] be saved: before all things it is necessary that he hold the Catholick Faith. Which Faith except every one do keep whole and undefiled: without doubt he shall perish everlastingly. And the Catholick Faith is this: That we worship one God in Trinity, and Trinity in Unity...".

Of course, by this time the Church had moved wholeheartedly and enthusiastically into that understanding of 'faith' which we criticised above: 'faith' equals 'belief', but now adding the idea that 'right belief' (orthodoxy) is necessary for salvation (implying that you can be as evil as you wish, so long as you believe the right things). Whilst concern for salvation was, as we have noted, one of the main drivers of doctrinal formulation ('we need to understand how it is that we are saved' and 'we need to be sure that we are saved'), it now becomes dependent on that very formulation. Indeed, despite continuing (apparent) concerns to show how Christ brought salvation, here the emphasis is on simple belief as the method: 'just believe what the Church tells you and you shall (or may?) be saved'.

The fundamental mistake of the Fathers was to assume as an *a priori* datum that salvation could only be granted *directly* by God, and so (logically) Christ the Saviour had to be God (a good example of an *a priori* argument failing due to the weakness of its premise). As we have seen, this goes directly against the understanding expressed in the OT when God uses his chosen agents as mediators of deliverance: the deliverance itself is from and of God, but the vehicle of its 'delivery' is always human. There is nothing to prevent us from understanding that whilst God is the giver of salvation it is (somehow) brought through the one he has chosen to offer it on his behalf. As we noted above:

> *"Isaiah 53 is not a prophecy of the Messiah but a portrait of how Yahweh's servant-prophet becomes the means of Israel's being put right with God, of Israel's personal renewal, and of the nations' coming to acknowledge Yahweh".*[69]

It is not only the case that Jesus doesn't have to be ontologically divine to be 'saviour' but that being ontologically divine so undermines his true humanity that (to end where I began) he becomes fundamentally irrelevant to us. If salvation is dependent on the 5th Century equivalent of 'believing six impossible things before breakfast' then the whole enterprise descends into triviality. But salvation is far too important to be treated like that; it is, primarily, the gift and work of God himself:

that is the source. The 'mode of delivery' is then a matter for serious theological discussion and that requires sensible and comprehensible expression. One such expression is to say that our salvation can only be found in and through a truly human representative of God (the Fathers at least recognised that side of the coin): otherwise why doesn't God grant salvation to all as a direct 'metaphysical' gift; why go to all the trouble of the Incarnation? In Christian understanding the gift of salvation is naturally associated with Christ (using variously helpful models), although taking belief as the main criterion seems bizarre and not only invites the question: 'if belief were, in itself, so important for salvation then, as noted in the introduction, why hasn't God – creator of an ambiguous universe – made things rather clearer?'. But it also removes the possibility of salvation from a huge proportion of the human race who are 'unbelievers' such as atheists or members of other Faiths (just as those of other Faiths may call us 'unbelievers'; so *kafir* is the somewhat crude, certainly inaccurate and somewhat insulting term used by some Muslims to describe non-Muslims). We might also wonder how, in the greater picture, a particular mental or intellectual or cognitive disposition is to be thought more important (say) than a compassionate, loving, unselfish nature and character.[70]

Whatever we may wish to say about Christ, and whatever philosophical categories we choose to use, the whole must hinge on its relevance to faith and how our reflections on our faith may be expressed intelligibly, so that they may make (at least some) sense in and to the 21st Century. Only in that way can any mission or evangelism have any hope of succeeding with those who wish to relate their faith to the real world. As we have seen: some Christians are happy separating these two worlds; but many of us are not. So can the Christology of the Councils do this; can the addition of an existential element rehabilitate those somewhat remote and often baffling concepts? Probably not, because the problem which I identified as my starting point is still there. Even with a mitigating existential analysis, we are faced with the problem of ontological divinity. Whilst it is clear that, for some, this doesn't undermine faith at all, and so there is that genuine existential element as well (the Second Person of the Trinity 'claims me for his own'), it will for others simply because of the insistence that Christ's divinity must be interpreted literally, coupled with an absolute failure to be able to explain what that means. Much Christian proclamation continues to make the simplistic claim: 'Jesus is God' and although this is technically a heresy many Christians are unbothered by such technicalities. As a result, the Christ who is proclaimed struggles to be recognised as human at all.

Whilst ontological enquiry is not rendered unnecessary with or irrelevant to a functionalist and symbolic Christology (in fact, attempting to show how Christ shares God's Being though action is a crucial part of the task), a focus on ontological identity between God and Christ, even with a redeeming element of existentialism, does not go far enough in – indeed, it hinders – the development of a clear idea of who Jesus was and how he mediated the presence of God in the world. This is because a Christ who is ontologically identical with God cannot be truly human: that is the ongoing and probably insoluble problem for the classical formulations. Existentialism does not rehabilitate the formulations of the Great Councils: but it can provide a more human dimension to our Christology (after all, what else do we have to bring to the task?) which can lead, with further reflection (taking seriously that the Councils are a starting point and not the end of discussion) towards an understanding of Christ in which his true, real, genuine humanity is protected. At the same time it allows us to understand why humanity may be worthy of saving, reflecting the Eastern tradition that atonement/salvation is brought simply by the Incarnation, not particularly by anything Christ did, including dying on the cross. The somewhat artificial distinction between Christ's Person (Christology) and his work (Soteriology) is laid bare as a totally misleading way of proceeding: it is in Christ's human response to the will of God in which salvation is both based and offered. For Paul Tillich "Christology is a function of soteriology"[71] and not *vice versa*.

Notes

1. op cit p. 114;
2. ibid. pp. 117 – 118;
3. When I was ordained, Bishop Eric Kemp of Chichester offered to buy each ordinand a book; I asked for Lampe's book, and his Chaplain asked me to think again as the conservative Kemp disapproved of Lampe; I held to my request, and received the book;
4. op cit p. 11;
5. ibid. p. 11;
6. ibid. p. 23;
7. 'On the Incarnation';
8. Lincoln op cit p. 279;
9. ibid. p. 280;
10. Hick J 'An Inspiration Christology for a Religiously Plural World' in ST Davis (1988) 'Encountering Jesus' pp. 6 – 7;
11. MJ Borg 'From Galilean Jew to the Face of God' in Borg (ed) 'Jesus at 2000' pp. 10 – 11;
12. CW Eucharistic Prayer E;
13. Goldingay 'Isaiah' p. 92;
14. Macquarrie J (1955) 'An Existentialist Theology' (henceforth 'AET'); (1972) 'Existentialism;'
15. 'Existentialism' p. 1;
16. AET p. 11;
17. ibid. p. 17;
18. ibid. p. 20;
19. 'Existentialism' p. 217;
20. AET p. 23;

21. In Chapter 7 we seek to make the traditional language of the Councils more meaningful and relevant by balancing their rather cold ontological/substance language with a touch of existentialism;

22. Macquarrie J 'AET' p. 7 ;

23. Macquarrie J 'Principles' p. 185 ;

24. Macquarrie J (1967) 'God-Talk' p. 203;

25. ibid. p. 206;

26. ibid. p. 207;

27. '...Blessed Trinity' as in the hymn 'Holy Holy Holy' (1861, Reginald Heber);

28. It may be that had non-metaphysical concepts been available at the time, then Unitarianism (fearing the loss of the human Jesus) would never have appeared, as it would not have been needed;

29. Horrell JS 'The Eternal Son of God in the Social Trinity' in Sanders F & Issler K op cit p. 55;

30. The Greek Fathers termed this *theologia;*

31. Peters T (1993) 'God as Trinity: Relationality and Temporality in the Divine Life" p. 83;

32. LaCugna C (1993) 'God For Us' p. 8;

33. Higton M (2008) 'Christian Doctrine' (SCM Core Texts) p. 93;

34. ibid. p. 99 – so confirming that what we believe is relatively unimportant, as we can never know it all (or indeed much at all);

35. Johnson E 'Trinity: To Let the Symbol Sing Again' in 'Theology Today' (1997) 54, 3 pp. 301 – 302;

36. Sanders F 'Trinity Talk, Again' in 'Dialog: A Journal of Theology', 44/3, 2005 p. 269;

37. Peters op cit p. 103;

38. Sanders art cit p. 269;

39. Simmons EL op cit pp. 107 – 108;

40; Sanders p. 270;

41. In Sanders & Issler op cit p. 47;

42. Simmons EL op cit p. 2;

43. 'The Trinity: a Liberal Account' in 'Modern Believing' Vol. 55, Issue 3, 2014, pp. 211 – 222;

44. ibid. p. 213;

45. ibid. p. 213;

46. ibid. pp. 215 – 217;

47. For those interested in such things, the verb was actually used with a different preposition: in Christology using *eis* + accusative; for Trinitarianism = *en* + dative i.e. a movement from the idea of **exchange**/permutation of properties to that of **a reciprocal indwelling**;

48. Collins PM 'The Trinity: A Guide for the Perplexed' p. 76;

49. Davis ST 'John Hick on Incarnation and Trinity' in Davis ST et al (1999) 'The Trinity', p. 272;

50. McFayden AI (1990) 'The Call to Personhood: A Christian Theory of the Individual in Social Relationships' p. 29;

51. In a fascinating, although difficult book (at least for those of us who are non-scientists/mathematicians), 'The Entangled God: Divine Rationality and Quantum Physics' (2011), Kirk Wegter-McNelly explores the implications of quantum physics for theology, particularly the phenomenon of 'quantum entanglement' (a kind of interpenetration/ perichoresis?) and how that might relate to God's self-revelation; he affirms the traditional understanding of the Holy Spirit as mediation between Father and Son and, furthermore, argues for a doctrine of creation in which, as opposed to *creatio ex nihilo* (creation out of nothing), God creates *ex relatione* (from relationship);

52. Phan PC (2011) 'Developments of the Doctrine of the Trinity' in Phan PC (ed) 'The Cambridge Companion to The Trinity', pp. 21 – 22;

53. 'Perichoresis: A Key Concept for Balancing Trinitarian Theology' in Wozniak & Maspero 'Rethinking Trinitarian

Theology' pp. 177 – 192;

54. ibid. p. 181;

55. Simmons EL op cit p. 2;

56. Hick J in Okholm & Phillips op cit p. 58;

57. Paradox: a statement or proposition which seems self-contradictory or absurd but in reality expresses a possible truth in the combination/juxtaposition of two apparent opposites e.g. 'less is more', 'a wise fool', 'be cruel to be kind';

58. 'Principles' pp. 309 – 310;

59. Schwoebel C 'Christ for Us – Yesterday and Today: A Response to "The Person of Christ"' in Holmes & Rae 'The Person of Christ' p. 182;

60. Implying that it may not be the same as 'yesterday' i.e. existential meaning is dynamic rather than static;

61. Macquarrie 'Principles' pp. 23, 182-185;

62. Mt 16: 13 – 20; some commentators may seek to interpret Jesus' question existentially i.e. 'what do I mean to you?'; if that were the case, then the answers are hardly appropriate because all they do is provide a variety of possible identities/titles which, of themselves, do not necessarily evoke any explicit personal commitment; in any case, it seems clear that the purpose of the incident, in the way that Matthew uses it, was to make explicit to his audience (perhaps in the light of Mark's apparent/supposed 'secrecy') that Jesus was indeed the Messiah; that obviously carries the implication: '…and you should follow him', but does not, of itself, require an existential response;

63. 2 Kings 2: 11 – we may compare the later tradition that (the fully human) Mary was taken bodily into heaven ('The Assumption'/'Dormition of the *Theotokos*');

64. Article by John Bowden in Bowden (ed) (2005) 'Christianity: the Complete Guide' p. 225;

65. See e.g. Hick & Knitter (2004) 'The Myth of Christian

Uniqueness';

66. Schwoebel op cit p. 184;

67. Evans CS 'Historical' p. 123;

68. "Its third and final death [in 18th Century British theology] was primarily due to a changing perception of the world [particularly 'new scientific thinking']" Wiles M (1996) 'Archetypal Heresy: Arianism through the Centuries' p. 164;

69. Goldingay J 'Isaiah'p.72;

70. See e.g. the parable of the sheep and the goats (Mt 25: 31 – 46) where the criteria for 'salvation' are all ethical: "...just as you did it to one of the least of these who are members of my family..." (v. 40, NRSV); or Mt 7: 21 "Not everyone who says to me, 'Lord', 'Lord', will enter the kingdom of heaven, but only the one who **does the will** of my Father in heaven" [what is God's will? "He has told you, O mortal, what is good; and what does the Lord require of you but to do justice and to love kindness, and to walk humbly with your God" Micah 6: 8]; or Mt 5: 16 "...that they may see your good works..."; or Mt 5: 48 "Be perfect...as your heavenly Father is perfect" [what kind of perfection is this?]; or particularly the very blunt Amos 5: 21 – 24 "I hate, I despise your festivals, and I take no delight in your solemn assemblies...Take away from me the noise of your songs... But let **justice** roll down like waters and **righteousness** like an ever-flowing stream" etc. etc.; texts such as these suggest that God is much more interested in how we live our lives (showing compassion and mercy, and working for peace, justice and reconciliation) than in our 'religious' activities: how do you think God views the intellectual atheist who lives a life of selfless service to others?

71. Tillich P (1975) 'Systematic Theology' Vol 2. p. 174.

Conclusion

My overall aim has been to formulate a meaningful Christology: one which, unlike the classic expressions, can offer ways of understanding Jesus Christ that are comprehensible and so able to convey the meaning and the truth of that remarkable, but very human life to a modern world. Much of the developed world in the 21ˢᵗ Century has turned its back on Christianity, believing it to be outmoded, obsolete and irrelevant to their lives. This dismissive attitude is in part the outcome of the Church's fixation with a quasi-medieval set of beliefs (particularly, but not only, its Christology), together with a reading of the Biblical text which, if not wholly fundamentalist, is at least simplistic and naïve in its failure to grapple with the historical and literary critical issues such study so obviously demands (consider the havoc being created across the world by fundamentalist, medieval and non-scholarly readings of the much younger and significantly less complex Qur'an). It is also due to the Church's refusal to address issues which are important to those outside, preferring instead to engage in a theological navel-gazing so often accompanied by an arrogant and damaging 'holier-than-thou' attitude towards 'non-believers' (a term which, for some Christians, may even include fellow church members).

In undertaking this task I have sought to:

1. take seriously Rahner's contention that the conclusions of the great ecumenical Councils are to be understood as a starting point rather than the final word on Christology;
2. reinterpret Nicene and Chalcedonian language by divesting it of its metaphysical baggage; but in so doing...
3. remain within the 'horizons' set by the Councils (what **must** be said to be authentically Christian) and so be faithful to the traditional 'grammar' of Christology, along

with some of its vocabulary; in so doing...

4. focus on what the doctrine of the Incarnation was originally intended to express: its core meaning concerning the absolute closeness of the personal relationship that existed between Jesus and Father God; so close that we can truthfully say: "God was in Christ reconciling the world to himself" (2 Cor 5: 19);

5. find ways in which Jesus' staggering impact might now be re-expressed seeking, in particular, to interpret 'divinity' using the categories of functionalism and symbolism, and so enable us to recognise how humanity itself can be uplifted to become what it has been called to be.

Most Christians *would* agree, and all Christians *should* agree (as this is 'official policy': orthodoxy, at which only the incurably docetic might cavil), that Jesus called the Christ, Jesus of Nazareth, Jesus the founder of the Christian movement (even if founding a long-term movement was not the aim of an eschatological prophet – if that was how Jesus understood himself) was **fully, completely and truly human**. He was 'one like us'. The fundamental argument of this study has been that this very proper affirmation of genuine humanity is at best undermined, at worst terminally denuded of meaning, by the equal affirmation that this same Jesus was also ontologically divine: that he was/is (somehow) God ('*homoousios* with the Father'). This Conciliar notion of shared ontological divinity not only lacks meaning today (if it ever did in the past, beyond being helpful devotional shorthand), but is nowhere to be found explicitly spelt out in the Scriptures. Such a claim would, in any case, have been unthinkable in the Jewish milieu in which Jesus was nurtured and in which he himself proclaimed the arrival of God's Rule and Authority, which he had been called both to proclaim and share: a vocation which was part of God's eternal plan of reconciliation.

My own proposal has been that a meaningful reinterpretation of the classic doctrines of Christ can be achieved through a functional-symbolic Christology, and that this kind of Christology not only more accurately represents the whole of the Biblical witness (rather than just selective parts of it), but is actually much easier to understand: 'Jesus worked for God' is a far more straightforward and meaningful assertion than 'Jesus was God'. It can, therefore, be a much more effective tool for evangelism than the simple repetition – ever louder and louder - of the proclamations of Nicaea and Chalcedon (and all stations between).

Furthermore, this kind of Christology doesn't set Christians against the findings and insights of modern scientists and philosophers, as do those 5th Century metaphysical conundrums; on the contrary, it is supported and illuminated by them. Most positively, it encourages Christians to explore the Biblical record in greater depth and with greater richness of interpretation, particularly that intense relationship between the 'Old' and 'New' Testaments, recognising just how much the latter relied on the former, and to be able to do so without feeling the need either to retire their cognitive functions or to think that such explorations are somehow impermissible or even impious. It also enables us to understand the central truth that the Bible is not itself God's revelation, but rather the witness to that revelation. In so doing, it replaces widespread Bibliolatry with the true subject of Revelation: God.

Although some may judge such an approach heretical, (I have argued that it not only meets the governing intentions of Nicaea and Chalcedon, but that it also keeps faith with the doctrinal 'grammar', and even some of the vocabulary, established by the Conciliar Fathers) it is certainly not as heretical as the manner in which the classic formulations have been both understood and expressed over the centuries, particularly within liturgies which use the literally foreign language and concepts of the

5th Century simplistically, uninterpreted and unmediated. If Docetism didn't actually 'win' in becoming embedded and implicit within orthodox pronouncements, it has continued to lurk in the background of Christian imagination and piety: most Christian 'portraits' of Christ are inevitably (due to the way his 'divinity' has been understood) at least quasi-docetic.

That Jesus is 'divine' has been treated as an unquestionable truth by the Church, although its meaning and the problems implicit in its assertion have seldom been explored outside the rarefied atmosphere of the academy. The gulf between academy and pulpit has often been as immense as that between pulpit and pew. Such Christian and Biblical education as has been provided by churches has been either of poor quality or sectarian, or both. Faithful churchgoers may have had questions, but the exploration of those questions has more often than not been discouraged: particularly in those churches where (because faith is mistaken for belief) to question means to doubt, and to doubt means having a culpably weak faith. That is why it is incumbent on those who continue to use the term 'divine' of Christ uncritically to explain what they mean. If it be argued that the categories used by the Conciliar Church do make sense, then let those who claim this explain how: specifically how a man can be divine or God can be human.

As demonstrated in the classic debates and their persistent propensity to fall into heresy (as with the Alexandrian tendency to neuter or even obliterate Jesus' humanity), divinity inevitably 'trumps', and so overwhelms, humanity because the divine Creator is exponentially greater in every respect than a human creature: a 'God-man' will always be a '**God**-man', never a 'God-**man**'. Sadly, the *'homoousion'* is not rescued from inevitable redundancy by the modern doctrine of 'Kenosis' which itself involves the same kind of logical fallacies: how can God – even 'just' the Second Person of the Trinity - cease to be Godlike: and if God did somehow manage to 'lose' his divine powers, what power would he then have to 'retrieve' them? In any case, is that actually what the famous hymn in Philippians 2 was seeking to claim; or is this just another huge theological edifice built upon shallow, sandy exegetical foundations (Mt 7: 24 – 27)?

As we have seen, one way of making sense of (giving meaning to) the Christ story-event (for our only access to the event is through the story) is to take the man Jesus seriously and without qualification as a Jew who, when living in Palestine a couple of millennia ago, committed himself totally to serving his (and our) Father God, even to the extent of laying down his life for his precious cause: to proclaim the coming of God's just and loving rule over against an unjust and oppressive imperial regime. He did so in such a selfless way and with such obedience to God's will that (to reconceptualise a traditional Jewish concept) he attained Christhood: in specifically Christian terms, the state of 'sinlessness' (properly understood), raising his, and potentially our humanity too, to the very life of God. For Christians he is the first-fruits of human transcendence, something available to us all as we are enabled through his life's work and by his example to transcend ourselves; furthermore, there is no *a priori* reason to suppose that there may not have been others before and since, of which we are not so aware, who have achieved the same. This flowering of human transcendence is just one of the reasons why it is right to hold onto the term 'divine', for it acts as a useful shorthand for 'humanity raised to the very life of God': the fullness of *homo sapiens spiritualis*. What that may ultimately mean for us all must inevitably be an eschatological mystery.

It is abundantly clear that the route to the conciliar verdict on Jesus' identity (from 'prophet of Nazareth' to 'Second Person of the Trinity') depended on and was the outcome of privileging the 'higher' Christology of the 4th Gospel over those of the other three Evangelists (who, despite Hays' arguments, expressed Christologies which were significantly 'lower': one only has to read the Four Gospels to recognise that there is a vast Christological gap between John and the Synoptics), even though there is sufficient evidence within the 4th Gospel itself to allow alternative conclusions to be considered. "The Father and I are one" is equally capable of a functional interpretation: Christ was one with the Father in the work he did, just as he was one with his disciples (across the ages) in their continued ministry which is rightly termed the 'extension of the Incarnation'. Had Jewish categories of thought been privileged over Greek philosophies: in particular, had a more authentically Jewish rather than a predominantly Greek understanding of John's '*Logos*' Christology been developed, and had the Synoptic witness been taken as seriously as that of the 4th Evangelist, then it is entirely possible that a way of understanding Jesus Christ would have emerged that did not require 'ontological divinity' to take on the status, in effect, of being the only way of expressing his relationship with God.

The 4th Century Arian controversy, during which both sides used scripture to bolster their arguments (sometimes even using the same 'proof' texts: Bishop Alexander and Presbyter Arius argued vehemently over the meaning of Proverbs 8: 22ff), demonstrates clearly enough that the Biblical witness is ambiguous about Jesus' identity. Perhaps most significantly, when the texts are explored and interpreted on their own terms instead of having externally-derived meanings imposed upon them, those who do not take a blinkered blik-like view of the Bible may even draw the conclusion that the Jewish scriptures actually have nothing specifically to say about Jesus at all. How could they, as the future cannot be known? There are only those generalised comments (which were then applied to Jesus by his followers after the event) about how God, at some undefined stage in the future, would send an equally undefined emissary – a 'chosen and anointed one': a Messiah.

But once the Councils had proclaimed that Jesus was not only this Messiah (Christ), but that he was also 'one in being' with

Father God, possessing 'two natures' and 'two wills/minds' in 'one person'; rather than encouraging further exploration into the question of 'Who do you say that I am?', it was assumed that the question had been answered for all time. Christological enquiry was effectively shut down. After all, when one believes that everything that matters is already known, what more needs to be said? In this regard the Church has often acted like criminal prosecutors who are so sure they have the right perpetrator, they no longer bother to follow where any new evidence leads: the plot of many good crime novels has been realised in Christography.

Certainly, from Chalcedon to the modern age, soteriological thinking (one of the main drivers of Christology) tended to take precedence. When it happened at all, Christological thinking (with certain honourable exceptions) consisted more of tinkering around the edges of the already designated 'divine Christ' (such as those medieval discussions as to whether the Incarnation would have occurred had there not been a Fall) than producing any significantly new insights into what scripture, as the record of God's revelation, might actually be saying. Scriptural assessments of Christ had either to support what the Fathers had decided, or else be judged heretical. Yet when the biblical evidence is viewed through the lens of modern scholarship, complemented by other modern disciplines, rather different conclusions can be reached which actually take their meaning from the scriptures rather than imposing their meaning upon them.

Perhaps we can now begin to move towards that more rounded and genuinely searching exegesis of the Biblical texts, previously constrained and contained by dogmatic certainties; one which recognises the diversity of Christologies to be found therein, of which only selected verses, pre-interpreted in line with 'orthodoxy', need lead us in the direction of a Nicaea or a Chalcedon. In so doing, we may be able to shed new light on the mystery of the Incarnation in a manner that can be better understood and which actually makes sense in and to a world brimming over with knowledge of God's vast and complex universe. Instead of saying: 'this is the truth and so it must be found in the Bible' we should rather ask: 'what is the truth to which these scriptures bear witness?' In this way, once linguistic usage has been accurately assessed, meaning can more easily lead to truth.

And what is that truth? Putting it at its most basic: Jesus was a man, divinely commissioned and appropriately (and prodigiously) gifted; spirit-filled, doing the very work of God; a human being as human beings were always meant to be, and still are called to be. His 'mission action plan' was very simple: to proclaim God's Kingdom as present and active in the world, but also as something requiring action: a personal response from the one challenged by his life and message. Yet, sadly, the Church often says (at least in practice): 'be baptised – you don't need to do anything about it afterwards; just have a good party', so forgetting the fundamental message of Jesus that God's work is often costly: even leading to a Cross.

This Jesus did God's work in such a manner that **it seemed to some 'as if' he, Jesus the Christ, were God.** Jesus spoke with an unusual authority and he brought healing to many who, in a variety of ways, lacked wholeness. For the Fathers of the Councils this signalled that he 'shared the Father's Being' (Nicaea) or that he 'united two natures in one person' (Chalcedon). Neither of these 'solutions' is required if we can simply affirm that in the life-task of embracing christhood (doing the work of the Father), he raised his (and our) humanity to its full potential which we might understand using terms such as divinisation or *theosis,* although we need to be clear what such ideas mean and, even more importantly, what they don't mean. It certainly doesn't mean that Jesus was or somehow became God; neither does it mean we will. It does mean for Christians that Jesus was the first-fruits of what some have called a 'new humanity' (*spiritualis*), but which is rather humanity as it was always intended to be.

Regarding this latter point, we have also seen that the (often alleged) gulf between divinity and humanity is more relative than absolute (as might be expected in the relationship between creator and creature, the very basis of Aquinas' use of analogy and of the doctrine of *theosis*), and that the idea of a human being raising his humanity (or having his humanity raised) to divinity through the quality of his God-driven life, rather than some kind of metaphysical origin, not only makes very good sense, but must give all humanity hope that, despite the myriad ways in which we go wrong, our entelechy and potential 'to be like God' (in an appropriately human manner) is a real possibility.

A more realistic variant of the exceptionally naïve and foolish, yet oft-quoted tag that Jesus must have been 'either mad, bad, or God' is this: **if Jesus didn't claim to be divine**, he must have either been **deluded** (he was divine but didn't know it – a possibility for a kenotic Christ, but does it really make sense?), **coy** (he knew he was divine, but didn't want to say so – in which case, just how real is his humanity if he were 'God dressed up'?), or actually **not divine at all,** at least not in the manner traditionally expressed by *homoousios*. There is now a hard fact to be faced: if Jesus was not divine in the sense that he shared the Father's 'substance' (so, as in the 'Gloria', he can be designated 'Lord God') then, clearly, the task of Christology needs urgently to be revisited by the whole Church. This is because we, as Christians, have thoroughly misunderstood both Jesus and God in several key aspects (normally parcelled up under the label: 'The Person of Christ'). If Jesus isn't God in any metaphysical or ontological sense, then we are probably guilty of some degree of idolatry. Of course, the Biblically ratified understanding that the identities of God and his agents may well be blurred mitigates this problem somewhat as, perhaps even more positively, does the symbol-symbolizandum distinction I have proposed, in which the former validly attracts the response properly addressed to the latter.

God did and (somehow) continues meet us in Christ; and we also meet him in Christ. It is for us 'as if' Christ were God and it is quite proper, with appropriate caveats and in the right circumstances (predominantly liturgical, because the liturgy is a linguistically and existentially expressive experience as well as a devotional one), to treat him 'as though he were' divine. But some of my Christian friends are so overwhelmingly Jesu-centric (or much worse: Paul-centric), that one sometimes wonders quite how and where the God proclaimed by Jesus ever fits into their schema. When the Proclaimer becomes the Proclaimed and God's agent is mistaken for God, then some kind of theological nuance would be helpful, if simply to keep our spiritual eyes glued to where they ought to be, and from whom Jesus' own eyes never wavered: on God.

Ultimately, and with due theological humility in the face of Ultimate Mystery, we have to recognise that we cannot fully comprehend God, nor his intentions, nor his ways. God, in Christ, has revealed (as it is often put) 'sufficient for salvation'. Perhaps one of the most relentless problems underlying much theology is the assumption that we really do know, if not everything, at least most things: thus some happily follow 'Rahner's Rule' that the Economic Trinity (how God appears) is exactly the same as the Immanent Trinity (what God really is): but how could anyone possibly know that? That is why the concept of an 'apophatic horizon' always needs to be before us. We can particularly see in the 21st Century (although history is easily mined for other examples) how blind belief can lead self-designated 'people of God' to carry out the most awful atrocities, when a moment's rational thought would ask why God 'the Merciful, the Compassionate' would want his followers to murder indiscriminately? That is the problem with irrational religion: and it is undeniable that many Christian beliefs as expressed today are equally irrational: some may even be immoral.

The corollary of what we have to say about God is the need

to enhance our theological understanding of anthropology: the nature of humanity. Not only *sapiens*, and sometimes, it would appear, not even *sapiens*. Presumably influenced by 'The Fall' (falling under Augustine's spell rather more than that of Irenaeus), theologians have often presented a 'dim and grim' view of humanity. Calvin infamously claimed that humankind is utterly depraved[1] and, certainly many, both in history and today, appear by their actions to be just that: many ordinary human lives are disordered and more or less immoral, or even amoral. But perhaps that is simply an aspect of our finitude and the accompanying freedom to reject God? Because we are 'enclosed individuals' it is natural to see things from our own perspective, because that is where we are, and we find it difficult to see beyond ourselves and our own needs. But equally, there have been and continue to be examples of goodness, kindness and self-sacrifice, regularly commemorated in celebrations of the lives of the Saints and public acts of Remembrance. Humanity is capable of that love which is the nature of God himself (1 Jn 4: 16) we just need to work on it. We have the capacity to 'go beyond' ourselves, to transcend our individualism so that 'we might be one' with God and with our fellow human beings. That is both the human vocation and its ultimate destiny.

In what I have thought through and in what I have written, I have 'questioned the Incarnation'. Not, as I have made clear, because I want to deny it; I just wanted to be able to understand it better. Whether the reader agrees with my arguments or not, I hope that they have, at least to some degree, shed new light on this central expression of Christian belief and source of our commitment. If any choose to be critical, please don't attack the writer (in my experience, a frequent response in the Church to things we don't like to hear): this presentation of my 'belief-that' is the outcome of genuine and committed reflection on my much more important 'faith-in'. Demonstrate, if you will, where the argument is lacking. I further hope that, in my writing, I have paid due respect to Jesus the Christ, 'Son of God', who calls his followers above all else to take responsibility for a mission that was not simply his, but is for every Christian generation: to proclaim, pray and work for the coming of Father God's Kingdom 'on earth as in heaven' and, in so doing, live lives of love, compassion and self-sacrifice. Lives which mimic the self-giving and 'letting-be' of God himself. Yet, as I also hope I have made sufficiently clear: this Jesus is no mere example to follow; he is not some passive exemplar who only shows us what human potential can be. He is one in whose life and work God is to be genuinely found (that is the essential nature of the Incarnation) and who, thereby, not only invites us to share in his transfiguration, but through that very work, enables us to do so. Not because God has 'intervened' and created a new kind of human being, but because in this particular and genuinely human individual God's will has been done, God's nature has been revealed, and as a result we have all been changed.

In this truly human life, we – not only those who knew Jesus, but the millions after who have come to recognise God acting in him - have been met and challenged by God. In this human life humanity itself has been given the potential to be raised to Godhood. This transcendent anthropology of which Christ is the first-fruits assures us of our own destiny: to be raised to a new life as we seek (continuing perhaps even beyond death) to conform our own lives to Christ-likeness and so to transform our self-centredness into God-centeredness. Jesus Christ, 'Truly God' and 'Truly Human' certainly; but please give a little more thought to what such slogans might mean, so that both God and also that part of God's creation made in his image, may be honoured. That is the challenge I humbly issue to the Church I joined as that enquiring child so many years ago, and in and through which I have never given up my quest for a more reasonable, believable and Biblically secure understanding of Jesus. Before its decline, at least in the developed world, becomes terminal.

Notes

1. "...everything proceeding from the corrupt nature of man [is] damnable"; Calvin J 'Institutes of the Christian Religion' II, iii;

CHRISTIAN
ALTERNATIVE

Christian Alternative
THE NEW OPEN SPACES

Throughout the two thousand years of Christian tradition there have been, and still are, groups and individuals that exist in the margins and upon the edge of faith. But in Christianity's contrapuntal history it has often been these outcasts and pioneers that have forged contemporary orthodoxy out of former radicalism as belief evolves to engage with and encompass the ever-changing social and scientific realities. Real faith lies not in the comfortable certainties of the Orthodox, but somewhere in a half-glimpsed hinterland on the dirt track to Emmaus, where the Death of God meets the Resurrection, where the supernatural Christ meets the historical Jesus, and where the revolution liberates both the oppressed and the oppressors.

Welcome to Christian Alternative... a space at the edge where the light shines through.
If you have enjoyed this book, why not tell other readers by posting a review on your preferred book site. Recent bestsellers from Christian Alternative are:

Bread Not Stones
The Autobiography of An Eventful Life
Una Kroll
The spiritual autobiography of a truly remarkable woman and a history of the struggle for ordination in the Church of England.
Paperback: 978-1-78279-804-0 ebook: 978-1-78279-805-7

The Quaker Way
A Rediscovery
Rex Ambler
Although fairly well known, Quakerism is not well understood.
The purpose of this book is to explain how Quakerism works as a
spiritual practice.
Paperback: 978-1-78099-657-8 ebook: 978-1-78099-658-5

Blue Sky God
The Evolution of Science and Christianity
Don MacGregor
Quantum consciousness, morphic fields and blue-sky
thinking about God and Jesus the Christ.
Paperback: 978-1-84694-937-1 ebook: 978-1-84694-938-8

Celtic Wheel of the Year
Tess Ward
An original and inspiring selection of prayers combining Christian
and Celtic Pagan traditions, and interweaving their calendars into
a single pattern of prayer for every morning and night of the year.
Paperback: 978-1-90504-795-6

Christian Atheist
Belonging without Believing
Brian Mountford
Christian Atheists don't believe in God but miss him: especially the
transcendent beauty of his music, language, ethics, and
community.
Paperback: 978-1-84694-439-0 ebook: 978-1-84694-929-6

Compassion Or Apocalypse?
A Comprehensible Guide to the Thoughts of René Girard
James Warren
How René Girard changes the way we think about God and the
Bible, and its relevance for our apocalypse-threatened world.
Paperback: 978-1-78279-073-0 ebook: 978-1-78279-072-3

Diary Of A Gay Priest
The Tightrope Walker
Rev. Dr. Malcolm Johnson
Full of anecdotes and amusing stories, but the Church is still a
dangerous place for a gay priest.
Paperback: 978-1-78279-002-0 ebook: 978-1-78099-999-9

Do You Need God?
Exploring Different Paths to Spirituality Even For Atheists
Rory J.Q. Barnes
An unbiased guide to the building blocks of spiritual belief.
Paperback: 978-1-78279-380-9 ebook: 978-1-78279-379-3

The Gay Gospels
Good News for Lesbian, Gay, Bisexual, and Transgendered People
Keith Sharpe
This book refutes the idea that the Bible is homophobic and makes
visible the gay lives and validated homoerotic experience to be
found in it.
Paperback: 978-1-84694-548-9 ebook: 978-1-78099-063-7

The Illusion of "Truth"
The Real Jesus Behind the Grand Myth
Thomas Nehrer
Nehrer, uniquely aware of Reality's integrated flow, elucidates
Jesus' penetrating, often mystifying insights – exposing wide-
spread religious, scholarly and skeptical fallacy.
Paperback: 978-1-78279-548-3 ebook: 978-1-78279-551-3

Do We Need God to be Good?
An Anthropologist Considers the Evidence
C.R. Hallpike
What anthropology shows us about the delusions of New Atheism
and Humanism.
Paperback: 978-1-78535-217-1 ebook: 978-1-78535-218-8

Fingerprints of Fire, Footprints of Peace
A Spiritual Manifesto from a Jesus Perspective
Noel Moules
Christian spirituality with attitude. Fourteen provocative pictures,
from Radical Mystic to Messianic Anarchist, that explore identity,
destiny, values and activism.
Paperback: 978-1-84694-612-7 ebook: 978-1-78099-903-6

Readers of ebooks can buy or view any of these bestsellers by clicking on the live link in the title. Most titles are published in paperback and as an ebook. Paperbacks are available in traditional bookshops. Both print and ebook formats are available online.

Find more titles and sign up to our readers' newsletter at
http://www.johnhuntpublishing.com/christianity
Follow us on Facebook at
https://www.facebook.com/ChristianAlternative